CLASSICAL PRESENCES

General Editors

Lorna Hardwick   James I. Porter

CLASSICAL PRESENCES

The texts, ideas, images, and material culture of ancient Greece and Rome have always been crucial to attempts to appropriate the past in order to authenticate the present. They underlie the mapping of change and the assertion and challenging of values and identities, old and new. Classical Presences brings the latest scholarship to bear on the contexts, theory, and practice of such use, and abuse, of the classical past.

Classical Culture and Modern Masculinity

DANIEL ORRELLS

OXFORD
UNIVERSITY PRESS

Great Clarendon Street, Oxford OX2 6DP

Oxford University Press is a department of the University of Oxford.
It furthers the University's objective of excellence in research, scholarship,
and education by publishing worldwide in

Oxford New York

Auckland Cape Town Dar es Salaam Hong Kong Karachi
Kuala Lumpur Madrid Melbourne Mexico City Nairobi
New Delhi Shanghai Taipei Toronto

With offices in

Argentina Austria Brazil Chile Czech Republic France Greece
Guatemala Hungary Italy Japan Poland Portugal Singapore
South Korea Switzerland Thailand Turkey Ukraine Vietnam

Oxford is a registered trade mark of Oxford University Press
in the UK and in certain other countries

Published in the United States
by Oxford University Press Inc., New York

British Library Cataloguing in Publication Data
Data available

Library of Congress Cataloguing in Publication Data
Data available

Typeset by SPI Publisher Services, Pondicherry, India
Printed in Great Britain
on acid-free paper by
MPG Books Group, Bodmin and King's Lynn

ISBN 978–0–19–923644–2

1 3 5 7 9 10 8 6 4 2

For Jayne and Brian Orrells

Contents

Acknowledgements

This book examines the relationship between teachers and their pupils, and could not have been written without the intellectual input and support of two teachers in particular: first, Simon Goldhill, who got me thinking about the history of masculinity the first time we met, when he asked me what the word *vir* meant; and, secondly, John Henderson, whose satirical and demanding intellectualism serves as a model for pedagogy: *nempe haec adsidue* . . . I could not have hoped for better teachers. Both have led and accompanied my education over the years, and more recently have kindly read and commented diligently on drafts of this book. Heartfelt gratitude is also due to Miriam Leonard, my friend and an exemplary scholar, whose reading of the book's penultimate draft caused me to think again.

I would also like to thank the Faculty of Classics and King's College, Cambridge, for both financial and intellectual generosity, which supported and nurtured my graduate training, which sowed the seeds of this book. I must mention the Department of Classics and Ancient History at the University of Warwick: my colleagues, in particular Simon Swain and James Davidson, have provided me room to explore my ideas. This book would not have been completed without research leave generously granted by the University. Further afield, parts of this book have been shared at seminars in Bristol, Reading, Glasgow, Canterbury, and London, and I have learnt much from the discussions.

Special thanks should also be paid to Jim Porter and Lorna Hardwick for their backing of this project, and providing this book with a home in *Classical Presences*. My thanks are also owed to Oxford University Press, in particular Hilary O'Shea and Taryn Campbell, as well as my highly adept copy-editor, Hilary Walford.

Closer to home, I have benefited endlessly from the kindness, advice, and support of friends over so many years: Aude Doody, Katie Fleming, Annelise Friesenbruch, Natasha and Manjit Marhia, Omar F. Okai, and Amanda Tidman. Rohan McCooty ensured that the final stages of writing this book did not induce insanity. And finally, for the warmth and love of my family, Jayne and Brian

Orrells, Kate and Paul, and now Harrison: my deepest thanks and respect.

This book meditates on what it means to learn from teachers one has never met. I should like to remember here Eve Kosofsky Sedgwick (1950–2009), whose written word has taught me so much.

Introduction: Knowledge and Desire, Ancient and Modern

Historians have long known about the once putative existence of a mysterious pamphlet entitled *Ancient and Modern Pederasty Investigated and Exemplify'd*. The last page of the April 1749 issue of *The Gentleman's Magazine* was dedicated as usual to a 'Register of Books' of the previous month's publications, in which item 14 notes: 'Pederasty investigated and exemplified. 1s.'[1] Since then, however, not a single copy of the document has appeared in a public sale, and not a single copy has been known to exist in a public or private library. In 1965 David Foxon brought together three documents that further attested the lost pamphlet. One is a now well-known letter, dated 13 November 1749, from the imprisoned novelist John Cleland (author of *Memoirs of a Woman of Pleasure*) to a Newcastle law clerk in which he compares his own case to that of the 'Son of a *Dean* and Grandson of a *Bishop*' who was 'mad and wicked enough to Publish a Pamphlet evidently in defence of *Sodomy*, advertised in all the papers'. Although Cleland divulges no names, the letter's receiver must have taken the hint, as Foxon records a letter from Newcastle to the attorney general, Dudley Ryder, asking Ryder to prosecute 'the Author of a most wicked, and mischievous Book'. The last document chronicled by Foxon is a petition some years later in 1755 from Elizabeth Cannon to the Duke of Newcastle requesting the charges against her son Thomas Cannon be dropped.[2]

As Hal Gladfelder has meticulously uncovered, John Cleland had been imprisoned for unpaid debts to two men, one being the nebulous Thomas Cannon. The nature of the debt and the relationship

[1] Gladfelder (2007a: 22).
[2] Foxon (1965: 54–5).

between Cleland and Cannon remain unclear, but it seems these one-time friends had fallen out. As part of the complaint that Cannon lodged against his erstwhile acquaintance, on 5 February 1749, was a further complaint about 'diverse scurrilous and libellous papers from the said Cleland greatly reflecting upon and abusing this Deponent And this Deponents Mother Elizabeth Cannon'.[3] And attached to the affidavit seems to be an example of such a libellous paper, in which Cleland apparently slanders 'that execrable white-faced, rotten cata-mite'. The note then continues to accuse Cannon and his mother of poisoning Cleland five times with arsenic.[4] Within a few weeks, Cannon paid a visit to a printer, John Purser, who agreed to publish his pamphlet *Ancient and Modern Pederasty*. We cannot explain what led Cannon to bring this pamphlet to publication, especially since he had recently brought a public complaint about Cleland's slander that clearly refers to it. But what is definitely known is that, in April, notice of its printing appears in the *Gentleman's Magazine*. Nothing further is known about the work until Cleland's letter of November, which led to the prosecution of Cannon. The trial was expected to take place in the spring of 1750, but Cannon absconded. Only Purser, the printer, was prosecuted, fined, imprisoned in the Marshalsea prison for a month, and exhibited in the pillory at both Charing Cross and the Royal Exchange, even though he claimed he did not know what he was printing.[5] According to Elizabeth's 1755 petition, it seems that Cannon went abroad, but after three years was forced to return to England, no longer able to finance himself. It would appear that Elizabeth's petition did the trick, when Thomas returned home: the last that is known of him is that he was living 'the most recluse life at Windsor' with his mother and sisters.[6]

But the story does not stop there. The careful archive work of Gladfelder has excavated the indictment of the pamphlet's printer, Purser, which includes long excerpts from *Ancient and Modern Pederasty* itself. And with Gladfelder's edition of the text,[7] Cannon's work (or most of it at least) has finally seen the light of day. The

---

[3] Affidavit of Thomas Cannon, 5 Feb. 1748/9, Affidavits for Hilary Term, 22nd George II, PRO, KB 1/10/1, quoted in Gladfelder (2007a: 25).

[4] See Gladfelder (2007a: 25).

[5] See Gladfelder (2007a: 26–8).

[6] Elizabeth Cannon quoted in Foxon (1965: 54) and Gladfelder (2007a: 28). Cannon is also mentioned in Harvey (1994: 125, 159).

[7] Gladfelder (2007b).

opening of the indictment presents the substance of the charge: Purser printed the pamphlet in order to 'Debauch Poison and Infect the Minds of all the Youth of this Kingdom and to Raise Excite and Create in the Minds of all the said Youth most Shocking and Abominable Ideas and Sentiments beneath the Dignity of Humane Nature'.[8] But, when Cannon's words do begin, he states: 'Among the many Unspeakable Benefits which redound to the World from the Christian Religion, no one makes a more conspicuous Figure than the Demolition of Pederasty.' And, because of the 'Unspeakable Benefits' that Christianity has brought on, Cannon feels that this '*Detested Love*' may be discussed 'with Freedom and the most philosophical Exactness'.[9] Cannon's witty rhetoric transfers the unspeakable 'Love' to the 'Unspeakable Benefits' of Christianity, to suggest that Christianity does not silence discourse on the subject, but actively encourages it. The drollness of Cannon's prose provokes Gladfelder to suggest that the text betrays Cannon's 'own arousal as it seeks to arouse the reader'.[10] It is now, of course, impossible to tell whether Cannon meant his writing to be pornographically titillating or not. But what we can say is that Cannon shows an uncanny anticipation of Michel Foucault's ideas about the 'repressive hypothesis'. That is to say, discourses that have sought to legislate, classify, and taxonomize sexual practices into licit and illicit categories, actually have proliferated discourse about sex, and have produced all the more the desires they sought to eradicate.[11] Cannon's little pamphlet makes a big point about how modernity can speak about antiquity in the first place: the interpretations that Christianity has brought to bear on ancient cultures had provided Cannon with the possibility to think of a polarity between antiquity and modernity, as expressed in the very title of his work. Cannon, then, shows an awareness of his position in modernity, irrevocably separated from the ancient world, but at the same time accessible to that world precisely because of the Christian discourses that seek to disconnect ancient and modern cultures.

This paradox is the subject of Cannon's pamphlet and the object of enquiry of *Classical Culture and Modern Masculinity*: modernity's self-conception through its reification of its relationship with

---

[8] Gladfelder (2007b: 39).   [9] Gladfelder (2007b: 40).
[10] Gladfelder (2007a: 29).   [11] See Foucault (1998).

antiquity. To be more exact, how have *ancient same-sexual desires* been utilized by modern intellectuals to understand that relationship? How has the pederastic relationship that putatively was supposed to transfer knowledge from one elder generation to the younger, as so many modern scholars have argued—how has that relationship informed the transfer and inheritance of the ancient world into the modern? How might the ancient pederastic teaching scene exemplify the production and transference of knowledge and culture from one generation to the next? Cannon, presumably a well-educated man (the son of the Dean of Lincoln and the grandson of the Bishop of Norwich and Ely, as Cleland's letter inferred), wrote a relatively short pamphlet that anticipated a sustained interrogation of these very questions between 1752 and 1930, especially in Germany and England, as this book will examine. But, before we turn to these later, altogether more scholarly works, let us remain with Cannon to unearth what he rather more wittily and satirically, yet also thoughtfully, made of the relationship between ancient and modern pederasty.

As Gladfelder has discussed, the text is a hotchpotch of stories and scenes, to the extent that, 'rather than referring to a single, insistently hierarchical model of male—male sexual relations, pederasty in Cannon's incoherent anthology becomes a figure for the undermining of fixed categories and roles'.[12] The first story Cannon summarizes comes from Lucian's tale of Jove's love for Ganymede and Juno's jealousy. Another is a digest of an episode from Petronius' *Satyricon*. Finally, one of the longest stories is of two figures called Amorio and Hyacinth set in modern London, which was apparently told to Cannon by Amorio. 'The classic pederastic relationship between a mature male . . . and a young boy'[13] is not straightforwardly presented in Cannon's text. As Gladfelder examines, Lucian's story is a love triangle between god, goddess, and boy; and his re-presentation of a scene from Petronius shows Eumolpus seducing a boy, who then reciprocates his desires, and, even though the latter is the passive partner in the relationship, he dominates the sex, wearying his old lover out. Cannon seems to play with the classic pederastic paradigm, 'unsettling the distinction between active and passive, subject and object'. Furthermore, Cannon 'included two anecdotes of pederastic heterosexual desire' in both of which 'a woman appropriates for herself the role of catamite . . . thus making a hash of the binarisms presumed to operate in both heterosexual and homosexual relations'.[14]

It is Cannon's story of Amorio and Hyacinth to which we will attend in more detail. The tale opens at a masquerade, where the 'young and blooming' Amorio is entranced by a beautiful young lady who recounts to him the sad narrative of her life. A maidenly Devonshire farm girl, she was seduced by an aristocrat and eventually abandoned by him in London, penniless and without friends. 'To relieve the Excess of my sadness,' she says, she took a walk in Somerset Gardens, where she met a 'genteel Fellow'. She told the same tale of seduction to him, and the gentleman asked her to become his mistress. He, however, proved a 'Tyrant', and she eventually managed to escape. And now that her Tyrant is 'in the Country', she says she would like to invite Amorio for supper at her chambers. Amorio is enthralled and so enjoys 'a delicious Repast' with the beautiful young lady. The evening goes so well that

the enraptur'd Amorio, snatching her up, speeds to the Bed, where Incumbrances quickly off, he finds in his Clasp a Body past Imagination delicate; but of Gender masculine. Surprize invades; yet predominates Desire; which becomes absolute, when Hyacinth (so let's name the guilty Boy) mortify'd at the Deliberation, then speaks in a Voice, to which every Melody lends it's Aid; My dear *Amorio* does not enfold a Woman; but one, who more than a Woman *Grasps*, and *Binds*. Penetrating *Love* takes the Meaning; and the most lib-d-nous Fire ever felt by our wondring Glower, seizes his panting Frame. He is quickly piloted into a Streight whose potent Cling draws all the Man in cl-mmy streams away . . . [Later] Hyacinth says, let me clasp that charming Amorio, who wou'd touch nothing, but a Woman. They love away an Hour or two, then rise and recruit with a long Breakfast.[15]

And so the story ends.[16] As with the Eumolpus tale, Gladfelder is again interested in 'Amorio's unmanning . . . He has been under Hyacinth's control from the start'—Hyacinth, whose 'potent Cling draws all the Man in cl[a]mmy streams away'.[17] Clearly, on one level, the story warns of (arousal by) the dangers of pederasty: the active

[14] Gladfelder (2007a: 31–2).
[15] Gladfelder (2007b: 50).
[16] For the complete story of Amorio and Hyacinth, see Gladfelder (2007b: 47–50).
[17] Gladfelder (2007a: 33).

male is drained of his virility. However, the story also poses an
interesting conundrum: was Amorio tricked into pederasty or was
he attracted to girlish boys all along—after all, Cannon calls him an
'antiquated Beau'?[18] Hyacinth's body is 'past Imagination delicate'
suggesting that Amorio had never fantasized about such a form
before. And Hyacinth (as the narrator christens him), concerned
about Amorio's 'Deliberation', speaks 'in a Voice', which convinced
Amorio to partake of this particular pleasure. Has Hyacinth awa-
kened a desire already there—was Amorio the one who was really in
disguise?—or implanted one that was never there before? The story
asks, what makes a pederast? What makes a man of love ('Amorio')
desire a Greek-looking boy, called Hyacinth?

A little later in the indictment, however, the story is recorded again,
with an additional coda:

They love away an Hour or two; Then rise and recruit with a long Breakfast.
The Lady's Story is the Subject of much Laughter. Amorio wants a Chair to
go dress. But Hyacinth insists upon sending for his Things. Having put
themselves in sallying order, they take Coach; and to Billiards.[19]

'The Lady's Story is the Subject of much Laughter': does Amorio's
and Hyacinth's laughter imply that Amorio was foolish for believing
the 'Lady's Story' in the first place, or is it meant to suggest that the
story was merely an amusing game, which both had already invented
and knowingly engaged in, as erotic foreplay? The narrative begins to
look like a modern, eighteenth-century tale of romance and adventure; then the scene on the bed suggests that these two figures more
closely resemble ancient pederasts (the author calls the boy 'Hyacinth'); but then the tale's coda brings us back to the modern world as
it implies that the whole 'Adventure' might have been mere play. The
narrative challenges the reader's expectations: it begins by suggesting
that what might look like a modern tale of romance between boy and
girl is actually a mask for ancient pederastic desires, thereby questioning the difference and distance between ancient and modern
passions; but it ends by positing the possibility that a return to
antiquity was itself pure charade, a role-play fantasy for men of
modernity. In fact what these two figures are meant to 'exemplify'
(to nod to Cannon's title) is extremely hard to say: their role-playing

[18] Gladfelder (2007b: 47).   [19] Gladfelder (2007b: 56).

pederasty does not resemble the classical model, nor do they look like what we might call gay men: does Amorio fancy boys who (can) look like girls, or girls who are really boys? Finally, we should not forget that it is Cannon himself who christens our protagonists 'Amorio' and 'Hyacinth': the former had apparently told him an 'uncommon story [which] by his permission I make publick, averring the Alterations to be only verbal'.[20] Do these names, then, sum up who these men 'really' are, in Cannon's mind, men who actually resemble ancient pederasts? Or does Cannon suggest these names as disguises for self-aware modern men, who self-consciously disguise themselves in fantasies about the (im)possibilities of desiring (like) ancient pederasts?

The tale of Amorio and Hyacinth, the longest episode in *Ancient and Modern Pederasty Investigated and Exemplify'd*, has deserved our attention precisely because of its ludic, yet sophisticated, interrogation of its modern reader's understanding of the relationship between antiquity and modernity. By presenting to his reader a story in which we are not quite sure whether Amorio—*Love* himself—is knowingly or unknowingly imitating ancient desires (why does he laugh about the 'Lady's Story'?), Cannon asks us what we think we might know about the historicity of our own desires: what do we know about the history that has enabled us to desire as we do? Indeed, this story causes the reader to question whether the ancient history of desires is factual and might thereby be reproduced in modernity, or is merely fantasies of the modern imagination. What would it mean to say that antiquity *has* informed the way men desire in modernity? Indeed, as we saw earlier, Purser the printer was indicted because this material was deemed inflammatory of the desires of 'Youth'. The story itself presents Hyacinth convincing Amorio to bugger him, with his melodious 'Voice'. What effect do stories of 'antiquated' desires have on the young man of modernity? How do they make him desire?

As Hal Gladfelder observes, '*Ancient and Modern Pederasty* . . . is significant as the most extensive and varied treatment of male same-sex desire in all of eighteenth-century literature'.[21] Its importance lies, however, not so much in what it tells us about how men 'really' did manage to administer their sexual pleasures in the eighteenth century.

---

[20] Gladfelder (2007b: 47).   [21] Gladfelder (2007a: 34–5).

Rather it is so significant because it considers at great length and sophistication what it means to say that ancient notions of desire were exemplary for modernity. *Ancient and Modern Pederasty Investigated and Exemplify'd*: Thomas Cannon's work (sure to become central to the canon of texts comprising the study of the history of sexuality[22]), asks its readers how *exemplary* are the tales of desire told: are they desires to be used as models? (The legal establishment clearly worried they were.) *The story of Amorio and Hyacinth is itself about whether antiquity was being used knowingly as an example or not.* And so Cannon's little tale brings us to larger, broader concerns. Although the pederastic relationship between Amorio and Hyacinth was not one based in a pedagogic setting, as so many scholars have understood classical pederasty, the issue of knowledge—of knowing what it is to be a pederast—is the story's central concern: what does it mean to know about ancient pederasty, and how does that knowledge inform modern masculinity? If Cannon was prosecuted for the influence this story might have over 'Youth', then precisely what might modern youth learn about ancient pederasty? This is the question to which *Classical Culture and Modern Masculinity* will turn and return.

SOCRATIC LEARNING AND PLATONIC TEACHING

For many modern male readers, knowing about pederastic desire, knowing what pederastic desire means, meant close attendance and examination of Plato's dialogues. As this book will show, male readers have repeatedly found inspiration, encouragement—and problems—in the works such as *Charmides, Lysis, Symposium*, and *Phaedrus*. Eighteenth- and nineteenth-century German classics professors, and Victorian and Edward English intellectuals and writers have all turned back to the Platonic texts whose characters are very often older men and male youths. But these texts have not simply furnished modern men with knowledge *about* ancient pederasty. Rather the philosophical enquiries into self-understanding and knowledge undertaken in these dialogues are often conducted in the context of an intensely charged scene between an older man and boy or youth.

---

[22] See Gladfelder (2007a: 36), for this pun on Cannon/canon.

That's to say, it is the words exchanged between an older man and a beautiful youth that facilitates the possibility for a more truthful philosophical investigation. The relationship between knowledge and pederastic desire becomes a complex and entangling one, as desires between males beget knowledge which in turn begets further desire.

Plato's dialogues repeatedly emphasize the *embodied* nature of knowledge: the Socratic model of pedagogy is one at which one has to be there—one has to hear Socrates' words. The emphasis on being present and close to the physical body of one's teacher, and the stress laid upon the phonocentric nature of the lesson, are cornerstones of Socratic pedagogy. Even though many will argue that an erotic charge between teacher and pupil is not necessary, what most readers can agree on is that it is the relationship between (at least) two embodied men, present to one another, able to hear each other's words, that conditions the possibility for true enquiry into knowledge in the works of Plato. And yet it is the putative presence of Plato at Socrates' philosophical conversations that problematizes this model straight-away, since it is Plato's very transcription of Socrates' words that has led to continual questioning about the reliability of that transcription. Our access to Socratic wisdom is facilitated because *and* despite of Plato's writing. Famously, in the *Phaedrus*, Plato has Socrates tell the story in which the Egyptian god Theuth informs his king (Thamous or Ammon as the Greeks called him) about his new invention, writing that he describes as a 'pharmakon' (274e6). However, this notorious word, which can ambiguously mean both 'medicine' and 'poison', reflects the king's reception of this new invention when he says to Theuth:

you, as father of letters [*patēr grammatōn*], have been led by your affection for them to describe them as having the opposite of their real effect. For your invention will produce forgetfulness [not memory] in the souls of those who have learned it, through lack of practice at using their memory...To your students [*mathētais*] you give the appearance of writing, not the reality of it; having heard much, in the absence of teaching [*aneu didachēs*], they will appear to know much when for the most part they know nothing...[23]

---

[23] *Phaedrus* 275a–b (Plato 1988: 123).

Socrates concurs with the king's opinion:

> So the man who thinks that he has left behind him a science in writing, and
> in his turn the man who receives it from him in the belief that anything clear
> or certain will result from what is written down, would be full of simplicity
> and would be really ignorant of Ammon's prophetic utterance . . . [W]hen
> once it is written, every composition is trundled about everywhere . . . in the
> presence both of those who know about the subject and of those who have
> nothing at all to do with it, and it does not know how to address those
> it should address and not those it should not. When it is ill-treated and
> unjustly abused, it always needs its father [*patros*] to help it; for it is incapable
> of defending or helping itself.[24]

Writing for Thamous and Socrates is an unstable entity—its
description as both medicine and poison expresses that. Writing
disenables the oral exchange between teacher and pupil, as it wanders
aimlessly without its author, its 'father' to protect it and speak in its
defence. Socrates' paternal metaphor attempts to naturalize the relationship between a speaker and his words: the learning he speaks is a
reproduction of what he thinks, as a child takes after his paternal
parent. Behind this genealogical metaphor hides another pairing: that
of Socrates and Plato. Even though the speaking Socrates underlines
his suspicions about the usefulness of writing for possessing knowledge and wisdom, it is Plato who writes these oral thoughts down.
Just as writing is an ambiguous *pharmakon*, so Plato's own writing
both makes Socrates' speech live (memorializes his wisdom) *and*
marks his death. The complexities of the transmission of wisdom
from father to son, from elder man to youth, from Plato and Socrates,
are already emphasized by Plato himself. Even though we might like
to think that true philosophizing is a *tabula rasa*, self-engendering,
present to us, created by the dialogues we have with one another in
the present, our ideas actually reflect a long *textual* tradition, a long
genealogy in which ideas are not simply passed down, but also
wilfully and mistakenly redirected, appropriated, altered, and
emended. Plato is all too aware that the *pharmakon*, writing, is a
help and a hindrance in the processes of educating the younger
generation in the ideas of the older.[25]

---

[24] *Phaedrus* 275c–e (Plato 1988: 123–5).
[25] Derrida (1981) explores these issues most fully. Derrida's reading of Plato has
itself spawned a long bibliography: see Naas (2010) for a close reading and debate.

This paternal metaphor is also explored by Plato in the *Symposium*. The picture Plato paints of the ideal teaching scene is so strange that it warrants brief but detailed examination. At this point in the dialogue—again a scene at which only learned *men* are learning—Socrates introduces a woman into the circle. Or rather Socrates reports what the prophetess from Mantinea, Diotima, told him about what *erōs* has to do with philosophy. Socrates' testimony of Diotima's lesson is set in a context in which various men are discussing the uses, glories, and pitfalls of *erōs*. Male-male *erōs* takes over a large part of the proceedings, but none of what the previous speakers had said would have prepared them for Socrates' speech.

Strangely, then, a woman, Diotima, is both present at, and absent from, Socrates' explication of love and philosophizing *between men*. But then it is the *female body* that is invoked in order to discuss this topic:

The point is, Socrates, that every human being is both physically and mentally pregnant [*kuousin . . . pantes anthrōpoi kai kata to sōma kai kata tēn psuchēn*]. Once we reach a certain point in the prime of our lives, we instinctively desire to give birth, but we find it possible only in an attractive medium [*en de tōi kalōi*], not a repulsive one—and yes, sex between a man and woman is a kind of birth.[26]

Bizarrely, *all* people can be pregnant—either in their bodies or in their souls, and this includes men. Even if we might think that Diotima/Socrates is speaking metaphorically here, the physical (male or female?) body repeatedly intrudes into the text:

proximity to beauty makes a pregnant person [*to kuoun*] obliging, happy and relaxed . . . Proximity to repulsiveness, however, makes us frown, shrink in pain, back off, withdraw; no birth takes place, but we retain our children [*to kuēma*, literally embryo, foetus] unborn and suffer badly. So the reason why, when pregnant and swollen, ready to burst [*tōi kuounti te kai ēdē spargōnti*], we get so excited in the presence of beauty is that the bearer of beauty releases us from our agony.[27]

As Kenneth Dover notes in his commentary, 'the vivid physical terms . . . describe equally the reactions of the male and of the female genitals to sexual stimulus and revulsion'.[28] It is not simply the sex of

---

[26] *Symposium* 206c. (Plato 1994: 48–9). All subsequent translations of the *Symposium* will come from this translation, unless noted.

[27] *Symposium* 206d (Plato 1994: 50).

[28] Dover (1980: 147).

these bodies that becomes questionable. Moreover, pregnancy comes *before* sex in Diotima/Socrates' narrative.

The story gets still more curious, as Diotima, through Socrates, fully explicates what *erōs* is:

mortal nature does all it can to achieve immortality and live forever. Its sole resource for this is the ability of reproduction constantly to replace the past generation with a new one...a person in fact never possesses the same attributes, but is constantly being renewed and constantly losing other qualities...no one's mental characteristics, traits, beliefs, desires, delights, troubles, or fears ever remain the same: they come and go.[29]

And so the conclusion to which we are leading is that men are 'in love with immortality'.[30]

Immortality is brought about in the following way:

Now, when men are physically pregnant [*egkumones...kata ta sōmata*], she continued, they're more likely to be attracted to women; their love manifests itself in trying to gain immortality, renown, and what they take to be happiness by producing children. Those who are mentally pregnant, however...I mean, there are people whose minds are far more pregnant [*en tais psuchais kuousin*] than their bodies, they're filled with offspring you might expect a mind to bear and produce. What offspring? Virtue and especially wisdom.[31]

The relation between men who are 'mentally pregnant' is nevertheless marked by physical desires: 'he'll never do it [give birth] in an unattractive medium. Since he's pregnant, he prefers physical beauty [*ta...sōmata ta kala*] to ugliness.' 'Physical beauty' is, literally 'beautiful bodies'. And it is in such a context that the mentally pregnant man 'can talk fluently...about virtue and about what qualities and practices it takes for a man to be good [*ton andra ton agathon*]. In short, he takes on this person's education.'[32] The Greek for 'education' here is the verb *paideuein*, which heavily implies a pederastic context, albeit with male bodies that have female traits. Furthermore, this relationship between two males looks very much like a full-blown love affair: 'For as I think, he clings onto/grasps/touches the beautiful

[29] *Symposium* 207d–e (Plato 1994: 50).
[30] *Symposium* 208e (Plato 1994: 51).
[31] *Symposium* 208e–209a (Plato 1994: 52).
[32] *Symposium* 209b (Plato 1994: 52).

(one) and associates with him/it' (*haptomenos yap oimai tou kalou kai homilōn autōi*) (209c): The clause is extremely difficult to render, as translators do not agree how much physical touch is intended by 'haptomenos'. Walter Hamilton coyly suggests 'by intimate association with beauty embodied in his friend'.[33] Robin Waterfield, on the other hand, offers: 'once he's come into contact with an attractive person and become intimate with him.'[34] Finally Christopher Gill gives us: 'when someone has made contact and formed a relationship with beauty of this sort . . . '.[35] What sort of contact is involved? Does 'tou kalou' refer to an individual, or 'beauty' itself? Indeed, the relationship between two males who are so invested in talking about 'the qualities and practices it takes for a man to be good' is, at least, very highly charged: 'he thinks of his partner all the time, whether or not he's there, and together they share in raising their offspring [*to gennēthen*].'

Scholars have already pointed out that this picture of human bodies and relationships is clearly at odds with the picture many have formed of more conventional Athenian pederastic relations and encounters. Evidence suggests that Athenians regarded sexual desire as an appetite, construing it as 'a longing for the possession and consumption of a desirable object'.[36] Whereas many scholars, since Foucault's *History of Sexuality: The Uses of Pleasure* (originally published in 1984), have underlined the asymmetrical nature of the pederastic relationship (positing active and passive, elder and younger partners), the picture of (possibly reciprocal) *paideuein* Diotima/Socrates presented here is quite different from that sort of pederasty.[37] What has been most pressing for readers is the possibility of translating the key terms in Diotima's vocabulary, especially the word *kuein* ('to be pregnant'). Vlastos has argued that this must always be rendered as I just have.[38] Burnyeat notes hesitantly that Plato 'allows no backing away from the implications of the metaphor'

[33] Plato (1951: 91).
[34] Plato (1994: 52).
[35] Plato (1999: 47).
[36] See Halperin (1990: 276).
[37] See Halperin (1990: 264–75). Foucault's and Halperin's work has, of course, been contested by the important critique of Davidson (2007). Although Davidson does discuss Socrates' speeches and Plato's writings in detail, he does not examine Diotima/Socrates in the *Symposium* in any detail in his work.
[38] Vlastos (1981: 424).

of pregnancy and conception, suggesting that he does not quite know how much we are meant to see in that metaphor.[39] Halperin, on the other hand, locates Plato's language 'as a male strategy for controlling reproductive politics', a strategy his anthropology uncovers in various places around the globe 'best studied in New Guinea'.[40] He goes on to note that this appropriation of female bodily attributes is paradoxical, since it had to be seen as 'symbolic, not real . . . their assumption of "feminine" capacities and powers' was to be understood as 'a cultural fiction, or (at the very least) a mere analogy'.[41] Halperin's Plato was fully aware of the actual biology of human reproduction.[42]

The problem in understanding the language of Diotima/Socrates here is reflected in Diotima's discussion *about* how we use language to describe love and desire, which prefaces her description of male pregnancy. She tells Socrates that we 'single out a particular kind of love and apply to it the term which properly belongs to the whole range. We call *it* "love" and use other terms for other kinds of love.'[43] Similarly, with being pregnant: the Greeks have applied the term *kuein* to a particular kind of pregnancy (that of women), when its real meaning covers a range of reproductions. Nevertheless the problem remains: how metaphorical are these pregnant male bodies in Plato's text? Did Plato actually attempt to envisage a radically different view of the (male) body here? How tangible are the bodies meant to be? How much touching occurs when Diotima/Socrates uses words like 'haptomenos'? Plato's images of pregnancy and reproduction neatly bring into focus the problems of the transmission of knowledge from teacher to pupil, from father to son, from one generation to the next. Male pregnancy is meant to guarantee that men will always know what makes a good man ('ton andra ton agathon') despite the fact that a man is always changing ('neos aei gignomenos' (207d)). But ironically it seems that the perfect, truthful reproduction of this image of perfect reproduction remains out of the grasp of Plato's readers: successfully translating and reproducing what this image of perfect reproduction is has eluded classical scholars. Instead, Plato's language has spawned *too many* translations, each contesting the

[39] Burnyeat (1977: 14 n. 5).
[40] Halperin (1990: 287, 286).
[41] Halperin (1990: 291).
[42] See Halperin (1990: 279). For a more recent explication of the text, see Penner (1992).
[43] *Symposium* 205b (Plato 1994: 47).

other about the exact meaning of terms like *kuein*. What pregnant men must look like and do in order to reproduce knowledge of what makes a man good eludes the reproductive strategies of modern translators.

Instead, the beautiful, pregnant bodies in the text have permitted numerous interpretations. For instance, Plato's writing can acquire heterosexist and misogynistic connotations: he paints a homosocial scene, from which women have been excluded, women whose reproductive capacities are nothing in comparison to the intellectual abilities of men. On the other hand, Plato's text could offer a positive picture for those men not sexually attracted to women, who are often doomed to feel inadequate for their inability to reproduce and procreate in the 'conventional' manner. Plato's extremely unusual depiction of male pregnancy has ensured that it is very difficult to know what sort of male bodies and desires are to be reproduced from this text. How knowledge is to be transferred from one male to another, how each is to educate the other, is an issue reflected in the structure of the *Symposium* itself. Rather than speaking in his own voice, Socrates is *reporting* the speech of a woman, Diotima. Furthermore, the *Symposium* is presented to us as Apollodorus' account of Aristodemus' account of a symposium (perhaps fictional) that had occurred many years before.[44] Who should we be thinking is speaking when Socrates speaks Diotima's words? Is it Diotima, Socrates, Aristodemus, or Apollodorus, or even Plato? As Plato's text on male pregnancy veers between theoretical abstraction and an emphasis on the physical aspects of the philosopher's body, the framing of Diotima's words through a relay of people who orally pass her terms from one person to the next underlines the fact that the production of knowledge occurs between embodied persons. 'For all its desire to deliver theoretical, depersonalized "truths", philosophy ultimately happens between people', ideally, pregnant men.[45]

The reproduction of knowledge, then, is tied to the issue of reproducibility of Greek men: Socrates' suspicion of Egyptian inventions and Diotima's paean to the pregnant male form has seen to it that many modern readers of Plato, since the eighteenth century, at least, have masculinized and Hellenized what it means to teach and to learn. But the difficulty in reproducing Platonic reproductive

---

[44] See Halperin (1992).   [45] Leonard (2008: 45).

technologies has also seen to it that the appropriation of Socratic elenchus and Platonic pedagogy has always been contested and debated. *Classical Culture and Modern Masculinity* examines how the examples of the Socratic method and various texts of Plato have provided ground for profound discussion about how best to educate and (re)produce modern men in eighteenth- and nineteenth-century German-speaking states and nineteenth- and twentieth-century Britain. Plato's texts showed modern readers how elastically complex the pederastic relationship could become in ancient Greek culture. On the one hand, highly charged relations between men were taken as a given in Plato's dialogues (even when a 'woman', Diotima, enters the context, her discourse is about male *erōs*), but, on the other hand, male—male *erōs*, in Plato, could take on all sorts of shapes, contours, and meanings. Plato's texts, then, were already engaged in examining whether knowledge can ever really be transferred from one male to another one generation to the next. What does it mean to say that the term 'translation' can ever be literally understood? What does it really mean to 'carry across' knowledge? What is at stake in saying that Plato is using the term *kuein* literally? Indeed, Plato's depiction of two young men intensely involved with the beautiful pregnancy of one another is a complex, messy affair, complicating the traditional view of asymmetrical Athenian pederasty in which the older male actively pursues and educates the younger passive one. Indeed the positions of 'teacher' and 'learner' are blurred, just as Socrates rejects the advances of Alcibiades as later described in the *Symposium*, precisely because Alcibiades thinks Socrates possesses some quantifiable knowledge that might be passed down from the elder man to the younger (215a–219e).

Despite the cluttered messiness of pederastic relations in Graeco-Roman antiquity, for many recent historians, the modern turn to ancient Greece was a response to the legal criminalization and medical pathologization of modern male—male desires. Since the work of Foucault, most have viewed such philhellenism between 1750 and 1950 in terms of 'counter-discourse'. Indeed, the reference to Greek homoerotics apparently formed something of an open secret, a euphemism everyone understood, but the knowledge of which everyone denied.[46] As Thomas Cannon had already inferred, the subject was

[46] See Dellamora (1990) and Dowling (1994).

generally unspeakable. Alfred Douglas and Oscar Wilde used the cumbersome phrase 'the love that dare not speak its name', and John Addington Symonds in his *A Problem in Greek Ethics* could 'hardly find a name which will not soil this paper'.[47] Historians have comprehensively shown that a few modern homosexuals were lucky enough to leave the northern climes, seduced by the Mediterranean. From Winckelmann's employment at Rome, to rich Grand Tourists, to Byron's visits to Italy and Greece, and to Pater, Symonds, Wilde, and Forster—all enjoyed the pleasures that the shores and cities of the Mediterranean had to offer.[48] *Classical Culture and Modern Masculinity*, however, asks what sense of history, what sense of the historicity of their desires, did these individuals have? The classical education and learning of scholars such as Winckelmann and nineteenth-century British classicists were sufficiently ample and wide-ranging, so that any straightforward identification with ancient Greeks was never going to be simple: we have already seen how difficult it has been to translate Greek. *Classical Culture and Modern Masculinity* examines the ways in which male classicists and classically trained intellectuals, between 1750 and 1930, really thought that they were and loved like ancient Greeks. Rather than uncovering a continuous history of covert, secretive (even subversive), homosexual identification with antiquity, we will see that Greek pederastic pedagogy permitted many sorts of men to admire and reproduce in various modes that highly intense form of education, men whom we will not straightforwardly be able to call 'homo-' or 'heterosexual'. In what senses, this book asks, did antiquity offer various 'truths' to those modern men who searched for the answer to the question 'who am I?' How did ancient pederastic relationships operate as models that informed the conceptualizations of their own desires? How did such relationships, seen by so many philhellenists as the context of ancient pedagogy and the conduit for the transfer of knowledge from one generation to the next, provide modern men with knowledge about themselves and their passions? If pederasty and pedagogy were seen to be so closely intertwined in ancient Greek culture at least, then, what was the relationship between knowledge and desire in

[47] Symonds (1928: 6).
[48] On Byron, see Crompton (1985), and, on the Mediterranean more generally, see Aldrich (1993). See also Bleys (1996).

modernity? And how would modern pedagogy in the classics inform men about modern pederasty, modern erotic desires?

HISTORICISM AND HOMOEROTIC DESIRES

Indeed, understanding Greek pederastic pedagogy became one of the most important ways in which modern thinkers could reflect upon the nature of the historicism of their knowledge. The seventeenth and eighteenth centuries witnessed the development of a particular historical method, through which intellectuals became increasingly concerned with postulating and formulating the nature of the relationship between the ancient and modern (European) worlds: how is modern Europe different from, and similar to, classical antiquity? In what areas of modern European life might it be possible and desirable to reproduce ancient culture? The various and varying German, French, and British discourses of historicism in the eighteenth and nineteenth centuries navigated the course between viewing antiquity as analogous and anachronistic to Western modernity.[49] Indeed the professional development of classical philology as a German university discipline exemplifies well these intellectual disputes. The period between 1750 and 1850 witnessed intense debate around the purpose of classical scholarship. Is the aim an idealistic *Bildung* of young men who might reproduce the glory that was Greece? Or should philology be seen primarily as scientific *Wissenschaft* whose positivism permitted historians to set aside their emotional and moral responses to antiquity, and produce a full picture of the ancient world, establishing the similarities *and* differences between ancient and modern? 'The historical study of the ancient world was supposed to produce *Bildung* in students by showing them the Greek and Roman national characters in formation.'[50] This objective, however, did not dovetail neatly with scholars' wishes 'to imagine, at once comprehensively and in minute detail, what it had been to write or act as the ancients did. They insisted that the true scholar abandon the assumptions and mental categories of his own world and time ... To men like Niebuhr, everything ancient was alien to

---

[49] See DeJean (1997) and Hartog (2003, 2005).   [50] Grafton (1983: 183).

him—and had to be understood in all its rich otherness.'[51] The ambition of German historicism was such that Anthony Grafton has labelled it *'the will to replace the text*...scholars tended to try to dissolve the texts before them in order to recreate something lost,' the lost, othered world of antiquity, to inhabit it in all its difference.[52] The tensions, then, between philosophies of *Bildung* and *Wissenschaft* ensured that the translatability and reproducibility of ancient knowledge into modernity were profoundly debated issues.

But if some classical scholars 'knew' the ancient world was imitable for certain *gebildet* young men, and if other scholars 'knew' antiquity was a historically inimitable, different world, then Greek pederastic pedagogy proved to be the limit case for all types of historicism. It was not firmly known whether they were imitating the Greeks in this area of culture or not. Indeed, it was Greek love that made historicism such an urgent concern. The question of the exemplarity of the pederastic—pedagogic relationship became one of the thorniest problems for the historicist projects of the mid-eighteenth century onwards, as that relationship offered both a model and an anti-model of the very context for the production of *Bildung* and *Wissenschaft*. One of the most famous moments in the history of the historicist method was Johann Joachim Winckelmann's *Geschichte der Kunst des Alterthums* (1764).[53] It was Winckelmann's description of his desires for an ancient statue of a beautiful male youth that focused the problems encountered by the scholars of historicism who attempted to adjudicate upon the meaning of modernity in relation to antiquity. The 'Apollo Belvedere' became one of the most widely admired and imitated statues of antiquity, after its rediscovery at the beginning of the sixteenth century. Winckelmann's paean to its beauties not only made it even more famous, but also became the stereotypical image of modern veneration of the ancient world. When he gazed at the statue, which supposedly evidenced the very highest abilities of classical Greek sculptors, Winckelmann felt 'himself transported to Delos and to the Lycian groves, places Apollo honoured with his presence'.[54] Such ebullient prose saw to it that Winckelmann came to

[51] Grafton (1983: 179–80).
[52] Grafton (1983: 181).
[53] Friedrich Meinecke makes Winckelmann a key figure in his classic study of historicism: see Meinecke (1959: 290–302).
[54] Winckelmann (2006: 334).

be viewed soon after his death in 1768 as a modern Greek—a modern thinker capable of intellectually travelling back and forth in time, able to see the timeless, truthful beauty offered forth by the 'Apollo'.[55]

But this reading of Winckelmann was already partial—it already read only part of his text. Winckelmann's readers quickly forgot that his ekphrasis of the 'Apollo Belvedere' occurs in a section titled 'Greek Art under Nero'. The statue was supposedly carried away from Greece by 'Acratus, an iniquitous freed slave, together with the half-learned Secundus Carinas', under the command of the Roman emperor. Nero 'gives evidence of an unrestrained desire [*ausgelassene Begierde*] for everything related to the fine arts—only it was a craving for collecting and not for having new works made'.[56] The 'Apollo' 'enters into the history of the decline of art in ancient Rome as an ideal that by that time could no longer be recreated but had to be pillaged from the past'.[57] That is to say, the 'Apollo Belvedere' is an exemplary work of art, but an example that could not be reproduced owing to the historical specificity of the politically free classical Greece. It is, then, the erotic beauty of the Greek male youth that puts into sharp focus the issues that historicist classical scholarship negotiated.

Interestingly, Winckelmann emphatically contrasts his own response to the statue with that of Nero. Nero's 'unrestrained desire' ('Begierde' implies lust) and his 'vile . . . bad taste [*übeln Geschmacke*]', together with the 'freed slave' Acratus and his 'half-learned' assistant evidence the inverse of Winckelmann's expert connoisseurship: Winckelmann's appreciation of the 'Apollo' does not represent the lustful, half-learned pleasures of men such as the freed slave Acratus who hover between freedom and abject servitude under the degenerate, rapacious Nero, whose desires have another freed slave decorate a portico 'with figures of gladiators in every possible position [*in allen möglichen Stellungen*]'.[58] Furthermore, Acratus' name is suggestive of the Greek *akratos*, used of unmixed, strong wine and violent and intemperate persons.[59] Winckelmann's eroticized translocation *from*

[55] See Hatfield (1943) and Namowicz (1978). See also Sünderhauf (2004).

[56] Winckelmann (2006: 332–3).

[57] Potts (1994: 64). See also Hartog (2003: 184).

[58] Winckelmann (2006: 333).

[59] His name is also suggestive of (though not etymologically linked to) *akrateia*, the Greek term for the loss of control of oneself and one's pleasures: see Foucault (1986) on *akrateia hedones*. Finally, is it possible to see the keel of the ship (the *carina*), which transported Nero's plunder, in the name of the half-learned Secundus *Carinas*?

his study in Rome to the groves of Greece is differentiated from Nero's 'completely insatiable [*vollends unersättlich*]' desires that sought to 'carr[y] away' statuary *from Greece to Rome*.[60] Nero's *Wegführen* goes in the opposite direction (spatially and temporally) to the *Wegrücken* of Winckelmann.[61]

On the one hand, then, Winckelmann's aestheticizing text aims to leapfrog over the centuries that separate his own time from ancient Greek culture, to show that this timeless sculpture can be understood *outside* historical processes. On the other hand, however, the statue is part of a history of the *Roman* acquisition of Greek art: what it is, is evidence of Nero's 'vile taste', making it part of a narrative that *historicizes* taste for, and admiration of, Greek art. Winckelmann is keenly aware that this timeless beauty of Greek art, the 'Apollo Belvedere', could be viewed as such only *because* Nero's 'vile taste' saw to it that it survived. It is because of this tension that Winckelmann must attempt to contrast his desires with those that Nero had on the statue. On the one hand, then, Winckelmann says that this statue should be viewed in its original context—as if at Delos, or the Lycian groves—it is a product of Greece and should be seen as such. Yet, on the other hand, it is only its *trans-latio*, its transportation to Italy, that shows us modern viewers that the 'Apollo' can look like the perfect work of art that it is, anywhere, transcendent of time, context, and framing. Winckelmann's appreciation, then, oscillates between seeing the statue within its historical context and outside any contextual framework. And, most crucially, it is Winckelmann's erotic desires that structure this tension between his historicism and his aestheticism. On the one hand, he presents his homoerotic response to the statue as a timeless response to the art (he feels himself in the 'presence' of Apollo in Delos or the Lycian groves). Yet, on the other hand, he seeks to differentiate historically his desires from those displayed by the Roman emperor Nero.

Winckelmann's paean to Apollo is so often seen as a covertly homoerotic response to the beauties of ancient statuary (classics becoming an alibi for expressing illicit sexual desires for beautiful men and boys), a subtle attempt to demonstrate the *ahistorical* nature

---

[60] To be more precise, Winckelmann argues that the statue was taken to Antium, Nero's birthplace. Winckelmann (1764: 391; 2006: 333).
[61] See Winckelmann (1764: 391, 393) for these terms.

of homoerotic desires. But this decontextualizing of the ekphrasis of the 'Apollo Belvedere' from its place in Winckelmann's *Geschichte* omits to consider Winckelmann's very serious interest in Nero's own decontextualization of the statue from Greece. For Winckelmann is quite concerned to distinguish historically the desires Nero had for beautiful male statuary from his own. Winckelmann sought to provide a space in which it was possible to explicate the difference between ancient and modern homoerotic desires for ancient Greek culture, while at the same time dehistoricizing his own desires. And it was the understanding of the (a)historicity of such desires that posed one of the greatest challenges for the modern historicist European academy. Greek love in all its various manifestations became an urgent concern for those formulating the intellectual and cultural relationship between classical antiquity and European modernity.

FOUCAULT'S PARADIGM SHIFT

Those scholars who have been invested in writing histories of secret codes, in which 'Greece' becomes the signifier for 'homosexuality', have been encouraged by the work of Foucault, who uncovered a 'paradigm shift' in the way in which the desiring self was conceived in the period between *c*.1750 and 1900.[62] The 'love that dare not speak its name' found a language in classical antiquity. We have just seen with Winckelmann, however, the identification with ancient Greece was a rather more complex affair. Let us turn to Foucault's work itself, then, to consider its usefulness for *Classical Culture and Modern Masculinity*. In a famous passage, Foucault writes:

As defined by the ancient civil or canonical codes, sodomy was a category of forbidden acts; their perpetrator was nothing more than the juridical subject of them. The nineteenth-century homosexual became a personage, a past, a case history, and a childhood ... [His sexuality] was everywhere present in him: at the root of all his actions because it was their insidious and indefinitely active principle; written immodestly on his face and body because *it was a secret that always gave itself away* ... the psychological, psychiatric,

---

[62] See Dowling (1989, 1994) and Aldrich (1993) on the Hellenic codes.

medical category of homosexuality was constituted from the moment it was characterized—Westphal's famous article of 1870 on 'contrary sexual sensations' can stand as its date of birth—less by a type of sexual relations than by a certain quality of sexual sensibility . . .

Homosexuality appeared as one of the forms of sexuality when it was transposed from the practice of sodomy onto a kind of interior androgyny, a hermaphroditism of the soul. The sodomite had been a temporary aberration; the homosexual was now a species.[63]

Eve Kosoksky Sedgwick has been one of the closest and wisest readers of Foucault's prose at this point in his argument. And, by tracing out her analysis of Foucault here, we will also introduce the history that *Classical Culture and Modern Masculinity* seeks to produce and examine. In her essay 'Gender Criticism', Sedgwick offers a particularly focused close reading of this passage, in which, as Sedgwick says, 'the metonym for *sexuality* that *The History of Sexuality* installs is *homosexuality*'.[64] She notes:

Foucault's discussion here of the invention of 'the homosexual' is presented as an exemplifying instance of a process of specification, of the emergence of *identities* where previously there had been *acts*, that also included 'all those minor perverts whom nineteenth-century psychiatrists entomologized by giving them strange baptismal names' . . . The newly reified homosexuality, in short, is but one representative example of 'these thousand aberrant sexualities' that came, in their plurality, to define sexuality itself.[65]

This exemplification of homosexuality makes the Victorian period look a lot like our own. That is to say, his concentration on the passage from sodomite to homosexual elides any discussion of zoophiles, zooerasts, auto-monosexualists, mixoscopophiles, gynecomasts, presbyophiles, sexoesthetic inverts, and dyspareunist women who were part of nineteenth-century sexological theory and psychiatric practice, but literally get but the briefest of mention in Foucault.[66] These 'minor perverts', as Foucault diagnoses them, played crucial roles in the history of the polarization of sexuality in the twentieth century into homo/heterosexual definition. These roles, however, are

---

[63] Foucault (1998: 42–3), emphases added.
[64] Sedgwick (1992: 281).
[65] Sedgwick (1992: 281, with quotations from Foucault 1998: 43, 44).
[66] See Foucault (1998: 43).

quite straightforwardly minoritized by Foucault, so that homosexuality is installed 'in a more than just metonymically representational relation to sexuality as a whole'. The story that Foucault does *not* tell, as Sedgwick discusses, is the disappearance of this throng of sexualities and its subsequent canalization of sexuality between the banks of homo- and heterosexuality.

Foucault's discussions of nineteenth-century sexuality seem to take very twentieth-century hues. He writes: 'What is peculiar to modern societies . . . is not that they consigned sex to a shadow existence, but that they dedicated themselves to speaking of it *ad infinitum*, while exploiting it as *the* secret.'[67] As Sedgwick notes, 'what could be less secret than the . . . particular secret within the open secret of sex, the one named by Christianity and multiple reinscriptions of Western law as the unspeakable itself'.[68] Indeed Foucault says in his famous paragraph on the homosexual that homosexuality 'was a secret that always gave itself away'. Homosexuality was, in effect, the most secret of secrets of that open secret that was sex. 'The particular case of homosexuality here marks an intensification of, but by the same token a certain discontinuity from, the knowing reification of "sex".'[69]

Sedgwick cites another highly revealing passage from Foucault, revealing precisely for what it conceals. We will re-cite a few of the most important moments:

Thus sex gradually became an object of great suspicion . . . the *fragment of darkness* that we each carry within us: a general signification, a *universal secret, an omnipresent cause, a fear that never ends* . . . there has evolved . . . a knowledge not so much of *his* form, but of that which divides him, determines him perhaps, but above all causes him to be ignorant of himself . . . Causality in the subject, the unconscious of the subject, the truth of the subject *in the other who knows, the knowledge he holds unbeknown to him*, all this found an opportunity to deploy itself in the discourse of sex.[70]

Although Foucault appears to be in the process of demystifying the history of sexuality and its utter importance to a Western sense of self, as Sedgwick elegantly examines, 'Foucault chooses not to make

---

[67] Foucault (1998: 35), quoted in Sedgwick (1992: 283), emphasis in original.
[68] Sedgwick (1992: 283).
[69] Sedgwick (1992: 283).
[70] Foucault (1998: 69–70), quoted in Sedgwick (1992: 283), emphasis added.

explicit the privileged referent of his "universal" noun phrases in the locus of a particular homosexual-heterosexual question.'[71] That is to say, the rhetoric of the text—the 'universal secret', the 'omnipresent cause'—clearly conjures up connotations of homosexuality, and the 'his' of 'his form' would most clearly refer, in Foucault's reader's late-twentieth-century mind, to the male homosexual *him*self, despite the fact that Foucault does not actually mention him. By closeting the homosexual in his text—by referring to him at the same time as not referring to him—Foucault has the homosexual become

'the unconscious' of the text . . . in the sense that the text's refusal to verbalize it forces its articulation or denial on the reader, whom the text thus interpellates as 'the other who knows . . . the knowledge [the text] holds unbeknown to [itself]'; Foucault founds the reader as the knowing Other of 'that which divides [the text], determines [it] perhaps, but above all causes [it] to be ignorant of [it]self'.[72]

Rather than demystifying the secret of sex, Foucault's text *repeats* what he sees nineteenth-century culture doing. By *implying* homo-sexuality, his own text expresses *and* represses, represses *and* ex-presses. The reader becomes a kind of psychiatrist, who is forced to judge whether the homosexual is perceptible behind the words 'his form', just as the nineteenth-century psychiatrist was positioned to perceive the truth of the homosexual, even though the homosexual perhaps did not realize his dark secret himself. The text itself, then, does not simply not 'come out', but seems to harbour its secret somewhat unknowingly.

Sedgwick uncovers two problems with the text of the *History* at this point, then. First, when Foucault exemplifies the homosexual openly, in expressing the predicament of the homosexual most blatantly, as in the famous passage quoted earlier,[73] he nevertheless makes homo-sexuality *unlike* the other 'minor' perversions, precisely because homosexuality can be exemplified. He does not discuss, however, this discursive gap that developed between homosexuality and other forms of sexuality. Or, to put this more precisely, he does *not* demys-tify the 'actual' story of the homosexual but presents the nineteenth-century homosexual as if he were the same as the twentieth-century

---

[71] Sedgwick (1992: 284).
[72] Sedgwick (1992: 284).
[73] Foucault (1998: 43).

model. The moment he expresses the homosexual's 'truth', he also suppresses the very particular history of what homosexuality has meant between 1870 and 2011. It becomes a history that dare not speak its name. Conversely (and this is the second problem Sedgwick identifies), when Foucault speaks of 'a universal secret' and 'an omnipresent cause' (as in the second passage quoted), he invokes the homosexual precisely by *not* expressly referring to him. That is to say, then, the moment Foucault discusses the homosexual most expressly and as an example, he actually *suppresses* the specific story of that individual; and the moment Foucault writes about nineteenth-century mystifications of sex, the rhetoric of his generalizations make it very hard for his readers *not* to see a homosexual being specified in the text, although Foucault never makes any such specific exemplification.

Rather than simply describing the formation of certain discourses that supposedly came to understand the truth of sex, Foucault's text *reiterates* the discursive movements made by these discourses. His exemplification of homosexuality on page 43 in Foucault's text makes homosexuality look like one perversion among many. This 'minoritizes' homosexuality, or, as Sedgwick explains, 'minoritizing [accounts of homosexuality] are those that attribute each of these desires [for example, homosexual desires] to a fixed, unchangeable segment of the population'. On the other hand, Foucault's subsequent failure to exemplify the homosexual clearly, even though it was half-clear that he was writing about the homosexual, has the effect of 'universalizing' homosexuality. That is to say, as Sedgwick elucidates, 'universalizing discourses are those that suggest that every person has the potential for same-sex, as for other-sex, desire or activity'.[74] 'Each kind of account [that] can underpin virulently homophobic and supportively antihomophobic ideological formations' has nevertheless been in conceptual deadlock ever since the so-called birth of the modern homosexual. Indeed, it is Sedgwick's contention that this incoherence is at the heart of the very conceptualization of homosexuality, and it is this incoherent conceptualization that structures the possibility of heterosexuality as well. What Sedgwick's reading of Foucault shows is that his very own discourse executes this very incoherence. As Sedgwick says: 'Foucault performs the emergence

---

[74] Sedgwick (1992: 285).

of homo-hetero as *the* defining axis of modern sexuality silently'.[75] If homosexuality has become *the* open secret of sex and sexuality, then Foucault's text repeats this open secret: when he talks about the homosexual, he is not really talking about him, and when he appears not to be talking about the homosexual, his text looks very much like it is. In effect, then, Foucault's own discourse re-performs much of the doubletalk chatter about the homosexual that has characterized both the nastiest homophobia and the most compassionate antihomophobia since 1870.

In *Epistemology of the Closet* Sedgwick analyses how 'the historical search for a Great Paradigm Shift may obscure the present conditions of sexual identity'.[76] The most interesting work to emerge since Foucault, in Sedgwick's opinion, comprises precisely 'ever more nuanced narratives of the development of homosexuality "as we know it today"'.[77] Despite these important scholarly advances, it seems to Sedgwick that such analysis 'has tended inadvertently to *re*familiarize, *re*naturalize, damagingly reify an entity that it could be doing much more to subject to analysis', that entity being homosexuality 'as we know it today'. Post-Foucauldian scholarship seems

to underwrite the notion that 'homosexuality as we conceive of it today' itself comprises a coherent definitional field rather than a space of over-lapping, contradictory, and conflictual definitional forces...for all their immense care, value, and potential, [such post-Foucauldian works] still risk reinforcing a dangerous consensus of knowingness about the genuinely *un*known, more than vestigially contradictory structurings of contemporary experience.[78]

In order to exemplify the 'contradiction effect' involved in the definability of homosexuality, Sedgwick shows that what counts as a homosexual in the history of the emergence of homosexuality differs wildly in different scholarly accounts. Foucault's famous depiction of the sodomite as a 'temporary aberration' and the homosexual as a 'species' provides the homosexual with a minoritized identity, as has already been discussed. Additionally, in the same paragraph Foucault describes (the nineteenth-century reification of) homosexuality as 'a hermaphrodism of the soul'. This depicts homosexuality in terms of

---

[75] Sedgwick (1992: 291).
[76] Sedgwick (1990: 44), title of 'Axiom 5'.
[77] Sedgwick (1990: 44).
[78] Sedgwick (1990: 45).

gender inversion. Putting it crudely, the male homosexual is a non-male (or, following Foucault's term, a hermaphrodite) encapsulated within a male body. 'This understanding appears, indeed, according to Foucault, to underlie and constitute the common sense of the homosexuality "we know today".'[79] David Halperin, on the other hand, offers a more intricate story in the grand narrative of homosexuality. For Halperin, the gender-inversion theory of homosexuality was soon superseded by theories that talked about 'sexual orientation independent of relative degrees of masculinity and femininity, [which] takes place during the latter part of the nineteenth century and comes into its own only during the twentieth. Its highest expression is the "straight-acting and -appearing gay male", a man distinct from other men in absolutely no other respect besides that of his "sexuality"'.[80] Sedgwick observes that it is Halperin's 'presumption of the reader's commonsense, present-tense conceptualization of homosexuality, the point from which all the thought experiments of differentiation must proceed [that] is virtually the opposite of Foucault's'. For Halperin, the modern (that is, contemporary) homosexual is the straight-acting male, whose male gender has no bearing on his sexuality, whereas 'for Foucault, it is, in the form of the feminized man or virilized woman'.[81] What characterizes *both* historians, Sedgwick demonstrates, is their emphasis that 'one model of same sex-relations is superseded by another, which may again be superseded by another'.[82] In Halperin's narrative the notion of sexual connotation replaced that of sexual inversion, and apparently any elements of the earlier model could be viewed as 'historical remnants whose process of withering away, however protracted, merits no analytic attention'.[83] Halperin's history moves from a minoritizing to a universalizing account of homosexuality. Similarly, but the opposite way around, Foucault posited the existence of a 'universalizing discourse of "sodomitic" sexual acts', which was superseded by a 'minoritizing discourse of sexual identity'.[84] *Epistemology of the Closet*, however, shows 'how issues of modern homo/heterosexual definition

---

[79] Sedgwick (1990: 46).
[80] Halperin (1989: 9) quoted in Sedgwick (1990: 46).
[81] Sedgwick (1990: 46).
[82] Sedgwick (1990: 47).
[83] Sedgwick (1990: 47).
[84] Sedgwick (1990: 47).

are structured . . . by the relations enabled by the unrationalized coexistence of different models during the times they do coexist'.[85]

Along with Foucault and since Sedgwick's own important analyses, there have been sustained and detailed attempts to do what Foucault did not do in *The History of Sexuality*—that is, offer a historical description of that paradigm shift: how did sodomitical acts become a homosexual identity in the early modern era? Several scholars have analysed the history of the rise and prevalence of sodomy trials in eighteenth-century England. Such historians have been interested in how this period witnessed a moral panic produced by war and living difficulties, and found a scapegoat in the form of the socially marginalized: 'mollies', prostitutes, and other undesirables.[86] Jeffrey Weeks's ground-breaking work (*Coming Out* (1977) and *Sex, Politics and Society* (1981)) has situated the legislation over 'homosexuality' in the context of modern social change, the processes of urbanization, industrialization, and capitalization, and the concomitant reorganization of the morphology of the family. Alan Bray and Randolph Trumbach have offered the most telling discussions of the historical development of sodomitical subcultures in the seventeenth and eighteenth centuries.[87]

Still more recently, again, Michael McKeon's *The Secret History of Domesticity: Public, Private, and the Division of Knowledge* (2005) has built on, *inter alia*, the research of Thomas Laqueur's *Making Sex: Body and Gender from the Greeks to Freud* (1990). Laqueur tracks scientific understandings of biological sex in order to demonstrate what he describes as a movement from a "one-sex" to a "two-sex" model.[88] Drawing on ancient medical texts and pre-seventeenth-century medical illustrations of male and female genitalia, he documents how it was common to think that women had the same genitals as men but inside, rather than outside, the body. The vagina was conceived as an interior penis, the labia as the foreskin, the uterus as the scrotum, and the ovaries as the testicles. And around the end of the seventeenth century, 'an anatomy and physiology of incommensurability replaced [this] metaphysics of hierarchy in the representation

[85] Sedgwick (1990: 47).
[86] See Gilbert (1978; 1980–1) and Harvey (1978).
[87] Bray (1988) and Trumbach (1977, 1987, 1989a, b, 1998). See also Bredbeck (1991) and Stewart (1997) on Renaissance and early modern sodomy; and Norton (1992) on eighteenth-century subcultures.
[88] Laqueur (1990).

of women in relation to men'.[89] Rather than being viewed as a deformed, less perfect version of man, woman came to be regarded as the polar opposite, with sexual organs that were fundamentally different.[90] This revolution in scientific 'knowledge' ensured that masculinity and femininity became biologically essentialized: one's 'sex' became a physiological object of analysis, and thereby became a separate area of study.

'Under the one-sex regime,' as Michael McKeon discusses,

> sodomy was condemned as a sinful behaviour that might be indulged by a variety of men. In fact, a normative aristocratic masculinity, defined by the crucial fact of superior power, could entail sexual relations both with women and with young male commoners... Under the two-sex model, by contrast, masculinity came to be consistent only with an anatomically gender-based differential and defined by sexual behaviour.[91]

McKeon compares the 'Renaissance institution of court pederasty' with the criminalization of the sodomite, which he argues coalesces into the homosexual:

> Pederasty names the kind of same-sex behaviour that required a decisive difference in generation, power, and status between its participants and that worked, like the patron—client relationship, to cement hierarchical super- and subordination through the performance of one man's dependence on another's power. From a modern perspective this is definitely a 'sexual' behaviour. Within early modern culture, however, pederasty was experienced as a political relationship of dependence and empowerment, a 'sexual' instance of subjection comparable, at least in this respect, to the subjection of the wife to the husband's power... As the devolution of absolutism made political subjects into ethical subjects [in the early-modern period]... so it relocated the increasingly antiquated political practice of pederasty within the general category of sodomy, a 'sexual'

---

[89] Laqueur (1990: 6).

[90] Laqueur notes (1990: 5) that the scholarly belief that a fundamental shift occurred at the end of the seventeenth century in the way that humankind viewed itself and its body is shared by a wide range of cultural historians. See also Foucault (1970) and Stone (1977). According to Laqueur, there was a whole host of ideologies that helped to usher in this change in viewing the body: the Enlightenment, the French Revolution, post-revolutionary conservatism and feminism, the rise of evangelical religion, Lockean ideas about marriage, new factory systems, the appearance of the free market. 'The remaking of the body is itself intrinsic to each of these developments' (Ibid. 1990: 11).

[91] McKeon (2005: 274).

practice that remains ethically abhorrent but politically neutral ... If to contemporaries pederasty bespoke not 'sodomy' in general but the absolutist order of hierarchical subjection, the subjective reciprocity of gender difference, bonded to a repudiation of sodomy that is more precisely a repudiation of pederasty, become intelligible as a rebellion against royal and aristocratic absolutism.[92]

The necessitation of the othering of the sodomite and the molly by the new *Bildungsbürgertum* and the middling classes ensured that those outsiders were subject to ever increasing, punitive methods of surveillance. But, as Thomas King has recently analysed, the 'molly house' was articulated as an open secret. On one level, it 'declared its own interest in the negative freedom of autonomy from the surveilling gaze of governmentality', and so 'the sodomites within the molly house were represented as having re-embodied the reciprocity of surveillance and subjection, publicity and privacy, as the condition and motor of pleasure'.[93] In other words, seventeenth- and eighteenth-century accounts of molly houses depicted mollies marrying in molly 'chapels', having sex and furthermore performing childbirth. Molly houses were seen as parodies of the normative private family space. This space was where every man was lord and master, enacting his privatized power over that space, as a subject equal in the eyes of the law, laws that putatively treated all men in public as modern and private equals, no longer part of a chain of antiquated aristocratic power relations.[94] The scientific essentialization of masculinity, discussed above, supposedly accompanied what King calls this 'levelling of masculinity'. Sodomites were ridiculed as profoundly different from modern man: their sexual practices stood for all that which modern men no longer had to endure. And so sodomy became associated with aristocratic regimes and spaces, upper-class foppery and dandyism.[95] And yet at the same time sodomites came to mimic the normative domestic scene all too closely and perilously. As Harry Cocks has recently analysed in *Nameless Offences*, the sodomite becomes eminently readable, a sign of that which is abject, *and* utterly unreadable, as it becomes impossible to identify the sodomite because

---

[92] McKeon (2005: 276).
[93] King (2008: 232).
[94] See King (2004).
[95] On the 'aristocratization of homosexuality', see King (2008: 64–90), and, on foppery, King (2004: 228–42).

he mimics the normative man so well.[96] Thomas King's important work seeks to show, then, that modern 'masculinities and femininities' are nothing 'but the performative and experiential spaces of the difference of private subjectivities from patriarchal and pederastic subjection'.[97] The modern male, as head of the modern family, balanced by the wife, who is mistress in her own complementary sphere, is at heart a reaction against the non-privatized life of the Renaissance court, which brought adult males into 'pederastic' relations. And yet, modern man is continually haunted by his doppelgänger, the sodomite and then the homosexual, who often looks just the way he does—is as modern and as masculine as he is.

Interestingly, what is not discussed in any detail by these historians is the modern interest in and concern over *ancient* systems of desire with society.[98] King refers his readers to the very pages of *Epistemology of the Closet* we discussed in detail above,[99] showing that 'old' sexual norms and behaviours are not straightforwardly replaced by 'new' ones. This is reflected in his very eloquent discussions about modern men's concerns about 'residual pederasty', sodomitical cultures that represent a hangover from an earlier period of history. As well as Sedgwick, other recent historians have also shown that there was *no single* model of 'the homosexual' in the modern period. Indeed the period that is subject to our analysis witnessed numerous, competing reifications of same-sex desires and masculinities. Theories of sexual inversion (female brains trapped in male bodies) jostled with theories of homosexuality (masculine men who might love other masculine men, making them narcissists, or younger, effeminate boys, making them look like pederasts). British intellectuals, like Edward Carpenter, also theorized the possibility that 'homogenic' men were a third gender.[100] Matt Cook, Harry Cocks, and Matt

---

[96] Cocks (2003: 77–114).

[97] King (2008: 399).

[98] King (2008: 75–82) discusses the modern reception of the *Belvedere Antinous*, including Winckelmann's description of the statue (2008: 80–2); and Boswell's 'rehearsal of Socratic pederasty' (2008: 315).

[99] See King (2008: 229).

[100] On the particularity of Carpenter's theories, see Sedgwick (1985: 202–15). On the competing theories of inversion and homosexuality, see Sedgwick (1990: 157–60), which remains one of the best discussions on the complex non-monolithic conceptualization of desire and masculinity in the nineteenth century. For Carpenter more generally, see Rowbotham (2008).

Houlbrook have all written recently on the various, often highly conflicting accounts of same-sex desire and masculinity in this period.[101]

Nevertheless, there is virtually no extended discussion about how intellectuals of the modern period might have conceptualized the historicity of masculinity in terms of the historical relationship between *ancient Greek pederasty* and *modern homoerotics and homosociality*. Winckelmann's discussion of the 'Apollo Belvedere' is merely one of the most famous moments in the period between 1750 and 1930, when an intellectual explicitly examined and discussed the antiquity and modernity of male erotic desire.

Classical Culture and Modern Masculinity does not seek to adjudicate in detail upon the grand narrative of the history of sexuality itself. This book is not concerned with tracing out The Emergence of Modern Male Sexuality: the historiography we have been tracing, inaugurated by Sedgwick's analysis of Foucault, has warned us against that. Instead this book is interested in characterizing its period of analysis (*c.*1750–1930) as one in which the relationship between ancient and modern masculinities was continually under scrutiny, the continual subject of debate. Furthermore, then, this book will *not* suggest at the end of the story that a homosexual identity we can 'know' 'actually' emerged, as if we could 'know' homosexuality, as nineteenth- and twentieth-century sexologists and psychologists have thought they could. Indeed, this period witnesses a sustained interest in learning about the formation of masculinity. That is to say, modern classical scholars have repeatedly turned back to the ancient pederastic—pedagogic relationship, in an attempt to understand what makes the man.

TOO MANY WORDS FOR UNSPEAKABLE LOVE

This period's philhellenism in German and British intellectual and cultural history was wide ranging and extremely complicated. In his discussion of the German context, Robert Tobin notes that 'the

---

[101] Cocks (2003); Cook (2003); Houlbrook (2005). See also Bristow (2007), a detailed review of these works.

"meaning" of Greek referents was unstable—it could mean sodomy or it could mean culture'.[102] Despite his either/or definition, Tobin himself goes on to show that, for various scholars and intellectuals, 'the terms "Greek", "platonic", and "Socratic" signified some sort of same-sex desire', even if what that desire precisely consisted in could not be specified and agreed upon.[103] Tobin recounts the story of the renowned and highly respected Swiss historian Johannes Müller. Müller wrote numerous letters to young male friends, which were later published, reflecting 'the notion that these letters could help transmit a culture of male—male bonding from one generation to the next'.[104] Indeed, Müller 'soon became a symbol of male—male desire for German intellectuals in the early nineteenth century'. His modern pederasty formed the context for his pedagogic relations with younger males. Nevertheless scandal attended Müller, as one of his pupils

mulcted Müller by inventing an epistolary lover who allegedly wrote under the pen-name 'Count von Batthiany'. Using letters supposedly from the lover, the young man convinced Müller to give him considerable amounts of cash, as loans supposedly guaranteed by the lover. When it finally became clear that there was no lover, Müller was broke and embarrassed. He was compelled to leave Vienna because of the scandal.[105]

Although Goethe, Müller's friend, was one of the figures apparently involved in the subsequent hiring of Müller at Weimar, Goethe later wrote in reference to the affair that 'Greek love,' was as old as humanity and so 'one could therefore say that it was rooted in nature and at the same time against nature'.[106] As Tobin examines, this description of pederasty as both part of nature and against nature becomes a *topos* for Enlightenment thinkers writing in German.[107] It is both something that is timeless and something that should not have to exist naturally—indeed it should be eradicated. Goethe's contradiction attests the existence of contorted debate about the historicity of 'Greek love' and its status in modern men's lives.

---

[102] Tobin (2000: 30).
[103] Tobin (2000: 34).
[104] Tobin (2000: 21).
[105] Tobin (2000: 22).
[106] Tobin (2000: 22 on Müller; 2000: 98 for Goethe).
[107] Tobin (2000: 98–9).

Tobin goes on to argue that the eighteenth- and early-nineteenth-century German interrogation of same-sex desire was the forerunner of later nineteenth- and twentieth-century accounts of homosexuality.[108] That modern sexuality could be said to have been 'made in Germany' is also interrogated in the essays collected in *Outing Goethe and his Age*, in order to show the centrality of the Age of Goethe for lesbian and gay archaeologies.[109] More recently still, Susan Gustafson, in *Men Desiring Men: The Poetry of Same Sex Identity and Desire in German Classicism* (2002), has sought to show how classical models were used by Winckelmann, Goethe, and other writers to invent the parameters of modern masculinity. 'The self they depict is one who *consciously* and *purposefully* decides to construct a language of, for, and about himself.'[110] And, although Gustafson agrees with Tobin that '*so far* no "highly self-conscious homosexuality" has been documented in the eighteenth century', the writers of this period nevertheless do represent, for Gustafson, 'an early attempt to express male—male desire in terms of specific personages, in terms of individuals with pasts and childhoods'.[111]

Classical Culture and Modern Masculinity is not concerned, however, with providing a teleological analysis, whereby the issues explored by German intellectuals are inherited by later British figures, in order to show how the earlier generation provided the building blocks for the later. Rather we will make profitable use of these scholars' work on the complications and incoherencies of eighteenth-century German writers, to show that these difficulties in reifying masculinity through Greek models was a continuous concern, which never resulted in a straightforward concrete, totalizing model of homosexuality. Gustafson herself refers to Immanuel Kant's 'Vorlesung über Ethik' ('A Lecture on Ethics'), in which the philosopher says:

Everyone shrinks from naming this vice, *every teacher* [*jeder Lehrer*] refrains from naming it—even with the best intention of warning his charges against it. Because it nevertheless occurs so often, one is here pressed and uncertain whether one should name it in order to make it recognizable and thereby prevent it from happening so often, or if one should not name it, in order not

[108] Tobin (2000: 195–215).
[109] Kuzniar (1996).
[110] Gustafson (2002: 31).
[111] Gustafson (2002: 35, 36).

to (by that means) provide an opportunity whereby one learns about it and commits the act thereafter ever more often. The cause of this shameful activity is that the more frequent naming of it familiarizes it so that one loses one's abhorrence of it and it becomes more tolerable.[112]

As Gustafson observes, Kant 'is unable to decide, ultimately, what the possible effects of its linguistic formation might be'.[113] As Kant shows, it is the one aspect of modern pedagogy about which 'every teacher' avoids speaking, but it is also 'the most abhorrent thing a person can commit', as Kant writes a few sentences before, and so demands pedagogical attention and instruction, perhaps more than any other topic.[114] The modern teaching scene is exactly the place where it should be discussed, but also where it cannot be. Kant's discussion brings us back to the issues raised by Cannon's story of Amorio and Hyacinth: what were modern intellectuals to make of the possibility that ancient Greek pederastic relations produced knowledge and its historical transmission from one generation to the next? What sort of (anti-)example was Amorio's lesson in love for Kant's modern pupil? Just as Kant can be seen to be worrying about the possibility that pederasty might make the man, so his lecture also explicitly suggests that knowledge itself, as transmitted from the teacher to the pupil, might bring about unspeakable desires themselves. The relationship between knowledge and desire is *the* key issue when considering the role of the teacher.

CLASSICAL CULTURE AND MODERN MASCULINITY

As other scholars have shown, the eighteenth and nineteenth centuries actually witnessed a profusion of terms to discuss male same-sex desire and identification that convey a Hellenic background: 'Sodomiterey'; 'Knabenliebe'; 'Männerliebe'; 'griechische Liebe'; 'Päderastie'; 'sokratische Liebe'; 'platonische Liebe'; 'Hyacinth'; 'Narcissist' . . . The list goes on.[115] Rather than bespeaking an unspeakability, this wealth of terms suggests that the relationship between ancient and modern masculinities

---

[112] Kant, quoted in Gustafson (2002: 17–18), emphases added.
[113] Gustafson (2002: 18).
[114] Kant, quoted in Gustafson (2002: 18).
[115] See Gustafson (2002: 24–5),with further references. See also Derks (1990).

was a highly vocal and multifarious concern. This book could have take any of the following topics as its subjects: the Age of Goethe; homosexuality in eighteenth-century literature; the poetry of Percy Bysshe Shelley, including his translation of Plato's *Symposium*; the poetry of Matthew Arnold; the Uranian writers; Bentham's essays on *paiderastia*; the place of Sappho in modern scholarship and modern discussions of same-sex desire; female erotic responses to antiquity; Heinrich Hössli and the subsequent German emancipation movement; the influence of Walt Whitman; the philosophy of Edward Carpenter; Henry Tuke's paintings of bathing boys; Simeon Solomon's words and images; nude Victorian painting and sculpture; the clandestine circulation of photographs depicting modern Mediterranean boys dressed as ancient youths.[116]

We will, however, take a deliberately restrained trajectory, to focus on the modern intellectual interest in, enjoyment and admiration of, and anxiety over, the ancient teaching scene. What sort of example was the pederastic teaching scene of ancient Greece for modern formations and distributions of knowledge? What did it mean to claim that we might be like the Greeks in everything but the pederastic relationship, that relationship that also formed the basis of ancient education and knowledge? Could these ancient pederastic desires really be said to have 'produced' in some way modern knowledge in that modern knowledge could be traced back to ancient wisdom? In short, what is the relationship between ancient pederastic desires and modern classical knowledge? Chapters 1 to 3 examine the historicist response to these questions in Germany and England between 1750 and 1895. These chapters examine how German and

---

[116] I offer a select bibliography here: on Goethe, see Kuzniar (1996) and Tobin (2000); on homosexuality in eighteenth-century literature, see Haggerty (1999); on Shelley, see Notopoulos (1969), Lauritsen (2005), and Nelson (2007); on Arnold's poetry, see Dellamora (1990); on Uranian writers, see d'Arch-Smith (1970) and Kaylor (2006); on other aspects, more generally, of homosexuality in nineteenth-and early twentieth-century literature, see Craft (1994); on Bentham, see Crompton (1978a, b, and 1985); on Sappho, see DeJean (1989) and Prins (1999b); on female responses to antiquity, see Olverson (2010); on Heinrich Hoessli, see P. Meier (2001); on the nineteenth-century German gay emancipation movement, see Kennedy (1988) and Sigusch (2000); on the significance of Whitman for nineteenth- and twentieth-century thought and letters, see Robertson (2008); on Carpenter, see Rowbotham (2008); on Henry Tuke, see Wallace (2008); on Simeon Solomon, see Cruise et al. (2005); on the Victorian nude, see Smith (1996, 2001); on the circulation of photographs of boys, see Aldrich (1993).

English scholars, seriously receptive to the lessons and challenges of historicism, attempted to uncover the truth about, first, Socrates' teaching methods; and, secondly, other pederastic relations in ancient Greece, which scholars scrutinized in their attempts to provide a comprehensive *Altertumswissenschaft*. Chapter 1, '*Paiderastia* and the Contexts of German Historicism', opens with the neo-Humanist inauguration of the modern university system at Göttingen, whose first classics professor, Johann Mathias Gesner, produced what some have called the first modern piece of scholarship on ancient pederasty. His treatise clearly betrays concern over the sort of example ancient teachers like Socrates might set for the brash, modern seminars offered at the University of Göttingen, which came to be standardized across Germany and the British universities. The chapter goes on to analyse how the academic discourse of historicism within the German academy took on particular inflections when the subject of pederasty was broached. The ability to describe and examine ancient pederasty in an objective manner was to become a token of one's unshakable historicism, but, all too often, the pederastic pedagogy of the Greeks became emptied of historical meaning and glorified as exemplary. The relationship between ancient pederasty and modern German pedagogy required careful elucidation.

Classical Culture and Modern Masculinity is concerned with modern constructions of ancient traditions of knowledge production and transmission—that is, pedagogy. And, so as we turn to Chapter 2, 'Translating the Love of Philosophy: Jowett and Pater on Plato', we will not be interested in simply recording how the ideas of German thinkers of the first chapter have been packaged and transferred to nineteenth-century Britain. (Indeed we have already seen how for some historians modern sexuality was 'made in Germany' and wrapped up ready for delivery to Britain.) Rather Chapter 1 will have made abundantly clear that the ancient pederastic—pedagogic scene proved that the transfer of knowledge from one generation to the next was fraught with difficulties. And so the British reception of German historicism will not be one that can be characterized straightforwardly in terms of 'influence', just as the German historicists themselves were not at all sure how 'influenced' they were by ancient teaching models and teacher—pupil relations. Chapter 2, then, takes Benjamin Jowett's Oxford as its subject. The Regius Professor of Greek was very interested in recent developments in German thought, and encouraged his students to read such writers—including some considered in Chapter 1. Not surprisingly, then, it was the historical transmission of ideas from one generation to another that preoccupied Jowett's thinking. His centralization of the Platonic dialogues in the Oxford classics curriculum ensured that his students learnt about what it means to learn. Furthermore, his reformation of the curriculum challenged his students to examine the relationships between ancient and modern thought and society. The Platonic œuvre has, however, always been difficult read. Socrates' injunction to his interlocutors to know themselves while also emphasizing that wisdom lay in knowing how little one really knew has ensured that Plato's texts have produced highly polarized interpretations about the possibilities of knowledge. Jowett's Platonic pedagogy was developed in changing times for Oxford. As the Greats curriculum was reformed through the nineteenth century, teaching provision was improved and the laicization of the university was under way, nineteenth-century Oxford opened its doors to the sons of the new commercial and industrial middle classes. The growth in the demand for places at Oxford and Cambridge saw to it that competitive scholarships and written examinations for matriculation and graduation became the norm. The principles of 'testable knowledge' were at odds with the notion of character building and formation at the heart of an Oxford education: the English universities were experiencing the conflict between *Bildung* and *Wissenschaft*. Jowett's emphasis on Plato in Greats responded to the dilemmas besetting the modern university: in his attempt to make classical antiquity seem 'relevant' in a self-consciously scientific Victorian age, he sought to prove that reading Plato made the man ready for duty for the British Empire, as his reforms on Oxford syllabi were accompanied by his constant interventions in the development of the civil-service tests. Plato's significance for the Victorian man was not that his writing straightforwardly 'influenced' the modern world, but that his dialogues depicted a teacher, Socrates, teaching young men how to think for and fashion themselves for a life ahead.

If Plato's Socrates taught not facts in an increasingly scientific era but a masculine sensibility and sociability for modernity, then the historical 'fact' of Socratic/Platonic pederasty proved for modern times, not surprisingly, one of the most difficult areas for Jowett to formulate. What sorts of male relationships would produce the knowledgeable man, ancient and modern? What is the relationship between Platonic *erōs* and knowledge? As we shall examine, Plato offers Jowett an image of perfect friendship the likes of which only a very few could obtain. In his attempts to find a space for male friendship that is loving but not sinful, Jowett describes a male love imitable and impossible, knowable and beyond knowledge, irrecoverably past and a model for the present. Jowett's Plato becomes awkwardly lodged in a historical past while at the same time tantalizingly a model for male sociability in the present, both an object of *Altertumswissenschaft* and an example of *Bildung*. And it is the (un)knowability of Platonic *erōs* that will interest Walter Pater, for whom homoerotic relations will be the key trope for understanding the relationship between (ancient) past and (modern) present. In his essay on 'Winckelmann', Pater argues that the German art historian's homoerotic responses to ancient art make him an ideal scholar: his love of the ancient Greek male body affords Winckelmann an affinity, an idealized knowledge of Greece. *Erōs* affords the truth. And yet, at the same time, Pater will show that Winckelmann's desires were continually frustrated, merely played out in letters to absent, non-reciprocating boys: Winckelmann's homoerotic desires mark an unending *erōs for* truth, knowledge, the attainment of one's desires.

As we shall also show, the unknowability of Greek love also meant for Jowett that such love was literally unknowable: Jowett openly admits to not knowing what Plato meant and thought about pederastic desire. This cues Jowett to produce his own parodies of the Platonic texts, imaginative explorations of what modern friendships and masculinities might look like. Jowett's creative rewriting of Plato's texts permitted Pater equally inventive views, as expounded in his book *Plato and Platonism*. Having received public critique for his intricate examination of Winckelmann's erotic feelings, Pater used his book on Plato to defend his ideas about homoeroticism and the (im)possibilities of understanding the relationship between ancient Greeks and modern Victorian men. Writing at the time when sexuality came to be seen as the secret truth of the self as Foucault has so famously analysed, Pater shows that the relationship between Platonic *erōs*, truth, and knowledge becomes very complicated. Pater portrays a Plato who was himself pondering over the influence of past models of male Spartan beauty and the possibilities of reproducing such beautiful men in his modern Athens. Just as Plato supposedly mused over how the Spartan past might live on and influence his Athenian present, so

Pater himself wonders how Plato's pederastic—pedagogic texts do not really teach facts but rather *form* the modern male self.

Jowett's and Pater's responses to German classical scholarship were sophisticated, sensitive, and thoughtful. As some Germans sought to grasp and know the historical truth of Greek pederasty, others chose to see it as a model for the production of truth and knowledge. Jowett and Pater similarly wondered whether Platonic *erōs* should remain inside or outside the history of modern men's lives. And it is in this context that the relationship between Jowett and Pater has been scrutinized through the course of the twentieth century and beyond: in what ways precisely were Jowett and Pater (not) friends? What impact did their Platonic teaching have on their friendship? It is the complex musings on the (un)knowability of male *erōs* that have caused their own relationship to become the object of unending enquiry. Rather than permitting us simply to know their selves and their sexualities, their discussions of Platonic *erōs* evidence two men in constant examination of what it means to know the truth about desire.

Chapter 3, 'The Case of John Addington Symonds's, another of Jowett's Oxford pupils, takes up this theme of the difficulty of Greek. We will see that Jowett was very keen to include a detailed essay on the subject of 'Greek Love' in his translations, but his ex-student Symonds warned against this. This chapter will examine how dangerous Symonds thought the learning of classics to be, both for those men who desired women and for those who desired other men. The chapter will look at how ancient Greece offered competing examples of same-sex desire for the modern Symonds: on the one hand, an 'Ionic' relationship between man and boy, and a 'Doric' relationship between two virile men. The profusion of types of ancient desire both fascinated and troubled Symonds: 'Greek love' was no simple model for modernity; instead it offered a worrying selection of options, causing a sense of fragmentation in Symonds's very soul. Symonds has often been taken as a case study for the emergence of the modern homosexual—identifying (with) Symonds as a gay man has seemed a straightforward exercise. However, as we shall see, Symonds himself was extremely wary about identifying with periods of history. His candid discussion of Greek love, the first ever to be written in the English language, offers up a choice of homoerotic desires none of which was easily translatable into Victorian Britain. Havelock Ellis, who included Symonds's essay in his controversial work *Sexual Inversion* (originally published in 1897), actually felt that Greek history could be little help with the modern issue of homosexuality: Symonds's emphasis on the formative nature of a classical education conflicted with sexological theories about the congenitality of sexual orientation. Reflecting his Oxford education, Symonds, unlike Ellis, became most interested in how reading Greek writers like Plato formed the modern male.

These opening chapters examine a series of intellectuals who were interested in constructing a *historical* reality from ancient evidence, and who also attempted to understand the actual purchase of that reality on the modern world. The German scholars sought to present as far as possible a literal picture of knowledge transmission from ancient teacher and pupil, and to characterize in as much detail as possible the pedagogic relationship, and the role that desire played in that encounter. Their English readers, Jowett, Pater, and Symonds, took up this scholarship and expanded it, by attempting to elucidate historically the literal transmission of pederastic pedagogy from ancient to modern worlds. The historicisms of the classics departments in the German and British universities, however, produced graduates who developed altogether more self-consciously rhetorical, metaphorical translations of ancient pederastic pedagogy. In the texts of Oscar Wilde, E. M. Forster, and Sigmund Freud, the Greek teaching scene becomes a far more flexible model for thinking about the formation of modern masculinity in relation to ancient counterparts. We saw at the beginning of this Introduction how difficult the Platonic texts have been to translate and reproduce. Although the historicizing scholars attempted to regulate the interpretation of those texts, they realized (and indeed, in the case of Jowett and his pupils, analysed why) the reception of Plato could never be controlled. As Foucault examined, by the end of the nineteenth century, the 'truth' of the self became a sexual truth. In eighteenth-century and nineteenth-century German scholarship, the question of the truth of historical scholarship became entangled both with telling the truth about ancient Greek pederasty and with how Greek pederasty itself supposedly told the truth about philosophy. At the end of the nineteenth century, the relationship between truth, sex, and Greek love became an urgent concern beyond the corridors of the university, as these intellectual debates spilled over into the law court, where the case of Oscar Wilde was being heard.

Chapter 4, 'Trying Greek Love: Oscar Wilde and E. M. Forster's *Maurice*', examines the result of this history of eighteenth- and nine-teenth-century 'knowledge' about ancient 'desire' as it is momen-tously expressed in the trial of Oscar Wilde. Wilde—the disciple of Pater, who himself was the pupil of Jowett, who himself learnt the lessons of German historicism before him—pronounced most pub-licly in 1895 on the platonic 'love that dare not speak its name'. Tellingly, Wilde has often been named *both* the first homosexual to be 'outed' in history, *and* the first queer figure to question modern notions of sexuality, the first gay/queer to tell the truth. On the other hand, Wilde has also been condemned by gay historians for lying in public: if only he *had* come out and told the truth behind the meaning of that troublesome phrase, then perhaps gay life in the twentieth century might have been so different. This chapter addresses this fissured reception of Wilde, to consider what Wilde might have 'understood' about the 'truth' of his 'sexuality'. If 'the love that dare not speak its name' speech has so often been taken to be Wilde's most public pronouncement on desire, then precisely what did he mean? As we shall see, this seemingly straightforward question has never stopped baffling historians. Was his paean to Platonic love a clever euphemistic reference to homosexuality, or did he 'really' think that he loved like a Greek? A close reading of the speech will show how tricky it is to comprehend. Despite repeated attempts across the eighteenth and nineteenth centuries to historicize Platonic love, Wilde's speech shows that the translation of ancient lessons into modern times and terms remained open to contestation and debate. Indeed, the heated debate about the 'genuineness' of Wilde's speech (Was he coming out? Was he offering up some queer wit? Was he utilizing the discourse of philhellenism in serious defence?) shows that the translation of Wilde's Platonic translation has been a fraught process, producing different Wildes through the twentieth century and beyond.

Wilde himself played a part in this process, with the posthumous publication of *De Profundis*, which this chapter also considers. In this long letter ostensibly addressed to 'Bosie', but which we are invited to receive as well, Wilde examines the misunderstanding brought to bear on the Apollo—Hyacinth letter, which he originally wrote to Douglas but which found itself as evidence in a trial for gross in-decency. It was the misdirected transmission of Greek love into the hands of people who had not read the *Symposium*, as Wilde acerbically notes—the mistaken reception of this letter—that led Wilde into shameful incarceration. Wilde questions the Marquis of Queensberry's version of events, in which the older man, Wilde, had corrosively influenced the youth, Alfred Douglas. Instead of a perverse form of Platonism, *De Profundis* relocates the truth of the history leading up to the trial in Douglas's contorted relations with his father and mother: it was the hereditary transmission of Queensberry's personality to his son and his mother's inability to teach her son any difficult lessons that led the younger Douglas on his crash course into Wilde. The Platonic relationship between an elder and a younger man was *not* the problem here: it was the perverse pedagogy of the Douglas family that taught its son his modern masculinity. With *De Profundis*, we examine how Wilde attempts to turn away from Plato to the Greek of the Gospel. We shall see, however, Wilde's hymn to Christ makes understanding who Wilde (thought he) was all the more difficult. This chapter, then, traces the movement of Hellenism from its context within academic discussions about historicism to a more public discussion about the politics of modern philhellenism.

The chapter closes with a reading of E. M. Forster's *Maurice* (originally written in 1913–14, but not published until 1971 after Forster's death). Although this novel was written explicitly *after* the Wilde scandal, the relationship between Clive and Maurice explores the *continuing* difficulty of what to make of the Platonic texts when considering one's own modern desires. As we shall see, it is their varying translations of Plato that bring about the heartbreak of Maurice and Clive. Oscar Wilde and his famous speech did not so much offer a solution for modern young men who desired other men as a problem to think through: what might Plato mean after 1895, wonder Forster's characters. The translation from Wilde's nineteenth-century pederastic desires into Forster's representation of young men in love was to be a difficult and bumpy transition. Indeed, the complicated reception of Wilde in the later twentieth century ((how) should contemporary gay people identify with Wilde?) is already registered by Maurice, Clive, and Alec, the three protagonists of Forster's novel—none of whom could be said to be straightforwardly identifiable with Wilde, none of whom could be said to desire (a man like) Wilde. Chapter 3 on Symonds sets up one man's torturous examination of the historical relationships between an 'Ionic', pederastic ethos, a 'Doric' manly companionship, and modern sexual orientation. The historical moment of *Maurice*, written in

1914, shows us that the self-examinations of Symonds no longer made sense: nineteenth-century pederasty was seen to be quite different from twentieth-century congenital homosexuality.

As we shall also see, the transmission and reception of knowledge about male desire is an issue continually figured through the writing of letters. Jowett, Pater, Symonds, Wilde, and Forster's Maurice and Clive all write letters, have letters written about them, or are asked to interpret letters, in which male friendship and love are expressed and discussed. Benjamin Jowett's letters to his friend Arthur Stanley, the letters he writes to Florence Nightingale, the letters Josephine Butler writes about him, as well as his biographers Abbott and Campbell all show a keen interest in the meaning of ancient and modern male friendship. In 1874 Walter Pater was apparently censured and threatened with exposure by Jowett, who received love letters Pater had written to the undergraduate student William Money Hardinge. John Addington Symonds records evidence in his *Memoirs* about pederastic letters Harrow's headmaster had written to a fellow-pupil and friend of Symonds, letters that saw the headmaster leave the school and embark on a career in the church. Furthermore, Symonds was himself threatened with blackmail while a fellow at Oxford for supposedly homoerotic letters he wrote. Most famously, Oscar Wilde was convicted partly on the 'evidence' in a letter about Apollo and Hyacinth he had written to Alfred Douglas, an issue he explores in his letter *De Profundis*. Finally, E. M. Forster's Clive sends a letter *from Greece to England* stating epigrammatically, 'against my will I have become normal. I cannot help it,' thereby ending his relationship with Maurice.[117] This last letter journeys 'down to the sea', which, Forster follows, 'would embark and voyage past Sunium and Cythera', past where the modern Romantic poet Byron supposedly signed his name, and past the island of Aphrodite/Venus—that is, *past Greek islands of romantic desire*. The writing of letters from Greece and with Greece in mind, concerning the loves and friendships between men, becomes a leitmotif in the period between 1870 and 1914: the course and destination of those letters, their designated reception, and their mistaken or wilful misreading, become crucial for the way in which men at this time conceptualized the reception of ancient Greek culture (in particular, ancient *erōs*) into modernity. Clive's letter

---

[117] Forster (1972: 104).

painfully shows that letters sent from Greece could never be guaranteed to arrive at their destination, that is, to be understood as intended, as Maurice writes back: 'I am very anxious about you on account of your letter . . . two sentences, which I suppose mean that you cannot love one of your own sex any longer. We will see whether this is so as soon as you arrive!'[118] The question of what letters can tell us about male desires, as opposed to the lesson to be learnt from the actual presence of a male body, is pondered by Maurice's reply, reflecting Plato's concern that letters or writing ('hoi logoi' (*Phaedrus* 275d)) are not a good substitute for the embodied teacher. The translation of textuality into sexuality, of Platonic Greek into modern desires and passions, becomes a highly problematic issue in the late nineteenth and early twentieth centuries.

Chapter 5, 'Freud and the History of Masculinity: Between Oedipus and Narcissus,' returns to the German context. Just as Chapter 4 discussed Ireland's and Britain's most famous pupil of classical pedagogy, so this chapter examines one of the most famous German-speaking pupils of the classics: Sigmund Freud. In particular, this chapter examines the significance of the intellectual context of the Viennese *Gymnasium* for Freud's thought: his schooling sought to produce a well-rounded individual, who could successfully master the arts and the sciences. The Viennese experimentation with the Humboldtian model produced a Freud who became most interested in the well-rounded artist-scientist Leonardo da Vinci. His 1910 psychobiography of the man was written explicitly after the Wilde trial (Freud says he does not want to besmirch the great man), and yet the picture he presents was far stranger than anyone could have anticipated. Under Freud's analysis, Leonardo becomes a figure who is both Narcissus and Oedipus, destined to love those who look like him, as well as to rival his oedipal father for the love of his mother. Where previous German accounts had been more thoroughly invested in historicist enquiry, in this chapter we witness Freud's turn to myth to elucidate historical processes. That is to say, men's historical, lived sexualities are nothing but the reproduction of the myths of Oedipus and Narcissus. And, as we shall see, whereas, at the beginning of his Leonardo study, the Renaissance man was seen as a historical oddity, by the end he becomes exemplary for all men, troublesomely stuck

---

[118] Forster (1972: 105).

between narcissism and oedipal desires, between the past and the future, ancient and modern, in the middle, in the Renaissance. Rather than clarify the nature of homosexuality, Freud's *Leonardo* questions the homo/hetero distinction, which contemporary sexologists were positing. Written against a canvas of classical historiography, Freud's position that our sexual desires and identities are mythical fundamentally questioned previous historicist accounts of the relationship between antiquity and modernity. Our personal histories of sexuality were to be far stranger. Indeed Freud's interest in child sexuality marks a sharp break from the versions of Greek pederasty and love circulating at the end of the nineteenth century. Freud famously abandoned his belief in the seduction theory, which posited the sexual seduction of a child by an adult (parent) as a common occurrence, and came to focus on the sexual curiosity of the child as directed at his and her parents. Rather than our paternal teachers tutoring us, their children, how to desire, it is the child that teaches the adult man, in particular Freud himself, the history of our sexualities. Furthermore, Freud departs from the nineteenth-century interest in Platonic pederasty between an elder and younger man, as articulated by Oscar Wilde. Here it is the *mother* who enters the scene: it is her presence in the young boy's life that alerts and alarms Freud. Indeed, Freud's text moves away from earlier conceptualizations of male desire. In *De Profundis*, Wilde chides Douglas's mother for not taking enough interest in the emotional education and development of her son: if she had done, he would not have ended up the way he did. With Freud, however, it is the mother's influence that is partially the cause of Leonardo's sexuality. Freud's study ensures that it is no longer so much the male homosocial space that should concern modern men, but the relationship a little boy has with his mother.

This final chapter elucidates a recurring issue: the knowability of our desires and our selves. In his shocking arguments for a repressed myth-history of infantile sexuality that contend that men are all Narcissus and Oedipus, Freud begs the question: do men ever really know what they want? If 1895 has marked the emergence of the modern homosexual for many historians, then Freud demonstrates that the very nature of homosexuality was debated, questioned, and contested straightaway. And these debates took place with continual consideration of the Greek example—or rather example*s*. By the end of the nineteenth century, sexuality came to be seen as the truth of the self. But Jowett, Pater, Symonds, Wilde, Forster, and

Freud problematized that notion through their neo-humanistic edu-
cations: the complicated relationship between knowledge and Greek
love as explored in German historiography saw to it that male desires,
friendships, and relationships would require continual attention.
Plato's complex exploration of the meaning of *erōs* and truth; the
Ionian/Dorian polarity; the exemplary friendship of Achilles and
Patroclus; the impossibly beautiful Spartans; the wonder of Christ;
and the narcissism of Leonardo: modern men were furnished with
numerous ways for conceptualizing histories of masculinity.

   This book, then, is not concerned with uncovering and diagnosing
various writers' 'sexualities', as if 'sexuality' in this period (indeed in
any period, as Sedgwick and others have suggested) were straightforwardly 'knowable.' Rather, just as the identification with ancients was
such a complex and knotted issue for men between 1750 and 1930, so
identifying modern gay and queer subjectivities with those of nineteenth-century, classically trained intellectuals becomes somewhat
difficult, and politically problematic. The highly charged relationships
between Greek men brought into sharp focus the contests of historicism in the modern period: ancient Greek pedagogy veered between
being seen as foundational, and as other to, modern European culture. Similarly, homosocial Oxbridge Hellenism has provided a possible and precious window into a gay past. But, just as eighteenth- and
nineteenth-century intellectuals were keenly aware of the historical
specificity of ancient Greece, so gay people need to be wary of
identifying with the specificities of late Victorian and early Edwardian
classicisms.[119] Our wish to have been present at their moments of
passion, the wish to get beyond the merely textual 'evidence' of
Victorian and Edwardian letters and scholarship, reflects those Victorians' and Edwardians' own wishes to see Greece 'as it really was',
which in turn reflects those ancient Athenians, such as Apollodorus,
who heard about Socrates' symposium and wished they had been
there too. Plato's text questions what it means to know about *erōs* in
the first place. Rather than simply knowing and feeling it, the writers
and intellectuals we will be considering all interrogate the nature of
desire: in what ways is it located in the body and/or the imagination?
Are our 'real' objects of desire that which we can touch or that which
we can only imagine? The oscillation of the ancient Greeks between

---

[119] See also Blanshard (2010: 159–63).

historical personages and mythical exemplars saw to it that the meaning of men's desires became a problem not a straightforward fact.

Although Pater, Symonds, and Wilde can all be viewed as gay
martyrs or heroes, repressed, expressive, or otherwise, they actually
negotiated their lives and desires in contexts that look both very
similar *and* very different from our own. As we shall examine, their
particular modes of identification with ancient Greeks makes them
look very modern, very gay, *and* very foreign, very past. Their continual attempts to dovetail their Hellenisms with Christianity, and
their huge valorization of pederastic relationships based on age difference should permit us to see that their notions about male desire
and companionship were very different from our own. Furthermore,
although their sharply racialized vision of beauty (white, marble boys
and men, or racially othered Mediterranean youths) finds important
echoes in contemporary Western gay culture, it cannot nevertheless
offer a very broad and inclusively positive message to today's and
tomorrow's gay men of colour. Indeed what is so 'homo' about
Victorian—Edwardian 'homosexuality' when the word was first invented? This period evidences numerous men desiring human objects
quite *dissimilar* from themselves: (pre)-pubescent boys and youths,
not men, and racially differentiated Mediterraneans, Italians, Greeks,
Turks, Egyptians, and Moroccans. Although these ephebophilic and
raciological discourses are still a part of contemporary Western gay
culture, they are profoundly contested and do not signify straightforwardly what it is to be gay or queer. Finally, the position of women in
the debates and lives of these men poses innumerable problems from
the perspective of twenty-first-century gay and queer sensibilities.
Victorians' and Edwardians' profound regard for the homosocial
context for Greek pedagogy and their particular theorizations about
female knowledge about desire, as we shall see, hardly resemble
modern gay man's reliance and precious need for a woman in his
life. Indeed, what gay man could survive without the learning and
knowledge that his female, best friend has bestowed upon him (be it
his mother, sister, aunt, or soul-mate who taught him how to be
himself)? *Classical Culture and Modern Masculinity* will show that it
is impossible to examine Pater's, Symonds's, and Wilde's desires
outside their beliefs about Christianity, race, and femininity, making
their conceptualizations about the historicity of their masculinities
very different from contemporary gay engagements with the past. As
we shall continually examine, various Christianities (and in Freud's

case, his Jewishness) formed crucial contexts, without which any comprehension of desire was impossible. Furthermore, the historical contours of their masculinities were inconceivable beyond colonialist-British and Imperialist-German discourses of race. And, finally, the debates about the politics of women's education in the nineteenth century formed an important framework, which conditioned the very possibility of these men's notions and suppositions.

The discourses of postcolonialism and feminism have profoundly changed the ways in which classical antiquity has been viewed and lionized. Indeed, these discourses have deeply altered what we want to gain by way of heritage from the ancient world. Our admiration of the Greeks, indeed gay admiration of the Greeks, needs now to be tempered and contextualized by an examination of the effects of male homosociality on ancient women. Indeed, the many institutional partnerships between departments of women's studies and those of lesbian and gay studies in the modern academy reflect the very different place women occupy in the worlds of gay men today. Furthermore, the debates that have spilled out from the publication of Martin Bernal's *Black Athena* have ensured that we should be wary about viewing the Greeks as desirable because of their putative 'race' (be it 'white', 'brown', or 'black').[120] The racialization of culture is a discourse—so prevalent, as we shall see, in the worlds of Pater, Symonds, and Wilde—which no one should have to live with now. In short, then, the Victorian—Edwardian masculinization and Hellenization that packaged up particular brands of Greek beauty are quite different from the rainbow-flag world that welcomes the contemporary desiring self.

But *Classical Culture and Modern Masculinity* is not designed to preach a lesson to gay men. Rather, it is gay men's particular predicament that should speak to all contemporary efforts aspiring to build a heritage with distant pasts, all aspirations to receive the classical past 'correctly'. On the one hand, the desperate need for gay men to locate a history makes it perfectly understandable that figures like Pater, Symonds, and Wilde should become iconic. On the other hand, however, the attempt to build a gay heritage in Victorian–Edward philhellenism is beset with perilous pitfalls. The transmission of Greek culture to modernity was such a profoundly important issue

---

[120] See Bernal (1987) and Berlinerblau (1999).

from the Enlightenment until the Second World War that it ensured continual meditation upon the possibilities of translating and re-packaging the messy specificities of the ancient Greek world into a modern self. Pater, Symonds, and Wilde were themselves highly self-conscious about the historical relationships they posited between ancient and modern. And so, contemporary gay people need be just as self-reflexive in constructing of gay pasts, when navigating the Scylla and Charybdis of positivist historicism and creative, poetic identification. The 'correct' reception of the classical past and the 'correct' reception of Victorian—Edwardian receptions of the classi-cal past are academic debates that acquire altogether more urgent significance for contemporary gay and queer people. The ways in which we write our histories profoundly shape our abilities to live and love. If modern Victorian—Edwardian philhellenisms offer poten-tially *both* so much *and* so little hope for shoring up a history for contemporary gay people, then it presses upon us to consider how we might and might not relate to those previous philhellenic identifica-tions and desires.

1

Paiderastia and the Contexts of German Historicism

non postulandum est, ut per omnia sapiant, ut graves sint pueri, hoc est, ut non sint pueri.

(Johann Matthias Gesner, *Isagoge in eruditionem universalem*, 1763)

The University of Göttingen is viewed as one of the first modern universities. Its founders' reorganization of theological learning, their expansion of philosophical areas studied, the explosion of *Geschichtswissenschaft* at the University, and the comparatively large law faculty, all marked a significant change in the composition of German—and indeed European—higher education. By the beginning of the eighteenth century, attendance at German universities had plummeted to an all time low (some seats of learning had well beneath one hundred students). The foundation of a Hanoverian seat of education was certainly audacious. Most notably, the brave, new Göttingen played a pivotal role in the ascent of the philosophical faculty, steadily shaping a scholarly ideal that paved the way for the secure establishment of the teaching of Latin and Greek as disciplines for their own sake. 'Whereas previously this faculty had been regarded largely as preparatory, it increasingly ... became the semi-autonomous enterprise, the harbinger of a new type of enquiry,' which sought to prepare students for professional employment and to augment the domain of knowledge through scholarly research.[1] And, although courtly training (dancing, fencing, and riding), which attracted rich nobles, did find a place on the original curriculum, this

---

[1] Howard (2006: 81).

later fell away and 'the new emphasis placed on the philosophical faculty remained a breakthrough in the university, with its emphasis on the subjective, rather than objective, benefits of study'.[2] The ethos at Göttingen, along with the other relatively recent foundations Halle and Erlangen, 'helped nurture new ideas about the goals of higher education, and for the professoriate, about the search for truth, resulting in the beginnings of a neo-humanistic orientation in teaching and a modern research ethic in scholarship'.[3]

It was the classical seminars of Johann Matthias Gesner and Christian Gottlob Heyne that modernized university teaching. The ideals of the neo-humanists moved the objective of education towards the creation and lionization of the individual being. The Göttingen system looked forward to the pedagogical philosophy of *Bildung*. The new *Bildungsbürgertum* marked and staked out its interests in the halls and corridors of the new institutions.[4] Although there has been debate about how modern neo-humanist thinking was, we should attend to the paradox that the revival of classical studies provided the impetus towards the future.[5] 'The fact that Göttingen, in the late eighteenth century, was a leader in the philological renaissance should not surprise us.'[6] The neo-humanist teaching of the classics was seen as vigorously modern. One of the special features of Göttingen's foundation was its gathering-together of nationally and internationally renowned intellectuals. The Hanoverian administration was concerned to collect a faculty that would attract not only the newly developing *Bildungsbürgertum*, but also the noblemen and other *Vornehme*. Johann Matthias Gesner was appointed as the very first professor of rhetoric and poetry at the University. (*Altertumswissenschaft* and *Philologie* were not yet terms used to designate professorial chairs of the classical subjects.[7]) Indeed, Gesner was the very first professor to have arrived in Göttingen, as well as the very first who publicly announced his lecture programme in 1734. The University was not officially open for business until 1737.[8] Gesner

---

[2] McClelland (1980: 45–6).
[3] McClelland (1980: 57). On the history of the modern research university, see, generally, Clark (2006).
[4] See McClelland (1980: 96–8).
[5] See Marchand (1996) and Carhart (2007: 121–34).
[6] McClelland (1980: 61).
[7] Schindel (2001: 10–11).
[8] Friedrich (1991: 43).

found himself at the origins of the modern moment of (classical) European pedagogy.

At the time of his appointment, Gesner was one of the most famous schoolteachers in eighteenth-century Germany.[9] He was in correspondence with major scholars across much of Europe.[10] Born in 1691, in Roth an der Rednitz, between 1730 and 1734 he was *Rektor* at the Thomasschule in Leipzig, where, together with Johann August Ernesti, he radically reformed educational policy.[11] There he became good friends with J. S. Bach, with whom he was supposed to have composed a cantata.[12] It was also here that he completed his important pedagogical work, the *Chrestomathia Graeca*. Gesner's book was one of the first of its kind. One historian claims that he is 'der eigentliche Erfinder diesen neuen Art von Lesetext'.[13] Another says that the *Chrestomathia* provided the fundamental basis for a renewal of Greek studies in German schools.[14] In 1734 Gesner was called to Göttingen, and there he remained until his death in 1761. He played an important role in the advertisement of the new university within an international arena. With the understanding of the Hanoverian administration, Gesner wrote an anonymous letter to an English nobleman in which he praised Göttingen's new professors, students, and buildings, adding friendly words about the town's inhabitants. The authorship of the letter became a great puzzle among the university professors. Although it was many years before the name of the writer was revealed (Gesner's handwriting was verified only in 1922), the letter did the trick in helping to establish a truly international reputation for Göttingen.[15]

Gesner has been called the 'Vater und unermüdliche Wegbereiter' of neo-humanism, a legacy that Christoph Gottlob Heyne, Friedrich August Wolf, and Wilhelm von Humboldt took on and appropriated.[16] Gesner's pedagogical methods were crucial for the educational reforms of the late-eighteenth and early nineteenth centuries, which culminated

---

[9] See Friedrich (1991: 31).
[10] See Friedrich (1991: 53).
[11] See Friedrich (1991: 33–41).
[12] See Friedrich (1991: 37). Modern musical historians now doubt both Bach's and Gesner's authorship of the piece.
[13] Schindel (2001: 14), noting that the neoplatonist Proclus provided an example for Gesner's work.
[14] Friedrich (1991: 39). See also Gericke (1911: 27), who writes 'dass er das Studium der Griechen in Deutschland wiedererweckt habe'.
[15] Friedrich (1991: 43).
[16] Friedrich (1991: 17).

in Humboldt's University in Berlin. Gesner's contribution to classical
scholarship does not come in the form of an edition of a text that
brought the philological *Wissenschaft* to new levels. Indeed, Pfeiffer
mentions Gesner only briefly as a predecessor of neo-humanism.[17]
His collection of *Scriptores Rei Rusticae* (1735) is a very conventional
commentary, loaded with *notis variorum* and learning. His editions of
Livy (1735) and Horace (1752) were almost unaltered texts of older
editions. What are more interesting in these works of scholarship,
however, are his thoughts about practical, pedagogical matters. In his
preface to his Livy edition, he discusses what he calls 'statarische Lektüre' and 'kursorische Lektüre'. The former type of reading is the
traditional, according to Gesner. The school pupils and university
students are statically suspended, engrossed in the analysis of a single
text: 'Jahre werden für ein einziges Buch von Ciceros Briefen aufgewen-
det.'[18] The university teacher brings a huge 'Apparat von Gelehrsamkeit'
and leaves nothing unsaid, so that the student entirely misses what the
author actually says, and an enjoyment in reading is extinguished.[19]
With 'kursorische Lektüre', on the other hand, 'one takes a classical text
in the hand and does not put it down again until it has been read the
whole way through'.[20] Even though the 'kursorische' reader is meant to
attend to details, he should expect not to understand everything at this
stage of reading. Instead he should pay attention to what the author says
and means, so that the text is meaningful in its entirety. Most notably, in
his still active edition of Claudian, he writes that he has not burdened the
book with commentary but has complemented it with notes that will
develop ('bilden') the taste of the young people ('Geschmack der Ju-
gend') reading the text. He alerts his young reader to what is 'schön und
würdig' and 'wahrhaft dichterisch'.[21] The beauty, the worthiness, and
the poetry of the text are all to be observed in Gesner's 'kursorische
Lektüre'. Moreover, Gesner admits to not understanding everything and
says that he will confess his ignorance to his reader in order to console
him or her and to stimulate further scholarship on a particular problem
and issue.[22] Gesner's commentaries offer a model of the exemplary
reader, one in which the pupil's difficulties and problems are taken

---

[17] Pfeiffer (1976: 168, 175).
[18] Gesner, quoted in Schindel (1989: 18).
[19] Schindel (1989: 18).
[20] Schindel (1989: 18).
[21] Gesner, quoted in Schindel (1989: 19).
[22] Schindel (1989: 19).

seriously. Gesner presents himself as the ideal pupil, showing the pupil how to proceed.

This method of learning is reflected in his pedagogical techniques at Göttingen. In 1734 he announced a 'Fragekolleg'.[23] This in effect was a private lecture in which the student would see Gesner on Wednesday and Saturday mornings (he would be available from eight o'clock onwards), so that the student could ask Gesner any questions he wanted about the texts he was reading. Gesner is quite explicit that he is not the omniscient teacher—he notes that when he does not have the answer he will endeavour to obtain it for the next time the student attends.[24] As Ulrich von Schindel remarks, we find here the seeds of what was to become the 'Seminarium Philologicum' four years later. Gesner's seminars established a fundamentally different mode of teaching, which moved away from the unidirectional model of teaching passing knowledge to pupil to a dialogic transaction in which teacher and pupil question each other. Although the Seminarium Philologicum began with mostly theological students, it soon became the environment in which Greek and Latin philology was tested and learnt. Gesner's seminar became the basis for a different emphasis in university teaching and spread through Germany and England as the eighteenth and nineteenth centuries passed.[25]

This transformation in the teacher—pupil relationship was to provide the context for an important shift in the way in which the relationship between antiquity and modernity itself was conceptualized. 'Dieses Seminarium', as Ulrich von Schindel has written, 'ist der Ausgangspunkt für ein neues Selbstverständnis der Philologie... nicht mehr Imitationstechnik oder Hilfsdisziplin für die Theologie ist sie, sondern auf dem Wege zu einer selbständigen, der allseitigen Menschenbildung verpflichteten Wissenschaft'.[26] Eighteenth- and nineteenth-century neo-humanists portrayed Renaissance humanists as dry imitators of antiquity. Gesner and his successors were not interested in mimicking the texts of the ancient world. Greek prose and verse composition was, for Gesner, superfluous.[27] Rather, the ancient world carried *exemplary* status, which is quite different from

---

[23] Schindel (2001: 12).   [24] Schindel (2001: 12).
[25] See Schindel (2001: 12–13).
[26] Schindel (2001: 16).   [27] Schindel (2001: 14).

being an original source designed to be merely copied. Similarly, Winckelmann, the intellectual who arguably did more than any other German-speaking figure to popularize the significance of classical antiquity, was extremely sceptical about the idea that modern art could and should mimic that of the ancient world.[28] The rising tide of positivist historicism dovetailed closely with the romanticist emphasis on the irrecoverability of antiquity. In his *Enchiridion, sive prudentia privata ac civilis* (1745), an edition with commentary of five Latin prose texts, Gesner professes that reading these works will inform the (male) student of the 'rechte Handhabung des ganzen privaten und öffentlichen Lebens'. He will learn to recognize this through 'wichtigen Regeln und *Beispiele*'—that is, precepts *and* examples.[29] In the *Enchiridion*, the reader—pupil is offered up several versions of exemplary masculinity: the citizen, the consul, the provincial governor, the soldier, and finally the emperor. Modern life is not reducible to a discrete set of rules, but needs to be informed by the complexities of exemplary ancient biography. From *Bürger* to *Kaiser* the Roman world, as well as the Greek, can offer the modern male German student all the possible models of masculinity available to him after the *Gymnasium* and the *Universität*, a world of public and private, citizen and state.[30] The masculinity of the education was designed to provide for an education in(to) masculinity. Boys are meant to be boys and should be educated as such: 'non postulandum est, ut per omnia sapiant, ut graves sint pueri, hoc est, ut non sint pueri.'[31]

The masculinist rhetoric of German philosophies of classical education at this time reflects the active exclusion of girls and women from most formal pedagogical processes in eighteenth-century

---

[28] See Potts (1994). Indeed Göttingen professors of classics were very much in contact with the ideas disseminated by Winckelmann: Gesner's successor Heyne was to incorporate Winckelmann's *Geschichte* (1764) into his lectures (see Howard 2006: 119).

[29] Gesner, quoted in Schindel (1989: 20).

[30] Schindel also observes that Gesner was very much preoccupied with grammars and composition books. His scholarship in this area was keen to stress that languages are learnt best *by example* and *not simply* by the memorization of abstract rules: 'Wir lernen ohne allgemeine und abgezogene Begriffe, *ohne Regeln, durch die blosse Erwartung und Einrichtung ähnliche Fälle*, jede Sprache, in welcher andere mit uns redden, recht verstehen und redden' (Gesner, quoted in Schindel 1989: 23, emphasis added). See also Gericke (1911: 16).

[31] Gesner, quoted in Gericke (1911: 14). See also Howard (2006: 117–19) on Gesner.

Germany. This period witnessed persistent debate about women's education, as Peter Petschauer has observed.[32] Nevertheless, most literature pertained to training young women in the arts of household management. By the second half of the eighteenth century, one finds authors speaking of housework in terms of a female 'profession', or 'Beruf', as the 'ideal "home" tended to assume a nuclear family... in which a man or a woman related on a more intensively emotional and, as visible in some writers, "equal" basis'.[33] Discussions of the possible entry of women into university education were, however, extremely restricted. Only a few scattered male voices suggested the establishment of female academies, and only one (anonymous) author suggested in print in 1747 a plan for a university designed specially for women.[34] And even these suggestions were hardly radical, as they contained the curricula within activities deemed the 'female arts, such as cooking, along with arithmetic, writing, drawing, music, dancing and languages'.[35] The classics were expressly *not* part of the syllabus: as Petschauer notes, 'the Greco-Romans... legalized this inferior status of women. And the modern Germans... took their inspiration not from the customs of their sensitive ancestors... but from their Roman neighbours'.[36] Furthermore, the exclusive and exclusionary philosophy of university education at the time was bolstered by the notion of male academic citizenship ('akademisches Bürgerrecht'), which dated back to the medieval university system. 'Through the matriculation ceremony, the new student was officially inscribed as a citizen of the university community,' as Patricia Mazón discusses: 'The bounds of "academical burgership" defined the perimeters of student life,' and established the student's position in the world after university. In German towns and cities, 'only burghers could own property or have a say in the town's governance. Like the townsman's citizenship, academic citizenship depended as much on keeping certain people out as on keeping others in.'[37] It was only in

[32] Petschauer (1986: 263) notes about 'two hundred and fifty books and essays in eighteenth-century Germany' were produced.

[33] Petschauer (1986: 268, 269).

[34] Petschauer (1986: 274).

[35] Petschauer (1986: 278).

[36] Petschauer (1986: 280). Petschauer notes that Tacitus' depiction of strong, powerful women in his *Germania* greatly interested eighteenth-century readers, although they were not keen revivify *that* area of the ancient world.

[37] Mazón (2003: 20, 21).

the second half of the nineteenth century that women's university education became more widely and seriously discussed. But it was not before the beginning of the twentieth century that women were admitted to higher education on the same terms as men in the German states.[38]

Gesner's educational philosophy and practice accentuated an 'allgemeine Bildung', an 'allgemeines "humanes"', exclusively for boys and young men. This meant that schoolboys should not be weighed down with 'Wortgelehrsamkeit'.[39] Education should not simply be religious in nature, but should also be embedded in 'Sprachen und Realien'.[40] Education is the training not of the intellect but of 'des Willens', 'die moralische Bildung'. We learn through examples of fully developed individuals, not through lists of grammatical regulations.[41] According to one historian of German education, Gesner's humanism was not so different from those that preceded it, except in the search for a 'Mittelweg' between an emphasis on religiosity and on childlike play.[42] A fundamental requirement, therefore, for education was: 'Whoever really loves children' would educate the child best.[43] Gesner's discourse of 'love' for the individuality of the child meant that he thought that the classics were not suitable for everyone and that they were not a requirement for becoming 'ein wissenschaftlich gebildeter Mann'. Schoolboys should not be forced into Latin and Greek and made to hate it. Only for certain professions in the *Bürgertum* were the classics necessary.[44] The emphasis on reality and exemplarity meant that Gesner's brand of humanism could advertise itself as a true humanism, as some of his scholarly supporters have celebrated him.[45] Paradoxically, a true humanism would really revivify the 'Geist der klassischen Humanität', which would enable the creation of a select elite of modern, 'neugeschaffen' individuals.[46]

---

[38] See Mazón (2003) and Rowold (2010: 69–151).

[39] Gericke (1911: 14).

[40] Gericke (1911: 14).

[41] Gericke (1911: 18). Gesner observes: 'apparet virtutem non tam praeceptis doceri quam adsuefactione posse.'

[42] Gericke (1911: 19).

[43] Gericke (1911: 19).

[44] Gericke (1911: 20). Gericke remarks: 'Gesner war eben ein völlig moderner Mann.'

[45] See Gericke (1911: 20). Gericke is also quoted verbatim in Friedrich (1991: 71).

[46] Gericke (1911: 26).

Making the ancients into examples implies a fundamentally different logic from that which is invested in the possibilities of mimicking antiquity. It suggests a question about the possibility of living up to the ancient example and takes seriously what emerges in the gap between ancient ideal example and modern reality. The neo-humanisms of the eighteenth and nineteenth centuries thereby established a *relationship* of negotiation, engagement, and confrontation between antiquity and modernity. This had significant implications for the teacher—pupil relationship: the lecture became supplemented by Gesner's seminar, which provided a place where the movement of knowledge might go back and forth, between one generation and another. The pupil was not there to copy the teacher but to be taught how to be self-taught, to learn not to need to learn from the teacher. In taking the experience of the pupil so seriously, Gesner's model of 'kursorische Lektüre' was designed to get the pupil to learn through his or her ignorance just as much as his or her knowledge. The pupil's *Bildung*, his self-development, was a continual, even unending process, not simply a set of rules by which one might live.

Just as the process of knowledge production and transfer became interrogated and problematized by the new pedagogic practices, so this provided the opportunity to reconceptualize modernity's relationship with antiquity. Now the issue was no longer one of straight-forward imitation, it turned into contrast and comparison. *Bildung* was facilitated through a logic of 'Vergleichung'.[47] That is to say, it was possible to speak properly for the first time of a *relationship* between antiquity and modernity. And this is reflected in the peda-gogy of neo-humanism: Greek and Latin texts could not be read without reference to modern ones and vice versa. The Göttingen Seminarium became more and more interested in comparing its findings with 'Teutschen Sprachverfassung'. Indeed, historians have traced the origins of the *Germanistik* of the Grimm brothers back to Gesner's seminar.[48] Christian Gottlob Heyne, Gesner's successor at Göttingen, had been educated in Leipzig by Johann August Ernesti, and was, so to speak, 'Enkelschüler Gesners'. He inherited and devel-oped Gesner's interest in viewing the ancient and the modern in

---

[47] Gericke (1911: 23).
[48] Schindel (2001: 17). To literalize the genealogical metaphor, it is interesting to note that Gesner's great-granddaughter, Henrietta Dorothea (known as Dortchen), married Wilhelm Grimm in 1825.

relational terms. Students' engagement with antiquity was mediated through English moral philosophy and sentimental literature, French tragedy, the *Bildungsroman*, and European painting. Titles of his lectures included 'Ursachen und Ausgang des Bürgerkriegs bei den Römern unter der Berücksichtigung des Kriegs mit den Amerikanischen Kolonie', and 'Vergleich der Deportation nach Neu-Südwales mit der Verbannung auf eine Insel bei den Römern'. In his lectures on Roman agrarian laws, Heyne talked about the expropriations made in revolutionary France.[49] It is not hard to see how Benjamin Jowett was able to formulate his reforms in Victorian Oxford (as we shall see in Chapter 2 below). The example of Göttingen among other German universities paved the way for the transformation of English classical pedagogy. Although the tale that Heyne was the first university student to graduate with a degree in Classical Philology is sometimes told, this is not actually true: the Göttingen *Matrikelbuch* contained the entry 'studiosus Philologiae' back in 1736. And, although the propaideutic status of classical philology persisted until the end of the eighteenth century, the steps made by Friedrich August Wolf in Berlin, August Boeckh in Berlin, and Karl Otfried Müller in Göttingen, to concretize classical philology as a discipline in its own right at the heart of the modern university, would not have been possible without Gesner's pedagogical techniques and reforms.[50]

We should not be surprised, then, to find that Gesner was interested in *ancient* as well as modern modes of pedagogy. Gesner's educational reforms would have placed the teacher—pupil relationship under greater scrutiny, and one of the most famous teachers in antiquity was Socrates. His open admiration of boys' physiques was, however, quite different from the way in which a modern educational establishment would have behaved. If Gesner's reorganization of classical pedagogy were to be thorough and comprehensive, he would have to confront the relationship between Socratic desire and Socratic philosophy. At least one recent and influential historian of sexuality has suggested that his lecture on the subject constitutes the first modern scholarly study of ancient pederasty, a study that was delivered originally on 5 February 1752.[51] If modern, neo-humanist intellectuals constructed their relationship with ancient writers and

---

[49] Schindel (2001: 18–19).
[50] See Schindel (2001: 20–3). See also Carhart (2007: 126–7).
[51] W. Davis (1996: 274 n.4). See also Derks (1990: 59).

thinkers in terms of a relationship of exemplarity, what ancient examples were available for the teachers themselves? Was there an ancient example of how to be a (modern) example to youths when teaching them? An example for the examples? (How) was Socrates going to teach the teachers how to teach?

GESNER, PEDAGOGY, AND PEDERASTY

The question of what Socrates could teach the modern world framed a vexing and contentious debate in the eighteenth century. Under-lining the problematic inimitability of the ancient pedagogue, Diderot famously exclaimed in the *Encyclopaedia* entry on Socrates: 'Ah Socrates! I am not much like you; but all the same you make me weep with admiration and joy.'[52] And Diderot's invocation of So-crates was not unusual. It has recently been observed that 'there were as many Socrateses as there were *philosophes* in the eighteenth cen-tury'.[53] There was a Socrates for Christians, another for pagans, one for democrats, and another for the anti-democrat.[54] It was Socrates' death in particular that captured the Enlightened imagination.[55] Indeed, 'ancient deaths were particularly interesting in a period that saw itself as decisively modern: the death of Socrates, Seneca or Cato could hint at the death of antiquity as a whole'.[56] 'The image of Socrates' was 'praised by the *philosophes* as a martyr for the good cause', *and* he was condemned as 'the Athenian citizen justly accused, judged and sentences for ἀσέβεια [irreverence for the gods] as re-vealed by the researches of the *savants*'.[57] Eighteenth-century intel-lectuals became most preoccupied with 'Socrates the *man*', a mortal 'individual rooted in a certain time and in a certain world in which he had found the conditions of existence', quite 'different from that sage of exemplary virtue beloved of the Italian Humanists'.[58] The

[52] On Diderot, see Wilson (2007: 181) and Goulbourne (2007: 230–1). See also Diderot (1975: viii. 313).
[53] Goulbourne (2007: 244).
[54] See Morris (2007).
[55] See Gay (1967–70: 82), Morris (2007: 209), and Wilson (2007: 170–91).
[56] Wilson (2007: 172).
[57] Montuori (1981: 15).
[58] Montuori (1981: 16).

excavation of the *historic* Socrates became a particular preoccupation of this period: 'his life, trial and death; his ethics, theology, metaphysics, dialectics and teaching; his daemon and pederasty; the Socratic sources and the reliability of Xenophon and Plato; the image of Socrates and his youthful studies of physics; his irony and maieutics... his physical appearance, his genius and prophetic gifts, his bigamy and his patience'.[59] Nicolas Fréret and Siegmund Fridrich Dresig 'began that subtle process of demythicizing the figure of Socrates', especially with their scholarship that investigated the justice of Socrates' trial and death.[60] Socrates' trial was, in effect, replayed several times over in the course of the eighteenth century, as his condemnation was judged and rejudged. Whereas, for some, Socrates' death represented the 'apotheosis of philosophy', for Fréret it was the Athenian judicial system that was brave enough to put such a man to death that represented philosophical apotheosis.[61]

Socrates' corruption of Athenian youth warranted particularly careful consideration. The myths of the earthly and heavenly *erōs* in the *Symposium*, the relationship between Alcibiades and Socrates in that dialogue, and the myth of the charioteer with two horses in the *Phaedrus* saw to it that modern interpreters posited *two* types of Greek pederasty, one purer than the other. Voltaire was especially loquacious on this topic. In the 1730s the *philosophe* and Frederick the Great cast themselves as Socrates and Alcibiades, respectively, causing scholars to speculate on the relationship between the intellectual and politician.[62] However, by 1764, when he published the *Dictionnaire philosophique* article 'Amour nommé socratique', Voltaire offered an altogether more negative opinion of Socrates' pedagogic passions, saying that they reflected a 'vice, which, were it widespread, would destroy the human race'.[63] And, in this very article, Voltaire also observed acerbically that 'a modern writer called Larcher dares to cite some book, in which Socrates is called *sanctus pederastes*, Socrates St. B . . .'.[64] Interestingly, Voltaire was referring to Gesner's lecture *Socrates Sanctus* παιδεραστής, which actually

[59] Montuori (1981: 16).
[60] Montuori (1981: 19).
[61] See Wilson (2007: 185–6). See also Rogers (1933) and Prior (1996) on the Socratic problem—that is, the recovery of the historic Socrates.
[62] See H. Mason (1981: 52–4) and Peyrefitte (1992).
[63] Voltaire (1968–: xxxv. 328).
[64] Voltaire (1968–: xxxv. 328).

suggested the opposite to that which Voltaire alluded. Gesner's Socrates was no 'bougre' but a 'saintly pederast'. Indeed, Gesner's canonization of the ancient philosopher refers back to Erasmus's famous 'Sancte Socrates, ora pro nobis'![65] Still more interestingly, however, Voltaire's misreading was anticipated by Gesner himself, when he wrote in his text that 'severe legislation is a requirement precisely because that love of boys, chaste, legal and saintly, might sometimes provide the cover [*obtentum*] for shameful practices [*flagitiis*]'.[66] The terms 'Religio, Pudor, Amor Patriae [and] Gloria', thanks to modern philosophers, 'have been reduced to the din of empty words', making saintly and immoral pederasty indistinguishable.[67] Indeed, Gesner opens his text saying that no man, however virtuous, is above suspicion.[68] Voltaire's misunderstanding of Gesner simply reinforces the professor's point. Gesner bemoans the Athenians' own distrust of pedagogues, which makes him insist all the more that 'παιδεραστία was most honourable and so saintly that it was the means by which men were believed to be incited to virtue, especially virtue in war, and whatever is beautiful'.[69]

Gesner's lecture, then, set out to prove with philological evidence that Socrates was a 'saintly pederast', despite the possibility that that chaste love of boys might indeed be a coverlet, blanket, or veil (*obtentum*) for other practices. So his text attempted to negotiate two different Socrateses: the mythical *exemplum* of the Renaissance and the historical individual of the Enlightenment. The very title of his lecture, *Socrates Sanctus Παιδεραστής*, reflects the equivocal nature of the project: the Latin *sanctus* suggests an anachronistic view of Socrates, the ancient philosopher as proto-Christian, whereas the untransliterated παιδεραστής implies the untranslatable nature of Socratic desire. Gesner's text—as well as its contemporary reception—makes very

---

[65] See Derks (1990: 57).

[66] Gesner (1877: 78–90). Quotations will be from the 1877 edition of the text, which includes a parallel French translation.

[67] Gesner (1877: 80).

[68] Gesner (1877: 2).

[69] Gesner (1877: 78, 88). Indeed, the difficulty of understanding the lecture of Gesner, the exemplary neo-humanist teacher, who sought to invoke the example of Socrates, is reflected in the need to translate his (Socratic) Latin speech into French prose, by Alcide Bonneau, who becomes in effect Gesner's Plato. Bonneau, at one time a priest, produced translations of erotica and curiosa with the French bibliophile Isidore Liseux, in the second half of the nineteenth century: see Adamy (2009).

explicit the difficulty in using Socrates as a model of pedagogy in the eighteenth century.

His text is preceded and conditioned by a very long history of thought comparing and contrasting Jesus and Socrates and their modes of teaching. One of the earliest Christians to appeal to Socrates' example was Justin Martyr (*c*. AD 100–65), in works where he establishes commonalities between the pedagogies of Jesus and Socrates. Such views provoked immense discussion and dissent in early Christian writing and art, with some expanding Justin's comparison, while others denounced it.[70] The relationship between Christ and Socrates was also a central aspect of Erasmus's humanism. In the *Convivium Religiosum* (1522), his version of the *Symposium*, Erasmus moves Plato's table talk from the urbane city into the idyllic gardens and home of the pious man Eusebius, where Christians learn how to converse and learn. The entrance of Eusebius' handsome property greets his visitors with a series of beautiful sights, including a statue of Jesus set in a shrine: 'he points to heaven with his right hand while with his left he seems to beckon and invite the passer-by [*velut invitat et allectat praetereuntem*]'.[71] Erasmus's revision of the *Symposium* rewrites Alcibiades' praise of the inner beauty of Socrates behind his supposedly ugly exterior. Here Jesus' beauty is there for all to see, as it 'allures [*allectat*]' all who view the statue. But it is the invisible beauty of God to which Jesus' right hand points that should capture our attention. The physical beauty of Jesus is to be seen through and beyond.[72] The allurement of appearances is a leitmotif in Erasmus's dialogue, in which one of the interlocutors, Nephalius, famously exclaims: 'St Socrates [*Sancte Socrate*], pray for us.'[73] Erasmus's affirmation of the beauty of Socratic teaching could be conceived only within a Christian frame—that is to say, prefaced by a lesson at the entrance of the textual property of Eusebius in how to admire the beauty of Jesus. And so it is this Christian framework to which Gesner's neo-humanist discussion of Socrates explicitly alludes. Gesner was, however, also encouraged by the close textual criticism executed by his friend and erstwhile colleague at Leipzig, Johann

---

[70] See Hanfmann (1951: 215–17) and Wilson (2007: 145–6).

[71] Erasmus (1997: 177).

[72] See Christian (1972) on Erasmus's Socrates. Erasmus's Latin here alludes to the praise of leisurely old age framed by the countryside in Cicero *De Senectute* 16, thereby further dampening down any overt eroticism in this image of Jesus.

[73] Erasmus (1997: 194). On St Socrates, see, Marcel (1951).

August Ernesti. This prodigious scholar was in the process of producing his important edition of Aristophanes' *Clouds* (which would appear in 1753). And he was more famously to direct his critical zeal to the Bible, whose texts he examined and annotated with the latest tools of rationalist philology.[74] Furthermore, we can see in Gesner a prognosis of the ascent of *Geschichtswissenschaft* that characterized Göttingen of the second half of the eighteenth century. Professors at Göttingen were among the first in Germany to receive chairs specifically designed for history.[75]

Gesner's lecture, then, represents the limit case in the history of attempts to unify *two* sorts of Socrates. His examination of the relationship between pederasty and pedagogy allowed him to attempt to unite into *one* man the most holy, disembodied, spiritual, Christianizing readings of Socrates with those that relentlessly viewed the philosopher as a physical, historical individual who might have been partial to the worst of bodily desires. Influenced by both Christian readings of antiquity *and* budding historicist techniques in scholarship, Gesner sought to combine the historical, embodied Socrates through close analyses of ancient texts, with religiously inflected humanism that sought to exemplify the Greeks. Gesner's saintly pederast tried to bring together the mythologized exemplary archetype with historical individual. This holy lover of boys was to stand as a pious ideal *and* as an embodied personage in history who supplies a real-life model for the homosocial milieu of classical education, which summarily excluded girls and women. Indeed, Gesner's career, which moved from schoolteacher to university professor, sought to transfer Socrates and the study of Greek from a threat to young boys to a serious adult education for men. In this way, then, Gesner anticipated the later debates about the relationship between *Wissenschaft* and *Bildung* (as discussed in the Introduction). The discussion of saintly pederasty underlined how urgent the debates about historicism had already become concerning the politics of turning ahistorical exemplars into historical personages, and vice versa.

Gesner's *apologia* for Socrates begins by claiming that the accusation of pederasty in antiquity is relatively rare, thereby plunging straight into obscure, learned texts. Porphyrius, quoted in Theodoretus, notes that Socrates 'removed this sort of behaviour with effort

[74] On Ernesti, see Grafton (1983: 166) and Howard (2006: 118 n. 276).
[75] See Howard (2006: 116). See also Iggers (1982).

and study'. The same Theodoretus, borrowing again from Porphyrius, who himself followed Aristoxenus, refers to his youth ('ad adolescentiam primam viri'), and to Archelaus, his 'honestus amator
(ἐραστής)'. But Gesner is explicit that Socrates' adolescence is *not*
the subject of his *sermo* ('adolescentiam . . . de qua nobis sermo non
est').[76] He is clear that 'nondum quidquam ex Porphyrio vel Aristox-
eno, quem ille auctorem sequitur, allatum est de horribili scelere,
Pæderastia'.[77] That Gesner sees his task to be the investigation of an
alleged *scelus* is significant: Socrates' pederasty is seen as an act *not* as
a special signifier of sexual orientation. (Indeed it would be incorrect
to suggest that Gesner thought he was defending Socrates from
imputation of 'homosexuality', since later in the text Gesner will
discuss Socrates' supposed bigamy.)[78] Gesner continues to note that
Cyril (like Theodoretus), an 'iniquus' critic of the father of philosophy, would not have passed over the accusation of pederasty in
silence, had he known of it. Even Aristophanes makes no mention
of this charge in his *Clouds* ('nec . . . huius criminis ullam mentionem
facit'). Indeed, there is no one in later antiquity or antiquity proper
('nec forte quisquam ex omni antiquitate remotiore illa, et tempor-
ibus Philosophi propinqua') who has brought this charge against him
('accusator huius criminis').[79] The very opening paragraph begins by
stating that nothing and no one is above suspicion, but Gesner then
moves to say that, apart from the 'alter Socrates', 'another Socrates'
(who falsely reports from Porphyrius), no one in antiquity actually
accused Socrates of the crime of pederasty. There is a marked contrast
between modern and ancient perspectives on Socrates.[80]

The only authors, according to Gesner, who do make adverse
comments regarding 'Socraticus amor Platonicusque' are Lucian
and pseudo-Lucian. On this matter he says that either Lucian was

[76] Gesner (1877: 8).
[77] Gesner (1877: 8). 'Nothing in Porphyrius nor in Aristoxenus, who follows this
writer, is related to that horrific charge, pederasty.'
[78] Gesner (1877: 112).
[79] Gesner (1877: 10).
[80] The reference to 'another Socrates'—that is, Socrates of Constantinople (born
about AD 380)—makes it clear that Gesner was invested in excavating the individuality
of Socrates the philosopher. He was exemplarily unique, and was not to be confused
with anyone else, even if Gesner was engaged in amalgamating several (mythical,
Christian and pagan, historical) Socrateses into his singular portrait. The later Socrates was famous for his *Historia Ecclesiastica*, a continuation of the work of
Eusebius: see Urbainczyk (1997).

writing mockingly ('lusit'); or he misunderstood Plato's *Phaedrus*; or any mention of pederasty in the *Amores* was said 'iocose et per calumniam'.[81] Maximus of Tyre had already refuted any 'ancient accusations' ('veterum criminationes') 'so that there might not seem to be any need for anything to be added'. There has nevertheless been a recent rise in malevolent opinion among both learned and good men regarding Socrates' pederasty ('*nuper* fuisse, et esse *hodie* homines eruditos, et bonos viros, qui pravam de patre illo Philosophiæ opinionem conceperint').[82] *Nuper* and *hodie* accentuate the modernity of the debate. Furthermore, this *opinio* is of major concern: it is 'harmful to virtue; contrary to the sense of good men; and moreover adverse to humanity itself [*humanitati*]'.[83] Socrates' alleged pederasty is not some obscure, academic issue. Rather, Gesner positions it as harmful to modern masculinity ('*vir*tuti noxiam'), and therefore as inimical to the collectivity of good men ('bonorum virorum'). Finally, the damage posed to *humanitas* refers not only to humankind in general, but also to the modern philosophy and practice of neohumanism itself.

For Gesner, the possibility that pederastic pedagogy might degenerate into pedagogic pederasty is brought about by the poor teaching and reading of Greek in the first place. The ancient archive about Socrates has been corrupted by the poor pedagogy of modern teachers, who are supposedly meant to conserve that archive and pass it onto the next generation. The corruption of the archive—poor pedagogy, which has ensured that the ancient archive is no longer understood—has ensured that it has become an archive of corruption. 'Magna pars doctorum etiam hominum legendi laborem fugit, legendi uno *tenore, continuata attentione, totos* veterum scriptorum libros.' To a large extent even learned men flee from the work of reading, of reading in one sitting, with sustained attention, ancient texts in their entirety. Students of the classical languages have become accustomed to reading merely excerpts of ancient texts 'velut compage vulsa', 'with only one eye on the text' ('mediocri attentione').[84] Although Gesner does not mention his methodology of 'kursorische Lektüre', it would have been clear to his Göttingen listeners and his

[81] Gesner (1877: 10–12).
[82] Gesner (1877: 12–14), emphasis added.
[83] Gesner (1877: 14).
[84] Gesner (1877: 16).

humanistic readers that Gesner took this opportunity to reinforce his
pedagogical philosophy. It was the reformed, modern pedagogy that
would resolve the (modern) problematization of Socrates' pederasty.
The teaching of the classics that focuses minutely on small sections of
classical text has created this problem. The reading of a text that
extends beyond grammatical interest to understanding what the
author actually says is required. And so Gesner commits himself to
offering an example of 'kursorische Lektüre', to show what an exemplary figure Socrates actually was. Socratic philosophy exemplifies
modern, Gesner's neo-humanism, just as Gesner's neo-humanism
exemplarily explains the exemplary status of Socratic thought.

Gesner's exercise in close reading brings him to Plato's *Phaedrus*
250e. Plato has just discussed how the philosopher grows wings and
becomes a lover of true beauty. At this point, Plato contrasts that
figure with 'the man whose initiation was not recent, or who has been
corrupted'. The corrupted man

does not move keenly from here to there to beauty itself, when he observes its
namesake here, so that he does not revere it when he looks at it, but
surrendering himself to pleasure does his best to go on four feet like an
animal and father offspring, and keeping close company with excess has no
fear or shame in pursuing pleasure contrary to nature.[85]

Gesner reproduces this text in Greek, complete with Latin translation,
so that, he says, those 'for whom Plato's text is not at hand or those
who do not want to bring down a heavy volume from the shelf, might
be able to think about the matter in complete certitude'.[86] The words
'contrary to nature' appear emphasized in capitals in both Greek and
Latin ('$\Pi APA \, \Phi Y\Sigma IN$,' 'PRAETER NATURAM'), as if proving that
Plato was anticipating modern discourses about 'crimes against nature'. Indeed, there is no discussion of the Socratic irony inherent in
the suggestion that animalistic sex should be something 'contrary to
nature'. Instead, Gesner adds in a footnote comparing the sentence
in *Laws* where Plato observes that sexual relations between males
were called '$\tau\grave{o} \, \Pi APA \, \Phi Y\Sigma IN \, \tau\acute{o}\lambda\mu\eta\mu\alpha$'.[87] Gesner's close reading
attempts to show that sexual activity between men is consistently

---

[85] *Phaedrus* 250e–251a, Plato (1988: 68–71).
[86] Gesner (1877: 38).
[87] Gesner (1877: 38–9 n. 1). See Plato, *Laws* 636c.

viewed as '*ΠΑΡΑ ΦΥΣΙΝ*' in the Platonic corpus, implying a constancy between the views on male desire espoused in texts such as the *Phaedrus* and *Symposium*, and those viewed reflected in the *Laws*. The reconciliation of Plato's texts on this point is, of course, a famous problem for scholars: the *Phaedrus* appears to sanction, indeed praise, male—male desire, whereas *Laws* seems to pronounce against them. Indeed that Plato is referring in the *Phaedrus* solely to male—male sexual practices is itself not clear. Ferrari notes that the 'surrender to pleasure (250e4) issue[s] in an attempt to achieve sexual gratification and/or the begetting of children'.[88] Gesner's translation of the Greek is actually somewhat different from Plato's Greek:

sed libidini se tradens, quadrupedis ritu inscendere *formosum* conatur, et genitale semen profundere[89]

but giving himself over to pleasure, he tries to mount a beautiful male like a four-legged animal, and to ejaculate into him

First, *Παιδοσπορεῖν*, meaning 'father offspring', becomes 'genitale semen profundere'. Secondly, Gesner inserts 'formosum' into his text, a grammatical and sexual object not there in the Greek. We are a long way from Plato's positive depiction of pregnant men fathering offspring in the *Symposium* (discussed in the Introduction). In his attempt to delimit the licit from the illicit, the saintly pederast from the demonized, Gesner, ironically, has to alter, subtly though significantly, the state of the text as it passes from Greek to Latin. Gesner thereby inserts a bestial sodomite into the text of Plato. Gesner's lecture set out to show that it is correct and cautious reading of the classical texts that ensured that the relationship between Socrates' pederasty and pedagogy would not become misunderstood and liable to corruption, abuse, 'obtentum flagitiis'. The corruption of the text would lead to corruption of the pupil. Yet, when Gesner does turn to the text, he corrupts its original meaning when he translates it from Greek to Latin, in order to ensure that his reader will no longer be corrupted by misreading of the ancient texts. The corrupt handing-over-of-oneself to pleasure is supposedly prevented by Gesner's corrupt handing-down of pleasure in the text. Gesner's invention of a corrupt tradition in the text is meant to check the corruption of the tradition of the text itself.

---

[88] Ferrari (1987: 146).
[89] Gesner (1877: 40), emphasis added.

If Gesner's deliberate mistranslation of the Greek reflects his wish to detach Socrates from any suspicion of physical desire for boys, he nevertheless makes up for this with close, explicit attendance to what ancient texts actually do say about Socrates' rumoured bigamy, voiced first by the biographer Diogenes Laertius. That is to say, when it comes to his relations with boys, Gesner is forced to alter the Greek text, but when he turns to Socrates' relationship to women, he feels quite comfortable confronting the ancient sources. Socrates' relationship with his wife had already been a cause of amusement in the Middle Ages: a popular myth circulated about an angry Xanthippe pouring the contents of a chamber pot over Socrates' head. And the alleged bigamy featured in a comic Italian operetta in 1680, and Georg Telemann reworked the theme in his opera *Der Geduldige Socrates* in 1721.[90] As before in his lecture, Gesner proceeds through the ancient evidence carefully and critically. Interestingly, however, here Gesner is *not* able to arrive at a judgement about Socrates' marital status. Unlike his discussion of pederasty, he feels able to respect the historical difference of antiquity: although Cecrops did not seem to have permitted bigamy in ancient Athens, the texts of Diogenes Laertius and Athenaeus do suggest that it was possible 'plures habere uxores', in order to increase Athens's dwindling population.[91] And so Gesner abandons the discussion, observing that, had Socrates committed bigamy, he would have been following the laws at the time, and that he would have been saving the daughter of Aristides, Myrto, from a life of poverty![92] Ultimately, Gesner is contented to respect the historical otherness of antiquity when it concerns men's relations with their wives. In the last word, Gesner notes that the great scholar Richard Bentley had already cast doubt on these aspersions.[93] Despite, then, concluding his lecture confident that he has cleared Socrates of all the charges set out, the accusation of bigamy nevertheless remains defensible in Gesner's text on grounds of the specificities of the Greek legal system and the particular situation of Myrto. The historical relationship between ancient and modern marriage is discoverable through correct philological

---

[90] On the reports of Socrates' bigamy, see Wilson (2007: 155). See also Diogenes Laertius, *Life of Socrates* 2.26.

[91] Gesner (1877: 118).

[92] Gesner (1877: 120). For a more recent discussion of Socrates and the daughter of Aristides, see Woodbury (1973).

[93] Gesner (1877: 120).

methodology. The matter of pederasty, the matter of erotic desires between males, however, is a far greater challenge for classical scholarship, and demands far greater philological erudition and sophistry. Indeed, Gesner's understanding of the relationship between ancient and modern social and cultural practices is framed by the difference in scholarly approaches he makes with regard to marital and pederastic relations.

The close reading of Gesner's close reading is not pedantic—rather it reveals an important theme in *Classical Culture and Modern Masculinity*. Gesner's exemplifying of Socrates attempts to ensure that he becomes both an impossible myth to follow *and* a historical individual one might imitate. *Sancta paiderastia* represents a relationship that every man and youth might partake of, but Gesner's text causes us to suspect that no one might do so, precisely because he says that no one is beyond suspicion. The Socratic exemplum is outside history—it is that which conditions the possibility of history, in that it provides a model for the ideal transfer of knowledge from one generation to the next, the ideal model of what tradition should look like. But, at the same time as a historical exemplum, Socrates is also placed within history—he is seen as the result of the proper transmission of knowledge, the incorruptibility of tradition itself. Gesner's text, then, bespeaks a deep tension: the pedagogic relationship between teacher and pupil is that which conditions an understanding of history—it is, in effect, what creates history. Ideally it should stand outside history, a relationship through which knowledge is repeatedly passed down correctly, without error. Yet, precisely because of the importance attached to such a relationship—it is that which preserves the archive—it then demands historical analysis and examination. It becomes an important concern for the developing historicism of mid-eighteenth-century classical scholarship. That which holds and conserves the archive of classical texts and their correct interpretations can no longer be beyond historical inspection. The way in which the archive is created and preserved ensures what that archive says and means. In the terms of neo-humanistic philosophy, the way in which the teacher teaches his pupil Greek will affect precisely how the pupil will behave, who the pupil will become, in his very individuality. Classical pedagogy does not simply conserve classical learning; it also (re-)creates that learning anew each time it teaches it. How the teaching of Greek has made modern masculinity and what the teaching of Greek has made of modern masculinity are the issues that confronted Gesner and his contemporaries, when they turned to that ancient pedagogue Socrates. The example of Gesner shows us not simply that there is no such thing as a purely objective translation of a text, without agenda. His *Socrates Sanctus Παιδεραστής* also demonstrates that it is pedagogy that actively *produces* the desires it teaches and legislates over. Gesner's version of a history of Greek desire *brings about* those desires as it attempts to reify the relationship between ancient and modern masculinities.

The difficulties involved in handing down knowledge properly—the corruption of the tradition—is the subject of Gesner's essay, which his own translation and reading of the Greek repeats, and this is also witnessed, as we have seen, by Voltaire's misunderstanding of Gesner's text. The misunderstanding of Greek brings about the corruption of desire, as the reception of Gesner's text shows, which itself wilfully (?) misreads the Greek. An interest in the erotics of pedagogy is witnessed by the proliferation of texts written in German in the eighteenth century on this very subject.[94] Furthermore, the mismatch between modern translation and ancient Greek text alerted the attention of another younger Göttingen scholar, the generation after Gesner, Christoph Meiners, Professor of Weltweisheit. Meiners wrote an essay on 'die Männerliebe der Griechen', which was published in 1775 in volume one of his *Vermischte Philosophische Schriften*. The exemplification of Socrates meant that the issue of the historical specificity of Greek pederasty demanded attention: was Socrates' lesson repeatable? As Carhart has discussed, Meiners 'represented antiquarian research at its highest levels in the 1770s and 1780s'.[95] His four-volume *History of the Origin, Rise, and Fall of the Sciences in Greece and Rome* became a highly influential history of ancient philosophy. 'Rather than discussing philosophers and their texts solely on their own terms, as if abstracted from their broader context, Meiners's chief interest was in the context itself. Philosophy was not eternal and objective Truth but an expression of a given nation'. The relationship between 'the eternal philosophical truths and the historical contingency of the human philosophers' occupied much of Meiners's scholarship on antiquity.[96] The rise of modern professional historiography at Göttingen in the second half of the

---

[94] See Derks (1990: 62–3).
[95] Carhart (2007: 198).
[96] Carhart (2007: 199).

eighteenth century provided a fertile environment for professors like
Meiners, whose interest in 'world history' 'hastened a dissociation of
historical enquiry from biblical chronology and eschatology'.[97] This
energizing intellectual context ensured that his work posed questions
also asked by his colleagues about 'how nations rose to greatness and
fell into decay, and more importantly why'.[98] Meiners's broad scholarly interests are also reflected in his *Geschichte der Menschheit*,
which contested the Kantian proposition of Pure Reason. For Meiners, 'there were no innate predispositions ... Even the passions and
emotions were learned.'[99] In its examination of the diversity of
human culture, his *Geschichte* argued that 'there were no natural
human tendencies ... If there was any essence to humanity, it was
that humanity was malleable.'[100]

Although Meiners's 'Betrachtungen über die Männerliebe der
Griechen' reflects his interest in historicism, it is the historical specificity of the Greeks that grants them quasi-mythical status in his
account. Taking up Gesner's lament, Meiners writes: 'I see from the
generally incorrect use of the term "Platonic love" how little concern
has been devoted to the true meaning of these words.'[101] This, however, is hardly surprising to the Professor of Weltweisheit: 'Sustained
attention has the same effects as magnifying glass: it shows a great
many things that the fleeting glance has not seen, a number of
varieties in things which were previously considered to be similar
and the same. Just as all savages have too often been viewed as
homogenous, so too have educated human beings and civilized peoples even been spoken of as homogenous opposites of the former.'[102]
Meiners's apparent sensitivity to human diversity is obviously under-
cut by his very use of the categories 'civilized' and 'savage'. But it his
preoccupation with the Greeks that concerns us here, since it is 'the
Greeks, through their spiritual male love alone, [who] are different
from all ancient and modern savage and civilized peoples of the
earth'.[103] For Meiners, their 'Metaphysik der Liebe'[104] sees to it that

[97] Howard (2006: 116). See also Iggers (1982).
[98] Carhart (2007: 198).
[99] Carhart (2007: 237).
[100] Carhart (2007: 247).
[101] Meiners (1775: 90).
[102] Meiners (1775: 63).
[103] Meiners (1775: 66).
[104] Meiners (1775: 66).

'a comprehensive comparison of this remarkable people with the civilized peoples of our time would be one of the most important contributions to the history of mankind'.[105] In his discussion, Meiners underlines the 'fantastical [*abentheuerlich*]' and 'unbelievable [*unglaublich*]' nature of the 'geistige Männerliebe' of the Greeks, even if presented to us 'in fiction'.[106] Indeed Meiners is aware that his account of this 'pure, irreproachable love of the soul'[107] will seem 'unbelievable' to many.[108] Nevertheless Meiners is certain that it is 'impossible that this love of the soul, in all states and throughout the ages, could have been merely a mask for an unnatural vice'.[109] 'Socrates loved . . . all his students with the purest fatherly love.'[110] Meiners's paean to Greek love clearly reflects the tension between a mythical and historical Socrates that emerged in Gesner's enquiry. That is to say, Meiners's apparent interest in the historicity of the Greeks enables him to grant them mythical eminence so that their love looks stranger than any fiction.

The Göttingen professors, Gesner and Meiners, represent two exemplary responses to the eighteenth-century examinations of the historical Socrates. For Gesner, the actual, historical existence of the ancient philosopher should ensure that such classical pedagogy could be reproduced in modernity—if it happened once, it could happen again. Meiners, on the other hand, felt that it was the historical contingency of the ancient Greeks that prevented the possibility of Greek love ever being felt or known again. Furthermore, the Göttingen professoriate introduces us to themes that will repeatedly emerge in the course of this book. First, for Gesner, Greek love could not be elucidated *without* thinking about its relationship to Christianity; secondly, Socrates' pederasty could not be examined *without* also elucidating his (marital) relations with women; and, thirdly, and finally, with Meiners, the issue of race firmly enters the frame of the debates. Instead of a religious context, the generation after Gesner at Göttingen, which sought to move away from biblical chronologies, operated within the context of increasingly more detailed raciological discourses: from the 1770s, it became impossible not to think about

---

[105] Meiners (1775: 64).   [106] Meiners (1775: 65).
[107] Meiners (1775: 82).   [108] Meiners (1775: 78).
[109] Meiners (1775: 81–2).   [110] Meiners (1775: 81).

the Greeks without also thinking about their relationship to civilization and 'savages'.[111]

It was against this intellectual background that the German universities received their second reformation at the end of the eighteenth and the beginning of the nineteenth centuries, culminating in Alexander von Humboldt's reordering of the school curriculum. His short tenure as the civil servant in charge of Prussian education policy between 1808 and 1809 saw to it that the learning of languages was centralized on the school timetable, with classical Greek dominating. Furthermore, the ancient languages were seen to substitute instruction in other subjects, such as philosophy and the history of art and classes in citizenship. Although each subsequent reform would reduce the burden of Greek from the timetable, Humboldt's reform was long-lasting.[112] Humboldt's educational philosophy and administration were accompanied by his thinking on sexual difference, as Catriona MacLeod has analysed. In 'Über den Geschlechtsunderschied', he posits the biological necessity of the two sexes. However, in another essay, 'Über die männliche und weibliche Form', he views the androgynous union of the two sexes as the ideal state for humanity: 'the most exact balance of form and matter, or art and freedom, of spiritual and sensual unity . . . is only achieved when the characteristics of both sexes are melted together in thought, and humanity is fashioned from the most intimate union of pure masculinity and pure femininity.'[113] Such an individual would reach the heights of genius, although the slim prospect of such an androgyne existing meant that, for Humboldt, only Sophocles could be placed in that category. As the essay proceeds, however, it becomes clear that the male child also 'occupies the fine line between the two sexes'.[114] And it is this balance between male creativity and female receptivity that is the perfect recipe for male *Bildung*.[115] It was with the intellectual context of the new *Gymnasium* system and renewed prestige of what had become *Altertumswissenschaft* that nineteenth-century scholars turned to consider Greek pederasty. Although Humboldt's androgynous boy referred back to Winckelmann's discussions on androgyny and aesthetics

---

[111] See Hartog (2005).
[112] See Landfester (1988) and Jeismann (1996).
[113] Humboldt, quoted in MacLeod (1998: 48). See also Humboldt (1960: 296).
[114] Ibid. quoted in MacLeod (1998: 50). See also Humboldt (1960: 308).
[115] MacLeod (1998: 51). See also Tobin (2000: 204–5) on Humboldt.

(as MacLeod shows[116]), it was the perceived androgyny of the Spartans that captured the post-Humboldtian generation.

MÜLLER'S DORIANS

The Spartans had, of course, received attention in both Gesner's and Meiners's works. Gesner observed that a Spartan man was punished if he did not have a younger beloved whom he might teach, who in turn might pass on those teachings again.[117] Gesner's interest in this aspect of Spartan legislation is hardly surprising, as it exemplifies the pedagogy to which he aspired, in its emphasis on the perfect transfer of knowledge from one generation to another. As well as noting this custom, Meiners also observed that 'the ephors of Sparta punished youths if they chose a wretched rich man as a lover instead of a righteous poor one'.[118] Both scholars had used Aelian's *Varia Historia* for these remarks. Aelian was also a source for Karl Otfried Müller. And, as hinted above, it was the androgyny of the Spartans, as Dorians, that interested this later generation of scholarship. As Müller wrote in *The History and Antiquities of the Doric Race* (originally published in 1824, with the English translation produced in 1839):

The Dorians were contented with themselves . . . They looked not to the future, but to present existence . . . They lived in themselves, and for themselves. Hence man was the chief and almost only object which attracted their attention . . . In short, the *whole race* bears generally the stamp and character of the male sex; the desire of assistance and connexion, of novelty and of curiosity, the characteristics of the female sex, being directly opposed to the nature of the Dorians, which bears the mark of independence and subdued strength.[119]

Müller contrasts this picture with that of Athens, where 'the love of the male supplied the place of that of the female sex'.[120] The masculine

---

[116] See MacLeod (1998: 50).

[117] Gesner (1877: 82–4).

[118] Meiners (1775: 78).

[119] Müller (1839: ii. 401–2), emphasis added. This work was originally published in 1824, entitled *Die Dorier*. We will be quoting from the English translation, which Müller himself helped to produce.

[120] Müller (1839: ii. 304, note (a)).

androgyny of the Dorians supposedly reflects their self-contentment and self-containment within the political boundaries and within their temporality. They had no thought for the future nor for novelty, and, as we shall soon see, nor for the past. Furthermore, their 'independence and subdued strength' suggest their political autonomy. In short, this masculine androgyny is the signifier of Doric wholeness and completeness. This is quite different from Müller's view of Athens as 'relatively modern', which contrasts with the archaic conservatism of the Spartans.[121] Similarly to Gesner, then, it is the gender relations of these Greek communities that characterize their historical specificity, in terms of the antiquity or modernity of these relations. But Müller reflects the growing nineteenth-century interest in racial sciences: the Dorians are typified *as a race*. Furthermore, in providing *two* models of ancient male—male desire (the Spartan, which consists of two masculine subjects, and the Athenian, which consists of a man and another male who is a substitute for the female sex), Müller makes very explicit his perception of the various *nationalisms* that comprised the ancient Greek world. This depiction of ancient male passion can be explained if we consider Müller and his particular intellectual context in more detail.

On the strength of his thesis on the history of the island of Aegina, Müller received the chair of classical philology in his early twenties, at Göttingen, a position previously held by Heyne and Welcker.[122] Here Müller, in a pre-eminent position within the classical—and more broadly scholarly—community, embarked upon a highly impressive publishing career. Two of the highlights of this—according to Martin Bernal, 'the works that became the pillars of *Altertumswissenschaft*'—were his three-volume *Geschichte hellenischer Stämme und Städte* (volumes two and three comprising *Die Dorier*), published between 1820 and 1824, and his *Prolegomena zu einer wissenschaftlichen Mythologie* of 1825. Müller has received much scholarly attention in the last twenty years since Martin Bernal's publication of *Black Athena*. For Bernal, Müller's scholarship was among the first to institutionalize what he calls the 'Aryan Model' of ancient history. Müller contested ancient accounts of the influences of Egyptian and near eastern civilizations on classical Greece. Müller's work, as Bernal examines, emphasized the autochthonous nature of ancient Greek culture. For Müller, the main foreign influence on Greece before later periods was the invasion of the Dorians from the north,

---

[121] Müller (1839: ii. 140).
[122] See Bernal (1987: 309) and Blok (1994: 28).

subduing and then mixing with the native population of Pelasgians. Bernal's depiction of a racist and anti-Semitic Müller has been tempered by Josine Blok, who has discussed Müller's genuine interest in Egyptology. In the light of this debate, Suzanne Marchand has written that it was a 'fateful combination of cultural nationalism, philological scepticism, institutionalized philhellenism, *and* the beginnings of racialist thought' that provided the context for Müller's writing.[123] However we might want to characterize Müller's views, then, it is certain that racialist— nationalist discourses were paramount in shaping Müller's scholarship. And, in doing so, such scholarship helped to formulate and concretize the belief that ancient Greeks and modern north-western Europeans shared not only cultural similarities, but also racial links.

As George Williamson has examined, with 'the ascent of Heyne at Göttingen and Wolf at Halle, philology had emerged as the model science for the research university'.[124] And the philological science, whose logic was to 'break down the wholes into their component parts',[125] is reflected in Müller's historical research. He was preoccupied with distinguishing between various different mythic traditions that had become mixed up and confused in Greek myth in order to discover the truly Greek element. The intellectual context for Müller's scholarship can be found with reference to the 'Creuzer affair'. Georg Friedrich Creuzer, a Heidelberg philologist, was the author of the four-volume *Symbolik und Mythologie der alten Völker* (1810–12). In this work, Creuzer argued that an esoteric symbolism, through a complex process of combination (reflecting the Greek *sumbolon*), had furnished the basis for religious and social life throughout the ancient world. This symbolism originated in ancient India and was diffused across Asia Minor, Egypt, and Greece. Creuzer's research profited from the recent surge of interest in India, with the 'discovery' of the links between Greek, Latin, and Sanskrit by William Jones in the 1780s, and the comparativist studies of ancient art, in the 1780s and 1790s, by French scholars such as Pierre-François Hugues (known as Baron d'Hancarville) and Charles Dupuis.[126] By the beginning of the nineteenth century, several German

---

[123] Marchand (1996: 44). See also Berlinerblau (1999: 64–5) on the debate around the politics of Müller's scholarship.
[124] Williamson (2004: 136).
[125] Williamson (2004: 137–8).
[126] On the late-eighteenth-century fascination with ancient Indian religious erotics, and its influence on Creuzer, see Mitter (1977: 73–104, 202–20).

scholars, including most prominently Friedrich Schlegel, had published work that traced the origins of religion back to India or the Caucasus.[127] Creuzer's book, which expressed a keen interest in the sexually explicit images of Indian deities, 'featured cross-dressing, enlarged phalluses, ritual intercourse, and orgies'. His view of antiquity made *Symbolik und Mythologie* 'a bold challenge to the profession of classical philology'.[128] His 'emphasis on the oriental antecedents to classical mythology threatened the individuality of Greek culture, the very premise on which neohumanism was founded'.[129] Although Creuzer had supporters, the reaction inside the academy and beyond was bitter and vitriolic. His violation of the rules of textual criticism that sought to dissect wholes into the constituent parts ensured his marginalization from other classicists, as Williamson analyses. Although Müller was interested in Creuzer's arguments, he thought that mankind's 'mythopoetic "sensitivity" [found] expression in contact with specific geographical and historical circumstances'. As Josine Blok discusses, 'the origin of myth is therefore due to an interaction between this special mental faculty' of symbol-formation and myth-making that Creuzer had posited, along with 'the historical experiences of the people in question'. For Müller, myth 'is an expression of the historical experiences of the people that created it'.[130] Although subsequent nineteenth-century scholars did not agree with the whole of Müller's description of the Spartans, his nationalization of ancient Greek culture and his further dissection of it into its component parts, Ionian (Athens and Asia Minor) and Dorian, became highly influential, as racialist thought became more prevalent in German and British nineteenth-century scholarship. Although Creuzer's notion of a 'transhistorical *Symbolik*' appeared unpalatable for most philologists, we will see in a later chapter how his ideas resurfaced with Freud's engagement with antiquity. For now, however, we can observe that it was Müller's that maintained a certain authority over the philological discipline. Indeed, Müller's sense of historicism was perceived as influential enough for Leopold von Ranke to have recognized his own affiliation to the work of the Göttingen professor.[131]

Müller's influence has also been traced through his students: Richard Lepsius, a significant figure in the history of Egyptology,

---

[127] Williamson (2004: 129).   [128] Williamson (2004: 131, 136).
[129] Williamson (2004: 136).   [130] Blok (1994: 41).
[131] See Walther (1998: 423). On Ranke, see the essays in Iggers and Powell (1990).

'stressed the autonomy of Egyptian civilization'.[132] Furthermore, Müller's death from sunstroke when visiting the Peloponnese in the summer of 1840 profoundly affected another of his pupils, Ernst Curtius, the classicist who went on to lobby for, and support, the Prussian archaeological excavation of ancient Olympia.[133] Indeed Curtius's own highly popular *Griechische Geschichte* (1857–67) positioned itself in 'the line from Wolf and K. O. Müller', as heir 'to the Prussian tradition of specialized, historicist philology' that led 'the retreat from speculation and comparativism, without, however, completely abandoning the aesthetic idealization of the Greek world'.[134] And, even though Heinrich Schliemann's exploration into Mediterranean prehistory had shown up 'Egyptian—Mycenaean stylistic commonalities' that 'could only vex the heirs of K. O. Müller', the Dorians, as depicted by the Göttingen professor, provided a highly evocative picture of a society that deserved further attention, as Curtius had shown with Olympia. Moreover, Müller's Dorians provided an excellent example to which the modern German scholar himself might aspire. As Marchand knowingly writes, 'the picture painted [of the professional philologist] is one of ceaseless toil, of a *Spartan* life-style commensurate with the Pietist—ascetic dedication to learning advocated (and practiced) by F. A. Wolf'.[135] Indeed Müller himself was a Pietist, and so Christianity remained an important framework within which to work, despite the expanding claims of purely historicist scholarship. And, finally, the homosocial nature of the classical community was marked by its inbred character: 'the very high proportion of father—son-in-law relations suggests that daughters of the *Bildungsbürgertum* still came with a dowry, now intellectual rather than monetary'.[136] Indeed, the importance of close ties between these men is illustrated in the bizarre marriage customs executed by these scholars in order to remain in (some sort of) proximity to one another: 'Ernst Curtius married a colleague's

---

[132] Marchand (1996: 64). On Müller's influence on Lepsius' austere, analytical method of Egyptological research, see Marchand (1996: 113).

[133] See Marchand (1996: 77–91).

[134] Marchand (1996: 109).

[135] Marchand (1996: 50), emphasis added. See Marchand (1996: 18) on Wolf, who 'is said to have staved off sleep by denying himself heat, submerging his feet in cold water and binding up one eye (to rest it, while the other read on)', in order to get through the classics as quickly as possible.

[136] Marchand (1996: 50).

widow in 1850 and her sister in 1853, after his first wife's death . . .
Richard Schöne wisely married a daughter of the successful publisher
Hermann Härtel, who had printed Schöne's dissertation; when she
died in childbirth, he married her sister.'[137] Interestingly, the transaction in women that thereby organized and regulated relations between
men is reminiscent of Müller's descriptions of the Spartans' own
marriage habits.[138]

Müller's scholarship, then, sought to specify a nationalized (even
racialized) historical particularity for ancient Greece and then to
examine its constituent parts, the Dorian and the Ionian. His discussion of *paiderastia* is to be situated within this context: it was a
historically specific national institution, particular to Dorian Greeks.
Like Gesner before him, the term παιδεραστία remains written in the
Greek alphabet, underlining its historicity. Indeed, it is the inclusion
of a discussion of παιδεραστία that apparently confirms for Müller's
readers his positivist objectivity. *Nowhere else* in *Doric Race* does he
say that he intends to 'state the exact circumstances of this relation
and then make some general remarks on it; *but without examining it
in a moral point of view, which does not fall within the scope of this
work*'.[139] At no other point does Müller emphasize quite so explicitly
that this is a historical enquiry and not a moral one. It is only on the
subject of pederasty that the historical nature of this book is underlined. It is the very subject of Greek pederasty that tests the limits of
nineteenth-century, German positivist historicism. Indeed, this book
would not truly educate its readers on the *history* of the Dorians, if it
did *not* educate them on the topic of pederasty. But, interestingly, it
was pederasty itself, according to Müller, that provided the context for
a Spartan education. The pedagogical benefits of nineteenth-century
German historicism are exemplified by a discussion on ancient Greek
pederasty, which itself furnished the necessary framework for Spartan
pedagogy. It is only within the context of nineteenth-century neo-
humanist historicism that ancient Greek pederasty can be made truly
visible, a relationship that Müller's text suggests is the *sine qua non* of a
Spartan education. Just as the nineteenth-century German or English
reader cannot be truly educated on the history of the Doric race

[137] Marchand (1996: 51).
[138] Müller (1839: ii. 295–6).
[139] Müller (1839: ii. 300), emphases added.

without reading an account of Spartan pederasty, so the ancient Spartans could not be educated without that pederastic relation.[140]

Müller then turns to consider the pederastic institution itself: 'At Sparta the party loving was called εἰσπνήλας, and his affection was termed a *breathing in*, or *inspiring* (εἰσπνεῖν); which expresses the pure and mental connexion between two persons, and corresponds with the name of the other, viz. ἀΐτας, i.e., *listener* or *hearer*.' Müller's text presents a phonocentric relationship. The connection between εἰσπνήλας and ἀΐτας is 'pure', not simply in the moral sense (although Müller claims not to be interested in the 'moral point of view'), but also in the sense that knowledge is perfectly transferred from the inspirer to the hearer. The relationship is pure in so far that it is mental—and the term 'mental' is not meant to be set in relation to an unmentionable sexual practice (indeed Müller will take us to the physical side of the relationship in a moment). It is pure and mental in that it is the perfect model for the transferral of knowledge from man to youth. The older man is seen as breathing into and inspiring the younger, as the double translation suggests.[141] The senior figure is precisely 'a model and pattern of life' for 'the youth [who] was constantly under the eyes of his lover'.[142] The younger figure, the ἀΐτας, is both listener and hearer, which is to say that he is one who not only simply hears but also pays attention, in his imitation of his 'model and pattern of life'.

The phonocentric nature of the relationship is emphasized here precisely because Müller himself underlines the Dorians' lack of concern for writing. We saw earlier how their androgynous masculinity was suggestive of a Dorian feeling of integrity and wholeness, which reflected their conservatism and political autonomy. Their disinterest in writing further reflected, for Müller, their disinterest in the written recording of history, bestowing upon the Dorians a feeling that they lived outside history. Some sixty pages after his discussion of pederasty, he turns to this issue: 'It has been shown in the preceding chapter [book four, chapter seven] that the national and original poetry of the Doric race was not the epic, but the lyric;

---

[140] Müller (1839: ii. 305–6). For comparison with Müller, for the latest scholarship on Spartan education, see Cartledge (2001b: 79–90); also Kennell (1995), which refutes the picture of conservative Sparta.
[141] Note the contrast between παιδεραστία, which does not receive a single translation, and εἰσπνήλας and ἀΐτας, which both receive *two* translations.
[142] Müller (1839: ii. 302).

which is occupied rather in expressing inward feelings, than in describing outward objects.' For Müller, this enables him 'to explain why history neither originated among, nor was cultivated by the Dorians. For both its progress and invention we are indebted to the Ionians, who were also the first to introduce prose-composition in general.'[143] 'This', Müller continues, 'naturally suggests the remark, that the Dorians paid more attention to the events of the past than of the present time; in which they are greatly opposed to the Ionians, and who from their governments and geographical position were more thrown into society, and interested themselves more in the passing affairs of the day'.[144] Müller's Dorians were a people for whom the past and the present have merged together. The conservative nature of Doric states, such as Sparta, ensured that the next generation is a reproduction of the one before. Müller implies that there was no need for sophisticated historiography in such an environment. And it was the pederastic relationship that guaranteed that the younger generation replicated the elder, and without this relationship, for Müller, there was no Spartan education, and, by consequence, no Spartan state.[145] Although Müller does not invoke Plato's discussions of pederasty, we can nonetheless detect here the influence of the Socratic suspicion about writing and the Socratic valorization of *oral* forms of teaching; finally, the remarkable image of pregnant men is re-formed through a Humboldtian emphasis on androgyny, as the ideal basis for *Bildung*.

The androgynous nature of the Dorians makes it necessary for Müller to consider the education of girls. He underlines the Spartan 'education of the [male] body . . . which was to harden the frame by labour and fatigue'.[146] Interestingly, 'the female sex underwent in this respect the same education as the male, though . . . only the virgins'.[147] Yet this accentuation on the virginity of the pupils, as

---

[143] Müller (1839: ii. 384–5).

[144] Müller (1839: ii. 385).

[145] Müller is repeatedly interested in the oral nature of Dorian society: the laws were unwritten; the debates in the Assembly were highly vociferous; and smooth operation of the army depended upon precise, oral communication between the rank and line of soldiers (Müller 1839: ii. 96–7, 125, 230, 250). We might also note here Müller's characterization of Doric religion as 'clear, distinct and personal', embodied in the god Apollo (Müller 1839: i. 409).

[146] Müller (1839: ii. 317–18).

[147] Müller (1839: ii. 321).

well as the keenness to show that it was 'highly improbable that youths and men were allowed to look on', demonstrate Müller's desire to erase any trace of heterosexual eroticism and admiration of the female physique.[148] Female education was *not* bound up in homosocial pederastic relations. The training of the beautiful male body, which was to be regularly viewed, registered, and regulated (as Müller explains[149]), fully contrasts with the invisibility of Dorian female education, which supposedly never extended beyond the loss of virginity.[150]

Müller supports his account of male pederasty by his discussion in chapter eight of the 'peculiar manner' the Dorian race had in

expressing itself, viz. by apophthegms, and sententious and concise sayings. The object [in all Doric discourse] appears to have been, to convey as much meaning in as few words as possible, and to allude to, rather than express the thoughts of the speaker. A habit of mind which might fit its possessor for such a mode of speaking, would be best generated by long and unbroken *silence*; which was . . . by Sparta enforced *on all youths during their education*.[151]

According to Müller, then, the famous laconism of the Spartans was literally true. And, furthermore, 'since in this apophthegmatic and concise style of speaking the object was not to express the meaning in a clear and intelligible manner, it was only one step further altogether to conceal it. Hence the *griphus* or riddle was invented by the Dorians.'[152] Interestingly, then, a Spartan boy's education is characterized by *both* the 'pure and mental connexion' of παιδεραστία in which the youth 'hears' or 'listens to' the elder, *and* a 'long and unbroken silence'. The pederastic relationship, as Müller presents it, is *both* open and publicized,[153] *and* wrapped in a veil of secrecy, as every example of speech is characterized by its lack of clarity and intelligibility. Indeed, the riddle perfectly exemplifies Spartan culture, as

---

[148] Müller (1839: ii. 321).

[149] Müller (1839: ii. 322).

[150] See Cartledge (2001b: 83–4) for a more recent account of the education of Spartan girls, which emphasizes how little we actually know about this topic.

[151] Müller (1839: ii. 386–7), emphases added.

[152] Müller (1839: ii. 392).

[153] Müller says that 'it appears to have been the practice for every youth of good character to have his lover; and, on the other hand, every well-educated man was bound by custom to be the lover of some youth' (1839: ii. 301); and that it was 'publicly acknowledged and countenanced by the state' (1839: ii. 304).

Müller characterizes it, in that it is both utterly secretive from the rest of the Greek world and at the same time very public. That is to say, the riddle is discourse that both manifests and conceals its truth simultaneously. The riddle simultaneously both says and does not say what it means. The pederastic relationship reflects this ability to hear that which is not said, as the ἀΐτας is apparently meant to listen to that which is merely breathed in (εἰσπνήλας).

This thematic of the public and the private reflects Müller's broader interests in the Dorians. What garners Müller's admiration in particular is the ability to balance public and private interest. He writes approvingly that 'there could not have been any accurate distinction between public and private economy'.[154] Similarly, marriage was a 'public institution' present for the good of society,[155] but he writes only a few pages earlier that, 'within [the household], the master of the house ruled as lord on his own ground; and the rights of domestic life, notwithstanding their frequent collision with the public institutions, were more respected than at Athens'.[156] It is not surprising, then, that a volume of essays examining Müller and his scholarship is called *Zwischen Rationalismus und Romantik*.[157] Müller's scholarship attempts an objective analysis, which nevertheless spills over into lionization of the object of his analysis. Gesner's concern that the word παιδεραστία had more than one referent (both saintly and more problematic) is also raised by Müller:

Now that the affection of the lover was not entirely mental, and that a pleasure in beholding the beauty and vigour, the manly activity and exercises of the youth was also present, is certain. But it is a very different question whether this custom, universally prevalent both in Crete and Sparta, followed by the noblest men, by the legislators encouraged with all care, and having so powerful an influence on education, was identical with the vice to which in its name and outward form it is so nearly allied.[158]

What παιδεραστία signifies is a *griphos* for Müller: the *one* term can signify *two* meanings. What παιδεραστία consists in is both clear (a 'systematic and regular' institution[159]) and veiled in secrecy, since it

---

[154] Müller (1839: ii.. 196).
[155] Müller (1839: ii. 295).
[156] Müller (1839: ii. 290–1).
[157] Calder and Schlesier (1998).
[158] Müller (1839: ii. 304).
[159] Müller (1839: ii. 303).

looks so much like its opposite. Just like Spartan society generally, it is both public and secret. Müller turns to Cicero for help: 'the Lacedae-monians brought the lover into the closest relation with the object of his love, and that every sign of affection was permitted *praeter stuprum*.' And then Cicero's text itself is cited: 'Lacedaemonii ipsi cum omnia concedunt in amore iuvenum praeter stuprum, tenui sane muro dissaepiunt id quod excipiunt: complexus enim concubitusque permittunt' (*Rep.* 4.4).[160] 'It was indeed a thin line which cordoned off that to which they took exception; for they permitted embraces and lying-together.' By merely reciting the Ciceronian text, Müller's sup-posedly rigorous, amoral, *historical* description *never* clarifies the difference between the close resemblance between παιδεραστία and the vice of the same name that also shares its outward form with the former, idealized relationship. Cicero's text is reproduced as if *com-plexus* and *concubitus* had only one connotation, as if they were clear and unambiguous signifiers. Furthermore, Cicero undermines any sense of lucid distinction when he says it is by a 'tenui muro', literally a 'thin wall', which is hardly literal and plain language itself: as an oxymoron, *tenuis* suggests thin or slender, whereas *murus* implies a division that is at least substantial. Müller's own text itself, then, re-performs the possibility that true and real Spartan παιδεραστία is not clearly distinguishable from the 'vice' of the same name.

Interestingly, then, παιδεραστία is situated in a complex position in Müller's project. First, its inclusion with historical analysis is neces-sary if Müller is to demonstrate the scholarly credentials of his work. Yet Spartan παιδεραστία is presented as a timeless, ahistorical—indeed ideal—institution by Müller that removes it from history, bestowing on it mythical status (as Gesner and Meiners had done before him). Secondly, Müller presents παιδεραστία as the context for a Spartan education, making it central to the historically specific Spartan state, yet its phonocentric and riddling nature makes it impossible to include within the historical record, since there is no literal archive of such παιδεραστία. In Müller's text, the Dorians, both public and private, both open and secret, both easy and difficult to understand, are situated both within and beyond the historian's grasp. Παιδεραστία provides a perfect image for historians to think about what it means to teach and preserve the classical archive, so

---

[160] Müller (1839: ii. 305).

that pederasty really requires historicizing, but, at the same time, German philology repeatedly ends up removing pederasty from the bounds of historical discourse. As an oral relationship, it was not recorded, and so it ends up being glorified. To put the paradox another way: it is presented as a model of what should be historicized—if one could write about pederasty, then one really could demonstrate one's scholarly abilities. Yet, at the same time, it becomes the idealized model for what the transfer of knowledge and the invention of tradition should look like. It is both inside and outside the historical archive.

Finally, we should note that it was the convergence of several discourses that enabled Müller to produce his picture of Dorian society in the first place: first, his Pietism is reflected in his ascetic, yet nurturing Spartans; secondly, the male homosociality of nineteenth-century classical scholarship and higher education is mirrored in the image of Spartan pederastic pedagogy (which also helped Müller downplay any sense of eroticism involved in the education of Spartan girls); and, finally, his emphasis on the European identity of the Dorians puts his account of pederasty within specific nationalist—racialist frameworks (just as Meiners had sought to differentiate the Greeks from uncivilized 'savages'). Müller's emphasis on the racial—cultural *links* between ancient Dorian and modern north European reflects his glorification of the phonocentric Spartan pederasty, through which wisdom and culture were perfectly passed down from one generation to the next. The intense, close male relations of whispers, riddles, and brachylogy become a metaphor for the racial—cultural links between ancient Sparta and modern Germany.

PURE HISTORICISM: MEIER'S PEDERASTY

The final German scholar to be examined in this chapter directly engaged with the perceived impasse of one term, παιδεραστία, having two meanings. Moritz Hermann Eduard Meier's attempt to resolve the problem was to suggest that this single term παιδεραστία referred to an institution that combined both noble and less edifying connotations: one word for one phenomenon. His provocations appeared in 1837 in J. S. Ersch and J. G. Gruber's *Allgemeine Encyclopädie der Wissenschaften und Kunst*. Voltaire was the first modern intellectual to include an entry on Greek love in an encyclopaedic work, in his *Dictionnaire philosophique*, as we examined earlier. However, Voltaire's satirical account was hardly a model of historicist scholarship. Ersch and Gruber's enterprise, on the other hand, represented a significant moment in the history of modern encyclopaedism. In its attempt to supply German readers with a reference work that collated together and organized the world's knowledge systematically, superseding the efforts of Diderot, Alembert, and Chambers, the first volume of the *Allgemeine Encyclopädie* appeared in 1813 and remained unfinished in 1889, by which time it had reached a gargantuan 167 tomes. It was viewed at the time as the epitome of German scholarly industriousness and endeavour, and more recently Robert Collison has called it 'the greatest Western encyclopaedia ever attempted'.[161] The entry on 'Griechenland' was the longest in the entire work, spanning eight volumes (80–7) and covering 3,668 pages.[162] Meier's article, then, was the first piece of modern scholarship to collate as much knowledge about Greek pederasty as possible.

Meier (1796–1855) was born into a Jewish family and later converted to Christianity. In 1824 he was made Professor in Philology at Halle, where he remained until his death. He was best known for his work *Der attische Proceß* (co-authored with G. F. Schömann), which won him a prize from the Berlin Academy. Furthermore, between 1830 and 1855 he was employed as co-editor on the *Allgemeine Encyclopädie*.[163] A highly respected scholar, then, Meier offers a truly encyclopaedic article on pederasty, which considered, as well as the Dorians, the Achaeans, the Aeolians, the Boeotians, the Elians, the Ionians, the Athenians, and Socrates, Plato, Aristotle, Cyrenaics, Cynics, Stoics, Epicureans, Plotinus and Lucian. Additionally he offered detailed information about sources and speculated upon the origins of Greek pederasty. Classical scholars still refer to Meier's work with approbation. Paul Cartledge, writing on the subject, notes that the essay 'is still of some value'.[164] And James Davidson writes more fulsomely: 'Meier's achievement was…quite remarkable, and some think his forty pages surpass anything written since.'[165]

---

[161] Collison (1966: 182).
[162] On the *Allgemeine Encyclopädie*, see Bahlcke (1997) and Rüdiger (2005).
[163] See Rüdiger (2005: 31).
[164] Cartledge (2001b: 207 n. 8).
[165] Davidson (2007: 107). Indeed, Davidson (2007) could not have been written without the knowledge gathered in Meier's essay. Interestingly, in 1930, a French

The inclusion of an article entitled 'Päderastie' in a work that would demonstrate its philhellenism with an eight-volume entry on 'Griechenland' was, then, certainly a bold and provocative move. Anticipating any concerns, Meier opened and closed his article, thereby framing it, with the admonition: 'den Teufel soll man nicht an die Wand malen.'[166] In asking us not to paint the devil on the wall, Meier encourages his readers not to be too pessimistic about the historical existence of Greek pederasty. Just like his predecessors on the subject, Meier is more than aware of the tensions between the equal demands of historical scholarship and culture-wide philhellenism. His response to this problem brings a quite different solution from those offered by Müller, Meiners, and Gesner. At the very beginning of the article, Meier writes a prefatory paragraph on 'unsere rein historische Aufgabe', 'our purely historical task'. He attempts to navigate a scholarly course between 'Unkunde, Leichtsinn oder Bosheit' and 'blosse Idealisirungen und Verklärungen dieses Verhältnisses', between 'ignorance, foolishness or stupidity' and 'sheer idealizations and glorifications of this relationship'. 'We need neither to set ourselves up as prosecutors [*Anklägern*] of the Greeks . . . nor do we need to whitewash a nation, which is indeed an object of wonder to us, of that stain'. 'Wir wollen Wahrheit und nichts als Wahrheit.'[167] Meier may not want to look like he is prosecuting or defending the Greeks, but he nevertheless speaks the 'truth and nothing but the truth'. The legal rhetoric, from this legal scholar, cannot be avoided.

So what is the result of Meier's 'pure historicism'? After considering, quite properly as befits his 'task', both possible extant and non-extant sources, Meier argues that 'die Knabenliebe der Griechen' was 'ein eigenthümliches Institut', an institution peculiar to the Greeks.[168] Like the scholars before him, then, Meier emphasizes that 'pederasty'

---

translation was produced with augmentations, suggesting that Meier's work was still worth reading. The epitaph on the title page, however, implies a very different context for Meier's work: 'I will be a pederast [παιδοφιλήσω]; for to me that is far better than marriage [γαμεῖν] (Seleucos).' By 1930, 'pederasty', or homosexuality, is seen as an *alternative* to heterosexual marriage, rather than as a practice alongside that institution, and Meier's scholarship is recuperated to demonstrate that position to a very different audience. See M. H. E. Meier (1930).

[166] M. H. E. Meier (1837: 149, col. 2; 189, col. 1).
[167] M. H. E. Meier (1837: 149, cols 1–2).
[168] M. H. E. Meier (1837: 150, col. 2).

was special to the Greeks, an emphasis that requires from us two observations. First, the contemporary academic position that underlines the *historical difference* between the Greeks and us is assumed by Meier. An accentuation on the historicity of the Greeks need not be the vehicle for a radical politics that aims to redefine contemporary living arrangements. The late-twentieth-century reference (inspired by the work of Foucault) to the Greeks that sees sexuality as a historically contingent phenomenon has a precedent in nineteenth-century historiography, but with a very different agenda: Meier argues for the peculiarity of the Greeks in order to bolster modern, nineteenth-century norms of familial domesticity. As we shall see, Meier will locate the origins of Greek pederasty in their domestic organization that differed radically from that of the modern *Bildungsbürgertum*.

This brings us to our second point: Meier observes that the 'vice of impure *Männerliebe* has been known in Sodom, by the Tyrrhenians, the Hebrews, even in Germany... the wilds of North America... and Peru', but ancient Greece has been the only place where a real 'Gemisch von Sinnlichem und Geistigem', a combination of the material and the spiritual, or intellectual, can be found.[169] The cultural-racial-historical specificity of the Greeks, which permits the classical scholar to exemplify them, as in Meiners, is reiterated in Meier's text here. After mapping out the distinction between 'reine und unreine Knabenliebe', 'pure and impure pederasty' (the latter is summed up in the vocabulary of sodomy, effeminacy and prostitution), Meier goes on to state: 'the noble [*edlere*] pederasty was for the Greeks not something purely spiritual/intellectual [*nicht etwas rein Geistiges*]' but 'something material/sensual [*etwas Sinnliches*] was mixed in'. The noble form of pederasty took 'pleasure/satisfaction [*Wohlgefallen*] in physical beauty [*körperlichen Schönheit*]'.[170] We might consider such relations between persons of the same sex 'disgusting' ('widerlich'), but we have to confront them, since these relations do not represent isolated incidents in the Greek world. It is a central part of their culture.[171]

Although Meier's amoral historicism might seem commendable, such discourse presupposes knowledge precisely of what is moral and

---

[169] M. H. E. Meier (1837: 152, cols 1–2).
[170] M. H. E. Meier (1837: 155, col. 1).
[171] M. H. E. Meier (1837: 156, col. 1).

immoral, pure and impure. 'Pure' historicism means, here, the open examination of pederasty that would be a mixture of what Meier's readers would have already considered acceptable and repugnant. His historicism is supposedly pure, because it excludes moralizing from its domain: 'Unsere *rein* historische Aufgabe *schützt* uns vor beiden gefährlichen Extremen.'[172] His purely historical task protects us from both those dangerous extremes of demonization and idealization. Nevertheless, the purity of (his) historicism is diluted as moral judgements slip back in, in order to shape Meier's very mapping and organization of his knowledge about the subject. The purity of modern historicism is explicitly set against the (im)purity of ancient pederasty. It becomes clear as the article proceeds (as we shall see) that Meier is most preoccupied with the contrast between ancient and modern methods of knowledge production and transfer.

Let us trace out a little further what Meier says with regard to the historicity of the Greeks and Greek pederasty. Straight after his 'purely historical' description of the 'edlere Knabenliebe', he makes some very interesting comments about the particularity and comparability of pederasty in relation to modern bourgeois romantic relations. This noble form of pederasty voices a 'pleasure over the physical proximity to the beloved, as well as pain at being distanced ... just as we [*wir*] know in sexual love [*Geschlectsliebe*]'. Furthermore, this passion produces 'jealousy [*Eifersucht*] not any different from that [produced] with the love of the opposite sexes [*nicht anders also bei uns in der Liebe der beiden Geschlecter zu einander*]'. If ancient Greek pederasty seemed to be 'eigenthümlich' to the Greeks just a little earlier in the essay, it is now directly comparable to the narratives of modern romances comprising man and woman. After discussing the sweetness of making up after a row ('die Verlöhnung ... so süßer wäre', and quoting Xenophon: note 90), closely comparable to a nineteenth-century bourgeois romantic melodrama, Meier writes: 'But the way the feelings of the lover express themselves ... in that their object is another man, is to us [*für uns*] still something that appears still stranger [*etwas Befremderes*] and is likely to make an embarrassing, indeed disgusting [*widerlichen*] impression on us [*auf uns*].'[173] At one moment, then, the reader is actively encouraged to engage with and compare Greek pederasty with modern romantic narratives of love,

172 M. H. E. Meier (1837: 149, col. 2), emphases added.
173 M. H. E. Meier (1837: 155, cols 1–2).

but at the next it is suggested to us that any such comparison is impossible. Indeed, the only way that Greek pederasty can be approached in a 'purely historical' manner is if one has *already* made a moral judgement about its *Widerlichkeit*.

Meier's attempts to locate the origins of Greek pederasty in the final section of his article are also instructive. The first and most important reason for Meier is the 'Absonderung des weiblichen Geschlechts', the 'segregation of the female sex'. 'Wives and girls were constricted to a life at home . . . and their daily tasks were akin to those of children and housekeepers [*Kindermädchen und Wirthschafterinnen*].' It is hardly surprising, Meier surmises, that men should have been interested in 'educated [*gebildeten*] hetairas or male youths capable of being educated [*bildungsfähigen*]', since their own wives were unschooled. The domestic and social arrangements of the ancient Greeks were such that the married relationship was not valorized in the way it came to be in Meier's nineteenth century. Hellenic antiquity and European modernity are, in Meier's eyes, quite opposed and as such, incomparable. Meier seemingly accentuates the non-repeatability of this Greek 'Institut', implying that 'Knabenliebe' could never regain such heights of cultural significance and popularity.

This incommensurability between ancient and modern is nevertheless tested when Meier then says that, although women were secluded in Ionian states, 'Knabenliebe' was 'kein Institut', and, in Dorian states where women were held in esteem, 'Knabenliebe' was indeed institutionalized. This troubling issue for Meier means that the organization of Greek domesticity and sociality cannot be the only reason for the importance of pederasty. Meier then argues that it is the *difference between ancient and modern education systems* that really explains the presence and absence of institutionalized pederasty in ancient and modern cultures. As well as mentioning *hetairai* and *syssitia*, Meier references the gymnasium; communal education in Doric states with the corresponding lack of paternal guidance ('den Mangel des väterlichen Einflusses'); and the accentuation on 'philosophischen Knabenliebe' in Athens, where there were neither 'Bildungsanstalten' nor 'speciellen Fachs- und Berufsbildung'. That is to say, modern, nineteenth-century *Bildung*, according to Meier, fundamentally differed from an ancient Greek pedagogy, which, in his words, basically consisted of the 'Anschließen eines jungern an einen bewährten älteren Mann', the joining of a youth to an approved older man. Whereas at the beginning of the essay Meier had accentuated the romanticism of the pederastic relationship, now, at the end, he argues that this relationship was a (poor) substitution for modern German *Bildung*: 'so vertrat die Knabenliebe gewissenmaßen die Stelle der hohen Schule.'[174] The position of ancient Greek pederasty in relation to modern Western culture is complex as presented in Meier's text. At first, it is presented as the ancient counterpart to modern privatized, reciprocal domesticity and complementarity of the sexes. At the end of the article, however, pederasty emerges not so much out of the dispensation of domestic and social arrangements, as out of a faulty education system, which conversely the modern German system has succeeded in putting right. The ancient gymnasia of Athens and Sparta had been replaced by the modern German *Gymnasium*.

Gesner set up Socrates as an example; Meiners questioned such a possibility; Müller's hardworking, industrious Spartans offered an altogether more manly model to follow for those disturbed by imputations made about Athenian pederasty. Furthermore, Müller's scholarship was among the first to initiate and promulgate the belief in a more direct—even racial—link between the ancient Greeks and modern north-western Europe. Finally, the most detailed account yet of Greek pederasty, Meier's, bears the traces of all these strategies to historicize the topic at hand. On the one hand, it was an institution quite peculiar to the Greeks, which does not undermine modern philhellenism, but in fact bolsters it; yet, on the other hand, it looks very much like a modern romance, questioning the particularity of the Greeks; and yet again, however, ancient Greek education systems bear but shallow resemblance to modern German schooling and higher education. Meier's essay veers between identifying Greek and modern cultures and accentuating historical difference.

For a Halle professor of philology to have written this in 1837 would certainly have been at the very least thought-provoking, not simply because of its subject matter. The accentuation on the *contrast* between ancient and modern pedagogical philosophies reopened the question of what sort of example Greeks might (have) set for European modernity. If the Humboldtian University and Gymnasium had ventured to centralize classical Greek on the curriculum, Meiers' argument problematizes the point of this policy: what is the relationship between ancient and modern *Gymnasien*? German philhellenism

[174] M. H. E. Meier (1837: 187, col. 2; 188, cols 1–2).

bequeathed the British scholars who engaged with this discourse a complex heritage: between the positions taken by Müller and Meier, the question arose of what sort of descendants of the Greeks are Germans and Britons. Müller's racialized discourse suggested a biological link, which was reflected in his emphasis on the careful handing-down of tradition from one generation to the next in the phonocentric pederastic relationship. Meier, on the other hand, while also attesting the racial particularity of the Greeks, ended up questioning the relationship between ancient and modern pedagogy.

The tensions between *Bildung* and *Wissenschaft* in the first half of the nineteenth century became all the more apparent when scholars attempted to historicize ancient pederasty. Was this institution or practice the way in which ancient knowledge was actually passed down into the modern world, or should it represent to modern historians precisely how different ancient Greek culture was? Furthermore, scholarly examination of these issues brought into sharp focus the significance of Christian belief, raciological discourses, and gender politics for modern historicist scholarship. Gesner could not frame his understanding of the historical outside Erasmus's Christianizing humanism. Meiners's interest in 'world history' saw to it that the Greeks were to be considered in terms of their difference from both civilized moderns and modern 'savages'. Conversely, Müller took up the racialist—nationalist framework of *Geschichtewissenschaft* in order to draw a close link between ancient Spartan and modern Pietist German, a linkage that (despite his own reliance on the Greeks' racial—cultural particularity) Meier again undermined and questioned. And, for all these scholars, pederastic pedagogy was unimaginable without comparison to men's relations with women: from Socrates' alleged bigamy, through Spartan education of virgins, to Meier's depiction of ancient pederasty as a modern romance. Sometimes, as we have seen, the position of ancient women is used to prove the historical difference of the Greeks; at others, ancient pederasty is closely compared to modern heterosexual relations (as with Meier), collapsing the difference between modern self and ancient other.

Just as German neo-humanism was so invested in the belief that Greek made the modern man, so a careful elucidation of the pederastic context of the pedagogic encounter was required. And it is precisely these issues that preoccupied Oxford's Hellenists, Jowett, Pater, Symonds, and Wilde, to whom we will turn in the next chapters. And, as we shall see, the German engagement with antiquity will form a crucial context for Jowett's reformation of the Oxford classics curriculum. That is to say, Oxford philhellenism of the second half of the nineteenth century will be seen to negotiate its classical heritage through the prism of the German scholarship we have been considering. Pater and Symonds will be able to analyse modern masculinity only in relation to ancient manhood through their reception of Müller and Meier especially. And it will be their complex appropriation and manipulation of this German scholarship on παιδεραστία that will question still further what it means to transmit and translate knowledge from one generation to the next, what it means to receive knowledge from one's teacher. What sort of ἀΐτας was Jowett, Pater, Symonds, or Wilde, to their εἰσπνήλας, German historicism?

2

Translating the Love of Philosophy: Jowett and Pater on Plato

... dialectic is a sort of inspiration akin to love ...

(Benjamin Jowett, *The Diaolgues of Plato*, 1892)

Pedagogy cannot but encounter the problem of imitation. What is example? Should one educate by example or by explanation? Should the teacher make an example of himself ...

(Jacques Derrida, *Of Grammatology*, 1976)

The place and influence of ancient Greek culture in modern society was a topic much imagined, debated, and contested in nineteenth-century Britain.[1] And Benjamin Jowett's Oxford was a focal point for the intellectual investment in the Greek example for the modern imperial nation state. His radical changes to the Greats curriculum saw to it that the Platonic dialogues became permanent and central fixtures on the teaching timetable. Furthermore, his promotion of the tutorial system at the University reflected his admiration of the Platonic teaching scene, the Socratic *elenchus*, between the older man and youth.[2] The Classics were to be the prescribed texts for those young men who wanted to run the Empire. Indeed, the racialization of the Greeks, already present in late-eighteenth-century Göttingen, then explored by Müller and Meier, was a discourse that had continued in the later nineteenth century, so that by the time of Jowett's ascendancy the Greeks were associated with civilized, civilizing, white masculinity. A classical education at Jowett's Balliol was

---

[1] See Goldhill (2002).   [2] See Evangelista (2007a: 210).

designed to prepare the Victorian student for life in the British and Indian Civil Service. In the 1850s Jowett assisted the Aberdeen administration to reform selection methods for the Civil Service, and Abbott and Campbell's posthumous edition of Jowett's letters contains extensive correspondence between Jowett and the India Office, in which he attempts to make the entrance requirements for service in India as conducive for Oxford graduates as possible. Furthermore, Jowett also had two brothers in the Indian army, who served and died there, making his interest in British imperialism both professional and personal.[3]

But Jowett's belief in the exemplary nature of Greek culture for British modernity was no simple-minded adoration. His curriculum challenged his students to study the relationship between ancient and modern societies and philosophies. In examinations, Jowett's students were asked, for instance, to compare the thought of J. S. Mill with that of Plato, or to consider the similarities and differences between ancient and modern shapes of domestic life. And it was German historicism that was to have one of the most significant impacts on the shape of Classics at Jowett's Oxford. The works of Müller and Ernst Curtius, among others, became standard reading for Jowett's pupils, who were guided by the Balliol Master to 'the highest honors in the Greats examinations and to such other glittering prizes as Oxford college fellowships... German historicist scholarship on Greece became in this way current among the most intellectually ambitious Oxford undergraduates and their tutors, for whom the Balliol model continuously operated as a standard.'[4] Still in 1914, when E. M. Forster came to write *Maurice*, 'the Germans' were seen as representing the most advanced classical scholarship. This can be seen in a caustic remark made by Clive Durham in conversation with another undergraduate about the Cambridge classical tripos: 'You can always learn something from an older man, even it he hasn't read the latest Germans.'[5] The knowing reader will see Clive favouring the ancient pederastic—Platonic mode of pedagogy over that of the modern German. That knowing reader will also remember, however,

---

[3] See Hinchliff (1987: 26, 153), and Jowett (1899: 156). On Victorian classical education and the Indian Civil Service, see Vasunia (2005).

[4] Dowling (1994: 75).

[5] Forster (1972: 39).

that it was precisely through 'the latest Germans' that Jowett's students came to learn about *paiderastia*.

Gregory Woods has cited Jowett's introduction of Plato into the Greats curriculum as a 'most significant event in the history of homosexual cultures in England'.[6] And it was because of Jowett that his pupils Walter Pater and John Addington Symonds were able to realign Plato's dialogues for their own purposes, which in turn allowed Oscar Wilde, who proclaimed himself inheritor of the teachings of Pater, to talk about Platonic love at his trial in 1895. In his introduction to Plato's *Symposium* in *The Dialogues of Plato*, Jowett refers his readers to 'the admirable and exhaustive article of Meier'.[7] And Müller's *Dorian Race* was prescribed reading, having been helpfully translated into English with further additions made by the author. The tutorial system itself, which Jowett so praised, was also in danger of 'replicating the erotic investment between master and pupil', as described in Plato.[8]

As one critic, among many, has observed: 'Plato's language infiltrated and shaped the very vocabulary through which an emerging homosexual identity was defined.'[9] The sexual subtexts and contexts of the Platonic corpus provided the space in which nineteenth-century scholars could consider the historicity of male—male desire and friendship. In a letter (of January 1874, cited by Stefano Evangelista[10]), the poet Swinburne describes the painter Simeon Solomon (who was later that year arrested for obscene behaviour in a public toilet) as a 'Platonist of another sort than the translator of Plato [Jowett]—"translator he too" as Carlyle might say, of Platonic theory into Socratic practice.' For Evangelista, 'Platonist' and 'Socratic' refer euphemistically to male homosexual practices.[11] In this chapter, we, on the other hand, will be concerned with Swinburne's interest in the issue of translation. Interestingly, Swinburne's comments attribute the 'truth' of Platonism neither to Solomon nor to Jowett. Rather, they are both types or 'sorts' of Platonists. The Platonic corpus could be translated, as Swinburne puts it, in quite different ways. For Jowett, the relationships that Plato depicted between *erasteis* and *eromenoi*

---

[6] Woods (1998: 4).   [7] Jowett (1892: i. 538).
[8] Evangelista (2007a: 210).   [9] Evangelista (234).
[10] Evangelista (2006: 235).
[11] See Dellamora (1990: 92), where Swinburne explicitly sees the term 'Platonist' as a 'euphemism'.

reflected 'mainly a figure of speech', whereas for John Addington Symonds and others they were realistic depictions of real people.[12] The issue of whether Platonism could live in the nineteenth century is embedded in Victorian Oxford scholarship, which itself asks whether these Platonic dialogues were themselves real-life depictions or not: were these relationships theoretical constructs used by Plato in order to think through his conceptualizations of the Beautiful and the Good, or were they actual, real-life exempla through which he came to imagine his philosophical positions? Precisely, what relationship between two males could give rise to absolute knowledge? (How) is it necessary to reproduce the conditions of the Greeks? The questions that exercised the minds of scholars in German *Gymnasien* and universities were reformulated and redirected at the Platonic dialogues with great intensity on the *Literae Humaniores* syllabus.

Indeed it is hardly surprising that these questions formed the focus of close Victorian readers. As more recent readers of Plato, such as Ferrari, have shown, 'Plato invents his cosmic myth' of the soul in the *Phaedrus* 'in order to illuminate—make us recognise—what happens when philosophers cope with contingency by attempting to gain the cosmic or impersonal perspective while maintaining their personal sense of who we are.'[13] As Ferrari explains:

Socrates declares that 'the whole discourse' [of his in the *Phaedrus*] so far has been working towards an account of what happens when the philosophic type comes face to face with beauty in this world (physical human beauty) . . . so to tell a story in which we become burdened by the contingency of embodiment, and to tell it as one's best stab at the truth, just *is* to take on the contingency of embodiment as a burden.[14]

Plato shows us that 'you can learn who you are by considering your unconsidered reaction to an encounter with someone beautiful, and thus gain the opportunity to foster and justify the life appropriate to the kind of character you take yourself to be'.[15] The vision of the beautiful boy in the eyes of the philosopher exemplifies the philosopher's 'double vision': 'the boy seems both more than he is—a god, or

---

[12] Symonds (1984: 100).
[13] Ferrari (1987: 129).
[14] Ferrari (1987: 138), emphasis in original.
[15] Ferrari (1987: 147).

beauty itself—and less than he is—a face, a shape, a block of stone.'[16] And this is the very point of Plato's Socrates speaking in allegories:

For if the philosophic lover is not seeing clear through the boy to the horizon of intent but becomes caught up in wonder at what the vision means for him, then the use of allegory perfectly captures his struggle to come to terms with himself. That is, if we have trouble figuring out just what the lover is feeling, this is because the lover is having trouble figuring it out for himself.[17]

We, the readers, are reading an allegory of how the philosophic lover reads—engages with—an allegorical representation of the Beautiful, the boy. Plato's *Phaedrus* is a dialogue that thematically focuses on what is at stake in gazing at a beautiful boy's body. Furthermore, the *Phaedrus* thematizes the issues of translation and translatability: how can the vision of the beautiful *eromenos* be translated into an understanding of the Form of Beauty? How is it necessary to translate the *mythical* allegory Plato presents to us about the contingency of embodiment into *historical* reality?

The representations of beautiful masculinities in the *Phaedrus*, as well as the *Lysis* and *Symposium*, alerted and aroused the attentions of Benjamin Jowett and one of his greatest pupils, Walter Pater. Just as Greek pederasty tested the historical methods of *Altertumswissenschaft*, so the pederastic context of the Platonic dialogue was to cast suspicions over Jowett's tutorial system at Oxford and his monumental translations of Plato. What sort of man would Platonic pedagogy produce in the nineteenth century? What sort of man was Jowett? What sort of man did Jowett's pedagogy produce in Pater? What was the relationship between that teacher and pupil? Furthermore, can we say what sort of influence Pater had on young men's formations? Indeed, can ancient texts produce modern masculinities and sexualities?

Jowett's and Pater's educational philosophies and policies ensured that they have both received a divided and complex reception. First, Jowett's curriculum reforms, with their emphasis on Platonic teaching within the arena of the college tutorial, basically a private conversation between tutor and pupil, caused Jowett to 'become associated with Socrates by colleagues and students at Oxford',

---

[16] Ferrari (1987: 161). See also (1987: 178, 180) on 'seeing double'.
[17] Ferrari (1987: 164).

making him 'liable to accusations of corrupting the youth; and worse, of having infiltrated the leading classes of the nation with a generation of degenerates'.[18] This ambivalent reputation reflects the contents of letters Jowett wrote and those written about him. As we marked out in the Introduction, the relationship between letters and male desire is an important one in the nineteenth-century British context. Jowett was a frequent visitor to the house of the Victorian feminist Josephine Butler, who, with her husband, received the professor, when they lived in Oxford. In one letter, recorded in Geoffrey Faber's 1957 biography of Jowett, she wrote about

an outbreak of abnormal immorality among a few young men at Oxford. To such he was (I know) the wisest, most prudent and gentlest of counsellors. He was extremely severe and tender at the same time . . . In these matters he was a help and blessing beyond what it is possible to publish . . . he never seemed to give any man up as hopeless, or beyond the reach of sympathy and help.[19]

The relationship between the Socratic Jowett and his Platonic pupils could not be put into letters. As Socrates said in the *Phaedrus*, and as Diotima's speech in the *Symposium* made clear, this relationship is between embodied men, present to one another, and cannot be recorded in writing without becoming misunderstood. Jowett's complex, idiosyncratic relationship with his pupils, 'beyond what it is possible to publish', also interests his first biographers, Evelyn Abbott and Lewis Campbell, as related in a letter from the latter to the former when Jowett had already died. With regard to Tennyson's 1850 poem written after the death of his beloved friend Arthur Hallam, Campbell writes on 17 September 1896:

I seem to have heard Jowett say something of that kind about *In Memoriam*. He had a 'horror naturalis' of sentimental feelings between men ('diabolical' I have heard him call them). This is one reason for his dislike of [John] Conington [one time Corpus Christi Professor of Latin at Oxford], whose influence on the elder [Henry] Nettleship [another Corpus Christi professor] he thought weakening. Nothing is more remarkable than his persistent attachment to J.A.S. [John Addington Symonds], though they differed so profoundly about this. I rather think that in the late note-books there are some entries that show a more lenient

[18] Evangelista (2003b: 221–2), with references.
[19] Faber (1957: 92).

view, confessing that he had exaggerated the evil. Of course nothing of all this is biographically available, but it is useful to think of it.[20]

Similarly for Campbell, then, Jowett's complex and shifting thoughts about same-sex friendship and love were not publicly transmittable, certainly not in their forthcoming biography.

Jowett's friendship with Symonds has been the subject of scholarly examination much more recently. Stefano Evangelista has uncovered evidence of a visit Jowett made to his ex-student, who was by then living in Switzerland. There they read and analysed Plato's *Symposium*. Evangelista discusses Jowett's eagerness to write an essay on Greek love as part of the introduction to his translation of Plato's text, but Symonds warned him off, suggesting that Jowett was 'sympathetic to sexual diversity but strict in his repression of its open manifestations among members of the University'.[21] Jowett's friendship with Florence Nightingale, again evidenced in letters, has also attracted scholarly attention precisely because of its unusual nature: Geoffrey Faber has described it as 'platonic', in the sense that it resembled Jowett's close relationships with other men, being of a 'noble, manly sort', as Abbott and Campbell noted.[22] Faber has also reprinted letters written (in autumn 1849) between Jowett and his friend Arthur Stanley (who would later become Oxford's Professor of Ecclesiastical History), in which Jowett's open and intense offer of a close friendship to Stanley was firmly rejected, leading Faber to comment: 'For the first time in his life he had jumped the conventional barriers, to be met with a deliberate rebuff,' learning 'not to expect of male friendship what it would not give'.[23] The epistolary exchange demonstrated to Jowett the dangers of writing down and putting one's desires into print, desires that should remain spoken between men.

More recently, Peter Hinchliff has criticized as 'unconvincing' Faber's depiction of 'Jowett's feeling for Stanley' as 'a homosexual one [albeit] repressed and unacknowledged'.[24] And, in 1991, Billie Inman, building upon the work of Laurel Brake and Richard Ellmann,

---

[20] Faber (1957: 90).

[21] Evangelista (2007a: 225). We will turn to Jowett's relationship with Symonds in more detail in Chapter 3.

[22] See Faber (1957: 89) and Abbott and Campbell (1897: 2: 108). See also Hinchliff (1987: 113).

[23] Faber (1957: 217).

[24] See Hinchliff (1987: 27).

transformed the image of Jowett as a kindly, sensitive figure, who had complex opinions about Greek love in the nineteenth century, into one of a blackmailing homophobe. Again the evidence emerges from letters written by Balliol undergraduates, as well as Arthur Benson's manuscript diary (Benson was Walter Pater's first biographer). The letters suggest that Pater (by 1874 a fellow at Brasenose) was involved in a sexual relationship with a Balliol undergraduate called William Money Hardinge, and that incriminating letters came into Jowett's possession, who sent Hardinge down and threatened to expose Pater if he sought any professional promotion within Oxford.[25]

In 1994, however, yet another interpretation of Jowett's relations with his pupils was offered on the basis of these letters, when William Shuter published an article that questioned Inman's story. Shuter believed Hardinge and Pater knew one another and that Hardinge might have flirted with Pater, attention that the elder man might have enjoyed. But beyond that nothing is certain.[26] The undergraduates' letters report only Hardinge's own letters (no longer extant), in which he writes about his unusual relationship with Pater, which even the undergraduates themselves do not know whether to believe. Hardinge was known in college to be unreliable, so say these letters. Any other evidence of a relationship with Pater is no longer available. Furthermore, Jowett's conversation with Pater, in which he threatened his ex-pupil, is attested only by entries in Benson's manuscript diary (between 12 November 1904 and 1 September 1905), in which he records hearing from his friend Edmund Gosse that Gosse had heard a rumour about Jowett being in possession of some letters, which he had threatened to use against Pater. Gosse had no further information about the letters.[27] For Shuter, all that is firmly known about Jowett's role in any of this history is that he sent Hardinge down from Balliol for 'discrediting the College'.[28]

Jowett's Platonic pedagogy has ensured, then, that his translation of ancient Greek culture into modern Victorian Britain became, and remains, controversial. The difficulty of translating the textual Plato into the modern educated Englishman is reflected by the difficulty of translating Jowett's letters into an embodied, feeling, historical

---

[25] B. A. Inman (1991).
[26] Shuter (1994: 485 n. 10).
[27] Shuter (1994: 483).
[28] Shuter (1994: 489).

personage. From intense and emotional friend, to repressed homo-sexual, to vindictive homophobe, both kind and cruel to young men attracted to other men, the words of this modern Socrates have begotten numerous translations. Finally, in a letter to Campbell after Jowett's death, Pater himself wrote that Jowett his ex-tutor 'seemed to have taken the measure not merely of all opinions, but of all possible ones, and to have put the last refinements on literary expression. The charm of that was enhanced by a certain *mystery* about his own philosophic and other opinions.'[29] Pater, in public—in writing to Campbell—presents Jowett as a 'mystery': one has to be in his pre-sence, and, even then, what he is really thinking remains an enigma.

This last letter was recorded by Arthur Benson in his 1906 book on Pater. The relationship between Jowett and Pater is embedded within a series of frames not dissimilar to the multiple-framed relationship of Socrates and Alcibiades in the *Symposium*, as the inner beauty of Socrates is reported by Alcibiades, whose words themselves are re-ported by Aristodemus, whose words are reported to us, the reader, by Apollodorus. Pater sent his letter to Lewis Campbell, who then reported it to Arthur Benson, who then transmits it to us. Similarly, Pater's relationship with the Balliol student Hardinge is reported by letters about Hardinge's letter about their relationship, as well as by a rumour that reaches Gosse, who reports it to Benson, who records it in his diary, which is then reproduced by Inman for us.

It was Benson who first publicly recorded the break between Jowett and Pater, the teacher who had once prophesied such great things for his pupil, with Benson writing elliptically that, 'whatever his [Jowett's] motives were, he certainly meant to make it plain that he did not desire to see the supposed exponents of the aesthetic philo-sophy holding office in the University'.[30] It was also Benson who would characterize Pater in a very similar way to Pater's assessment of Jowett: 'he passed through life in a certain *mystery* though the secret is told for those who can read it in his writings.'[31] Since then, the emergence of the epistolary evidence about Pater and Hardinge has produced several translations of their 'relationship'. Richard Della-mora describes Pater as 'spooning' Hardinge—that is, 'sentimentally falling in love'. Linda Dowling sees 'a sexually predatory Pater', while

[29] See Benson (1906: 56), emphasis added.
[30] Benson (1906: 55).
[31] Benson (1906: 188).

Billie Inman speaks of Hardinge's 'self-effacing adulation for a superior man', and, finally, William Shuter believes that Hardinge was a
flirt, whom Pater found 'attractive', finding the attention 'flattering'.[32]

Like his teacher Jowett, Pater the teacher has received highly
conflicting depictions. Similar to the Regius Professor, Pater was
regarded as an enigmatic figure by his students, a Socratic *agalma*.
Arthur Benson records the words of Humphry Ward (husband to the
famous novelist): 'even those of us who were most attracted by them
[his philosophy and ideas], and men like myself to whom Pater was
personally very kind, found *intimacy* with him very difficulty . . . His
inner world was not that of any one else at Oxford.'[33] The myster-
iousness of Pater has produced numerous characterizations through
the twentieth century. Robert Seiler suggested that Pater suffered
from 'a mixture of disorders originating in his repressed homosexual
tendencies'.[34] Dowling has argued that Pater is best situated within
Eve Sedgwick's theory of the 'homosocial continuum', positioning
him in an environment in which the sexological categorization of
men would have made no sense.[35] Dellamora has seen a Pater more
affirmative (albeit subtly) about his desires, beyond the homosocial
continuum, which 'stands in the way of homosexual awareness and
self-identification among males'.[36] And Shuter prefers 'to speak of his
homoerotic or even of his Hellenic sensibility', which, unlike those
other homo- terms, is 'purely Greek'.[37] The depiction of Pater slips
between ancient Greek homoerotic, Victorian homosocial, and modern (repressed?) homosexual. Charles Martindale and Stefano Evangelista read Pater's aesthetic writings more positively still: the
aesthetic becomes 'the sphere of the revolutionary and of pure modernity'; and for Pater, 'intensity and clarity of [aesthetic] vision are
located in unorthodox forms of sexual pleasure', which 'shows that
the study of Greece can be put to a much more radical use than was
allowed for the curricula of educational institutions'.[38] Finally, the
influence of Pater's teachings over twentieth-century writing (both

[32] Dellamora (1990: 60, 230 n. 13); Dowling (1991: p. xi); B. A. Inman (1991: 18);
Shuter (1994: 485 n. 10).
[33] Benson (1906: 26), emphasis in original.
[34] Seiler (1980: p. xxx).
[35] Dowling (1989: 5).
[36] Dellamora (1990: 194; see also pp. 169, 187–8).
[37] Shuter (1994: 505).
[38] Martindale (2005) and Evangelista (2009: 50–1)

literary and philosophical) has been a hotly debated issue. For some, Pater was neglected by modernist authors, whereas others have suggested that literary modernism was profoundly marked by Pater's presence.[39] Denis Donoghue writes: 'Pater is a shade or trace in virtually every writer of any significance from Hopkins and Wilde to Ashbery.'[40] Late-nineteenth-century decadents, early twentieth-century modernists, postmodernists, and even deconstructive critics have all perceived the influence of Pater on their work.[41]

The reception of both Jowett and Pater—indeed the reception of the significance of their teacher—pupil relationship—has been shaped by the issues of Platonic philosophy and Greek pederasty explored in their writings. Their scholarly explorations of what Plato might say to modern masculinities have seen to it that their own masculinities have been subjected to intense historical analysis. Just as the historical truth of Platonic *erōs* and its impact for Victorian men confronted Jowett and Pater, so the historical truth of the relationship between Jowett and Pater and its impact on the modern history of sexuality confronts us. From Benson and Gosse through to the present day, there has been continued discussion about what sort of influence Jowett really did have over Pater: what does it mean to say that Pater might owe his intellectual development to his Balliol tutor's teaching of Plato? Did Jowett block Pater's career prospects? What did Jowett actually say when he interviewed Pater about Harding's letters? Much later, in the 1890s, it was reported in correspondence that Jowett greatly admired Pater's last book, *Plato and Platonism*, an account that expressly alludes to Plato's homoeroticism, as we shall soon see.[42] So what actually happened, then, in the conversation in which Jowett praised Pater's *Plato and Platonism*?

Rather than locate a sexual truth behind those nineteenth-century letters, we will see that the relationship between Platonic *erōs* and truth was a complex one for Jowett and Pater. The translation of ancient text into modern man was not going to be simple. In his

---

[39] Harold Bloom has argued that the modernist disregard for Pater should be seen in terms of oedipal repression (Bloom 1974), a theory that itself has influenced several critics, including Meisel (1980), and indirectly Higgins (2002). Alternatively, other critics have contended that Pater's legacy is clearly traceable in modernism: see Shuter (1994: 138 n. 45, with further references).

[40] Donoghue (1995: 6).

[41] On deconstruction and Pater, see Fellows (1991) and Loesberg (1991).

[42] See Evangelista (2007b: 71).

discussions of the highly charged context of the pedagogic encounter, Jowett tries to find a space for an intensely close male friendship that is neither a vice nor like marriage. In his attempts to describe such a relationship, Jowett describes a male love imitable and impossible, irrecoverably lost in the past *and* a model for the present. Indeed Jowett admits to not really knowing what Plato thought about peder-astic desire. Greek *erōs*, then, shifts between the known and the unknowable. Rather than explain Plato's texts, then, Jowett writes his own creative parodies: just as Plato has Socrates praise male love in the *Phaedrus*, so Jowett praises male friendship over marriage. And, just as it becomes difficult for Jowett to know what Plato really meant, so Jowett's own texts become difficult to understand: what exactly is this friendship like that the Regius Professor so admires? Just as Socrates exhorts his listeners to know themselves while at the same time invoking his ignorance as knowledge, making it difficult to know what we are to learn from Plato's texts, so it is difficult to know precisely what Jowett's own writing sought to teach.

Pater hears his ex-tutor's difficulties in knowing Greek love. And so, for Pater, Greek homoeroticism becomes the key trope for exploring the relationship between the past and the present. In his 1867 essay 'Winckelmann', and his 1893 book *Plato and Platonism*, Pater expli-citly attempts to defend Greek homoeroticism in the eyes of its critics by distancing it from contemporary stereotypes of abnormal mascu-linities. As we shall examine, Pater's Plato looks very different from, and very similar to, that of his teacher, Jowett. In his attempt, then, to demonstrate the significance of Greek love for modern masculinity, Pater ends up showing that the difference between proscribed and prescribed masculinities is very difficult to tell, causing some readers to proclaim that Jowett praised Pater's book, whereas others have seen explicit critique of his old teacher's Platonism.[43] The difficulty of

---

[43] Mary Duclaux, in her recollections of Pater, wrote that Pater's lectures signified a glamorous and triumphant return to Oxford: 'Pater's old adversaries . . . surrendered their arms, and Jowett, having impeded the career of one of his favourite students, then repudiated. Jowett, the chief Platonist at Oxford, exulted to see one of the flock who had been too long misguided by the glamour of art return to the fold' (quoted in Evangelista 2007b: 71). Duclaux was a close friend of the author and critic Vernon Lee (Violet Paget). See also Gosse's *DNB* entry on Pater, quoted in Faber (1957: 380). See also Small (1972) on Jowett's influence on Pater. On the other hand, Lesley Higgins (1993) and Stefano Evangelista (2007a) see in Pater's critique of Jowett a defence of homosexuality (Higgins) and of counter-cultural lifestyles (Evangelista).

understanding what sort of relationship between men Plato valued has ensured that Jowett's and Pater's relationship has become so debated.

SYMPOSIUM IN THE CHAPEL

Jowett's translations are, of course, hesitant and sometimes opaque. For example, his Socrates says near the opening of the *Lysis* (204c): 'Simple and foolish as I am, the Gods have given me the power of understanding affections of this kind.'[44] In his *Plato and Platonism*, on the other hand, Pater offers a more explicit translation: 'Poor creature as I am, I have one talent: I can recognise, at first sight, the lover and the beloved.'[45] Recently, scholars have most commonly observed Jowett's heterosexualization of Greek friendship: 'In this, as in other discussions about love, what Plato says of the loves of men must be *transferred* to the loves of women before we can attach any serious meaning to his words. Had he lived in our times, he would have made the *transposition* himself.'[46] That quotation comes from Jowett's introduction to the *Phaedrus*. In his introduction to the *Symposium*, he readdresses this issue again, but this time coming to a slightly different conclusion:

The Platonic Socrates...does not regard the greatest evil of Greek life as a thing not to be spoken of; but it has a ridiculous element (Plato's Symp. 214), and is a subject for irony, no less than for moral reprobation (cp. Plato's Symp. 218 D, E). It is also used as a figure of speech which no one interpreted literally (Xen. Symp. 4.57).[47]

Interestingly, then, the pederastic relationship was *both literally there* in the Platonic text requiring transferral, transposition, and translation, *and merely a metaphor, a subject of irony*, not to be taken seriously. Either Plato provides a metaphorical account of desire, which we must translate into a more literal meaning, or he offers us a literal account, which we must transpose accordingly.

[44] Jowett (1892: i. 50).
[45] Pater (1910: vi. 133).
[46] Jowett (1892: i. 406), emphasis added. See Higgins (1993).
[47] Jowett (1892: i. 534).

Jowett found himself entangled in a double bind. If he did not translate Plato how he wanted, the stain of pederasty would remain on the page. Yet, if he were to translate Plato's words about pederasty into praises of marriage, then he would have shown that Plato could be appropriated howsoever the reader might choose. Jowett did not solve the issue: pederastic references remained in the translations, while in his introductions he suggested their removal. For Jowett, who was writing in the wake of the debates about historicism in Germany's classics departments, deciding which position would be the more accurate was a troubling concern: the translation of pederasty, a historically specific phenomenon, into modern marriage, or positing pederasty as a necessary part of the Platonic text? Indeed, the Socratic elenchus, which questioned the knowledge of both pupil and teacher, of both Socrates and his interlocutors, poses a problem for the reader: does Plato teach us to imitate or to think for and fashion ourselves? If Plato's texts were seen not as teaching facts but as offering a model for self-formation, then the question of whether we should receive an ancient text from tradition 'as it is', or appropriate it and use it as we see fit, becomes an urgent issue with those texts, featuring pederastic desires and relationships, and love between men. The presence and intense discussion of homoerotic desires in Plato's texts made the question of the usefulness of Greek in modernity all the more pressing: was it these desires that made Plato all the more antiquated or not? Indeed, this is a key area of the Platonic text, which Jowett suggests could be more profitably rewritten. It is one of the few moments when Jowett cannot decide whether he is reading or (re)writing Plato, whether he is teacher or pupil, whether he is ancient Platonic philosopher or modern translator. Jowett cannot decide whether the friendship he traces out in Plato is a truly timeless ideal to be imitated or a historical phenomenon that modern men can use to form and fashion their own masculinities.

Jowett's introductions to the dialogues clearly show a Victorian professor contending with his Christianity. Indeed, it would be easy to suggest that his religious beliefs blurred his scholarly vision. However, by the time Jowett came to publish the first edition of his Platonic dialogues in 1871, he was already well known in educated circles for his outspoken thoughts about the interpretation of scripture. In fact, the portrait of a curmudgeonly old scholar misses the energy and verve with which Jowett entered the public debates about Christianity in the middle of the nineteenth century. Rather than blinding him from what is supposedly there in the Platonic text, his incursions in the 1860s into theological dispute actually helped Jowett to formulate his ideas about history and the interpretation of ancient texts. Before turning to Jowett's Plato, then, we need to consider how his theological scholarship accompanied his Platonic labours.

The Oxford that Jowett had inhabited as a student and young man had been riven by theological doubt and dispute. The leaders of Tractarianism at Oxford, such as John Henry Newman, argued that Anglicanism was simply one 'branch' of the Catholic Church and encouraged the restoration of many aspects of medieval liturgical practice, believing that the Church had become too plain. Newman's 'Tract 90' went further than this to argue that the doctrines of the Roman Catholic Church were compatible with the Thirty-Nine Articles of the sixteenth-century Church of England, causing him to convert to Roman Catholicism.[48] The 'Romanizing' tendency of Newman and his followers was accompanied by an intense debate in Oxford about Christian manliness: '[Thomas] Arnold's ideal, on the one hand, stressed the importance of activity, both mental and physical, of the participation in worldly affairs and the applicability of knowledge to everyday life; Newman's, meanwhile, emphasised the benefits of the contemplative over the active life, retreat from the world and the value of knowledge for its own sake.'[49] Previous German discussions about *Bildung* and *Wissenschaft* became inflected, in the English context, through contests over gender politics.

These debates at Oxford looked back to the inauguration of the Greats syllabus following the institution of the Examination Statute in 1800. The syllabus reformers were criticized for churning out young men whose 'mental exertion must end in religious scepticism', as Sydney Smith wrote in the Whig *Edinburgh Review*, thereby encouraging a lack of manliness. Defenders of the new *Litterae Humaniores* curriculum in turn claimed that the degree course was designed to produce 'the manly reasoner'.[50] The concern about the Christian masculinity of the Oxford graduate was anticipated in the insistence that divinity be a compulsory part of the Greats examination from the beginning. Both Thomas Arnold and John Henry Newman were educated in this intense Oxonian mix of sacred and secular knowledge. And both men criticized the other for the lack of manliness produced

[48] On Tractarianism, see Faught (2003).
[49] Ellis (2007: 46–7).
[50] Ellis (2007: 47–8).

by their pedagogic philosophies and policies. Newman's paradigm was the 'contemplative, secluded, scholarly' academic, whereas Arnold believed that a university education should produce an 'active, practical and hard-working' man.[51] Each thought that the ideas of the other robbed the young man of his masculinity.[52]

Arnold praised the Examination Statute of 1830, which included the teaching of ancient history on Greats, and also criticized the Oxford rule, which necessitated the subscription to the Thirty-Nine Articles for matriculation and graduation at the University. Furthermore, he supported the admission of dissenters to Oxford. Newman firmly disagreed with Arnold's positions. For him, subscription guaranteed orthodoxy, and the arrival of history on the Greats syllabus marked a movement towards the application of scholarship to modern, everyday, practical life. It was Arnold's hope that the reading of Plato might play a larger role on the curriculum that influenced Jowett, among others. Arnold's sense of masculinity had been awoken by his reading of the *Republic* while in the sixth form at Rugby.[53] (As we shall see, the sixth-form enjoyment of Plato would become a formative experience for male Victorian and Edwardian readers.) Jowett's suspicions about scholarly research and his enthusiasm for the application of ancient philosophy to modern life, with due consideration for the historicity of such applications, encouraged the Balliol man to bring Plato into the Oxford tutorial.[54] Furthermore, Jowett was most apprehensive about modern forms of Christian dogmatism. In May 1848 he wrote, with his friend Arthur Stanley, a pamphlet entitled *Suggestions for an Improvement of the Examination Statute* in which he argued for a more open approach to theology (Jowett also wanted religious, doctrinal tests to be abolished). It was in the preface to this pamphlet that he first publicly suggested that the Bible should be interpreted 'like any other book'.[55] 'For Stanley and Jowett religious truth was to be discovered and tested rather than accepted and learnt.'[56] Although the new theology school was not

---

[51] Ellis (2007: 60).
[52] On Christian manliness, see also Vance (1985) and Hall (1994). On the reception of Newman's masculinity by other manly Christians, notably Charles Kingsley, see Buckton (1998).
[53] Ellis (2007: 51).
[54] See Evangelista (2007b: 72–3).
[55] Hinchliff (1987: 31).
[56] Hinchliff (1987: 32).

accepted, Jowett did manage to get Plato on the syllabus in 1850, when the Greats syllabus was reformed.

Jowett became Regius Professor of Greek at Oxford in 1855, the very year his Pauline commentaries appeared. As these made clear, as did his controversial essay 'On the Interpretation of Scripture' (1860), 'the Bible,' Jowett thought,

ought to be treated as any other book would be treated in its context and as expressing the mind of a particular author, an era, and a cultural setting. He wanted to get rid of the complex patterns of symbolic, traditional, and allegorical interpretation which, he maintained, had been read into, rather than out of, the actual text. He thought that trying to 'prove' doctrinal positions from scripture was an ill-conceived and impossible task,

as Peter Hinchliff has argued.[57] For instance, with regard to Paul, Jowett's commentaries sought to turn him 'from a text into a real person . . . he treated them [Paul's words] as the remarks of a man who *felt* what he was writing not as a man who was laying down in advance what would have to be believed two thousand years ago'.[58] Jowett, then, using his philological skills, sought to discover the original meaning intended by the authors. And yet, at the same time, Jowett was keenly aware of the difficulty (or impossibility) of doing just that. Following arguments set out in Thomas Arnold's *Principles of Church Reform* (1833), Jowett emphasized 'the very personal nature of belief, the uncertainty of ideas, which cannot be empirically demonstrated, the futility of trying to "prove" doctrines from the Bible'.[59] Most problematically, Jowett's famous 1860 essay was largely negative in its approach, in that it repeatedly outlined doctrines that could no longer be believed, but did not set out what could. And so modern man's relation to Christ was an awkward one: on the one hand, Jowett thought it was useful for Christians that 'the life of Christ was only partially known. "We have enough to assist us and not enough to constrain us."'[60] Yet, at the same time, he believed that Christ's life was there to be imitated. As Hinchliff has summarized: 'He was freeing Christianity from its historical roots while claiming that he believed the facts of history to be of crucial importance. He was also insisting

---

[57] Hinchliff (1987: 73). See Jowett (1860: 404).
[58] Hinchliff (1987: 46).
[59] Hinchliff (1987: 49).
[60] Jowett, quoted in Hinchliff (1987: 138).

that one should model oneself on Christ at the same time as he was
asserting that one could never actually know what Christ was like.'[61]

Jowett's wide reading in German historiography, philosophy, and
theology found him attempting to dovetail his appeal to *Wissenschaft*
(going back to the sources objectively) with his ardent belief in
Bildung (the ancient world offered models for modernity). Viewing
Jesus both as a singular historical figure and as exemplar reflected
Jowett's own complex positioning at Oxford: he was the first master
of Balliol *not* to go on to an important office in the Church *after* his
mastership. He was never tempted away from Balliol by ecclesiastical
appointment. 'That transformation—"from clergyman to don" as the
title of Engel's book [1983] describes it—Jowett *almost* epitomised.'[62]
If Jowett is now notable for his attempts to Christianize Plato,[63] in the
nineteenth century he was lambasted for his attempts to Platonize
Christianity. William Fremantle, an admiring pupil who was later to
become Dean of Ripon, produced editions of Jowett's chapel sermons
after the master's death. In one he opens the preface: 'The most
notable fact as to Jowett's doctrinal position is that he lays very little
stress on the Church system, either the system of worship or that of
dogma. From this it has been concluded that he held lightly by
Christianity itself and was content with a vague theism, in which
Plato counted for as much as Christ himself.'[64]

On becoming master, Jowett also became the official college
preacher. Henry Scott Holland, a pupil at Balliol (who would later
become Regius Professor of Divinity at Oxford), recorded his im-
pressions of Jowett's preaching:

[Jowett] preached yesterday in Chapel amidst great excitement, 110 people in
Chapel. He looked so fatherly and beautiful and brought out the best bell-like
silvern voice with quite rich tones . . . though I felt how beautiful it was in its
way, it was most unsatisfying to me. It was just Platonism flavoured with a
little Christian charity: Christianity is gutted by him: it becomes perfectly
meaningless . . . I admire the Symposium with all my heart and soul; but
I must have something more to have brought God down to death to procure
for me.'[65]

---

[61] Hinchliff (1987: 139). See also Barr (1982).
[62] Hinchliff (1987: 107). See also Engel (1983).
[63] See Higgins (1993) and Evangelista (2007a, b).
[64] Jowett (1901: xi).
[65] Holland, quoted in Hinchliff (1987: 116). See also Paget (1921: 33–4).

Christian preaching had turned into Socratic teaching. Indeed it seems that the smaller his audience the better.[66] The congregation resembled a symposium. Indeed, Holland's words are now difficult to interpret: does the Platonism of 'fatherly, beautiful' Jowett make Christianity seem too arid and abstract or is the reference to the *Symposium* a hint that his theology harboured irreligious beliefs?

In *Sermons on Faith and Doctrine* (1901), Fremantle prints Jowett's sermon on 'Friendship' that was delivered in Balliol College chapel sometime in 1873, two years after the first edition of the translation of Plato, and two years before the second. To exemplify friendship for his young audience, he delves into classical literature, observing that 'the school of Socrates was quite as much a circle of friends as a band of disciples'.[67] The pederastic context of ancient friendship is brought precariously close to the scholastic setting of modern male relations. 'It is in youth,' Jowett underlines, 'when life is first opening upon us, we easily form friendships.'[68] Our look back to such youthful bonds is explicitly likened to the modern age's admiration of ancient friendships: 'There will be no other opportunity in after life like that which he has here [at university] . . . The pleasant days of youth will be cherished by us in imagination thirty or forty years hence.'[69] Similarly, classical friendships are hard to repeat in a later age: 'this is an ideal of friendship which is rarely attained in this world.'[70] And so, then, just as Jowett implies the impossibility of resuscitating the likes of such ideal, ancient friendships, the men in Jowett's chapel will nevertheless look back at their own friendships '*in very ancient days*' never to be repeated later on in life.[71] The singular pleasures of ancient friendship are indeed explicitly known by every Victorian boy: 'For everyone in youth knows the delight of having a friend. Who has not felt his heart beat quicker, standing at the door of the house at which he expects to meet him after a long absence? How many things have we to say to him; how much to hear from him, protecting into the night our conversation with him, which seems as if it would never end'. Just as it was difficult for modern nineteenth-century historians to characterize the Greek pederastic relationship (as we saw

---

[66] Hinchliff (1987: 148): 'Jowett was far happier to see thirty volunteers early on a Sunday morning than a more or less compulsorily full chapel later in the day.'

[67] Jowett (1901: 340).

[68] Jowett (1901: 341).

[69] Jowett (1901: 342–3). Does 'after life' hint that life after university is like death?

[70] Jowett (1901: 347).

[71] Jowett (1901: 354), emphasis added.

with Müller and Meier), so it is hard for us in the twenty-first century to understand the intensity of the singular relationships between young men in Victorian England. Jowett's translation of ancient friendship into nineteenth-century Oxford depicts a chaste, yet romantic relationship that is hard to translate into our present day. Indeed, it is the historical singularity of such modern friendships that Jowett seeks to vaunt, just as at the same time he emphasizes the impossibility of living up to antique ideals. The cultural—historical relationship between ancient and modern is, then, conceptualized by Jowett through a modern man's memory of his intense, youthful, 'ancient' friendships. And this is how Jowett tries to dovetail *Wissenschaft* with *Bildung*: antiquity was a singular historical moment and remains a repeatable model—repeatedly lived through in childhood but at the same time an ancient memory, a Balliol man's child becomes antiquity.

We have already examined how Jowett's Socratic persona produced a complex, fissured reception of him and his work. And what we are to learn from Jowett's chapel sermons remains problematic: was his Christianity a veil for an irreligious Platonism or was his Platonism a vehicle for his Christianity? When the Oxbridge clergyman was becoming the professionalized Oxbridge don, Jowett looks like the last in a line of Oxford men who attempted to rein Plato's œuvre into a Christian framework and the first of a generation invested not in inculcating its students with doctrine but in inspiring a genuine intellectual curiosity that would not presuppose an answer, a dogmatic truth. Hearing precisely what Jowett intended to teach was always already hard to heed. Christianity should not be seen, then, as a repressive counterweight to the pagan joys of Hellenism in mid-Victorian Oxford. Rather than suppressing discussion, Jowett's sermons produced a space for debate. Jowett's emphasis on the impossibility of interpreting scripture dogmatically, thereby opening it up to endlessly competing interpretations, prepares us for a similar move with his Plato, who would provide modern man with 'numerous applications'.

JOWETT'S PLATONIC PARODIES

The *Lysis* is the second dialogue to appear in Jowett's edition of translations. And it is its examination of friendship that makes it such a worthwhile read for modern students. For Jowett, the *Lysis* suggests 'a few problems of Friendship . . . which he [*sic*] who wishes to make or keep a friend may profitably study'.[72] Platonic philosophy can apparently offer practical advice about friendship for the Victorian reader. In particular and most interestingly for us, Jowett is concerned with comparing ancient pederasty with modern marriage. The Professor remarks: 'We may expect a friendship almost divine, such as philosophers have sometimes dreamed of: we find what is human. The good of it is necessarily limited; it does not take the place of marriage; it affords rather a solace than an arm of support.'[73] Jowett, then, sets male—male friendship in opposition to marriage, but at the same time suggests that they are mirror images of each other—one has merely replaced the other in modern society. Although one might interpret Jowett as translating ancient Greek pederasty into modern marriage, the relationship between the two is more complicated. Jowett thinks that men have unrealistic expectations about friendship ('we expect a friendship almost divine'). Male friendship might 'not take the place of marriage', but Jowett's text also explicitly implies that marriage is a mere surrogate for a male—male relationship. 'We' might 'dream' of a 'divine' friendship with another man, but 'we' will have to settle with second-best, modern marriage. Men, who might expect—which is more than just hoping for—a friendship that outstrips marriage, must realize that marriage is the more suitable option. At the same time, then, as extolling the virtues of marriage, Jowett also explicitly acknowledges the great allurement and attractions of friendship between men.

Jowett goes on to wonder 'whether friendship can safely exist between young persons of different sexes, not connected by ties of relationship, and without the thought of love or marriage; [and] whether, again, a wife or a husband should have any intimate friend, besides his or her partner in marriage'.[74] Jowett responds to his own questions (and we need to quote him at length here):

The answer to this latter question is rather perplexing, and would probably be different in different countries (cp. Sympos. p. 182). While we do not deny that great good may result from such attachments, for the mind may be drawn out and the character enlarged by them; yet we feel also that they are attended with many dangers, and that this Romance of Heavenly Love

---

[72] Jowett (1892: i. 48).
[73] Jowett (1892: i. 47).
[74] Jowett (1892: i. 47).

requires a strength, a freedom from passion, a self-control, which in youth especially, are rarely to be found. The propriety of such friendships must be estimated a good deal by the manner in which public opinion regards them; they must be reconciled with the ordinary duties of life; and they must be justified by the result.[75]

Interestingly, then, Jowett does *not* even try to answer the first question (can young people of different sexes be friends?) and moves straight onto the second (can a wife or husband have 'any intimate friend' outside marriage?). And the answer itself perplexes Jowett, as he suggests that friendship seems to be a culturally bound and constructed relationship varying 'in different countries'. His reference to *Symposium* 182 focuses the question on whether *married men* can be intimate friends with other men outside their marriage: that section of the *Symposium* sees Pausanias discussing the variation of institutionalization of male—male friendship across the Greek-speaking world: 'In Elis and Boeotia . . . the law is simply in favour of these connexions, and no one, whether young or old, has anything to say to their discredit . . . In Ionia and other places, and generally in countries which are subject to the barbarians, the custom is held to be dishonourable.' With regard to Athens, Jowett's Pausanias remarks, 'the explanation of it is rather perplexing [*ou rhadion katanoesai*]. For observe that open loves are held to be more honourable than secret ones, and that the love of the noblest and the highest, even if their persons are less beautiful than others, is especially honourable.'[76]

Jowett's perplexity is matched by that of his Pausanias. And, although his answer is not altogether positive, it is certainly not wholly negative either. 'This Romance of Heavenly Love' (making the reference to Pausanias' speech on male love all the more explicit) 'requires a strength' that is 'in youth . . . rarely to be found'. Although the possibility of such love is rare, it can nevertheless happen. Jowett's highly suggestive prose seems to offer a discreet nod of approval to his married friend and ex-pupil, the scholar John Addington Symonds, with whom he earnestly discussed the meaning of Greek love.[77] And, although Jowett's 'perplexing' answer of cultural variation seems to

---

[75] Jowett (1892: i. 48).
[76] Jowett (1892: i. 552).
[77] See Evangelista (2007a) on Jowett's and the married Symonds's conversations about same-sex desire, and *infra*, Chapter 3.

match Pausanias' own 'perplexing' explanation of Athenian friendship, which commends 'open loves' and condemns 'secret ones', Jowett is actually in direct contrast. He emphasizes the need for modern friends to hold and keep secrets from each other: 'in friendship too there must be reserves . . . '.[78] Finally, Jowett does *not* criticize intimate male—male friendship *per se*. Rather, he comments that the 'propriety of such friendships' is mostly 'estimated' by 'public opinion', and such friendships, therefore, should be managed 'with the ordinary duties of life', and they can even be 'justified by the result'. Jowett implies that the problem is not such friendship itself but the modern perception of it. Yet, if the results of such a friendship could be justified, then it could indeed play a role in modern society.

Subtly and quietly, then, Jowett's text slips from invoking the paradigm of modern marriage over ancient male—male friendships to suggesting that, if one could be discreet about such friendships and show self-control, ensuring the goodliness of such a friendship's outcome, then this sort of relationship could be part of the modern world alongside one's marriage. Jowett is tantamount to proposing the possibility of modern men living double lives . . . [79]

Some of Jowett's most remarkable writing about Plato comes in his introductory essay to the translation of the *Phaedrus*. For Jowett (and his nineteenth-century readers, as he positions and manipulates their responses to Plato), one of the primary difficulties in reading this dialogue was telling whether the pederastic background was a seriously integral factor in the comprehension of Platonic philosophy. In his introduction to his *Symposium* translations (which follows directly on from his *Phaedrus*), he ponders: 'It is difficult to adduce the authority of Plato either for or against such [pederastic] practices or customs, because it is not always easy to determine whether he is speaking of the "heavenly and philosophical love, or of the coarse Polyhymnia"' and he often refers to this (for example, in the *Symposium*) half in jest, yet 'with a certain degree of seriousness'.[80] Rather than offering a straightforward analysis of the problem, Jowett himself re-enacts and re-performs that (nineteenth-century) difficulty in

---

[78] Jowett (1892: i. 46).
[79] Jowett's discreet tolerance of passionate friendships between married men is evidenced in the respect he shows for his ex-pupil and fellow classicists, John Addington Symonds. See, *infra*, Chapter 3.
[80] Jowett (1892: i. 536).

reading Plato. In his discussion of Socrates' parodies of Greek oratory in the *Phaedrus*, Jowett remarks: 'Plato had doubtless a higher purpose than to exhibit Socrates as the rival or superior of the Athenian rhetoricians. Even in the speech of Lysias there is a germ of truth and this is further developed in the parallel oration of Socrates.' Jowett goes on:

Socrates, half in jest and to satisfy his own wild humour, takes the disguise of Lysias, but he is also in profound earnest and in a deeper vein of irony than usual. Having improvised his own speech, which is based upon the model of the preceding, he condemns them both. Yet the condemnation is not to be taken seriously, for he is evidently trying to express an aspect of the truth.[81]

The Socratic parody gives Jowett leave to write *his own* parody of Platonic speech, on a subject he already examined in his introduction to the *Lysis*:

We may raise the same question in another form [in reference to Lysias' speech and Socrates' response]: Is marriage preferable with or without love? 'Among ourselves,' as we may say, a little parodying the words of Pausanias in the Symposium, 'there would be one answer to this question: the practice and feeling of some foreign countries appears to be more doubtful'.

We have already seen Jowett refer to *Symposium* 182 in his essay on friendship. Now Jowett sets up a 'modern Socrates' (that is, Jowett himself) to ask this question about modern marriage in this 'little parody'.[82] The 'modern Socrates' would wonder of 'two inexperienced persons, ignorant of the world and of one another, how can they be said to choose?' Their so-called love, the argument goes, would grow stale quickly:

Better, he would say, a 'little love at the beginning', for heaven might have increased it; but now their foolish fondness has changed into mutual dislike...How much nobler, in conclusion, he will say, is friendship... Besides, he will remark that there is a much greater choice of friends than wives—you may have more of them and they will be far more improving to your mind.[83]

Just as Plato hid himself behind the ancient Socrates, so Jowett positions himself behind a modern version. Like the ancient Socrates,

---

[81] Jowett (1892: i. 405–6).
[82] Jowett (1892: i. 406).
[83] Jowett (1892: i. 407).

Jowett gives no indication as to how seriously this parody is to be taken. He apparently just provides the argument for the preference of friendship over marriage.

Jowett then goes on to offer a 'palinode' for marriage, 'for the injustice done to love Helen'. Then the 'modern Socrates', says Jowett, would argue that the

> true love of the mind cannot exist between two souls, until they are purified from the grossness of earthly passion: they must pass through a time of trial and conflict first; in the language of religion they must be converted and born again . . . When they have attained to this exalted state, let them marry (something too may be conceded to the animal nature of man); or to live together in holy and innocent friendship. The poet might describe in eloquent words the nature of such a union . . . how in a figure they grew wings like doves, and were 'ready to fly away together and be at rest'.[84]

Jowett offers his readers a Socratic defence of marriage that is imbued with Christianizing discourse ('language of religion . . . converted . . . born again . . . they grew wings like doves') but at the same time, problematically, resembles the intense, yet controlled friendship of the ancient Greeks that Symonds recommends and that Jowett says can exist on rare occasions ('live together in holy and innocent friendship'[85]). Jowett then muses on his impression of Socrates (and it is necessary to quote at length):

> So, partly in jest but also 'with a certain degree of seriousness', we may appropriate to ourselves the words of Plato. The use of such a parody, though very imperfect, is to *transfer* his thoughts to our sphere of religion and feeling, to bring him nearer to us and us to him. Like the Scriptures, Plato admits of numerous applications, if we allow for the difference of times and manners; and we lose the better half of him when we regard his Dialogues merely as literary compositions. Any ancient work which is worth reading has a practical and speculative as well as a literary interest. And in Plato, more than in any other Greek writer, the local and transitory is inextricably blended with what is spiritual and eternal. Socrates is necessarily ironical; for he has to withdraw from the received opinions and beliefs of mankind. We cannot separate the transitory from the

---

[84] Jowett (1892: i. 408–9).
[85] See above on passionless Greek friendship, and Jowett (1892: i. 48).

permanent; nor can we *translate* the language of irony into that of plain reflection and common sense.[86]

Just as Jowett would have trouble in deciding how serious Plato was in his myth of the soul ('Was he...serious? For example, are we to attribute division of the soul to the gods? Or is this merely assignable to them by way of parallelism with men?'[87]), so Jowett's own reader will inevitably face the dilemma of how earnest these parodies of Socrates were. If they were indeed 'half in jest but also "with a certain degree of seriousness"', then which bits were in jest and which were serious? What these parodies do show, Jowett suggests, is the applicability of Plato 'like the Scriptures', as long as 'we allow for the difference of times and manners'. Jowett's intention is to demonstrate the 'practical interest' gained from studying Plato. Yet Jowett then seems to admit that that which is culturally specific to Socrates and Plato ('the local and transitory') is 'inextricably blended' with the timeless truths expounded by Platonic philosophy (the 'spiritual and eternal'). The pederastic context, which is necessarily different from the pedagogical context of nineteenth-century Oxford, *is*, then, in some way 'blended' with the eternal spirit of Platonic thought. But then, rather mysteriously, Jowett pronounces that 'Socrates is necessarily ironical; for he has to withdraw from the received opinions and beliefs of mankind'. Socrates must couch his philosophy in the ironies of pederastic discourse simply because he must 'withdraw from... received opinions'. And then again Jowett notes that we cannot 'separate the transitory from the permanent', the culturally specific pederastic context from the timeless philosophical truths. And, finally, Jowett admits that he and we cannot '*translate* the language of irony into that of plain reflection and common sense'. Jowett is unable to translate away the pederastic irony of Socrates despite any desire to do so. Instead, it must either remain (as it does in his actual translations) or he can provide his own parody of Socrates' irony 'half in jest but also "with a certain degree of seriousness"', unable to provide an analysis of what Socrates meant in 'plain reflection and common sense'. Just how serious *was* Jowett being in his parodies? In this paragraph, he moves from suggesting that the 'use of such a parody, though very imperfect, is to *transfer* his thoughts to our

---

[86] Jowett (1892: i. 409), emphasis added.
[87] Jowett (1892: i. 412).

sphere of religion and feeling', to saying that he cannot '*translate* the language of irony into that of plain reflection and common sense'.

In seeking to stake out a space for male friendship that is neither liable to vice nor replaced by modern marriage, Jowett shows that this space in modern Oxford is nevertheless precarious. Plato's text is prone to appropriation and transformation, as Jowett himself demonstrates. The multiple Jowetts we detected earlier are all present in his texts: defender of passionate friendship, sympathizer with Greek lover, severe critic of sodomitical vice. Indeed, it was the pederastic context of Plato's dialogues that provided room for Jowett's various and shifting positions. We might go as far as saying that it was this context that 'begets' much of the Victorian debate about the use of an ancient text on a modern university curriculum. And the interpretative freedom that Jowett's Plato encouraged—the freedom to think for oneself—was a lesson that Walter Pater learnt from his old tutor. The 'mystery' of Jowett's 'philosophic opinions' provided Pater with an alibi to produce his own rendering of Plato, which both resembled and differed from the translations of his teacher.

FROM WINCKELMANN TO PATER

Walter Pater's scholarly and literary engagement with ancient Greece began in 1867, when his essay 'Winckelmann' was published anonymously. This was included in the first edition of his book *Studies in the History of the Renaissance* in 1873, the same year that Jowett was preaching on friendship in Balliol College chapel. 'Winckelmann' was altogether more explicit about Greek homoeroticism in its praise of Winckelmann's history of ancient art. Indeed, Winckelmann's homoerotic response to the Greeks was central to Pater's understanding of the reception of antiquity in modernity. The essay artfully argued that 'the fulfilment of homoerotic desire is integral to the process of understanding ancient art'.[88] As Stefano Evangelista observes: 'Winckelmann's active desire for the male body is presented as an important stage in the development of his understanding of ancient sculpture.'[89] 'That his [Winckelmann's] affinity with Hellenism was

---

[88] Evangelista (2009: 33).
[89] Evangelista (2009: 34).

not merely intellectual, that the subtler threads of temperament were inwoven in it, is proved by his romantic, fervent friendships with young men.'[90] Later in the essay he also writes: '[He] apprehended the subtlest principles of the Hellenic manner, not through understanding, but by instinct and touch... [H]e fingers those pagan marbles with unsigned hands, with no sense of shame or loss.'[91]

At the same time as viewing Winckelmann as a 'relic of classical antiquity', however, Pater 'is also at pains to remind us', as Elizabeth Prettejohn argues, 'that Winckelmann, living in eighteenth-century Germany and Rome, did not have access to the more recent discoveries that had fundamentally changed the canon of Greek art... Thus Winckelmann's special intuition of Greek art, while it permits him to break free from the conventions and orthodoxies of his own period, nonetheless remains historically contingent.'[92] Furthermore, Pater was keenly aware that Winckelmann's own writing reflected a marked ambivalence about the possibility of modern art, and therefore life, successfully imitating the ancients. The crucial text that informed Pater's complex response to Winckelmann's work was Goethe's famous 1805 essay 'Winckelmann und sein Jahrhundert'. And for Pater, taking up Plato's metaphor from the *Symposium*, it was Goethe, 'then in all the pregnancy of his wonderful youth', who takes on the philosophy of Winckelmann, which itself is likened to 'a fragment of Greek art itself, stranded on that littered, indeterminate shore of Germany in the eighteenth century'.[93] Learning from Jowett's lessons, Pater saw that ancient Greece was both a perfect(ed) example *and* a fragment that permitted Goethe 'the sense of freedom'. '*Im Ganzen, Guten, Wahren, resolut zu leben*'—that is, to live resolutely in integrity, goodness, and truth.[94] Rather than mimicking ancient culture and lifestyles, the Romantic fragments of Greece, like Winckelmann's fragmentary, unfinished *Geschichte* (1764), should provide the catalyst 'to mould our lives to artistic perfection. Philosophy serves culture, not by the fancied gift of absolute or transcendental knowledge, but by suggesting questions which help one to detect the passion, and strangeness, and dramatic contrasts of

---

[90] Pater (1910: i. 191).
[91] Pater (1910: i. 124, 143).
[92] Prettejohn (2007: 265).
[93] Pater (1910: i. 228).
[94] Pater (1910: i. 231, 228). Pater misquotes Goethe: 'Wahren' should be 'Schönen', 'beauty.' See Pater (1980: 439–40).

life.'[95] In 'passion', 'strangeness', and 'dramatic contrasts', Pater's language suggests a modern performative exploration of freedom from contemporary social strictures that clearly includes erotic experimentation. Just like Socratic elenchus, philosophy should provide not the answers but the questions. Both exemplar and fragment, a 'fusion of aesthetic perception and historical (re)inter-pretation', Greece, 'liberated from the remote past but always only half-known, is the ur-text that is forever being rewritten through history and that forever proves the inexhaustibility of meaning and the possibility of radical rereading'.[96] The 'Winckelmann' essay moves from a position in which we see Winckelmann erotically feeling (like) a male Greek (statue), towards viewing ancient Greek culture and the modern Winckelmann himself as fragments, which can give birth to all sorts of counter-cultural individualities, beyond those that are purely homoerotically inclined, as exemplified by the polymath Goethe, whose knowledge, sexual and otherwise, extended in numerous directions.[97]

Pater's Winckelmann, then, looks like both the classical ideal and a romantic fragment, an incomplete project that inspires Goethe to improve upon it. Indeed, this ambivalence about Winckelmann is present throughout the essay. And, just as it is Winckelmann's homo-eroticism that bridges the gap between ancient and modern, so it is also his erotic desires that mark the impossibility of getting in touch with antiquity. At one point Pater quotes a letter Winckelmann had written to a beautiful young nobleman, Friedrich von Berg:

Our intercourse has been short, too short both for you and me; but the first time I saw you, the affinity of our spirits was revealed to me: your culture proved that my hope was not groundless; and I found in a beautiful body a soul created for nobleness, gifted with the sense of beauty. My parting from you was therefore one of the most painful in my life . . . your separation from me leaves me no hope of seeing you again.[98]

For Pater, 'Winckelmann's letters, with their troubled colouring', make 'an instructive but bizarre addition to the *History of Art*'.[99] But textuality does not translate straightforwardly into sexuality.

---

[95] Pater (1910: i. 230).
[96] Evangelista (2009: 50). See also C. Williams (1989).
[97] On Goethe, see Kuzniar (1996), Tobin (2000), and Gustafson (2002: 37–67).
[98] Pater (1910: i. 191–2).
[99] Pater (1910: i. 193).

Winckelmann's Platonic/platonic text is not an aperture onto modern sexual desires and sensibilities. Rather, his letter marks the separation from Berg and, therefore, his inability to re-create Greek love in modernity. Goethe's essay, the text through which Pater approaches Winckelmann, underlined Winckelmann's life in letters, which he describes as a 'Selbstgespräch', a monologue, and literally a discussion about the self.[100] As Goethe notes, Winckelmann was constantly revising his work, and therefore himself: 'weil er sich immer wieder umgeschrieben [hat].'[101] But it is Winckelmann's inability to write his self in his letters that interests Goethe: Winckelmann is merely a 'Silbenrätsel', a charade, or literally a puzzle of syllables.[102] 'In Goethe's opinion,' as Susan Gustafson has observed, 'Winckelmann never completed the decipherment and reformulation of himself as a man desiring other men'.[103] His letters perform and experiment with identity, as they muse platonically on the possibility of ever knowing oneself. They repeatedly suggest the impossibility of writing down one's desires: it is only words spoken between two men present to one another that will do. 'Out of the fullness of my soul,' he wrote to one male friend, 'I wanted to speak to you [*mit Dir sprechen*]; what I have to say to you [*Dir zu sagen*] is unbelievably vast'.[104] In another, his first letter to Berg, he says: '[I] explain myself in strong words and words inexpressible in writing [*schriftlich unaussprechlichen Worten*].'[105] Modern episto-lary discourse cannot communicate what the spoken word between an elder and a younger man can voice and transmit. For Winckelmann, his letters were no substitute for the embodied Platonic encounter, just as the *Phaedrus* made clear.

These issues are specified by Pater from the very opening sentences of his essay:

Goethe's *fragments* of art-criticism contain a few pages of strange *pregnancy* on the character of Winckelmann. He speaks of the *teacher* who had made his career possible, but *whom he had never seen*, as of an abstract type of

---

[100]   Goethe (1985: vi. ii. 198).

[101]   Goethe (1985: vi. ii. 370).

[102]   Goethe (1985: vi. ii. 375).

[103]   Gustafson (2002: 62).

[104]   Winckelmann (1952–7: i. 134). The letter is dated 29 September 1747.

[105]   Winckelmann (1952–7: ii. 233). This letter is dated 9 June 1762. See Gustafson (2002: 56–9) for detailed readings of these letters.

culture, consummate, tranquil, withdrawn already into the region of ideals, yet retaining colour from the incidents of a passionate intellectual life.[106]

Despite what Pater will go on to say about Goethe's expansion of Winckelmann's Hellenism, Goethe is himself always already a fragment. And so Pater's essay sets up layer upon layer of missed encounters between generations of men: Pater and Goethe, Goethe and Winckelmann, Winckelmann and his young male friends, and, ultimately, Winckelmann and Plato. It has been the fate of modern man to be taught by a 'teacher . . . whom he had never seen'. It is only the letters of men generations before that can inform later generations of their selves and their desires. And yet it is this historical contingency, the impossibility of ever truly knowing Plato, Winckelmann, and finally Goethe, that demonstrates to Pater the continuing possibility of expanding upon and rewriting their texts. It is the imperfect transmission of knowledge from one generation to the next in the form of their texts that gives birth to new formulations of living in the modern age: 'Goethe's fragments of art-criticism,' just like Winckelmann's fragmentary *Geschichte*, which must be supplemented by his letters, which themselves speak of the fragmentary nature of desire, 'contain a few pages of strange pregnancy'. Pater reproduces Plato's discussion of male reproduction in the *Symposium, but with a difference*. Just as Pater reproduces Plato's imagery, so he also changes it: now it is the *non-encounter* between an elder and a younger man that 'strangely' begets self-knowledge. By both following and adapting Plato's text, Pater shows that the younger man's response to the 'pregnant text' is both imitative and creative, negotiating a dialectic of sameness and difference. The teachers that have never been seen both invite identification and become irrevocably lost objects of desire. Winckelmann's modern homoerotic response to antiquity signifies the blurring of ancient and modern, the love of the same, the complete, aestheticized absorption of the modern self in the beautiful, ancient other. And yet at the same time Winckelmann's modern homoeroticism grows from a historicized sense of loss, frustration, and the intangibility of the object of desire. Homoeroticism signifies both atemporal sameness and historicized difference. Winckelmann's desires were the love of the same *and* of the different.

---

[106] Pater (1910: i. 177), emphases added.

From the beginning, Socrates' lessons distanced the teacher from, as much as brought him into contact with, his pupil: Socrates' attempts to teach young men to become capable of teaching themselves begged the questions, what does it mean to follow that lesson, and what does it mean to think for oneself? This dilemma led Pater to examine how modern men might negotiate the poles of pure mimicry and radical transformation of the texts of their dead teachers. Indeed, Pater's whole theory of the reception of art and text by a viewer and a reader is informed by his reading and use of Plato. For Pater in *The Renaissance*, we are indelibly marked by the past, but at the same time we receive that past subjectively and re-create it according to our own desires.[107] It is Winckelmann's homoerotic desire for the Greek male body that addresses most directly Pater's dialectic of the sameness and difference of the past to the present. The German's desire for Greece is one of close affinity and sameness—the homoerotic response to art is essential for a truthful 'aesthetic' response to art (αἴσθησις meaning sensory and mental perception and understanding). Yet, at the same time, Winckelmann's homoerotic desires signify the historical disjunction between object and viewer, leading to the necessity of understanding the meaning of the object in terms of its effect on the viewer and not in terms of the intention of the original maker.

Despite Pater's sophisticated conceptualization of reception, he worried about the influence that his own book *The Renaissance* might have. This anxiety caused Pater to suppress the final essay in the book, the 'Conclusion', from the second edition, conceiving that 'it might possibly mislead some of those young men into whose hands it might fall'.[108] *Studies in the History of the Renaissance* came to be seen in the press as a manifesto for a philosophy of amoral hedonistic aestheticism, garnering for the Oxford don a mounting notoriety. In his posthumous portrait of Pater, Edmund Gosse relates a remark Pater apparently made to him in 1876: 'I wish they wouldn't call me "a hedonist"; it produces such a bad effect on the minds of people who don't know Greek.'[109] Perhaps Pater was also thinking of Hardinge's 1874 letters of desire, written a year after, and therefore influenced by,

---

[107] See Pater (1910: i. 233 n. 1).

[108] Pater (1910: i. 233 n. 1).

[109] Gosse (1896: 258). On the divided and at times hostile, moralizing contemporary reception of Pater's book, see Evangelista (2009: 51–3).

his *Renaissance*.[110] In 1877, however, the *Contemporary Review* published an article entitled 'The Greek Spirit in Modern Literature' by the rector of St Mary Magdalen, Oxford, St John Tyrwhitt. In it, Symonds's work *Studies of the Greek Poets*, written under the influence of Pater's *Renaissance*, receives harsh criticism. (We will come to Symonds in the next chapter). Tyrwhitt cleverly quotes a section of Jowett fulminating against Greek love ('there is a great gulf fixed between us and them [the Greeks]').[111] Richard Dellamora has suggested that the article was an important factor in neither Symonds nor Pater obtaining the Oxford Professorship of Poetry, for which they were both candidates.[112] Pater's Greek was perceived by some at least, then, as dangerous knowledge.

PATER'S PLATO

Pater's examination of the transformation of ancient textual knowledge into modern embodied masculinity in terms of an elder man's pregnant text was a metaphor that he would develop most fully in the final book he published, *Plato and Platonism: A Series of Lectures* (1893). This work coincided with the publication of the fourth and final edition of *The Renaissance*, suggesting to us that the two books, spanning the beginning and the end of Pater's career, should be read together. The seed of Pater's metaphor about Goethe's pregnant writing becomes fully expanded in his mature and fully grown discussion of Plato and his influence over the history of philosophy. Pater's interest in Plato concerns how the original seed of the Platonic text could have given birth to such a wide range of interpretations. Implicitly punning on his own name (*patēr* is 'father' in classical Greek), Pater also causes us to consider how his own text might 'father' numerous young men, his students at Oxford and the readers of his book. Whereas in 1876 Gosse listened to Pater worrying about the impossibility of controlling the reception of his texts by young

---

[110] Gosse was himself writing his portrait of Pater in 1896 a year after Oscar Wilde's desires had been exposed in a letter about Greek love to Alfred Douglas. We will return to Wilde's letter in Chapter 4. We should also remember that it was Gosse who told Benson about the letters and Jowett's threats to Pater.

[111] Tyrwhitt (1877: 565).

[112] Dellamora (1990: 160–3). F. T. Palgrave was awarded the position.

male readers, by 1893, with the 'Conclusion' having been reinserted into *The Renaissance*, Pater explicitly confronts this issue about the transmission of knowledge between elder teacher and younger male pupil. Furthermore, Pater also encourages us to think of him as the son, as his book repeatedly comments upon its relationship to the work of his old teacher Jowett. As we have already mentioned, this has invited some readers to suggest that Pater should be seen as the intellectual offspring of Jowett, imitating his Socratic master, whereas for others his book demonstrates a man thinking for himself and criticizing Jowett's lessons. Deciding whether Pater was a copy of his teacher or a self-fashioned man reflects Pater's more general interest (as expounded by Jowett) in what Plato's lessons have to teach modernity: the coordinates for imitation or creative rewriting and appropriation. As we shall now see, Plato's description of male pregnancy and reproductive strategies will furnish Pater with the opportunity for defending Plato's love of the male form, and the significance of that love for modern men. Pater will speak back to his critics like Tyrwhitt.

Pater situates Plato and his work at a crossroads in history. Platonic philosophy is nothing but 'a palimpsest, a tapestry' that has woven together and synthesized all those previous philosophical schools (Heraclitus, Parmenides, Pythagoras, and Socrates), to produce a body of work from which all philosophical debates have since emerged in the history of Western philosophy.[113] Plato's texts are a product of their historical environment *and* producer of history—both product of history and history's condition of possibility. As such they are both modern and ancient. Plato is son and father, pupil and teacher, a blend of imitation of what came before and a creator of what will come in his wake. Taking up the Platonic metaphor of impregnation, Pater writes:

So, the seeds of almost all scientific ideas might seem to have been dimly enfolded in the mind of antiquity; but fecundated, admitted to their full working prerogative, one by one, in after ages, by good favour of the special intellectual conditions belonging to a particular generation, which, on a sudden, finds itself preoccupied by a formula, not so much new, as renovated by new application.[114]

[113] Pater (1910: vi. 8).
[114] Pater (1910: vi. 18–19).

Indeed Plato's very texts are themselves (like) seeds. A seed is a tiny fragment, a remnant, the remains of that which produced it, *and* at the same time that which contains everything that is to come in the future. Just like Winckelmann before, Pater at once inserts Plato into history and extracts him from it. And it is this peculiar place and lack of place that Plato occupies in history that has allowed him to produce his theory of Forms, which for Pater are historically, empirically sensible, and mentally, universally intelligible. And it is the image of the seed that Pater uses to describe Plato's theory:

> Take a seed from the garden. What interest it has for us lies in our sense of potential differentiation to come: the leaves, leaf upon leaf, the flowers, a thousand new seeds in turn. It is so with animal seed; and with humanity, individually, or as a whole, its expansion into a detailed, ever-changing, parti-coloured history of particular facts and persons.[115]

True beauty is to be seen in microscopic absorption and distilled concentration on the smallest of empirical objects and moments, just as each object also encourages the attentive viewer to attend to what is beside it. The observation of true beauty is the continuous oscillation between romantic fragment and classical whole, both of which are signified by Pater's seed: the leftover remains of that which produced it and the perfectly formed package containing the formula for everything in its wake. That profoundly absorbed contemplation marks an attempt to efface empirical space and time to touch the Form, and, at the same time, that beautiful particularity leads the viewer on to compare it and subsume it into a perfect, synthesized essence with the objects around it. For Pater's Plato, then, the Forms are perceived by a viewer who is continually oscillating between aestheticizing and historicizing viewpoints. 'Generalisation . . . is a method, not of obliterating the concrete phenomenon, but of enriching it, with the joint perspective, the significance, the expressiveness, of all other things beside it.'[116]

If Plato's text is a seed, both the result of a history and history's condition, embryonic and fully developed, Plato encourages perfect imitation *and* creative, autonomous self-fashioning from his offspring, his learner—readers. Plato's philosophy signifies an ancient historical tradition within which to situate oneself as well as a philosophy to initiate a new epoch in modern history. It is important to

---

[115] Pater (1910: vi. 155).
[116] Pater (1910: vi. 159).

note that Pater's metaphor reflects his dialectic of sameness and difference, already explored in his essay on Winckelmann. The seed suggests an almost biological relationship with the ancient world, a genetic sameness between antiquity and modernity, while at the same time emphasizing the idea that the modern age is a development and expansion from the ancient world, underlining historical differences. In conjuring up ideas about racial ancestry and biological relations, this image ponders upon the question of modernity's relationality with the ancient world. Pater's image of the seed suggests genetic relations between ancient and modern bodies as well as evokes metaphors about cultural pedigree and transformation from antiquity. That is to say, in what sense should we see the ancient world as the seed of the modern?

Pater's ambiguous rhetoric about antiquity being a seed from which modernity was grown was highly deliberate. In begging the question as to whether that historical relationship should be seen as literal/biological or metaphorical/cultural, so it is the relationship between ancient and modern erotics that puts this issue into focus for Pater. And it is Pater's examination of Plato's own life as a history of Plato's desires that formulates Pater's understanding of the relationship between ancient/youthful and modern/mature love. On the one hand, Pater explicitly emphasizes Plato's knowledge of 'all the ways of lovers, in the literal sense', having been 'ἥττων τῶν καλῶν — subject to the influence of fair persons'.[117] But at the same time they are what led him on 'the pathway, the ladder, of love, its joyful ascent towards a more perfect beauty than we have ever yet actually seen'.[118] It is the youthful sight of physical beauty that permitted the possibility that Justice itself could then 'become almost a visible object, and had greatly solemnised him'. Pater dates this historical moment to Plato being 'about twenty-eight years old' having 'listened to the "Apology" of Socrates'.[119] His youthful desires for the physical are both the same and transformed in his maturity:

The lover, who is become a lover of the invisible, but still a lover, and therefore, literally, a seer, of it, carrying an elaborate cultivation of the bodily senses, of eye and ear, their natural force and acquired fineness—gifts akin

[117] Pater (1910: vi. 136).
[118] Pater (1910: vi. 135).
[119] Pater (1910: vi. 138).

properly to τὰ ἐρωτικά, as he says, to the discipline of sensuous love—into the world of intellectual abstractions...[120]

The 'lover of the invisible' possesses gifts that are actually related to those used in the appreciation of physical beauty—as Pater says, 'gifts *akin properly to τὰ ἐρωτικά*'. Yet again Pater uses a metaphor of familial relations to emphasize the closeness of fit between Plato's juvenile and mature loves, just as he is trying to explain their historical development. Plato's homoerotic youth is a part of his past, and yet it is somehow differently present in his adulthood. Plato's youthful homoerotics are seen in an ancestral relationship to his maturity, both the same and different, which leads Pater to comment that 'Plato's style...in its turn promotes in others, that mental situation'—that is, seeing the invisible as if it were the visible.[121] Just as Plato's homoeroticism was his past and yet lingered on, unchanged and yet changed, into his adult present, so Plato's very text encourages the survival of that erotic sensibility, although modified, in the present day of the nineteenth-century reader. The issue of translating Plato into modern England, translating ancient Platonic textuality into modern sexuality, was, then, already anticipated by Plato himself in his negotiation between his youthful, physical loves and his mature love of the invisible. Just as the example of Plato confuses the relationship between visible and invisible, abstract and concrete, so Pater's imagery of seeds and familial relations questions the difference between sexual and textual reproduction: how do written inscriptions of desire (not) relate to physical, desiring bodies?

The seed of Plato's homoeroticism, which informed all that would follow in his philosophical career and yet required nurturing and development, put into neat focus for Pater, then, how Plato's very text, as a seed, might relate to modernity. Benjamin Jowett saw that Plato's texts taught the student to imitate the teacher *and* to get the student to think for himself, and that was a lesson heeded by his old pupil Pater. Pater understood that ancient Greek pederasty could not be revived in nineteenth-century English schools and universities, but at the same time he took very seriously that it was Plato's actual erotic encounters with other males that facilitated his philosophical enterprise, and that those encounters had played an important part in creating modern men

---

[120] Pater (1910: vi. 139–40).
[121] Pater (1910: vi. 140).

in the nineteenth century. Pater also understood that his defence of ancient erotics would be greeted with similarly hostile reviews as those that addressed his examination of Winckelmann's desires for the male body. Since 1873, many writers had been inspired by *The Renaissance*. Pater's discussion of the reception of art as a subjective matter encouraged Oscar Wilde to examine that notion in his novel *The Picture of Dorian Gray* (1891). In the same year Wilde also issued *Intentions*, a set of philosophical dialogues, which utilized Pater's theories to question the notion of authorial intent and the idea of a moral message behind art. The use of the form of the Platonic dialogue freed Wilde from moral responsibility: *Intentions* was to raise questions rather than to solve them, as Pater suggested true philosophy should do in 'Winckelmann'. It was *Dorian Gray* that was to push Pater's ideas to their extreme, where Lord Henry's beautiful 'yellow book' is seen to corrupt the impressionable Dorian. Wilde's work was viewed as contending that it is art that makes the man (and not the other way round). Although a reductive reading of the complexity of *Dorian Gray*, this contemporary reception saw to it that the novel itself was viewed as perniciously influential. Pater did not want his philosophical position to be associated with the reaction to Wilde's book, and, in a review in November 1891, Pater praised it but also criticized it, saying that Henry and Dorian lose 'too much in life to be a true Epicurean'.[122] Whereas Wilde was seen to overemphasize the influence of art on life, Pater underlined a more complex understanding of the influence of an older man's text over the life of a youth. That is to say, Pater's *Plato and Platonism*, written in the wake of the controversial publication of *Dorian Gray*, suggested that Plato's erotics crucially informed his philosophy but at the same time required maturing and development, just as Plato's texts were the seeds that have shaped modern men to teach and fashion themselves.

Wilde's gothic tale about Dorian Gray's narcissism, a disturbing story about the collapse of art and life into one another, provoked Pater to find a more positive model for his exhortation that one should make one's life a work of art. And so, with the publication of the fourth edition of *The Renaissance* (including 'Winckelmann' and the 'Conclusion', which broadcast that message), Pater used *Plato and Platonism* to depict another type of male love for the male form. That is to say, Pater depicted another type of Dorian. Wilde's 'Dorian'

----

[122] Pater (1891: 59–60).

alluded to Karl Otfried Müller's book *The Doric Race* and the discussion of pederasty in that volume, scholarship that Wilde knew well from Oxford.[123] Although this was a reference for only the most educated of Wilde's readers, Pater saw that the public image of Platonic love was in need of reformulation. And so Pater argued at length in *Plato and Platonism* about the importance of *Dorian* culture for Plato's *Republic*, a central text on the Oxford Greats syllabus. Chapter eight of Pater's book on Plato is an imaginary portrait of what a young Athenian student at Plato's Academy would have seen if he had visited ancient Sparta. 'Lacedæmon' appeared in the journal *Contemporary Review* in June 1892, only a year after *Dorian Gray* and seven months after his review of that novel. This essay was then inserted into *Plato and Platonism*, to be published in 1893.

Pater explicitly makes use of Müller's scholarship contesting Wilde's satirical notion that Dorian Gray might find his heritage in ancient pederastic Dorian society. In utilizing Müller's work, Pater offers another sort of link between ancient and modern masculinity, which develops upon his idea that Platonic philosophy was the seed from which modernity had grown. That is to say, Pater repeated Müller's inferences about the racial connections between ancient Dorian and modern white masculinity. Indeed, Müller's scholarship had become more widely accepted as the nineteenth century progressed, bolstering the 'Aryan Model' of ancient history.[124] We saw in Chapter how the academic philosophy of *Altertumswissenschaft* emphasized the possibility of recovering and accurately recording the lives of the ancients. This translation of information from primary source material into German scholarship was seen to reflect the Dorians' own exemplary pedagogic practices, which were a model of how to transmit knowledge from one generation to the next. Müller, however, was troubled by the meaning of Spartan παιδεραστία: just as the phonocentric nature of that relationship was viewed as exemplary

---

[123] See Cartledge (2001b). Evangelista (2009: 136) discusses Wilde's undergraduate essay 'Hellenism', which makes use of Müller's work on ancient Sparta. On the theme of narcissism in *Dorian Gray*, see most recently Craft (2005) and Ohi (2005).

[124] See Pater (1910: vi. 217): 'Patient modern research, following the track of a deep–rooted national tradition veiled in the mythological figments which centre in what is called "The Return of the Heraclidæ", reveals those northern immigrants or invaders, at various points on their way, dominant all along it.' See Shuter (1982) on Victorian scholarship on Dorians and Ionians. See Bernal (1987) on the 'Aryan Model'.

by Müller, so the lack of written records for what was actually said and done by pederastic partners ensured that including it within the historical record would remain impossible. Pater picks up on this difficulty of knowing ancient Sparta and the ensuing difficulty of knowing whether modern northern Europe could locate its ancestry there, reflecting his sophisticated discussion about the (non-)affinity between Germany and Greece in 'Winckelmann'. He emphasizes not only how little the nineteenth century knew about Sparta but also how sparse Plato's own knowledge was.[125] Both present and absent, exemplary and fragmentary, the influence of archaic Spartan society over Plato's classical ideal is seen to mirror the ancient world's complex influence over the modern. Pater's picture of Lacedæmonian education, which sought to make its young men into works of art, depicted a society both historical and imaginary, a society between real life and art, quite different from the world of *Dorian Gray*. And his translation of Müller's scholarship in his own beautifully written, highly artistic description, indeed a virtuoso example of Pater's prose, attempted to ensure that Dorian culture would be both historical example and impossible fantasy for modern boys and men in England's schools and universities. Pater's beautiful Dorians could not have been more different from Wilde's Dorian Gray.

Where Wilde simply did not mention Dorian's schooling and university days, only to concentrate on the contending Platonisms of Basil and Lord Henry over Dorian's young mind, Pater's portrait of the Spartans is almost entirely given over to their education. It was 'a peculiar kind of barrack life . . . a sort of military monasticism . . . The place of deference, of obedience, was large in the education of Lacedæmonian youth.' This was a strictly hierarchical society, 'a constant exhibition of youthful courage, youthful self-respect, yet above all of true youthful docility . . . an implicit subordination of the younger to the older [youth], in many degrees'.[126] At the same time as their enthralment to authority, Spartan youth were themselves served upon by slaves, who were '*Greeks*: no rude Scythians, nor crouching, decrepit Asiatics, like ordinary prisoners of war'.[127] Whereas at one moment the relationship between master and Helot is one that

---

[125] See Pater (1910: vi. 198, 234) on Plato's imaginative, romanticized depiction of the Spartans.
[126] Pater (1910: vi. 220, 206, 221).
[127] Pater (1910: vi. 204).

included 'a sort of bodily worship' by 'the young servitor' of his
'youthful lords', at another the 'personal beauty' of a slave 'was so
greatly prized' that 'his masters are in fact jealous of him'.[128] Pater
depicts a dark and violent world:

Whips and rods used in a kind of monitorial system by themselves had a
great part in the education of these young aristocrats, and, as pain surely
must do, pain not of bodily disease or wretched accidents, but as it were by
dignified rules of art, seemed to have refined them . . .

That common Greek worship of Apollo they made especially their own,
(but just here is the noticeable point), with a marked preference for the human
element in him . . . which resulted sometimes in an orgiastic, an unintellectual,
or even an immoral service. He remains youthful and unmarried . . . other
gods also are, so to speak, Apollinised, adapted to the Apolline presence;
Aphrodite armed, Enyalius fettered, perhaps that he may never depart thence.
Amateurs everywhere of the virile element in life . . . Lovers of youth they
remained . . . 'passing even the love of woman . . .'[129]

Pater's idiosyncratic picture contains close references to erotic, sado-
masochistic nineteenth-century writing, blurring the boundary between pleasure and pain.[130] Master—slave relationships, the whips
and rods, the orgiastic, unintellectual, and immortal reverence of
Apollo, Aphrodite in arms and Enyalius in fetters, make this very
clear. The worship of Apollo could not be more different from
Winckelmann's serene veneration in his *Geschichte*: the Spartan
Apollo looks altogether more Dionysian.[131] Pater's allusion to the
biblical tale of David and Jonathan (whose affection 'passed the love
of a woman' (2 Samuel 1: 26)) also reflects Pater's 1870s essays on
Demeter and Dionysus in which the latter's suffering is compared to
that of Christ.

At the same time, however, Pater's Spartans look very much like
English public-school boys. The Spartan youth was drilled in the
history of its nation 'as in our own classic or historic culture of
youth'.[132] The secluded exclusivity of Spartan education is mirrored

---

[128] Pater (1910: vi. 217, 205).

[129] Pater (1910: vi. 206, 227–8, 231).

[130] See Evangelista (2003b: 185).

[131] Note, however, that Winckelmann himself also observed the congruence between Apollonian and Dionysian religion, which influenced Pater in his story 'Apollo
in Picardy', which also appeared in 1893: see Dellamora (1990: 167–92, and 177 on
Winckelmann).

[132] Pater (1910: vi. 223).

in modern British schooling. Neither 'young Spartans' nor 'our own academic youth' are permitted to go to the market; furthermore, both ancient and modern boys have 'their "public school slang"'.[133] Indeed the monitorial system, the corporal punishment, and the intense competition, which included the highly charged and desirous hero-worship of older boys, were central to public-school mythology and practices.[134] Finally, Pater underlines the martial context of male love: 'The beloved and the lover, side by side through their long days of eager labour, and above all on the battlefield, became respectively, ἀΐτας, the hearer, and εἰσπνήλας, the inspirer . . .'.[135] Homer's theatres of war were scenes that boys built for imperial rule were taught to emulate.[136]

Pater's description, then, is a masterpiece in ambiguity. Pater's Sparta looks dangerously foreign and reassuringly familiar—looks both past and present. Pater paints a place that would be idealized by the English public-school system at the same time as being erotically alluring. It is hardly surprising that Pater's reception in the twentieth century should have been so contested: from repressed, to hesitantly homoerotic to affirmatively homosexual, and radical and revolutionary aesthete. Pater manages to find a space that would look both traditionalist and seductively subversive. We, however, do not need to locate a single meaning or message behind Pater's text. Instead we should note that Pater sought to depict a world of intense male love that fervently values the physicality of the male body *and* meets the approval of readers such as Benjamin Jowett. In such a way, then, Pater explicitly defends Plato's homoeroticism in the face of the hostility to the aestheticism of Wilde's *Dorian Gray*. Pater's aestheticism has become fully and explicitly masculinized: at the end of the portrait, Pater asks what the point is of 'this laborious, endless, education, which does not propose to give you anything very useful or enjoyable in itself? An intelligent young Spartan might have replied: "To the end that I myself may be a perfect work of art, issuing thus into the eyes of all Greece."'[137] Pater attempts to show a Greece where the nineteenth-century ideal of masculinity founded on work,

---

[133] Pater (1910: vi. 215, 222).
[134] See M. M. Martin (2002) and Weaver (2004) on Victorian schoolboy fiction.
[135] Pater (1910: vi. 231–2).
[136] Shuter (1997: 87).
[137] Pater (1910: vi. 232).

competition, and financial success could be dovetailed with an aesthetic masculinity that strove to be a work of art.[138] In a later chapter Pater makes explicit that this Spartan masculinity is to be distinguished from any contemporary pathologization of loving male relations, a condemnatory discourse that had been building through the 1880s, building upon the Christian fulminations of figures such as Tyrwhitt in the 1870s: 'Manliness in art' is to be opposed to what 'must be called the feminine quality . . . to what is literally incoherent or ready to fall to pieces, and, in opposition to what is hysteric'.[139] Ultimately Pater seeks to defend himself as 'a scholar, formed, mature and manly': he and his work are bolstered by *Altertumswissenschaft*, he is *gebildet*, and his desires are mature—Dorian, not quite those of erotic Platonic youth.[140] Pater's text, then, inhabits a historical moment in which it was possible to claim that erotic enjoyment in the male body should be commensurate with the pursuits of the imperial battlefield—that is, Pater was writing before the Wilde trial of 1895, which supposedly concretized and essentialized the 'homosexual' and his desires. Yet, in casting his Spartans as racial ancestors of his readers, personages recorded by history *and* half-known, fragmentary works of art that can be re-created only imaginatively, Pater already implicitly asked his readers, whether Dorian culture was a realizable possibility or an impossible ideal—what presence should Dorian culture have in nineteenth-century England? What might be the relationship between invisible Dorian works of art and visible modern male bodies?

Pater shows *Plato himself* already contending with these difficulties: how much could Spartan life actually be an influence on Athens or was it just a fantasy for the imagination? It is hardly surprising, then, that Platonic textuality should have produced so many contesting accounts of Jowett's and Pater's own masculinities and sexualities: Plato ultimately raised more questions than answers for these Victorian men and their readers. Pater's complex depiction of the Spartans (both racial—historical ancestors and artistic constructs) reflects his conceptualization of the relationship between ancient past and modern present: do (classical) texts create us or do we create classical texts

---

[138] See Evangelista (2009: 49) on normative Victorian models of masculinity. See also Adams (1995). Finally, see Shuter (1994: 499) for a brief mention of the ambiguity of Pater's prose.

[139] Pater (1910: vi. 280–1). On sexology in culture, beyond its scientific reception, see Bland and Doan (1998).

[140] Pater (1910: vi. 280).

when we receive them? The Spartans are portrayed both as a modern Englishman's racial heritage and as an invisible artistic ideal to be imagined and fashioned subjectively in the modern present. They are both tangible, muscular bodies and perfect works of art. Indeed, Pater's entire aesthetic theory stems from his reading of Plato, including Jowett's lessons. Jowett's dilemma about what to do with the Platonic text (read or rewrite the pederasty) put into urgent focus the question of what sort of presence the ancient world has in the modern. Were the pederastic contexts of the *Phaedrus* and the *Symposium* a sign of historical difference (the perfect object for *Altertumswissenschaft*) or a model for modern male relations (the example for *Bildung*)? That is to say, is it the task of modern scholarship to create the classical world in its texts, or was it the pederastic relationship of Plato's texts that founded a model for modern pedagogy, back to which modern scholarship could trace its roots? Again, do modern, nineteenth-century men create the texts of antiquity or do those texts create nineteenth-century men? Indeed Plato brought those questions up perhaps more urgently than other classical writers with his depiction of a teacher, Socrates, who teaches the reader to teach themselves. Between influence and reception, Plato's dialogues are both models for imitation and motors for self-fashioning and self-invention.

What is so interesting, finally, about Jowett's and Pater's readings of Plato is the complete avoidance of discussion about women's education in their work. From reading these two classicists, one would not believe that they were writing in a context of great upheaval at Oxford, and at Cambridge: the new presence of female students at British universities. Peter Hinchliff cites an anonymous 1897 article in *Blackwood's Edinburgh Magazine* that mentions Jowett's opposition to women undergraduates at Oxford, and he briefly discusses an 1874 memorandum by Jowett on university reform that suggests that higher education for the working classes and women could be located in England's industrial cities, but certainly not in Oxford.[141] As we have seen from Jowett's readings of Plato, even when he came to discuss marriage, his analysis turned into an analysis of male—male friendship. It is tantalizing to wonder whether Jowett had ever read Amy Levy's poem 'Xantippe' (1884) in which Socrates is thoroughly criticized for being such a poor husband and friend to his

---

[141] See Hinchliff (1987: 100, 150).

wife.[142] Furthermore, the possibility that *women* might be teachers and leaders is given very little attention. As Nathalie Bluestone has observed, Jowett and Pater (among others) downplayed and disregarded Plato's provocative proposals for women rulers and philosophers in his *Republic*.[143] Moreover, in his introduction to the *Symposium*, Jowett shows no interest in the fact that Socrates received his knowledge from a woman. Diotima is described as 'some Hebrew prophet or other Eastern sage'. Diotima's knowledge suggests to Jowett that 'the so-called mysticism of the East was not strange to the Greek of the fifth century before Christ'.[144] Jowett's casting of a woman's knowledge in racialized terms further reflects his difficulties in understanding how Plato's wisdom about love might relate to Victorian empire-builders. Pater's depiction of pedagogy is also an exclusively male homosocial scene. 'Winckelmann' continually values male over female beauty. And, in his *Plato and Platonism*, when he quotes from Diotima's speech, he does not even mention her name, saying instead: 'a certain Sibylline woman namely, from whose lips Socrates in the *Symposium* is supposed to quote what follows . . .'.[145] The possibility that Socrates and ultimately Plato could have learned from a woman is merely something that 'is supposed' to have happened. As we have seen, Pater the 'father' was far more interested in the metaphors of male pregnancy and impregnation.

The learning of Greek was seen in the Oxbridge context as a masculine pursuit. The arguments that raged from the 1870s about the compulsory Greek requirement at the ancient universities were linked to the debate about admission of women to higher education. Although Greek values were cultivated as universal, they were also seen as unique and individualizing (a paradox we have attended to in detail in this chapter). And this issue was reflected in discussions about educational opportunities in the Victorian (and Edwardian) period: Latin should be available for all, girls and boys, whereas Greek should be available for all gentle*men*.[146] Greek was often seen to 'unsex' women.[147] Isobel Hurst records the hostility of male undergraduates who were concerned over

[142] On Levy, see Olverson (2010: 54–82).
[143] Bluestone (1987: 5).
[144] Jowett (1892: i. 533, 532).
[145] Pater (1910: vi. 121).
[146] See Stray (1998: 162–3) and the essays in Stray (1999).
[147] See Olverson (2010: 15). See also Prins (1999a: 47–8) on the perceived maenadic qualities of women who read Greek at the end of the nineteenth century.

women reading works such as '*Oedipus Rex*, which is distinctly spicy in parts'. The 1888 undergraduate journal from which Hurst quotes goes on to discuss the comical embarrassment facing male lecturers explaining to female students the 'chaste complications' of Sophocles' play.[148] If the all-male homosocial teaching scene raised tricky questions, these were nothing compared to the problems raised between male tutor and female undergraduate.

Despite the opposition, women did gradually gain admittance into the universities, although on very unequal footing with men. And the year Jowett published his third edition of his Platonic dialogues, the year Pater wrote and published 'Lacedæmon', and the year that saw him write up his Plato lectures into *Plato and Platonism*, was also the year—1892—that saw Emily Penrose (later the Principal of Somerville) become the first woman to win a first in Greats.[149] Notwithstanding Penrose's achievement, the lack of Greek taught at girls' schools put female undergraduates at a significant disadvantage in the linguistic examinations in Oxford Moderations and Cambridge Tripos Part I. This encouraged women students and scholars to investigate other areas of the ancient world, especially its visual and material culture. Among the first generation of such intellectuals, Jane Harrison and Eugénie Sellers (later Strong) have become the most important and well known.[150] This exciting new fervour for classical art and archaeology was partly inspired by Pater's own interest in aesthetics. His essays were particularly informative for Harrison, and for the poets Katharine Bradley and Edith Cooper, aunt and niece who lived together in a close, loving, erotic relationship, writing under the name of Michael Field. The relationship between the elder Katharine and the younger Edith was envisaged in pederastic terms in at least one poem they wrote.[151]

Yet, despite the influence of Pater, it was not his work on Plato and pedagogy but his essays about the primitive, Bacchic rites of Dionysus and Demeter that mostly interested these writers and scholars.[152]

---

[148] Hurst (2007: 18).

[149] Hurst (2006: 97). Agnata Ramsey was the first woman to achieve a first-class result in Part I of the Cambridge Classical Tripos in 1887 (see Hurst 2006: 88).

[150] See Beard (2000), Hurst (2006: 89–92), Evangelista (2009: 75–80), and Olverson (2010: 22–4).

[151] See Olverson (2010: 120–1).

[152] See Prins (1999a; 1999b: 74–111), Evangelista (2009: 93–124), and Olverson (2010: 111–44).

And, although Pater's work offered these women space for thought, he was in the end not enough. Harrison notes in her *Reminiscences of a Student's Life* (published in 1925) that, having once visited the Oxford don, she found a 'soft, kind cat' who 'purred so persuasively that I lost the sense of what he was saying'.[153] The symbolic difficulty of understanding and applying Pater's Greek knowledge to the female scholarly and literary domain was also reflected in Katharine Bradley's journal published posthumously in 1933: 'One sentence of Mr Pater's which I would not say I could never forgive, because I recognised its justice; but from which I suffered, and which was hard to bear—that in which he speaks of the scholarly conscience as male.'[154] The problems in locating a positively feminine subjectivity from ancient Greece were a constant theme for 'Michael Field', two women in a relationship together writing as one man, 'Michael Field', who had adopted the voice of Sappho. Finally, we may note that Vernon Lee's (Violet Paget's) writing, which has often been seen as produced under the influence of Pater's aestheticism, was also highly critical of Pater's male, homosocial, narrow Hellenism.[155]

Pater's relationship with women and feminist politics is complex. Some scholars have found Pater protesting against the social and political marginalization of women in his scholarship, whereas others have seen his female characters in his fiction as two-dimensional, overly simplistic stereotypes.[156] Indeed, Pater's relationships with his sisters, Clara and Hester, are rarely mentioned by Pater's readers. And it is perplexing to square the absence of women from *Plato and Platonism* with the important presence of these sisters in Pater's life, especially since Clara read both Latin and Greek and coached female students in classics at Somerville and taught Virginia Woolf among others at the ladies' department in King's College, London. She was active on the Committee of Oxford Lectures for Ladies from about 1873 onwards, as well as being an active participant and committee member of the Association for Promoting the Higher Education of Women in Oxford, founded in 1878. Finally she also

---

[153] Harrison (1925: 46).

[154] Field (1933: 137).

[155] See Evangelista (2009: 55–92). It seems that Bradley is referring to the moment in *Plato and Platonism* when he talks of art being produced by 'a scholar, formed, mature and manly' (Pater 1910: vi. 280).

[156] Dellamora (1990) for Pater's protests and B. A. Inman (1991) on Pater's two-dimensional women.

served as a term as Acting Principal of Somerville College in the autumn of 1880.[157] The precise contours of Walter's and Clara's relationship remain mysterious. From an undergraduate letter saying that 'Miss Pater' was one of the agents of the expulsion of Hardinge from Balliol, Billie Inman has proposed that 'Clara or Hester Pater happened to see in Walter's room letters written by Hardinge', and, fearing that her brother would be disgraced, saw to it that Jowett received the letters.[158] Although we cannot verify this account, it demonstrates the exclusivity of Oxford's homosocial environment: we can only speculate upon what Oxford women knew about Platonic love in the 1870s. At this moment in our story, we have very little information about what women (mothers, sisters, and friends) might have taught their sons and brothers about love. As we shall see, the Freudian stereotype of the mother's dangerously overbearing influence over her son has not yet entered the debate. The knowledge of wives and mothers will also become an important concern, as we shall see, with Wilde and Forster.

Finally, just as Pater's relationship with women and feminism is difficult, what his lessons about male love might teach young men is also problematic. As we examined, Pater situated his discussion of Spartan love in a military context, founded upon the institution of slavery and imperialist encounters. Furthermore, his explicit use of Müller's scholarship would, by the end of the nineteenth century, be seen as a valorization of white, north European masculinity. And so, just as Pater's Dorians seem like an irrecoverable fragment from the past *and* an example for the present, so Pater himself has seemed like an eternally lost moment of masculinity and an inspiration for contemporary gay sensibilities. His discourse of the aesthetic has been viewed as directly influential over the persona of the homosexual aesthete from the *fin de siècle* onwards into the twentieth century and beyond.[159] Yet at the same time, his aesthetics should be contextualized within their moment. They are ultimately an aesthetics that takes a social and sexual pleasure from the imperial encounter: Pater revels in the possibility that men can be masters over slaves. We should not forget that Pater was writing at a time when the decline of Anglicanism as a central institutional feature of the Oxbridge system

---

[157] Brake (2004). Hester's biography remains unwritten.
[158] B. A. Inman (1991: 13). See Shuter (1994: 488) for further discussion.
[159] Evangelista (2009: 35–6).

saw to it that Britain's imperial subjects (African, Indian, and Caribbean) would potentially be able to attend the universities, a possibility that pamphlets such as the 1891 *The Moslem in Cambridge* worried about.[160] Although it is not possible to ascertain Pater's precise views about female education and British imperialism, his Spartans remain problematic for a gay heritage. As we shall see in Chapter 4, Pater's enslaving, virile Spartans will provide erotic allure *and* anxiety in E. M. Forster's novel *Maurice*. Furthermore, Pater's paean to the hyper-virile Spartans could never be a straightforward depiction of modern masculinity after Oscar Wilde's trials, which occurred only two years after *Plato and Platonism* was published. Before we get to the Wilde trial in 1895, however, we now need to turn to another of Jowett's students, John Addington Symonds, who learnt a very different lesson from his Greek tutor.

---

[160] See Stray (1998: 163–4).

3

The Case of John Addington Symonds

a stifled anachronism

(John Addington Symonds, *Memoirs*, 1984)

John Addington Symonds's *Memoirs* have been called 'the single most important surviving document of nineteenth-century homoeroticism'.[1] And in this document we get a view of Jowett's teaching scene. Although Pater finds it possible to make a great deal of use out of Jowett's teachings and texts, Symonds's depiction makes Jowett's pedagogy seem perhaps stranger than we might have imagined. In tutorials, Symonds writes, Jowett

said very little and gave me no tips. But somehow he made me comprehend what I had to aim at, and how I had to go about it. The contact of his mind enabled me to use my reading in Greek for the purpose of writing. We learn not so much by what is dictated to us or by set instruction as by sympathy and effused influence.[2]

Symonds presents the tutorial in mysterious terms. It is not even clear that he can remember how he even learnt: '*somehow* he made me comprehend.' It seems that there was a mystical bond between master and pupil, 'contact of the mind . . . sympathy and effused influence'. Jowett, apparently, did not require words to teach his pupil. His lack of loquacity made him a revered priest-like but altogether enigmatic figure. Symonds pictures himself trying to pry Jowett open, in order to reveal the secrets within. Symonds is describing what Abbott and Campbell, Jowett's early biographers, called, 'Jowett-worship'.[3]

---

[1] W. Davis (1999: 188).   [2] Symonds (1984: 225).
[3] Abbott and Campbell (1897: i. 126).

Not unselfconsciously, Symonds makes himself look like Alcibiades to Jowett's Socratic *agalma*. And, just as Symonds seeks to historicize Jowett's pedagogy for his reader, so he ends up mythologizing it, and putting it beyond his memory: '*somehow* he made me comprehend . . .'. Just as we saw Pater responding to the slipperiness of Jowett's teaching, so Symonds re-presents that scene in equally elusive terms: how *did* Jowett's Platonic pedagogy produce homoerotic Platonists? It seems that Symonds is unable to remember that for the historical record. The Platonic—pedagogic context for the production of Symonds's knowledge ('the contact of his mind enabled me to use my reading in Greek for the purpose of writing'—this very *Memoir*) remains beyond historical understanding.

Jowett's taciturnity is, however, contrasted with his verbosity over the subject of ancient Greek love, which proved a great concern to Symonds. Jowett had planned to write an essay specifically on Greek love in his new edition of *The Dialogues of Plato* (that is, the third edition in 1892, the edition we were reading in the previous chapter). In 1888, Jowett visited Symonds, who was by this time living in Switzerland. As Evangelista has uncovered, Jowett notes in his notebooks for that year that their conversations were certainly charged and intense: 'Their conversation culminated in a moment of great emotional intensity when Symonds kissed the astonished Jowett on the lips and then on his hand.'[4] Symonds's purpose is now no longer clear, but we read in a letter reproduced in the *Memoirs*, written in 1889, to his 'dear Master: I am glad to hear from the last letter you wrote me that you have abandoned the idea of an essay on Greek love. Little good could come of such a treatise in your book'. Symonds continues: 'the study of Plato is injurious to a certain number of [erotically] predisposed young men . . . When, therefore, individuals of the indicated species come into contact with the reveries of Plato . . . the effect upon them has the force of a revelation.'[5] Whereas the 'contact' between Jowett and Symonds was one of 'the mind . . . sympathy and effusive influence,' the 'contact' with Plato for some young men who are predisposed to erotic desires for other men is a real danger. 'What you call a figure of speech, is heaven in hell to him—maddening, because it is stimulating to the imagination; wholly out of accord with the world he has to live in: too deeply in accord

---

[4] Evangelista (2007a: 221).   [5] Symonds (1984: 100).

with his own impossible desires'.[6] Interestingly, then, Jowett is presented as the pedagogue all too keen to effuse on the topic of ancient Greek love, but Symonds the homosexual is eager to avoid mention of the topic, precisely because of the impossibility of reliving the ancient Greek experience. Symonds's letter to Jowett underlines the *difficulty of understanding the Platonic text*: 'Eros Pandemos is everywhere. Plato lends the light, the gleam, that never was on sea or shore. Thus Plato delays the damnation of these souls by ensnaring the noblest part of them—their intellectual imagination'.[7] Whereas Pater seemed to celebrate the polyphonic nature of the Platonic texts, Symonds feels that they were perilous for their readers precisely because they unleashed the 'intellectual imagination'. Jowett, a modern Socrates, would endanger the minds of the young. As always, then, the Platonic encounter was one at which one had to be present. Its relation to history, to the processes of historicization, was to remain problematic.

This chapter addresses the case study of John Addington Symonds. The rediscovery of his *Memoirs* in the archives of the London Library and their subsequent publication have ensured, for many, a securer history of modern homosexuality: from reading Symonds we might even come to identify with him. His *Memoirs*, being currently one of the very few, pre-twentieth-century first-person accounts of an individual who was sexually attracted to members of their own sex, unsurprisingly, has become an *exemplary* document for modern gay people and gay historiographers. But this exemplarity that comes with reading and sympathizing with Symonds's biography bears a risk, for two specific reasons. First, bearing witness to the 'truth' of his (homo)sexuality involves an investment in the sexological theory, which Symonds himself found so troubling. As we shall see, his histories of Greek aesthetics and desires will *not* help to prove the theorems of contemporary sexology. The making of Symonds into a 'case study', then, risks viewing his case history as paradigmatic and exemplary of Victorian male homosexuality. Symonds, however, considered himself a little more unusual, as we shall see. Indeed, the rarity of first-person accounts in the form of lengthy, detailed memoirs from the nineteenth century makes it difficult even to suggest that Symonds was in fact exemplary in any realistic, empirical sense. We should, then, be more cautious, circumspect, and self-aware

---

[6] Symonds (1984: 102).   [7] Symonds (1984: 101).

about how and who gets our label 'homosexual'. Secondly, it is risky to exemplify and identify (with) Symonds as The Victorian Homosexual, precisely because he himself found it so difficult to identify (with) ancient Greeks, their desires and sexual practices. Ancient Greek culture offered the well-read Symonds highly conflicting paradigms of exemplary Greek love, rather than a utopia of a homosexual identity. Symonds expressed to Jowett grave concern about what happened to a boy when he read Greek. In this chapter, we will use Symonds as a case study for *that* problematic. That is to say, what happened to Symonds, a Victorian boy, when he read Greek? What desires or paradigms of self and sociability did that reading provide him with? Rather than ancient Greek culture offering a solution to the enigma of one's (sexual) identity, Greek arts and literature confronted Symonds with some bewildering questions about his identity and his place in history. Greek love will be no straightforward metaphor, or 'open secret', for a hidden and repressed homosexuality. Rather Symonds's investment in Greek, as providing the building blocks of one's sense of self as his teacher Jowett taught him, will cause Symonds to ponder very deeply on which aspects of Greek culture really do and do not form one's character. What we should hold on to, when we read Symonds, is how easy it was to misread, and how tricky it was to understand, classical Greek texts and images. Without proper tuition, a boy could let his imagination run wild: reading an essay by Jowett would not be enough. It is the *difficulty* of Greek that Symonds will emphasize. It will never be easy for him to identify with ancient Greek culture. This chapter will consider Symonds's account of his desires in his recently published *Memoirs*, followed by a discussion of two scholarly essays, 'The Genius of Greek Art' and *A Problem in Greek Ethics*. If exemplifying anything, Symonds's life and work will exemplify the Victorian obsession with the belief that we might become who we are from learning to read and view ancient Greek culture.

THE TRUTH OF SYMONDS'S MEMOIRS

Symonds, who expressed his worry about boys reading Plato, had already proven his point in his *Memoirs* about the revelatory experience of reading Greek philosophy. Early in the narrative of the *Memoirs*, he remembers the following scene:

We were reading Plato's *Apology* in the sixth form. I bought Cary's crib and took it with me to London on an *exeat* in March. My hostess, a Mrs Bain, who lived in Regent's Park, treated me to a comedy one evening at the Haymarket... When we returned from the play, I went to bed and began to read my Cary's Plato. It so happened that I stumbled on the *Phaedrus*. I read on and on, till I reached the end. Then I began the *Symposium*; and the sun was shining on the shrubs outside the ground-floor in which I slept, before I shut the book up.[8]

We seem to have been given access to a most private moment in the formation of a Victorian individual, a scene of nocturnal, clandestine reading. It is hardly surprising, then, that historians should have considered Symonds's autobiography such a significant document. Nevertheless, we should perhaps be cautious about what we think we might be recovering and discovering. Bearing in mind what Foucault has said about the 'truth' of sexuality, what does it mean to discover (the truth of) Symonds's sexuality? Phyllis Grosskurth, the editor of the *Memoirs*, discusses her own discovery of the autobiographical manuscript while researching for her Ph.D. at the University of London. When Symonds's literary executor, Horatio Brown, died in 1926, he bequeathed the manuscript to the London Library with instructions that it not be published until 1976, fifty years after his death. The rhetoric of the exploration and discovery of the manuscript that mark Grosskurth's account designedly suggest to the reader that very few people had even clapped eyes on Symonds's memoirs, and that Grosskurth's publication does indeed mark a significant event in the history of Symonds studies in its public revelation of new material from the depths of the archive. Grosskurth's voyage of discovery romantically begins:

Some years ago, rummaging in a second-hand bookshop in Broadstairs, I chanced upon a copy of H. F. Brown's 1895 biography of John Addington Symonds... I bought the book, took it back to my hotel and sat up most of the night reading it. Why, I kept wondering, did Brown... choose to write a biography of Symonds comprised largely of excerpts from Symonds's autobiography, rather than simply publish the autobiography?[9]

---

[8] Symonds (1984: 99).   [9] Symonds (1984: 9).

Interestingly, Grosskurth's discovery of Symonds's biography mimics Symonds's discovery of Plato: Grosskurth 'chanced upon' the biography of Symonds, which she read for 'most of the night', just as Symonds 'stumbled on' Plato, which he read until the following morning. And, just as Symonds had not been taught all of Plato, so Grosskurth had not been told the full story about Symonds. Grosskurth's subsequent discovery of Symonds's homosexuality replicates Symonds's own discovery of Plato. Her narrative of discovery—the very words that open her edition—programmes the reader of the *Memoirs*: Symonds's sexuality is the truth of this archive, just as the erotic pleasures lay at the heart of the truth of the Platonic texts.

Despite Grosskurth's notable editorial achievements, other readers have also shown scepticism about what sorts of truths are depicted in this text. Sarah Heidt observes that Symonds describes his subjectivity as split, between an inner (private) and an outer (public) self: 'It has been my destiny to make continual renunciation of my truest self, because I was born out of sympathy with the men around me, and have lived a stifled anachronism.'[10] And yet Grosskurth herself, as Heidt examines, ends up dissecting Symonds's subjectivity more exhaustively than Victorian society could ever have done, despite being 'in the grip of a compulsion to unearth everything about the man I could possibly find'.[11] Indeed, her outing of the (sexual) truth of Symonds was more of a production of that truth. Although Grosskurth fully admits to cutting out parts of the manuscript for her edition, she is not entirely truthful about what suffered under the editor's knife. Most potently, as Heidt discusses, 'she silences Symonds's own reflections on how (or even whether) autobiographies can speak truly about their subjects'. As she shows, Symonds ponders with great concern that an autobiography 'has to be supplemented . . . in order that a perfect portrait may be painted of the man'.[12] Furthermore, Symonds noted that the autobiographer was handicapped by the fact that 'no man can see himself as others see him'.[13] And it was the very documents 'supplementing' Symonds's *Memoirs* that Grosskurth excised for her edition. That is to say, Symonds's manuscript is a composite item

---

[10] Symonds (1984: 218). See also (1984: 82, 86). See Heidt (2003: 16).
[11] Symonds (1984: 9).
[12] Symonds, quoted in Heidt (2003: 8).
[13] Symonds, quoted in Heidt (2003: 17).

comprising his autobiography with other accounts of Symonds's life by other people who knew him, included in the manuscript so that they might '"correct" his account of himself'.[14] Grosskurth's edition covers over the fact that Symonds 'found it impossible or at least undesirable to represent the "truth" of his inner self without recourse to others' supplementary or "corrective" accounts'. Paradoxically, then, 'those textual materials connected to Symonds's external self' become 'the innermost secrets of the manuscript'.[15] Whereas Grosskurth's edition depicts a Symonds who must hide the full truth of himself from his wife, the manuscript sitting in the London Library actually includes two long diary entries by Catherine Symonds, through which Symonds 'lets "Catherine herself... speak"', which 'provide[s] a crucial corrective to his self-representation'.[16] As Heidt discusses, the manuscript shows that 'his internal and external selves are indissolubly interconnected and cannot be neatly schematized as true and false existences; instead Symonds presents both himself and his autobiographical text as composites of uneasily coexistent, disparately true affective lives'.[17]

With this in mind, then, let us return to the moment when Symonds uncovers the Platonic dialogues that were not prescribed study for the sixth form. Indeed Symonds's rhetoric of accidental discovery is very deliberate and considered. The fortuitous finding of Plato's *Symposium* and *Phaedrus* is designed to depict a scene whereby one is uncovering an intact past, an uncovering that the discoverer has in no way anticipated or invented. The truth of Symonds's memoirs and Plato's dialogues were just lying there in the archive, waiting to be received in the hands of its discoverer. Symonds's sexual orientation, as he perceives it, was, apparently, in no way influenced by his reading of Plato. Rather, as Symonds constructs his narrative, Plato simply confirms and acts as proof of what Symonds already knew/suspected. (We, of course, saw that, for Jowett and Pater, on the other hand, Plato's texts could not help but be influential, open to 'numerous applications'.) Symonds's very identity, as he narrates it, is a 'congenital' affair, not at all shaped by

---

[14] Symonds, quoted in Heidt (2003: 17).
[15] Heidt (2003: 19).
[16] Heidt (2003: 26).
[17] Heidt (2003: 26). Grosskurth does, however, include one long entry of Catherine's diary (Symonds 1984: 160–2).

the reading and study of ancient texts. And, yet, the artifice of Symonds's account of his Platonic midnight snack is paraded in his allusion to the closure of the *Symposium* itself: just as Socrates went on into the following morning discussing the relationship between tragedy and comedy, so Symonds supposedly read these dialogues until 'the sun was shining on the shrubs'. Just as the *Symposium* ends with the comic entrance of Alcibiades, with his satyric portrait of Socrates and with Socrates' own discussion of theatre, so Symonds's reading of that dialogue is prefaced by a comedy at the Haymarket. Furthermore, Symonds's narrative is constructed with a highly symbolic trajectory in mind: he depicts himself as moving away from the *Apology*, the text in which Socrates answers his accusers' charges of introducing new gods and, more significantly, corrupting Athenian youths, towards the Platonic texts of beauty and pleasure, *Phaedrus* and *Symposium*. The sun 'shining on the shrubs' has us imagine Symonds as being reborn in this bright new morning:

Here in the *Phaedrus* and the *Symposium*...I discovered the true *liber amoris* at last, the revelation I had been waiting for, the consecration of a long-cherished idealism. It was just as though the voice of my own soul spoke to me through Plato, as though in some antenatal experience I had lived the life of [a] philosophical Greek lover.[18]

If in a past life Symonds was living in classical Athens, he has now been resurrected to live again. This morning witnessed the emergence of a new Symonds, in the 'sixth form' (as he says), on the cusp of manhood, an *ephebe*, undergoing a *rite de passage*. As Symonds paints it, this night was pivotal:

The study of Plato proved decisive for my future. Coming at the moment when it did, it delivered me to a large extent from the torpid cynicism caused by the Vaughan episode. At the same time it confirmed my congenital inclination toward persons of the male sex, and filled my head with an impossible dream, which controlled my thoughts for many years.[19]

The rhetoric of deliverance portrays 'the study of Plato' as a salvation from the brutal and abusive sexual regime of Harrow, overlooked by the pederastic headmaster, Charles Vaughan. Indeed chapter five, in

---

[18] Symonds (1984: 160–2).   [19] Symonds (1984: 100).

which this episode is situated, opens with an explicit, but no less rhetorical, description of the 'moral state' of Harrow when Symonds attended it: 'Every boy of good looks had a female name, and was recognised either as a public prostitute or as some bigger fellow's "bitch".'[20] But there is a marked tension in the possible realization of 'a long-cherished idealism': that is, it is 'an impossible dream'. On the one hand, the reality of who Symonds is becomes confirmed; yet, on the other hand, 'the study of Plato' merely filled Symonds's head with 'an impossible dream', merely a vision of what could never really be. We can see, then, that the experience of reading Plato was not actually confirmatory of a 'congenital inclination', but really foundational in the retrospective invention of Symonds's identity, his writing of his *Memoirs*. 'The study of Plato' did not simply evidence Symonds's 'inclination'; it actively 'filled [the] head' of Symonds, profoundly influencing and shaping who he thought he was. Indeed, Symonds says as much himself: '*For the first time* I saw the possibility of resolving in a practical harmony the discords of my instincts. I perceived that masculine love had its virtue as well as its vice, and stood in this respect upon the same ground as normal sexual appetite.'[21]

Symonds can only know himself—he can only know what he desires—*through the study of Plato*. It is not simply, as the Foucauldian argument makes clear, that one's sexuality produces the inner truth of history (here, Symonds's secret sexual desires form the truth of autobiography). It is also the historical archive itself (Plato's dialogues) that produces the inner truth of sexuality. The textuality of the historical archive produces sexuality just as much as sexuality produces the historical archive, his need to write his *Memoirs*. Symonds the boy reading Plato is both the product and the producer of history: he is the boy, who comes at the end of a long line of men who love men as defined by Plato (product of history); and he is also the historian, who understands the history of male–male love ('I understood, or thought I understood'[22]—producer of history). The discovery of his sexuality is also the discovery of the archive of

---

[20] Symonds (1984: 94).
[21] Symonds (1984: 99), emphases added. Buckton (1998: 79–80) has also observed the literariness of Symonds's 'conversion'-to-homosexuality narrative: it also alludes to Augustine's *Confessions* and Newman's *Apologia Pro Vita Sua*.
[22] Symonds 1984: 99).

sexuality. The boy who desires to know is at the same time the historian who knows how to desire. Event and the archive of that event coincide: he is the character in the story—the boy reading Plato—but also the learned historian always already, the boy–historian reading Plato correctly. Symonds reflects Pater's complex account of the relationship between ancient textuality and modern sexuality in his essay 'Winckelmann' and his reading of Plato. Is it Symonds's sexuality that permits him special access into the ancient text; does his sexuality create the ancient text? Or was it Platonic textuality that told, and explained to him, his sexuality?[23]

The issue of the successful discovery of the 'truth' of Symonds's sexuality is also a theme of Oliver Buckton's analysis, who has also questioned what should count as the truth in Symonds's document.[24] Buckton has discussed the Vaughan episode (alluded to above) in some detail. He argues that the autobiography is a 'duplicitous text', in the sense that a 'central part of the work of the *Memoirs* . . . is the displacement of transgressive desires onto other characters in the narrative, figures that are constructed for their own rhetorical project of sexual self-definition'.[25] That is to say, Symonds constructs a dichotomy between the Platonic model of same-sex desire and the 'dark figure of sexual exploitation' embodied by 'C. F. Vaughan, headmaster of Harrow School'. Buckton discusses how 'Vaughan functions

---

[23] Symonds knew Pater's aesthetic writings well: see Evangelista (2009: 129–39). There is actually an earlier literary scene, Symonds's reading of *Venus and Adonis*. Until then, Symonds had dreamed of 'shaggy and brawny sailors', but, on reading Shakespeare's poem, he started dreaming of Adonis. As with the Plato scene, the literary text does not simply confirm an already present sexuality; it also teaches Symonds how to desire: Venus' 'hot wooing taught me what it was to woo with sexual ardour' (Symonds 1984: 63). Symonds concludes: 'Character might be described as the product of inborn proclivities *and* external circumstance' (here literary texts) (emphases added). In a note that follows this section on his early sexual feelings and his reading of Shakespeare's poem, Symonds observes fascinatingly that he 'was not aware how important they [these recollections of my earliest sexual impressions] were for the proper understanding of *vita sexualis*', since he 'had not then studied the works of Moreau, Tarnowski, [and] Krafft-Ebing' (Symonds 1984: 63–4). Symonds, then, had to be taught what counted as the truth, as truthful autobiography, a truth that was recognizable as such only in retrospection. We should also note that Venus the female teacher of the boy is a model of pedagogy in which Symonds learnt to identify with Venus in the poem. And it is not accidental that this poem should have been so meaningful to Symonds: the object of desire, the ancient Adonis, moves tantalizingly in and out of the arms of the (modern) lover.
[24] See Buckton (1998: 64–9), with his criticisms of Koestenbaum (1989).
[25] Buckton (1998: 69).

in the narrative as the first in a series of "doubles" for Symonds himself, acting out explicitly pederastic desires which Symonds could not, for various reasons, acknowledge himself and which become an obsessively recurring theme of the autobiography'.[26]

During the chapter on Harrow, Symonds relates how, during the last year at Harrow, 'in the month of January 1858 Alfred Pretor wrote me a note in which he informed me that Vaughan had begun a love affair with him. I soon found that the boy was not lying, because he showed me a series of passionate letters written to him by our headmaster'.[27] Symonds did not reveal the information he now possessed. Only later at Oxford did Symonds open up. Symonds had become quite friendly with his Latin tutor, John Conington, who, notes Symonds altogether ambiguously, 'sympathized with romantic attachments for boys'.[28] Conington (who held the chair of Latin) had passed on to Symonds a copy of a poetry book entitled *Ionica*, first published in 1858 by William Johnson (later Cory), a book that contained several poems on pederastic subjects. One afternoon in the summer of 1859, while on a reading trip in the Lake District, Symonds 'was talking . . . with Conington about *Ionica* and what I then called Arcadian love'. During this conversation, Symonds revealed 'Vaughan's story' to his Latin tutor. According to Symonds, Conington said: 'My father ought to know the fact, whatever happened.'[29] And so Symonds informs his father of the letters he had received, and Dr Symonds promptly contacts Vaughan to suggest he retire from Harrow quickly. Symonds's own feelings were, he records, deeply mixed. On the one hand, he has polarized his Platonic desires and those of the other Harrow boys. On the other hand, however, he also 'felt a deeply rooted sympathy with Vaughan'.[30]

As Buckton explains, this polarization between the Platonic Symonds and the pederastic Vaughan collapses later in the *Memoirs*, when Symonds (a fellow at Magdalen, Oxford) finds himself being blackmailed by a younger man at Oxford, C. G. H. Shorting, who came into possession of Symonds's correspondence that suggested that he shared Shorting's desires for choirboys. Although Shorting

[26] Buckton (1998: 72).   [27] Symonds (1984: 97).
[28] Symonds (1984: 109).   [29] Symonds (1984: 110–11).
[30] Symonds (1984: 112).

had sent extracts to six Magdalen fellows, Symonds was not judged to have transgressed any rules. Nevertheless the near scandal propelled Symonds out of Oxford, out of a conventional academic career. Buckton observes: 'It was by means of a letter that Symonds had discovered Vaughan's relationship with Pretor at Harrow; and it is by means of Symonds's own incriminating letters that Shorting attempts to ruin his reputation at Oxford.'[31] Indeed, by the end of the *Memoirs*, Symonds comes to look like Vaughan all the more, when he becomes engaged in a relationship with Norman Moor, a Bristol sixth-former: 'It was for Moor's sake that Symonds took steps to get a teaching appointment at Clifton School, where he delivered the series of lectures on Greek literature that would eventually be published as *Studies of the Greek Poets* (1873–76).'[32] Grosskurth's edition of the *Memoirs* leaves the very last word to Moor himself, in appendix four, a letter from Moor to Symonds, in which the former young beloved (who later married and became a schoolmaster himself) writes that 'the paiderastic instinct...was not in any way caused by the reading of G[ree]k lit[erature], but was rather chastened and directed by a literary education'.[33] Grosskurth's edition, then, ultimately redeems Symonds's troubled desires. But Buckton underlines 'Symonds's attempt to split his sexual self into two distinct personae—one secretive and sinister, the other aesthetic and idealized'.[34]

We can push this analysis further to suggest that it was the competing *exempla* provided by ancient Greek culture and literature that were the source of Symonds's problems of self-definition. That is to say, Symonds presents himself as enjoying *both* Ionic, pederastic relationships with youths *and* Doric, comradely relationships with highly virile men. One of the best-known scenes in the *Memoirs* is a description of a sexual encounter Symonds has 'with a brawny young soldier'. Their relations, Symonds describes, were 'comradely and natural...I thoroughly enjoyed the close vicinity of that splendid naked piece of manhood'.[35] And, at the end of the *Memoirs*, we see Symonds settling into a longer-term relationship with the gondolier Angelo Fusato, a man much younger than Symonds, but a man

[31] Buckton (1998: 93). [32] Buckton (1998: 95).
[33] Symonds (1984: 297). [34] Buckton (1998: 91).
[35] Symonds (1984: 253–4).

whom Symonds describes in highly virile terms. Symonds's assignation with the soldier mirrors the sex scene he describes with Norman Moor. Rather than use the Whitmanesque vocabulary of comradeship, here it is Moor's youth that is emphasized: 'Shy and modest, tender in the beauty-bloom of ladhood, is his part of sex . . . the lad turns pleadingly into my arms as though he sought to be relieved of some delicious pang.'[36] At some points in the narrative, then, Symonds is the pederast, whereas at others he is 'an *"anderastes"'* (a man-lover) with 'a passion for soldiers'.[37]

Symonds's ambivalent reaction to Vaughan neatly reflects his complex identification with ancient Greek desires: the sexuality of an elder generation of men—the sexuality of the past—is one that repulses Symonds but also one with which he feels (using a Greek word) 'sympathy'. Just like Pater and Winckelmann before him, Symonds would feel both close to and distant from ancient Greece. Indeed, his conflicted feelings about relationships between an elder man and boy are reflected in his horror, on the one hand, about Vaughan, and his happy acceptance of a pederastic poetry book from John Conington. Furthermore, it is the relationship between the bodies of lovers and their inscribed letters of love that returns here, an issue we have already explored with Jowett and Pater. That is to say, physical relationships between men and boys were imagined and realized through texts, through the letters between Vaughan and Pretor, the poetic letters Conington passed on to Symonds, and the letters Symonds supposedly wrote about Magdalen choristers.

Other historians have also noticed Symonds's quite particular subjectivity. In his essay on child sexuality in Victorian Oxford, George Rousseau discusses Symonds's 'attraction to the 11-year-old chorister Walter Goolden', along with other adult males who had relations (of whatever sort) with boys. Rousseau does not diagnose these individuals as '(in our sense) paedophiles: two men in their early twenties attracted to pubescent boys without whom they have physical–genital relations'.[38] But at the same time Rousseau inevitably gets himself into definitional difficulties, describing such men's sexuality as 'child love . . . or some other phenomenon for which we have no

---

[36] Symonds (1984: 210).
[37] Symonds (1984: 192). The term *anderastes* is, of course, not classical Greek. It is made up by Symonds's friend Claude Cobham.
[38] Rousseau (2007c: 179).

name'.[39] Yet a few pages later Rousseau can say that 'Symonds was doubtlessly homosexual',[40] although earlier in the essay he had already remarked upon 'the Victorian riddle about same-sex relations'.[41]

In *Plato and Platonism* Pater wrote about a Dorian and an Ionian strain of Greek culture, following Müller's definitions: Ionian reflected an eastern Mediterranean mentality associated primarily with the modernity of Athens, whereas Dorian culture was seen as archaic and conservative. We can also note that Pater's Plato was particularly invested in improving the Athenian state using the model of Sparta. And so, just as Pater sought to clear his aestheticism of any detrimental charges of hedonism and effeminacy in the 1890s, so Pater's Plato sought to redefine male–male love, away from an 'Ionian or Asiatic tendency' towards a more 'effectual desire towards the Dorian order and *ascêsis*'.[42] In his defence of Platonic homoeroticism Pater sought to correlate it with Western, manly, virile love, and to distance it from effeminate, orientalizing connotations.

By the 1850s, it seems, the Ionian/Dorian polarity had entered the vocabulary of the homosocial institutions of Oxford and Cambridge. And the evidence from Symonds's *Memoirs* seems to suggest that 'Ionian' implied pederastic relations, as attested in ancient Athens, whereas 'Dorian' involved two virile men. The *Memoirs* make clear that William Johnson's *Ionica* was being passed between tutors and students at Oxford. Johnson (later Cory) was a Classics master at Eton, 'a born teacher who was "apt to make favourites"', as one historian has euphemistically noted.[43] In 1872, Johnson was asked to leave Eton in mysterious circumstances. Some have read between the lines to suggest that this was due to improper relationships with his pupils, whereas others have suggested that yet again an incriminating letter was involved.[44] It is hardly surprising, then,

---

[39] Rousseau (2007c: 183).

[40] Rousseau (2007c: 186).

[41] Rousseau (2007c: 181). See Rousseau (2007b) on relations between dons and undergraduates in Georgian Oxford.

[42] Pater (1910: vi. 103, 110).

[43] D'Arch Smith (1970: 4), quoting A. C. Benson's introduction to his 1905 edition of *Ionica*.

[44] Honey (1977: 190). See also Kaplan (2005: 109–65). After leaving Eton, Johnson took women as private pupils. Hurst (2006: 68–9) notes that Johnson sometimes scandalized his new students with the eroticism of the poetry they read—Catullus in particular.

that Johnson's *Ionica* 'went straight to my [Symonds's] heart and inflamed my imagination'.[45] Privately printed in 1858, Johnson's verses pondered upon the beauty of youth in contrast to his own old age: 'And wrinkles gather on my face, And Hebé [sic] bloom on thine.'[46] One poem, 'The Swimmer's Wish', anticipating (and likely to have been influential over) the painting of bathing boys by Henry Scott Tuke, depicts a boy emerging 'fresh' from the river, who addresses the clouds with: 'I wish I could fly.' The poem continues:

> Laugh, if you like, at the bold reply,
> Answer disdainfully, flouting my words:
> How should a listener at simple sixteen
> Guess what a foolish old rhymer could mean
> Calmly predicting, 'you will surely fly'.[47]

The 'foolish old rhymer', Johnson himself, addresses the boy 'at sweet sixteen', a 'listener' (reminiscent of a Dorian ἀΐτας?) who does not understand that he will one day 'surely fly'. The oblique reference to the winged soul of Plato's *Phaedrus* is perhaps matched by an equally oblique reference to mature ithyphallic potency. Johnson's pubescent object of desire, who has not yet acceded to (sexual) knowledge, is contrasted in other poems with a sense of loss felt by Johnson himself over boys no longer in his care. In several poems he will 'regret that wooing, wedlock and children force a boy's heart to change and forget the loyal adolescent friendships'.[48] 'To Ageanax', which alludes to Theocritus *Idyll* 7, describes a youth on a journey, 'your princely progress is begun', on to maturation.[49] Another poem, *'ΑΛΙΟΣ ΑΜΜΙ ΔΕΔΥΚΕ*' ('The Sun Has Sunk for Us'), mourns the separation of Johnson from his young lover, although he is consoled by the fact that 'I play with those that still are here', under his pedagogic care.[50] The final poem in the book, 'An Apology', sums up Johnson's tome of erotic loss. This poem, which, despite the title, actually offers no Socratic defence, describes his desires as 'the temple of my love'. But by the end Johnson writes:

> The trophied arms and treasured gold
> Have passed beneath the spoiler's hand;

[45] Symonds (1984: 109).   [46] [Johnson] (1858: 79).
[47] [Johnson] (1858: 81).   [48] D'Arch Smith (1970: 11).
[49] [Johnson] (1858: 83).   [50] [Johnson] (1858: 86).

> The shrine is bare, the altar cold,
> But let the outer fabric stand.[51]

The relationships themselves have passed, but their shell, Johnson's poetry itself, like ruins of a temple, still stands. An empty ruin, empty words... Johnson's *Ionica*, then, meditates upon the untimeliness of pederastic desires in the nineteenth century. Not only do his poems hope that 'two minds shall flow together, the English and the Greek',[52] suggesting that modern England might never be (like) ancient Greece, but Johnson's poetry also observes that the pederast will always feel at loss: either his beloved is too young to reciprocate his desires (consider the swimmer at 'simple sixteen', who wishes he could fly), or the beloved is too old (the poems depict a separation that has already happened and separations that will inevitably come). Indeed, it becomes all too clear that this loss does not hinder Johnson's impossible desires but fuels them all the more.

Symonds, whose own poetry bears the marks of Johnson's influence, was caught between Ionic and Doric desires.[53] This chapter, then, is concerned not with discovering Symonds's 'true' sexuality, but with examining the complexity of the competing discourses of Greek love, which made it difficult for Symonds to understand (his) sexuality in relationship to modern sexological science. The boy–historian, who read Plato through the night, represented both sides of Symonds, a person who was both innocent and knowing, both Ionic and Doric, a sixth-former open to pederastic relations and desirous of Platonic comradely love. If Symonds saw himself split between an inner and an outer self, then his inner 'truest' self was itself split asunder. His *Memoirs* depict an ancient pederast and a modern homosexual, an individual whose desires are divided between ancient Hellenic exempla and modern sexological explanation. No wonder, then, that Symonds saw himself as a 'stifled anachronism'. Indeed, concerning his memoir, he wrote that it was 'a very singular book—perhaps unique, in the disclosure of a type of man

---

[51] [Johnson] (1858: 116).   [52] [Johnson] (1858: 25).
[53] On Symonds's Uranian (i.e. pederastic) poetry, see D'Arch Smith (1970: 12–18). Johnson's poetry was reprinted in 1891 and became somewhat more widely available as 'an inspiration and an example' (D'Arch Smith 1970: 11) to numerous Uranian poets between the 1890s and c.1930.

who has not yet been classified'.[54] He wrote his autobiography
only in the wake of his reading the work of R. von Krafft-Ebing,
K. H. Ulrichs, and other sexologists, and it was their 'scientific'
writings that 'first awoke Symonds to the existence of this own
sexual type'. But at the same time he 'expresses his dissatisfaction
with their theories'.[55] 'It appears to me that the abnormality in
question is not to be explained either by Ulrichs' theory, or by
presumptions of the pathological psychologists.'[56] Indeed, contemporary sexological theorizing suggested that those attracted
to children and adolescents were generally *not* homosexuals or
sexual inverts. As James R. Kincaid has observed, when the Victorians 'happened to speak about the attraction to children, they
tended to mark its *difference* from homosexual behaviour'.[57] For
Havelock Ellis and Albert Moll, paedophilia was actually 'a form
of inversion which comes closest to normal sexuality', since 'the
child attract[ed] the male adult because of its resemblance to a
woman'. Krafft-Ebing went further: "Practically speaking, acts of
immorality committed on boys by men sexually inverted are of the
greatest rarity".'[58] In his own essay *A Problem in Modern Ethics*,
Symonds himself distinguishes between adult male–male sexuality
and the corruption of boys:

It is the common belief that boys under age are specially liable to
corruption. This error need not be confuted here. Anyone who chooses
to read the cases recorded by Casper-Liman, Casper in his Novellen,
Krafft-Ebing, and Ulrichs...will be convinced of its absurdity. Young
boys are less exposed to dangers from abnormal than young girls from
normal voluptuaries.[59]

The Greeks did not offer a simple solution or Arcadia for Symonds.
As we shall see in this chapter, Symonds's reading of the Greeks
furnished him with conflicting paradigms for thinking about the
structures of male–male relationships. Rather than being a euphemistic expression for 'homosexuality' or 'sexual inversion', 'Greek

[54] Symonds (1967–9: iii. 642; MS 1943). The quotation comes from a letter to
Horatio Brown dated 29 Dec. 1891.
[55] Buckton (1998: 70).
[56] Symonds (1984: 65).
[57] Kincaid (1992: 191).
[58] Ellis and Krafft-Ebing, quoted in Kincaid (1992: 191).
[59] Symonds (1928: 109).

love' suggested a troubling series of contesting exempla for his nine-teenth-century desires. We have seen in the *Memoirs* how Symonds attempts and fails to polarize the pederasty of Vaughan and Shorting against the chaste Platonic love he read about in the sixth form. Symonds's identification with his Platonic sixth-form self cannot help turning into the desire for another sixth-former, Norman Moor, later on in life. Let us now turn to 'The Genius in Greek Art' and *A Problem in Greek Ethics*, to see precisely how problematic the Greeks were for Symonds.

A CHILD'S-EYE VIEW OF GREEK ART

We have already observed that Symonds was interested in the idea of writing the lectures that eventually became the book *Studies of the Greek Poets* because of his attraction to a sixth-former at Bristol's Clifton College, Norman Moor. Symonds was later to divulge to Horatio Brown that 'it was prompted by romantic feeling that I wrote on the Greek Poets, and whistled my soul's self-scorn to the winds—love having lent those frail things wings to fly by'.[60] Symonds's comments to Brown encapsulate the complex interface between sexuality and the textuality of the historical archive: it is apparently 'romantic feeling' that causes the existence of the history of the *Greek Poets*, a history whose topics, Symonds hopes, will help to shape and nurture the romantic feelings of its young readers. Sexuality and history are the grounds of each other.

Michael Doylen has already examined the final chapter of *Studies*, 'The Genius of Greek Art': 'Symonds distinguishes the "aesthetic morality" of the ancient Greeks—which encouraged free male citizens to shape their lives in ways that those citizens perceived as beautiful—from the "theocratic morality" of modern Western nations—which judges individuals according to *a priori* standards of right and wrong behaviour.'[61] 'Whereas the Christian regulates his instincts through ascetic practices of self-mortification, the Greek moderated his ac-cording to a "true artistic sensibility" that was the "ultimate criterion" in ethics no less than in aesthetics'. As Doylen shows, according to

---

[60] Symonds (1967–9: ii. 782).
[61] Doylen (1998: 145).

Symonds, 'health and good taste controlled the physical appetites of [the Greek] man'.[62] Symonds's work has clearly been situated within the Oxford discourse of aesthetic ethics, which we have already seen thematized in Jowett and, especially, Pater.[63] What has not been addressed so far is a central issue of the essay, the issue of adult–child relations. Here we take the context of the text (a set of lectures for sixth-form students) as crucial.[64]

Even if this text has been read by an audience beyond the sixth-formers for whom it was originally intended, the veiled allusion to masturbation is a permanent reminder to any reader that Symonds's writing was invested in 'the bloom of health' of young people:

The Greek no less than the Christian might need to cut off his right hand—to debar himself like Pericles from the pleasures of society,—or to cast aside the sin that doth so easily beset us—like Socrates who trampled under foot his sensual instincts,—for the attainment of that self-evolution which gave him the right to be one note in the concord of the whole, one colour in the prism of humanity.[65]

The danger of a boy's right hand is akin to the perils that faced Pericles and Socrates. But, if the boy's own body represented one of his greatest problems, the ancient Greek's body also represented one of their greatest hopes and possibilities: 'The one thing needful to him was, not belief in the unseen, nor of necessity holiness, but a firm resolve to comprehend and cultivate his own capacity, and thus to add his quota to the sum of the beauty in the world.'[66]

The interest in, and concern over, the youthful and infantile body is a recurring, indeed central, theme of the essay. Symonds opens just as he means to carry on: 'The Greeks had no past: "no hungry generations trod them down": whereas the multitudinous associations of immense antiquity envelop all our thoughts and feelings. "O Solon,

---

[62] Doylen (1998: 146).

[63] See Doylen (1998: 146) and Evangelista (2009: 129–34).

[64] See Holliday (2000: 89) for a brief mention of Symonds's interest in youthful beauty.

[65] Symonds (1920: 565). Doylen (1998: 176–7 n. 4) rightly notes that Symonds 'gradually eliminated the scent of homoeroticism' through each edition of the *Studies*. For our purposes, however, the third and final edition (from which our quotations come) is just as explicit and forthright on the beauty of children and adolescence as the first.

[66] Symonds (1920: 565–6).

Solon," said the priest of Egypt, "you Greeks are always children!"[67] In alluding to Plato's *Timaeus* (22b), where an Egyptian priest calls the Greeks 'children', Symonds depicts the Greeks as without a past, as infants. A people without a past, children, are people, then, without a (sense of) history. Conveniently ignoring the historical discourses that were prevalent in ancient Greek culture, Symonds is preoccupied with the conditions that have facilitated historicity itself. For Symonds, it is the relationship between the child and the adult that offers for us the possibility of conceptualizing our position in modernity vis-à-vis the Greeks in antiquity: 'The world has now grown old; we are gray from the cradle onwards, swathed with the husks of outworn creeds, and rocked upon the lap of immemorial mysteries. The travail of the whole earth, the unsatisfied desires of many races, the anguish of the death and birth of successive civilisations, have passed into our souls.'[68] The metaphor of Greece the child and the modern West as adult is, of course, not original to Symonds. But at the same time this is no rhetorical ornament to a deeper point. The very transience of time and the very possibility of history are unthinkable apart from the image of the aging adult's eroticized relationship with the child: 'How shall we, whose souls are aged and wrinkled with the long years of humanity, shake hands across the centuries with those young-eyed, young-limbed immortal children?'[69] Indeed, it is modern man's (in) ability to touch children that will absorb much of Symonds's attention in his essay.

He paints a portrait of the ancient Greek:

Like a young man newly come from the wrestling-ground, anointed, chapleted, and very calm, the Genius of the Greeks appears before us. Upon his soul there is no burden of the world's pain . . . nor has he yet felt sin. The pride and the strength of adolescence are his . . . the alternations of sublime repose and boyish noise . . . Of these adolescent qualities, of this clear and stainless personality, this conscience whole and pure and reconciled to nature, what survives among us now?[70]

Symonds's text slides from describing someone 'like a young man', to 'adolescence', to someone of 'boyish noise'. As the description proceeds, the object of gaze becomes younger and younger, in order to

---

[67] Symonds (1920: 554).   [68] Symonds (1920: 554).
[69] Symonds (1920: 554).   [70] Symonds (1920: 554–5).

culminate in a question that emphasizes the utter distance between
ancient (child) and modern (adult). The smudging of the exact age
suggests an impressionism that refuses to yield a photographic picture of the male: he is merely '*like* a young man', 'boy*ish*'. What he
'actually' looks like is not revealed. This is surely deliberate, as
Symonds laments the intangible qualities of the youthful culture of
the Greeks a little further on: 'Yet after all, when the process of an
elaborate culture has thus been toilsomely accomplished, when we
have trained our soul to sympathise with that which is so novel and so
strange and yet so natural, few of us can fairly say that we have
touched the Greeks at more than one or two points.'[71] The desire,
clearly enunciated in the text, of modern man is to touch the child
(of Greece), reflecting Pater's playful reference to Winckelmann's
'fingering' of Greek statues. Symonds's text moves subtly from identifying modern man with the ancient child (the history of man is the
unfolding of a lifespan, from child- to adulthood), to an active desire
for the child. This is sensed more colourfully when Symonds turns to
look for 'the reliques of Greek literature' in the contemporary 'Bay of
Naples, the coast of Sicily'.[72]

These late descendants of Greek colonists are still beautiful—like moving
statues in the sunlight and the shadow of the boughs. Yonder tall straight girl,
whose pitcher . . . might have been filled by Electra or Chrysothemis . . . Her
body sways upon the hips, where rests her modelled arms . . . And where, if
not here, shall we meet with Hylas and Hyacinth, with Ganymede and
Hymenaeus, in the flesh?[73]

It is not only in 'the sunlight of the South'[74] that Symonds can find
modern versions of beautiful ancient children:

If we in England seek some living echo of this melody of curving lines, we
must visit the water meadows where boys bathe in early morning, or the
playgrounds of our public schools in summer, or the banks of the Isis
when the eights are on the water, or the riding schools of young soldiers.
We cannot reconstitute the elements of Greek life; but here and there we
may gain hints for adding breath and pulse and movement to Greek
sculpture.[75]

[71] Symonds (1920: 556), emphasis added.
[72] Symonds (1920: 556).   [73] Symonds (1920: 557).
[74] Symonds (1920: 556).   [75] Symonds (1920: 560).

This portrait of England is also notable for the diversity of ages inferred in the text: the image of boys bathing is reminiscent of the paintings of Henry Scott Tuke (a friend of Symonds[76]) as well as the poetry of William Johnson Cory; we then turn to older males in the 'playgrounds of our public schools'; and then we are to imagine Oxford students; and finally 'young soldiers', that is, men, in 'the riding schools'. Symonds was, of course, interested in all these objects of desire (as has been discussed). At first the child seems distant, beyond Symonds's ever desirous touch; but, as the text proceeds, he turns to the modern world, and follows the maturation of the beautiful boy (and girl) into the beauty of the adult male.

The possibility and impossibility of the adult–child relationship, of touching the child, are exemplified in his discussion of Greek art. Straight after his portrait of English desirability, Symonds considers 'the adornment of a circular hand-mirror', which is reproduced in Karl Otfried Müller's *Denkmäler der alten Kunst* (plate LXI).[77] 'The central space is occupied by four figures—on the right the boy Dionysus, who welcomes his mother in heaven, on the left Phoebus and a young Paniscus playing on the double pipes.'[78] Decorating this hand-mirror are images that are meant to reflect back at us, just as they might reflect each other. Various hierarchical relationships, one between mother and child, the other between lover and beloved, are to be compared and contrasted. On the one side, 'Dionysus is thrown backward; both his arms are raised to encircle the neck of Semele'; on the other side, 'the little Paniscus is seated, attending only to his music, with such childish earnestness as shows that his whole soul goes forth in piping. Phoebus, half-draped and lustrous, stands erect beside a slender shaft of laurel planted on the ground.'[79] The double image seemed exquisite to Symonds: one presents an adult kissing a child, an act that is chastened, since it is between mother and child, whereas the other is overlaid with eroticism, which is nevertheless deferred, since the infant is gloriously unaware of the phallic Phoebus standing 'erect' beside his 'slender shaft of laurel'. It is only between themselves, as mirror images, that is, inversions of one another, that

---

[76] D'Arch Smith (1970: 14).
[77] Symonds (1920: 560, with note). In addition to the *Dorian Race*, Müller's work on ancient Greek art and archaeology was also well read by British scholars: see Müller (1832). On Müller, see the essays collected in Calder and Schlesier (1998).
[78] Symonds (1920: 560).
[79] Symonds (1920: 560–1).

Figure 1. Müller (1832), plate 61. By permission of The British Library.

these two images present a picture of adult–child erotic relations. The exquisite subtlety of deferment, as it is presented in Symonds's text, deftly exemplifies the tantalizing adult–child relationship that this text advertises but also fences off. Although Symonds does not mention it, the infant figures are depicted as bringing Apollo and Semele together: the boy-piper plays a seductive melody, just as Dionysus leads his mother to the beautiful Apollo: children are presented as knowing and desiring agents in a potentially sexual engagement.[80]

Symonds's interest in the relationship between child and adult, and ancient and modern, is also reflected in his discussion of the relationship between Greek and Christian cultures: 'In the adolescent age of the Greek Genius, mankind, not having yet arrived at spiritual self-consciousness, was still as sinless and simple as any other race that lives and dies upon the glove, forming a part of the natural order of the world.'[81] Symonds continues: 'With the Romans, humanity . . . began to wax wanton . . . The bestial side of our mixed nature encroached upon the spiritual, and the [Greek] sense of beauty was perturbed by lust . . . It was at this moment that Christianity convicted mankind of sin.'[82] This grand narrative, long familiar by the last quarter of the nineteenth century, especially since Matthew Arnold's ruminations on Hellenic and Hebraic culture, has very particular consequences in Symonds's essay, clarified by his conclusion. He says that this long history has had a direct effect on modern, nineteenth-century children:

After all, the separation between the Greeks and us is due to something outside us rather than within—principally to the Hebraistic culture, we receive *in childhood*. We are taught to think that one form of religion contains the whole truth, and that one way of feeling is right, to the exclusion of the humanities and sympathies of races no less beloved of God and no less kindred to ourselves than were the Jews. At the same time the literature of the Greeks has for the last three centuries formed the basis of our education.[83]

---

[80] We can note that Symonds eroticizes Müller's original, chaste description of the image: for the German scholar, the image is 'charmingly composed [*anmutig componirten*]' as Semele's 'maternal' arms rest 'prettily' on her son (see Müller 1832: 40 n. 308).

[81] Symonds (1920: 568).

[82] Symonds (1920: 568). See Sedgwick (1990: 136–41), on how Greek homoeroticism in the nineteenth century was unthinkable without rhetorical contrast with Christian ethics.

[83] Symonds (1920: 569–70), emphasis added.

Symonds's text hints at the idea that modern children might be brought up by *two fathers not one*. Indeed, the metaphor of the father figure surfaces explicitly in the very next sentence of the text: 'Some will always be found, under the conditions of this *double culture*, to whom *Greece is a lost fatherland*, and who, passing through youth with the *mal du pays* of that irrecoverable land upon them, may be compared to visionaries, spending the nights in golden dreams and the days in common duties.'[84] Symonds's appropriation of Arnold's Hellenism–Hebraism synthesis portrays the possibility of a modern child who might have a 'double culture', two fatherlands, one Greek, the other Judeo-Christian.[85] If such a double culture might be possible, then this 'must place the men of the future upon a higher level and a firmer standing ground than the Greeks'. Symonds hints, then, at the possibility of curing his homesickness (a subtle allusion to the sexological pathologization of homoerotic desires): 'days in common duties', that is, Christian works, will be compensated by erotic 'nights in golden dreams', dreams of an eroticized childhood, stimulated by night-time reading of Plato. Indeed the 'lost fatherland' of Greece emphasizes the foreignness of that land: a place of Ionian pederasty. The very final sentence of the essay highlights the centrality of child–adult relations for conceptualizing our history: 'The tact of healthy youth will be succeeded by the calm reason of maturity.'[86] But this mature state should be one 'under the conditions of this double culture' both childlike/Greek and adult/Hebraic.

It was no rhetorical accident, then, that Symonds's essay should slide between desire for the (ancient) child and a desire that that child might grow up and mature into healthy manhood. 'The Genius of Greek Art' concerns the ideal maturation of the modern British child, acculturated in both Greek and Christian learning; the drive of history ensures that we can never return to the childhood of Greece—instead we should progress to the 'calm reason of maturity', under the conjoined aegis of Greece and Christianity. Symonds's picture of England from 'boys bath[ing] in the morning' to 'the riding schools of young soldiers' demonstrates his historical teleology from

---

[84] Symonds (1920: 570), first and second emphases added. It is hard not to see Symonds referring to himself here, especially after having read his nocturnal Platonic reading.

[85] For Symonds, Goethe represents the 'hope of future reconciliation' (Symonds 1920: 570).

[86] Symonds (1920: 571).

boyish healthiness to manly adulthood. But, as we have seen, the desire *for* the child haunts this text, from the oblique reference to adolescent masturbation, to Symonds's eroticized gaze at the (archaically named) 'reliques of Greek literature' in the contemporary 'Bay of Naples'. Symonds, of course, himself suggested that the essay reflects his desires for the sixth-form student Norman Moor. Interestingly, around the time when Symonds was working on *Studies of the Greek Poets*, he was also reworking a manuscript he had originally conceived and attempted between 1866 and 1868 after he had left Oxford because of the Shorting affair.[87] And this work, *A Problem in Greek Ethics*, takes a very different position on the possibilities of making the Greeks an example for modern teachers and their pupils. In its proposition that it is impossible to return to the conditions of Greece, which is accompanied by its encouragement to allow the beautiful child to mature, 'The Genius of Greek Art' discreetly suggests that modern men move on from pederastic relations defined along axes of age, to relations that appreciate the beauty of adult men. As we have seen, however, Symonds never ceases to be attracted to the child of Greece, to relations of pederasty. Despite his historicism, which suggests that we are in a historically different moment from classical Athens, Ionian pederasty does, nevertheless, haunt Symonds's sense of modernity, as *A Problem in Greek Ethics* makes clear.

SYMONDS'S PROBLEM

In March 1877, as we saw in the previous chapter, Richard St John Tyrwhitt published a public attack on the 'Greek attitude' of certain Oxford dons. Tyrwhitt lambasted the 'fleshly' and 'effeminate' writings of aestheticians. Just as Symonds pondered on how we might 'bridge over the gulf which separates us from the Greeks', so Tyrwhitt quotes a choice chunk of Jowett to say that 'there is a great gulf fixed between us and them'.[88] *A Problem in Greek Ethics* offers another apologia for same-sex passion in 'wholly analytical and scientific

---

[87] Blanshard (2000: 103).
[88] Tyrwhitt (1877: 565). See Doylen (1998: 150–1) and Dellamora (1990: 162–3).

language'.[89] 'Symonds may have thought', surmises Michael Doylen, 'that the "fleshliness" of *Studies* made that work a target for the same accusations of morbidity and effeminacy being directed against the aesthetic movement and that, in order to be persuasive, his defence of same-sex passion needed to be written in a hardier and more manly tone'.[90]

Symonds's interest in the scientificity of the study of same-sex passion reached a fever pitch towards the end of his life, when he embarked on a collaborative project with Henry Havelock Ellis on the subject. This was first published in Germany in 1896 under the title *Die konträre Geschlectsgefühl*, better known to the Anglophonic reader as *Sexual Inversion*, published in England the following year. Ellis's project was designed to refute the law that criminalized sexual relations between men, by proving that such relations reflected natural, congenital identities, and were therefore involuntary and should not be outlawed. Several historians have already told the story of Ellis squeezing Symonds out of the project, a story that epitomizes the expunging of alternative theories of same-sex love by the dominant and domineering discourse of late-nineteenth-century sexology.[91] Ivan Crozier has shown, however, that the relationship between these two intellectuals, who only ever conversed with one another through the letters they wrote to each other, was far more complex, accommodating, mutually critical, and supportive.[92] Yet again, then, male sexuality is produced and contested textually in letters. Although *A Problem in Greek Ethics* became an appendix to *Sexual Inversion*, their correspondence shows that the question over how to integrate sexological theory with classical history was a key issue. If, for Symonds, it was impossible to think about modern masculinity without reference to classical culture, then this certainly was not the case for Ellis. In one letter to Ellis (dated 7 July 1892), Symonds writes: 'no survey of Sexual Inversion is worth anything without an impartial consideration of its place in Greek life.'[93] However, just a few months later, in another letter to Ellis (1 December 1892),

---

[89] Symonds (1967–9: ii. 934). See also Ellis and Symonds (2008: 227 n. 1). Symonds's thematic of aesthetic beauty in this essay is nevertheless very reminiscent of Pater's own rhetoric.

[90] Doylen (1998: 156).

[91] See Koestenbaum (1989: 57), Bristow (1998), and Doylen (1998: 141).

[92] Crozier (2008).

[93] Quoted in Crozier (2008: 40).

commenting upon the latter's proposed chapter organization of *Sexual Inversion*, Symonds notes a 'great difficulty': it might not be 'possible to conceal the fact that sexual anomaly (as in Greece) is often a matter of preference rather than of fixed physiological or morbid diathesis'. Or, as Crozier elucidates,

this fact . . . would make the argument against the legal position of homosexual acts in England unsound, as he realized that if inversion has been shown to be an act of will in Ancient Greece, then it must also be considered an act of will in England (indeed, it was so considered by the law), and therefore it would be of limited use in arguing that homosexuality was a natural occurrence which should not be outlawed.[94]

This indeed was Ellis's contention, as it is expressed in much of his correspondence with Symonds, as Crozier demonstrates. 'The biggest difference, as is made clear in Ellis's letters, was that he did not agree that Symonds's Greek chapter shed much light on the modern problem of homosexuality, especially as it challenged the idea that homosexual desires were beyond volition, which he thought were the strongest arguments against the law', which criminalized sexual relations between men.[95] Interestingly, although Symonds's *Greek Ethics* has most often been read as a treatise designed to argue for the timeless naturalness of homosexuality,[96] Ellis himself actually felt that the essay argued for quite the opposite—that is, that ancient Greek same-sex passion had little purchase on the debates concerning modern sexual inversion and homosexuality.

We would be wise, then, to take Ellis's lead, if we are interested in detecting contemporary, that is, nineteenth-century conceptualizations of male–male desire. If Ellis thought that Symonds's treatise broadcast a mixed message, then we should attend to the complexity of his work, rather than take him at his word on the supposed subject of the treatise (that is, the timeless nature of homosexuality), as twentieth-century readers have sometimes done. That is to say, the relationship between classical scholarship and sexology was an uneasy one. Symonds's work that aimed at scientificity was nevertheless profoundly influenced by the idea that one's desires were teachable.

---

[94] Crozier (2008: 43).
[95] Crozier (2008: 85).
[96] See Weeks (1990 [1977]: 52) and Doylen (1998: 157).

His letter to Jowett reproduced in his *Memoirs* warns his old teacher about the dangers of professing the truth of Greek love, since it would have a detrimental influence on modern boys and men. Despite his accentuation on the ahistorical nature of same-sex desire, then, Symonds is also highly invested in the idea that there is no such desire—no pederasty—without pedagogy. As Symonds's midnight scene with Plato showed, there would be no sexuality without textuality. Symonds was firmly attached to the belief that the classics really did shape one's individual character, one's *Bildung*. And, ironically, it was the Greek pederastic relationship that seemed to exemplify, rather worryingly, the idea that pedagogy was literally character building.

A Problem in Greek Ethics opens: 'For the student of sexual inversion, ancient Greece offers a wide field for observation and reflection.'[97] Even if the text has not always been read by persons who might define themselves as 'students', it nevertheless apostrophizes the reader as such and attempts to fix them into such a subject position. This is not accidental: the subject of this text, ancient Greek *paiderastia*, concerns the handing-down of knowledge from an older man to a younger man or boy, and Symonds's construction of his relationship with his reader as one between a teacher and his pupil attempts to ape that pederastic–pedagogic structure. If there is an unbroken tradition of male–male desire, then it is epitomized in the *erastes–eromenos* relationships of ancient Athens that enforced and regulated the very possibility of tradition. That is to say, such relationships made traditional the very idea of tradition. By turning his reader into his 'student', Symonds thereby places himself at the opposite end of such a tradition, in which older men hand down knowledge to their young(er) counterparts. On the one hand, then, 'student' is a simple, harmless word referring to anyone with an interest in studying sexual inversion; but, on the other, 'the student of sexual inversion' also suggests that Symonds's text is for someone who wants to study how to be one. The slippage in the very opening works is significant and programmatic: will this book just tell the reader about 'sexual inversion' or will it make him into a sexual invert? What is at stake in the modern reader reading about ancient Greece?

[97] Symonds (1928: 11).

As with Walter Pater, the work of Karl Otfried Müller also deeply informed Symonds's writing. The Dorians are central for *A Problem in Greek Ethics*, because they 'gave the earliest and most marked encouragement to Greek love'.[98] And, like Pater, Symonds makes his debt to Müller's work explicit: 'What I have to say, in the first instance on this matter is derived almost entirely from C. O. Müller's *Dorians*'.[99] Handing down historical knowledge himself, Symonds shows how the Dorians exemplified the intergenerational pederastic–pedagogical relationship that constructed history itself: 'It would appear that the lover was called Inspirer, at Sparta, while the youth he loved was named Hearer... Consequently we find that the most illustrious Spartans are mentioned by their biographers in connection with their comrades. Agesilaus heard Lysander; Archidamus, his son loved Cleonymus; Cleomenes III. was the hearer of Xenares and the inspirer of Panteus'.[100] Indeed, Symonds's prose itself reflects this ideal of the perfect transmission of knowledge, since it lists the *very same names* of Greeks as Müller did.[101] And, just like Müller before him, Symonds's account reflects the phonocentric nature of the relationship between Spartan man and youth, further emphasizing the notion that Symonds's own text is part of the tradition he is analysing. And again for Symonds, as for Müller before him, the exemplary pederastic relationship produced an exemplary understanding of the past, just as an exemplary understanding of the past is productive of ideal pederastic love.

Symonds's romanticized picture of Dorian invaders coming from the North into the Greek peninsula, however, quickly turns into a picture of how this glorious love degenerated:

Instead of a city-state, with its manifold complexities of social life, they were reduced to the narrow limits and social conditions of a roving horde. Without sufficiency of women, without the sanctities of established domestic life, inspired by the memory of Achilles, and venerating their ancestor Herakles, the Dorian warriors had special opportunity for elevating comradeship to the rank of an enthusiasm... when the Dorians had settled down upon their

---

[98] Symonds (1928: 26).
[99] Symonds (1928: 26).
[100] Symonds (1928: 26–7).
[101] Müller (1839: 301). When we turn to Wilde in the next chapter, we will see that the catalogue of Greek friends will be an important, but problematic, rhetoric, for the expression of same-sex desires in the nineteenth century.

conquered territories, and when the passions which had shown their more heroic aspect during a period of warfare came, in a period of idleness, to call for methods of restraint, then the discrimination between honourable and base forms of love, to which Plato pointed as a feature of the Dorian institutions, took place. It is also more than probable that in Crete, where these institutions were the most precisely regulated, the Dorian immigrants came into contact with Phoenician vices, the repression of which required the adoption of a strict code. In this way, paiderastia, considered as a mixed custom, party martial, partly luxurious, recognised by public opinion and controlled by law, obtained among the Dorian Tribes, and spread from them through the states of Hellas.[102]

Symonds, then, is interested in explaining 'the mixed form of paiderastia called by me in this essay Greek love'.[103] These Dorian settlers were supposedly socially organized for martial purposes. Their single-sex communities, not conducive to cross-sex marriage, were, however, incubators for close-knit relations between manly comrades. But the 'problem' of the essay lies in understanding the form of pederasty as it appears in the historical record in classical Athens. Earlier in the essay, Symonds had posited the ancient discrimination between two forms of love, 'Ouranios (celestial) and Pandemos (vulgar, or *volvivaga*)'.[104] 'Heroic comradeship remained an ideal hard to realise, and scarcely possible beyond the limits of the strictest Dorian sect. Yet the language of philosophers, historians, poets and orators is unmistakable. All testify alike to the discrimination between vulgar and heroic love in the Greek mind'.[105] On the former variety, Symonds merely says that he 'shall have little to do in this essay' with it. What does concern him is 'that mixed form of paiderastia upon which the Greeks prided themselves, which had for its heroic ideal the friendship of Achilles and Patroclus, but which in historic times exhibited a sensuality unknown to Homer'.[106]

Symonds offers an explanation of what he means by this 'mixed form': 'In treating of this *unique* product of their civilization I shall use the term *Greek Love*, understanding thereby a passionate and enthusiastic attachment subsisting between man and youth,

---

[102] Symonds (1928: 30–1).   [103] Symonds (1928: 31).
[104] Symonds (1928: 17).   [105] Symonds (1928: 18).
[106] Symonds (1928: 19).

recognised by society and protected by opinion, which, though it was not free from sensuality, did not degenerate into mere licentious-ness.'[107] The very uniqueness of this cultural achievement was, how-ever, a double-edged weapon for Symonds's apologia. On the one hand, it exemplified how male same-sex passion could be successfully integrated into society. This exemplary situation is contrasted, on the other hand, with numerous other societies around the world in which male same-sex passion is associated with effeminacy, transvestism and female impersonation, or sodomy. Symonds's very exemplifica-tion of Greece makes it a model to adopt but also a model impossible to imitate.[108]

Yet again, however, Symonds's text does accentuate the closeness of fit between ancient and modern, as exemplified by the palaestra, a key site for Symonds's analysis: 'the palaestra was the place at Athens where lovers enjoyed the greatest freedom...Boys and men met together with considerable liberty in the porches, peristyles, and other adjuncts to an Attic wrestling-ground.'[109] At the same time, however, Symonds observes that the 'Attic gymnasia and schools were regulated by strict laws'. 'Still, in spite of all restrictions,' Symonds continues, 'the palaestra was the centre of Athenian pro-fligacy, the place in which not only honourable attachments were

---

[107] Symonds (1928: 19), emphasis added.

[108] For Symonds, 'it was just this effort to elevate paiderastia according to the aesthetic standard of Greek ethics which constituted its distinctive quality in Hellas' (ibid. 1928: 33). The Hellenic situation is contrasted to that of 'various savage tribes...the Scythian impotent effeminates, the North American Bardashes, the Tsecats of Madagascar, the Cordaches of the Canadian Indians, and similar classes among Californian Indians, natives of Venezuela', where 'the characteristic point is that effeminate males renounce their sex, assume female clothes, and live either in promiscuous concubinage with the men of the tribe or else in marriage with chosen persons' (1928: 32). Symonds adds: 'For similar reasons, what we know about the prevalence of sodomy among primitive peoples of Mexico, Peru and Yucatan, almost all half-savage nations throws little light upon the subject of the present inquiry' (1928: 33). Just as Symonds was influenced by the work of Müller, so it is clear too that the article written by Meier also informed his thought. Nevertheless, in the 1897 edition, we read in the following footnote: 'It was only when I read the Terminal Essay appended by Sir Richard Burton to his translation of the *Arabian Nights* in 1886 that I became aware of M. H. E. Meier's article on Pederastie...My treatise...is a wholly independent production. This makes Meier's agreement...with the theory I have set forth...the more remarkable' (Ellis and Symonds 2008: 227). The fact that both Symonds and Meier would have read the same sources (such as Müller) does, however, make the coincidence in their thinking less remarkable. Symonds's orient-alism is clearly informed by Richard Burton's writing.

[109] Symonds (1928: 56).

formed, but disgraceful bargains also were concluded.'[110] The homosocial environment of the palaestra closely resembles that of modern,
Victorian public schools and universities. Far from repressing sexual
desire, the regulations that framed the gymnasia and schools in
Athens actually created spaces and opportunities for male–male
erotic interaction. Furthermore, Athens itself comes to resemble the
Victorian city of London, that city of dreadful delights: 'The shops of
barbers, surgeons, perfumers, and flower-sellers had an evil notoriety,
and lads who frequented these resorts rendered themselves liable to
suspicion.'[111]

   Symonds wavers, then, between an Athens that represented a
unique moment in time, in its careful accommodation of, and legislation over, same-sex relationships; and a city that contained a full
range of licit and illicit desires and passions, much like the nineteenth-century metropolis of London. As Symonds sees it, the central
problem for Athenian men was how to live up to the example of the
Dorians, as especially embodied in Homer's representation of
Achilles and Patroclus. Straight after his introductory paragraph,
Symonds observes to his reader: 'The first fact which the student
has to notice is that in the Homeric poems a modern reader finds no
trace of this [same-sex] passion.'[112] Moreover, 'the love of Achilles for
Patroclus added, in a later [i.e. classical] age of Greek history, an
almost religious sanction to the martial form of paiderastia'. Later
Greeks both were formed by the Homeric texts and reformed them in
their own images: 'The Homeric poems were the Bible of the Greeks,
and formed the staple of their education; nor did they scruple to wrest
the sense of the original, reading, like modern Bibliolaters, the sentiments and passions of a later age into the text.'[113] The historical
relationship between the Homeric texts and their classical Greek
readers was, then, a highly complex one, as Symonds himself was
most aware. In effect, his account eschews a linear model of history
and emphasizes instead how

Homer stood in a double relation to the historical Greeks. On the one hand,
he determined their development by the influence of his ideal characters.

[110] Symonds (1928: 61).
[111] Symonds (1928: 62). See Walkowitz (1994).
[112] Symonds (1928: 11).
[113] Symonds (1928: 12). See Turner (1981) on nineteenth-century ideas about
Homeric epic as the ancient Greek Bible.

On the other, he underwent from them interpretations which varied with the spirit of each successive century. He created a national temperament, but received in turn the influx of new thoughts and emotions occurring in the course of its expansion.[114]

Just as the classical Greeks 'stood in a double relation' to Homer, so, it can be said, Symonds's modernity stood in a similarly double relation to Hellenic antiquity. Just as Homer and the classical Greeks created each other, so Symonds's writing betrays a similar concern. Have the Greeks really formed and influenced us? Are the Greeks really precursors of modern sexual inversion? Or do we moderns make the Greeks? Do we make them into sexual inverts for our own purposes? Just as the Athenians mythologized about Achilles and Patroclus to formulate their structures of their desires, so Symonds mythologizes about the ancient Athenians so as to understand the reality of his sexual and social desires.

For Symonds, modern men are hybrids, descendants of two fathers, two cultures, Matthew Arnold's Hellenic and Hebraic. Utilizing the scholarship of Meier, he portrays the ancient Athenians as similarly mixed. Although Symonds is suspicious about 'the nomenclature of Semitic, Aryan, and so forth', his writing betrays raciological assumptions and connotations.[115] His image of Greece moves between a northern Dorian culture, which reproduces itself with unerring accuracy, and an Athenian culture, which is both similar and different from its Dorian ancestor—that is to say, a culture that looks like a racial hybrid, an imperfect reproduction. Symonds projects back onto Athens a very Victorian concern—that of racial miscegenation, an anxiety that accompanied the projects of nineteenth- and early twentieth-century sexology. Havelock Ellis was famously unsatisfied with the term 'homosexual', which he described as 'a barbarously hybrid word'.[116] In a discussion on the vocabulary of same-sex desire in the 1915 edition of *Sexual Inversion*, Ellis went further to say that *homosexual* 'has, philologically, the awkward disadvantage of being a bastard term compounded of Greek and Latin elements'.[117] Tellingly, Ellis was a public advocate of eugenics: in pamphlets he wrote for the British National Council for Public Morals, he supported the

[114] Symonds (1928: 13).   [115] Symonds (1928: 83–4).
[116] Ellis and Symonds (1897: 1 n.)   [117] Ellis and Symonds (1915: 2).

sterilization of the 'unfit' in the best interest of 'the race'. It is not surprising that Ellis should have been concerned about any hint of racial hybridity being attached to the homosexual: homosexuality was commonly viewed as a sign of racial degeneracy at the *fin de siècle*, and Ellis's work was an attempt to depathologize homosexuality.[118]

Symonds similarly, then, shows a concern about 'mixed' Athenian pederasty, developing Meier's implicit interest in the race of the Greeks and replaying Müller's admiration of the Dorians (discussed in Chapter 1). In his own efforts to match his sexual desires with the Dorians, Symonds ends up showing that Athens is a much more useful example for his predicament. Ellis professed concern over how a bastard, hybrid term might signify the love of the same, love between members of the same sex. Symonds's texts also betray this concern, as they oscillate between love of the virile same and the boyish other. We saw Pater's Winckelmann wavering between an affinity with ancient Greece and a frustration at its irrecoverable otherness. In *Plato and Platonism*, this sense that Winckelmann loved both what was the same and what was different from him becomes Plato's interest in the genetic–cultural relationship between Sparta and Athens, and Sparta and modernity. For Symonds, the question becomes still more contorted: which is his (racial) ancestor, which is his other? Dorian/Spartan or Ionian/Athenian? In which way is ancient Greece the same as him and different from him, when he identifies himself as someone who loves the same as himself?[119]

Symonds's use of the language of race and heredity can also be found in his discussion of 'sexual inversion among Greek women'. In contrast to male paiderastia, 'feminine homosexual passions were', according to Symonds, 'never worked into the social system, never became educational and military agents'.[120] Greek women, according to Symonds, were excluded from the pedagogical encounter. Although 'Greek logic', as exemplified by Aristophanes' myth of the *Symposium*, 'admitted the homosexual female to equal rights with the

---

[118] See Somerville (2000: 31–2) for a detailed discussion of the raciological contexts for much sexological theory.

[119] Just as Symonds's texts locate themselves within two traditions, the Dorian and the Ionian, so they are also literally German and English (Ellis's work, as mentioned, was published in both languages). Symonds, as a writer, would have looked like one who wrote in a German scholarly Dorian tradition and an English Ionian one, represented by English Uranian poets.

[120] Symonds (1928: 95).

homosexual male', Symonds can find 'no recorded example... of noble friendship between women'. Even 'Æolian women', such as Sappho, 'did not found a glorious tradition corresponding to that of the Dorian men. If homosexual love between females assumed the form of an institution at one moment in Æolia, this failed to strike roots deep into the subsoil of the nation.'[121] The language of 'tradition', 'roots', 'subsoil', and 'nation' is redolent of Symonds's investment in a Greek race or nation, to which he, as a man, can trace his origins. He does not grant that privilege to modern women. Indeed, his disapproval of lesbianism could not be clearer when he writes: 'while the Greeks *utilised* and ennobled boy-love, they left Lesbian love to follow the same course of *degeneracy* as it pursues in modern times.'[122] He applies to female same-sex desire exactly the language that Ellis sought to deflect from homosexuality in general. Moreover, the only explicit discussion of phallic sexuality comes in this section. Remarkably, Symonds's so-called scientific study does not mention any male homosexual interest in the penis. Instead, the only mention of the membrum virilis comes in his account of strap-on dildos in Lucian's *Amores* and Herodas' sixth mimiamb.[123] Ancient and modern female homosexuals are presented as a sterile, degenerate race, incapable of reproducing themselves in a 'glorious tradition', seeding the earth as Dorian men had done—indeed, they merely mimic the fecundity of the phallus with 'monstrous instruments of lust'.[124]

It is hardly surprising, then, that Ellis might have found the integration of Symonds's classical history into his sexology problematic. First, Symonds's paean to a Dorian self-reproducing tradition, virile and devoid of women, reminiscent of Pater's imagery of male

---

[121] Symonds (1928: 96).

[122] Symonds (1928: 96; emphases added).

[123] Symonds (1928: 97).

[124] Symonds (1928: 97). Heike Bauer does not discuss Symonds's use of the language of race and heredity in her discussion of his sexology, which 'challenged contemporary ideas about marriage and sexual health' (Bauer 2009: 65). German homosexual rights movements at the time were also highly disapproving of lesbian sexuality: see Rowold (2010: 140–1). We can also note here Symonds's description of 'vulgar love' as 'volvivaga', (Symonds (1928: 17)) meaning a 'womb that wanders', suggesting hysteria and/or promiscuity. Did Symonds deliberately misspell Lucretius' 'vulgivaga' ('inconstant,' 'wandering' (9.532))? The Latin does not appear in Symonds's original 1883 edition (see Symonds [1883]: 10), an edition limited to ten copies. Incidentally, the 1883 edition does not contain a section on female homosexuality.

impregnation and Plato's *Symposium*, would not have sat well with a sexological expert interested in the *literal* reproduction of racialized human beings. Secondly, Symonds's emphasis on the idea that through *studying ancient texts* we achieve sexual and social maturation, and *not* because of a congenital predisposition, contradicted Ellis's theories. Symonds writes: 'Young men studied the *Iliad* as our ancestors studied the Arthurian romances, finding there a pattern of conduct almost too high above the realities of common life for imitation, yet stimulative of enthusiasm and exciting to the fancy.'[125] Although the Achilles–Patroclus relationship never appears within history, it is nevertheless the condition of the possibility of 'the historical manifestations of this passion'—that is, Dorian love, 'inspired by the memory of Achilles', a Dorian love, which itself was the model for Athenian pederasty.[126] Potentially more troubling still for Ellis's project would have been the *inimitability* of Achilles and Patroclus. That is to say, Symonds's text argues that the historical Greeks utilized the Homeric, mythic example of Achilles and Patroclus as the model for real, historical relationships, for classical Greek *paiderastia*. And so, must Ellis have wondered, if Achilles and Patroclus proved such an impossible example to follow for classical Greeks, then what sort of example do the classical Greeks themselves provide for the modern, Victorian men, Symonds's readers?[127]

It is precisely this question that bedevilled and baffled Symonds himself. We have observed that the *Memoirs* bespeak a tension between two conflicting models of Greek same-sex relations, Ionian pederasty and Dorian masculine love. The essays 'The Genius of Greek Art' and *A Problem in Greek Ethics* both reflect that problematic. First, the essay 'The Genius of Greek Art' offers an account of how the modern child might grow into the healthy adult. It is not difficult to see that Symonds was interested in moving beyond ancient pederastic relations into adult homosexuality, balanced and tempered

---

[125] Symonds (1928: 13).

[126] Symonds (1928: 14, 30).

[127] In the original 1883 edition of *A Problem in Greek Ethics*, Symonds concluded with a section entitled 'Is Greek literature fit to remain the groundwork of the highest education in a modern commonwealth?' Just as Pater suppressed the 'Conclusion', because he was worried about its influence on his young male readers, so Symonds suppressed his conclusion, which examined the influence of a classical education on modern boys. Clearly, his view that reading Greek was responsible for sexual inversion would not have sat well with Ellis's views.

by Greek and Christian ethics. However, *A Problem in Greek Ethics* suggests that the history of Greek culture actually went in reverse of that process: Greek love began as a manly, comradely, martial pursuit, but changed into a rather more sensuous, but still pedagogic, pederasty in Athens. Symonds, under the influence of Walt Whitman, wrote about a love that would blend 'Social Strata' and abolish 'class distinctions'. It would 'further the advent of the right sort of Socialism'.[128] But readers of Symonds have not been slow to detect that this rhetoric veils an 'assertion of social privilege and the unapologetic fetishization of working-class male bodies'.[129] The complexity of ancient Greek sexuality, then, produces a problem for Symonds, rather than a solution for his desires and for the science of sexology. On the one hand, Dorian love is stuck so far in the past that both ancient Athenians and modern Europeans and Americans find it hard to revivify; on the other hand, however, Athenian pederasty seeps into, and haunts, the present, so that Symonds's assertions about masculine love look very much like a cover for desires based in relationships highly hierarchized along the axes of age and class.

For Symonds, then, the Greeks were exemplary for modern men precisely because they themselves examined the politics of exemplifying masculinity. Similarly to Pater's Plato, for Symonds, the Greeks themselves were struggling to synthesize two models of male–male relationship, and it is this problematic that finds itself voiced in Symonds's own thoughts about his own subjectivity, between pederasty and pure masculine love.[130] Blanshard has suggested that 'everyone ... knew the game which Symonds was playing' when he penned *A Problem in Greek Ethics*.[131] The rhetoric of Greek love was supposedly a thinly veiled metaphor for an *apologia* for modern homosexual relations. We have seen, however, that Symonds was never so certain about the meaning and historicity of his, and his Greeks', desires. Symonds, writes one historian, was 'torn ... between Hellenistic ideals and hellish desires'.[132] Ellis's *Sexual Inversion* sought to

---

[128] Symonds (1967–9: iii. 808). The letter is to Edward Carpenter, dated 21 January 1893.
[129] See Doylen (1998: 163).
[130] On the Athenians' own bewilderment: 'We may, indeed, fairly presume that, as is always the case with popular ethics, considerable confusion existed in the minds of the Athenians themselves' (Symonds 1928: 67).
[131] Blanshard (2000: 117).
[132] Kemp (2000: 60).

be the first book written in the English language that argued against
the criminalization of sex acts between men, since those acts were
grounded in a congenitally founded sexual identity. *A Problem in
Greek Ethics*, which was originally written in response to critics like St
John Tyrwhitt, eventually found itself literally appended to Ellis's
highly controversial text of 1897.[133] Yet its inclusion into his project
troubled the sexologist's theories about sexual identity: Symonds's
text offered conflicting conclusions, suggesting, first, that homoerotic
desires were teachable (institutionalized as they were in sanctioned
pederastic relationships), but also, secondly, that the example of virile,
chaste Achilles and Patroclus seems to be unrepeatable. If Symonds
found the examples of the Greeks so difficult to utilize for modern life,
so *we* should perhaps be cautious in celebrating (or demonizing)
Symonds as one of the first modern homosexuals in history, using
his *Memoirs* as evidence for the truth of his sexuality. Symonds's self-
characterization as 'a stifled anachronism' suggests that both labels,
'ancient' *and* 'modern', are ultimately unhelpful for locating Symonds
'within' the history of sexuality. That Symonds depicted himself as the
ephebe reading Plato's *Phaedrus* should not surprise us. Just as the
beloved 'is indeed in love, but with what, he is at a loss to say'
(*Phaedrus* 255d), so Symonds himself always found it hard to theorize
and envision truly his object of desire.

---

[133] Note Brady (2005: 194): 'Symonds' family ensured that all copies of the first
edition of *Sexual Inversion*, with Symonds' authorship, were withdrawn from publication. Ellis' second edition of the work, with Symonds' name removed, was banned
in 1898 as a work of obscene libel.'

4

Trying Greek Love: Oscar Wilde and
E. M. Forster's *Maurice*

The Platonic ἔρως· the dialectical energy of thought . . . 'it is the
child of wealth and Want· never poor, never rich: a mean
between ~~ignorance and knowledge': (Symposium) it is the spirit~~
~~of scepticism the force of contradiction and the~~ negative: the
Hegelian dialectic· the inquietude poussante of Leibnitz.

(Oscar Wilde, Commonplace Book,
Oscar Wilde's Notebooks, 1989)[1]

'And so Wilde created himself at Oxford,' as Richard Ellmann has
written. Under the diverse influences of the Greats curriculum of
Ruskin, Pater, and Jowett, the young and talented Irishman found his
feet.[2] And it was the classical training he received at Oxford (and
under John Mahaffy at Trinity, Dublin, who took Wilde the student
to see Italy and Greece[3]) that has provided us with one of the most
(in)famous moments in the history of modern (homo)sexuality:
Wilde's 'love that dare not speak its name' speech, his paean to
Platonic love in court in 1895. In the previous chapter we saw how
John Addington Symonds's history of Greek love engaged with medical theories of sexuality; in this chapter we examine the tension
between Greek explanations of modern desires and legal discourses
of sexual acts and practices.

We have seen that German and Oxford scholars' interest in Greek
pederasty lay in how that relationship provided a suitable context for

---

[1] Wilde used Greek semicolons as a way of emphasizing certain terms in his
notebooks. See Smith and Helfand (1989: 2).

[2] Ellmann (1988: 95).

[3] See Ellmann (1988: 53, 67).

the transmission and production of knowledge from one generation to the next. Gesner, Meiners, Müller, and Meier all made serious attempts to historicize the classical world, and displayed scholarly credentials by their abilities to confront the historical difference of Greek pederasty. In the wake of German debates about *Bildung* and *Wissenschaft*, Jowett examined what it meant to translate pederasty into the modern world. Pater, in turn, saw that male homoerotic desire was a key trope for understanding the relationship between past and present. Symonds attempted to produce a wholly scientific study of ancient Greek pederasty, which would contribute to the depathologization of sexual inversion and homosexuality. The usefulness of his scholarship was, however, compromised because of his emphasis on the influence of education on the formation of the sexual subject, as opposed to hereditary factors, as proposed by Havelock Ellis. What was to be known about Platonic love—how Platonic love might be knowable—was a crucial question for understanding modern masculinity. Wilde's Oxford notebooks (quoted at the head of this chapter) make clear that it was Platonic *erōs* that facilitated an academic understanding of the historical difference of the past: the seemingly endless journey towards truth, as outlined by Diotima/Socrates, suggests that secure knowledge always remains outside one's grasp, just like the beautiful object of one's desire, known and unknown.[4] Pater's influence is most visible here: Winckelmann's affinity with the Greeks and his awareness that they are an irrecoverably lost beautiful culture provided Pater with a model for thinking about how modern scholarship both knows and does not know the Greeks. As we saw in Chapter 2, however, Pater was greatly concerned about the influence of his own teaching over his most famous disciple—over a whole generation gone Wilde.

Although Oscar Wilde did not meet Pater in person until his third year at Oxford, he often called Pater's *Renaissance* his 'golden book', and in *De Profundis* he comments upon the 'strange influence over my life' it had, alluding to Pater's discussion of Goethe's strangely pregnant art criticism. Indeed, he read Pater closely all through his life: he requested copies of his books while in prison.[5] It was only in 1877, after Wilde had sent Pater a copy of a review he had written of an exhibition at the Grosvenor Gallery, that the young protégé was

[4] See also Evangelista (2009: 149–51) on Wilde's interest in Platonic *dialektikē*.
[5] See Wilde (2005a: 102) and Ellmann (1988: 46, 469).

introduced to the fashionable Oxford don. Wilde concludes his review by saying that 'that revival of culture and love of beauty . . . in great part owes its birth to Mr Ruskin, and . . . Mr Swinburne, and Mr Pater, and Mr Symonds, and Mr Morris, and many others, are fostering and keeping [it] alive, *each in his own peculiar fashion*'.[6] His observation shows the complexity of the neoclassical revival in the second half of the nineteenth century. Pater replied to Wilde approvingly, and, although the two 'were not slow to become friends',[7] their friendship was always awkward and difficult. Wilde commented that 'poor dear Pater has lived to disprove everything he has written', and that 'Dear Pater was always frightened of my propaganda'.[8] Wilde clearly enjoyed the idea that it was his work that compelled Pater to suppress the 'Conclusion' in the second edition of *The Renaissance*, even though Pater and Wilde did not meet until the year of that edition's publication. Although Wilde clearly took pleasure in constructing a teacher—pupil relationship with Pater in retrospect, we have already seen that it was *The Picture of Dorian Gray* that caused the Brasenose don enough concern to put pen to paper.

Pater taught his pupils and acolytes to engage with art subjectively and to ask what they saw of themselves in the artwork at hand, but found himself perturbed by the direction in which Wilde took his Platonism. As well as a response to Jowett, Pater's text can be seen to be replying to the Platonisms bandied around in Wilde's novel, Platonisms we will soon examine.[9] By the time Frank Harris was writing his sensationalized account of his friend in 1916, *Oscar Wilde: His Life and Confessions*, the relationship between Pater and Wilde had become mythologized. According to Harris, Wilde had told a story about how one day he and Pater 'were seated together on a bench under some trees in Oxford. I had been watching the students bathing in the river: the beautiful white figures all grace and ease and virile strength.' Harris's Wilde goes on to talk about how he explained

---

[6] Wilde (1877: 126), emphasis added.
[7] Ellmann (1988: 80).
[8] Ellmann (1988: 81). Wilde also had fun mocking Pater's work: see Ellmann (1988: 284).
[9] See also Monsman (2002) on how the Platonic 'theory of influence' structured Pater's and Wilde's intellectual relationship. Monsman, in particular, makes clear how *Gaston de Latour* was written in response to *Dorian Gray* (2002: 36–41). See also Riquelme (2000) and Evangelista (2009) on the influence of Pater on Wilde's writing.

to Pater the history of the reception of Christianity in the modern world: 'I really talked as if inspired, and when I paused, Pater—the stiff, quiet, silent Pater—suddenly slipped from his seat and knelt down by me and kissed my hand.'[10] In Harris's account the positions of teacher and pupil are reversed (his Wilde says that 'everyone sat at my feet even then' at Oxford[11]). And, although we do not need to see much truth in this tale, Harris's interest in the significance of the pedagogic relationship between Pater and Wilde is clear. His tall tale again reflects the desire to be physically present at the Platonic teaching scene, as he paints a portrait of the provocative Wilde—Alcibiades and statue-like *agalma* Pater—Socrates.

Wilde's own message has been difficult to hear. His rewriting of the Platonic dialogues, *Intentions*, 'complicates ideas of voice, meaning, and intentionality (an issue to which readers are alerted by the title), freeing the speaker from responsibilities to logic and truth—a vexed topic in Victorian criticism'.[12] *The Picture of Dorian Gray* also asks its readers whether a message can be securely conveyed from author to audience. Does Lord Henry's yellow book really corrupt Dorian? What is the source of his corruption? Wilde's paradoxical examination of how an older man can teach and influence a younger male friend provoked intense discussion about what Wilde himself meant and intended. The one moment Wilde did apparently speak out and look like a teacher, the one moment he did talk publicly about pederastic—pedagogic relations, was his 'love that dare not speak its name' speech in court in 1895. We will remember the Socratic suspicion about textuality and praise about the voice in Plato's *Phaedrus*: learning is best undertaken in the actual presence of one's teacher. Wilde playfully provoked that Socratic suspicion in his own writing. But, when it comes to hearing Wilde's voice, trying to teach an audience in his presence, understanding what Wilde meant then has proved just as difficult. For many historians who detect the real emergence of a real homosexual identity in history, the outing of Oscar Wilde through the course of his three sensationalised trials epitomizes that moment. This gay identification with Wilde has swept into popular gay culture most publicly, at least, since the 1960s.[13] Jeffrey Weeks has memorably

[10] Harris (1918: i. 49).   [11] Harris (1918: i. 48).
[12] Evangelista (2009: 150).   [13] Kaye (2004: 216–19).

written: 'The downfall of Oscar Wilde was a most significant event for it created a public image for the "homosexual", a term by now coming into use, and a terrifying moral tale of the dangers that trailed closely behind deviant behaviour.'[14] Weeks's rhetoric of downfall rehearses a familiar leitmotif in the biographical and literary—historical analyses of Wilde.[15] As Michael Foldy notes, Wilde is seen, 'by some today, as the first celebrity "poster boy" and martyr for what would later become . . . the "gay liberation movement".'[16]

In his speech, Wilde defended his male friendships by comparison with Plato, Michelangelo, and Shakespeare. This turn to the past has provoked other historians to eschew stable conceptualizations of 'gay' identity in their identifications with a queerer sort of Wilde. The cover of the English edition of Alan Sinfield's *The Wilde Century: Effeminacy, Oscar Wilde and the Queer Moment* (1994) makes this point demonstrably: Outrage's 'Queer as Fuck' T-shirt depicts Wilde as the symbol of queer politics. Sinfield's reading of Wilde's story 'The Portrait of Mr W. H'. elucidates his identification of Wilde as queer. This tale, as Sinfield recounts, follows the quest to identify the subject of a portrait as Willie Hughes, 'a boy in Shakespeare's theatre and the supposed addressee of the Sonnets'.[17] It turns out, however, that the painting is a forgery. 'The characters strive to establish the existence of Willie Hughes but it cannot be done'.[18] Although this story might have aroused suspicions about Wilde's sexuality, this tale 'depends upon the fact that the existence of Willie Hughes cannot be demonstrated'. 'The idea of a queer identity is ill-founded, the story seems to say'. The tale suggests Wilde's 'scepticism about how that [discovery of a homosexual identity] might be achieved'.[19] Just as for historians of homosexuality, for Alan Sinfield, Wilde's queer fiction provides a political strategy for our time, which 'might involve claiming same-sex eroticism without accepting the terms and conditions, social and psychological, of being "gay"'.[20]

---

[14] Weeks (1989 [1981]: 103).
[15] Cohen (1993: 3): 'Wilde's "downfall" has provided *and effectively continues to provide* a de facto "official version" . . .'.
[16] Foldy (1997: 91).
[17] Sinfield (1994: 18).   [18] Sinfield (1994: 19).
[19] Sinfield (1994: 19).   [20] Sinfield (1994: 20).

Neil Bartlett has turned Wilde from a voice at court into a text from which we can take whatever we want in a more creative (re)construction of a gay past. Bartlett's highly imaginative examination of Wilde's times discusses his complex reception in the twentieth century. For some, 'he lied, and he lied at a crucial moment in our history, just when we were about to appear', whereas others choose to 'celebrate' him and not 'dwell unnecessarily on the contradictions of Oscar's social position'.[21] In his re-enactments of 1890s gay London culture, Bartlett asks: 'Does any of this (1890–94) mean anything to me, now (1981–88)?'[22] And discussing *Dorian Gray*, he observes: 'Gray was imagined in 1890. Wilde first met Douglas in January or June 1891. He was the man for whom he gave years of his life, the man for whom he would have died, the greatest love of his life. He was his *type*. He was a fiction, one that already existed in his books.'[23]

Our desires for other people are nothing but attempts to attain an imagined image we have read in a text or seen in a picture. At the beginning of the history of (gay) sexuality, there is nothing but a fiction. Bartlett's language makes it unclear who 'he' was, 'the man for whom [Wilde] gave years of his life': Dorian or Alfred Douglas? This leads Bartlett to wonder:

I'm not sure, now, if my first 'gay experience' was with that man, or occurred when I was a boy watching an old film on television, watching an actor ride a white horse through a river. I'm not sure which image provides the truest text by which I now evaluate my loves, which set of features I now remember and recognize.[24]

Bartlett's point echoes Pater's and Symonds's interest in the influence of texts on the formation of one's identity. Reading Plato did play a crucial part in Pater's construction of aestheticism and Symonds's anxieties about the possibilities of imitating the Greeks. Bartlett similarly ponders self-consciously on what sort of gay sexuality a late-twentieth-century gay man can excavate from nineteenth-century textuality: 'like Wilde, I was scrutinizing an imagined historical London to see if it would reveal the face and ancestry of my own lover. When I sat there with the books, at midnight, I knew what

---

[21] Bartlett (1993: 33, 35).   [22] Bartlett (1993: 57).
[23] Bartlett (1993: 196).   [24] Bartlett (1993: 196).

I wanted from them.'[25] Just as Wilde plundered the ancient past for models of how to live in his present, so Bartlett shows that Wilde 'himself' is nothing but a mosaic of texts from which people pick and choose what they want to find of themselves.

Tellingly, then, for some historians, Wilde is one of the first men out of the closet to be definitively identified as homosexual or gay, whereas for others he is one of the first men *not* to be identified as such. This chapter traces out how Wilde and his writing could have been appropriated for such contesting political agendas of male same-sex desire. How has it been possible for Wilde to be(come) *both* the progenitor of modern homosexuality *and* the ironic, sexual dissident that questions the reification of sexual identity? Our focus will be one of the most famous episodes of the trials, trials that for many historians (as we have seen) 'outed' the writer and his works: the 'love that dare not speak its name' speech. We will examine how difficult it has been for historians to uncover precisely what Wilde was getting at. Was he actually lying about Platonic love in order to proffer a covert defence of modern homosexuality? Or could it be said that Wilde was telling what he thought was the truth? What does it mean to praise the 'great affection of an elder for a younger man' in a law court in London in 1895? If Wilde's pronouncement on such affection constituted one of the most public proclamations in British history on the subject of male—male relations, then understanding what that declaration meant has involved divining Wilde's own intentions in making the oration: just what did he think he was doing? Getting at what Wilde meant in his speech will prove tricky, however, even for the most careful of historians. Rather than proving to be a moment in the history of ideas where we can note a paradigmatic shift of conceptualizations around male—male desire, Wilde's speech creates a problem for the way in which subsequent writers and intellectuals reified the historicity of such desire. Michel Foucault's influential study of the nineteenth-century truth of sex, which viewed the secret of the self within one's sexuality, has explored the pervasive dissemination of sexological research in this period.[26] For Wilde, educated at Oxford, however, 'Platonic ἔρως' was to be viewed as 'the dialectical energy of thought . . . a mean between ignorance and knowledge . . .

---

[25] Bartlett (1993: 197). Bartlett's nocturnal reading is reminiscent of Symonds's night-time pleasures with Plato.
[26] See Foucault (1998).

the spirit of scepticism'. Wilde's speech about Platonic love was to provoke more questions than answers about the relationship between knowledge and desire.

In previous chapters, we have analysed scholarly historical accounts of Greek pederasty and the consequences of those accounts within the exclusively homosocial environment of the German universities and Oxbridge colleges. In this chapter, we continue by examining what it meant for Wilde to teach a lesson about Plato in public, to an audience of men and women, most of whom had never read Greek at an Oxbridge tutorial. What was Wilde trying to teach his audience—if anything at all? Who were meant to be the recipients of his message? Just who are Wilde's pupil—heirs? If the earlier chapters in this book looked at scholarly, academic discussions of pederasty, this chapter examines how Greek pederasty became a metaphor for thinking about the formation and production of modern masculinity more generally. This chapter will continue in a discussion of Wilde's own analysis of his Hellenism. As we shall see, in his prison letter addressed to Lord Alfred 'Bosie' Douglas, *De Profundis*, which appeared in expurgated form first in 1905, Wilde attempts to qualify and redirect the public discussions around his relationship with Bosie. The issue will revolve precisely around whether Wilde should be viewed as a Socratic/Platonic teacher who corrupts a younger male friend. In his attempts to deny the truth of this interpretation of his relationship with Douglas, Wilde becomes drawn to the figure of Christ, offering another model of pedagogy. *De Profundis* was not, then, a confession to his supposed misdemeanours, and, consequently, this text's opacity produced a huge response in Edwardian England—Frank Harris's 'confession' being just one of them. One of the most important writers to have written in the wake of the trial and the posthumous publication of *De Profundis* was E. M. Forster, who penned his 1914 novel *Maurice*, a literary work that ponders on what 'Platonic love' means for modernity. Far from being a signifier for the signified 'homosexuality', 'Greek love' at the beginning of the twentieth century remains an unstable category. As we shall examine, *Maurice* shows that 'Greek love' continues to be a complex, multifarious set of strategies, providing competing models and conceptualizations of same-sex passion. We will see that Wilde's speech, that most public expression of 'Greek love', did not create a unifying image in which modern homosexuals could see themselves. Rather, Forster's *Maurice* will show how difficult it was and still is to understand what one means when one compares one's (modern, unconventional) desires to those of the ancient Greeks.

PLATONIC LOVE ON TRIAL

At the second trial involving Wilde (the first for which he was tried for gross indecency), Charles F. Gill, the Chief Counsel for the Prosecution, read aloud the concluding lines of Alfred Douglas's poem 'Two Loves', which had been published in the *Chameleon*, an Oxford undergraduate publication (in the issue of December 1894). Gill asked Wilde to explain the final line: 'I am the love that dare not speak its name.' Wilde's reply was the following:

'The love that dare not speak its name' in this century is such a great affection of an elder for a younger man as there was between David and Jonathan, such as Plato made the very basis of his philosophy, and such as you find in the sonnets of Michelangelo and Shakespeare. It is that deep, spiritual affection that is as pure as it is perfect. It dictates and pervades great works of art like those of Shakespeare and Michelangelo, and those two letters of mine, such as they are. It is in this century misunderstood, so much misunderstood that it may be described as the 'Love that dare not speak its name', and on account of it I am placed where I am now. It is beautiful, it is fine, it is the noblest form of affection. There is nothing unnatural about it. It is intellectual, and it repeatedly exists between an elder and a younger man, when the elder has intellect, and the younger has all the joy, hope and glamour of life before him. That it should be so, the world does not understand. The world mocks at it and sometimes puts one in the pillory for it.[27]

Classicists and historians of theatre will know that one of the most frustrating aspects of research in this area is the dearth of evidence about contemporary reception of performance. Wilde's public tragedy is a rare moment when we know the audience's response: Montgomery Hyde notes the speech was greeted with a mix of boos, hisses, *and* applause.[28] That is to say, then, right from the very beginning of our story, knowing what Wilde meant was open

---

[27] Hyde (1973: 201).   [28] Hyde (1973: 201).

to debate and discussion: Wilde's voice was always already appropriated by his audience.

Michael Foldy's *The Trials of Oscar Wilde* (1997) represents one of the most detailed discussions of the events of 1895, including a close reading of the speech itself. Foldy's analysis will exemplify the difficulties readers have since had in understanding what Wilde actually intended. For Foldy, the speech 'contained a loose paraphrase of Socrates' espousal of the pederastic ideal of love in Plato's *Symposium* . . . The irony in Socrates' speech consisted in the fact that love for him contained a meaning which was spiritual, and therefore quite different from the meaning of love for the common man, which had sexual connotations'. Not dwelling upon Foldy's interpretation of Socratic irony, we turn, as he does, to his next sentence, where he writes: 'In contrast, the irony in Wilde's speech consisted in his inversion of Socrates. The Platonic relationship described by Socrates was precisely the opposite of the kind of (sexual) love that Wilde has sought with [Charles] Parker, [Alfred] Wood and the rest of the young men'.[29] Wilde's lies, then, were very clever. But the man's duplicity does not stop there: 'There was a truth' in this speech, just 'not the whole truth. Wilde's rhetoric was at once duplicitous and honest, but the "code" necessary to distinguish fact from fiction was withheld . . . The speech "addressed" sexuality by not addressing it, and by sublimating it instead'.[30] Foldy seems to see right through the veil of Wilde's metaphors to detect the 'sexuality' (the word Foldy uses) lurking behind.

Foldy then changes direction, as if troubled by Wilde's slippery rhetoric. He says (and I must quote at length):

I *believe* that Wilde's behaviour with Charles Parker, Wood, and the other young men can be best understood if his sexuality is discussed within the aesthetic context of the ancient Athenian discourse on male homosocial desire . . . As a prize-winning classicist at Trinity and Oxford, Wilde had been weaned academically on the culture of ancient Greece and Rome, and was thoroughly steeped in its virtues. The values and ideals of the ancient Hellenes were a tremendous influence on the development of his own aesthetic, and their attitudes towards sexuality were incorporated—in modified form as I will show—within it. [Foldy then offers a summary of Halperin's Foucauldian account of Athenian pederasty.] . . . Wilde's gender and sexual identities were *completely in concert* with the ancient Athenian pederastic

[29] Foldy (1997: 118).   [30] Foldy (1997: 119).

model and its correlative ethos of domination and penetration. Wilde's gender role was masculine and his phallocentric protocol was, as far as we know, insertive. Had Wilde lived in ancient Athena, his sexual object choices (young men) would have been appropriate and commensurate with his social position. As it was, however, it would have been ludicrous for Wilde to try to explain his behaviour in 1895 by appealing to the authority of the ancient Greeks, for his tactical objective was not to tell the truth, but to stay out of prison.[31]

Such apparently insignificant words as 'I believe' assume great significance. For all Foldy thinks he might *know* about the truth behind Wilde's lies, it is ultimately just a belief. But, more troublingly still, this belief sits very awkwardly with his previous reading of the speech. At one juncture in his analysis, Foldy detects Wilde's underlying 'sexuality'—his homosexuality—even though it is not addressed directly, and then at the very next, Foldy can say that Wilde's 'gender and sexual identities were completely in concert with the ancient Athenian pederastic model'. At one moment, Wilde lies in order to avoid directly revealing his homosexuality; at another, he lies because his 1895 public would not have understood that his identity was actually that of the ancient Athenian model, and they would have believed erroneously that he was really homosexual. So, even though it is apparently clear that Wilde was lying, the truth behind those lies is far from clear.

Our close attendance to Foldy's reading is not designed to criticize a scholar whose work has provided us with a fascinating and detailed account of the Oscar Wilde trials. Rather we have found that even an analysis as careful as Michael Foldy's has been disrupted by the tricksiness of the oratory of Oscar Wilde. For all his attention to detail, Foldy is somewhat bowled over by Wilde's rhetoric and does not actually attend to the language of the speech itself. The cunning of the speech lies in its explicit expressiveness about the impossibility of explicitly expressing what is meant by the 'love that dare not speak its name'. Wilde emphatically accentuates that it is 'in this century misunderstood, so much misunderstood', and that 'the world does not understand' it. The speech gives as it takes away: it claims to tell the world about that 'affection of an elder for a younger man', but then openly says that this is misunderstood, that the world does not

---

[31] Foldy (1997: 119–20), emphasis added.

understand it. The language of the speech short-circuits its own explicatory powers. The only thing that this speech gives to be understood is that the subject of this speech is not given to be understood. Platonic love is neither knowable nor definable within a legal context—it is a desire that the Law cannot comprehend. It is hardly surprising, then, that Foldy's analysis should be so troubled by the speech, as its very language is designed to disrupt efforts to pin down its sense.

Foldy frames his analysis of Wilde's self-presentation at the trial as 'performative', in the sense that Judith Butler has redefined the word. Foldy writes:

> Within this larger interpretive framework, we can represent the trials as a *'performative'* event in which Wilde's identity was effectively constituted and evaluated. Wilde's locutionary acts within the courtroom, in conjunction with the evidence provided by his written works, and the further evidence of his sexual practices as they were revealed in the testimony of witnesses, all served to 'construct' Wilde's identity in a public way.[32]

This 'brilliant extemporization' of a speech, as Foldy says, is 'performative' in that its saying performs the act of constituting Wilde's identity, making such a speech act performatively iterable. But this surely is a very strange performative speech act. There is no such thing as a performative event that does not depend upon a previous performative event: such a speech act by definition cannot be extemporized. What would it mean to confess publicly for the first time to be homosexual, when the conventions for a felicitous performance are not known and stabilized? Even though Foldy might introduce his discussion of Wilde's performance at the trial as performative, how his speeches create a concrete understanding of his identity at the trial is far from clear, as is evidenced from Foldy's own reading. As we have seen, Foldy sees *both* modern homosexuality *and* ancient Greek pederasty lurking behind the rhetoric: either Wilde was lying about his homosexuality or he was telling the truth about Platonic love.

Foldy's position might, however, be defended—though again by qualifying his notion that Wilde's speech was extemporization. That is to say, it is possible to trace previous performances of this speech, making it a repeatable execution of a speech act that

---

[32] Foldy (1997: 94), emphasis added.

expresses one's homosexual identity. It has indeed been shown that Wilde was quoting *himself*. Neil Bartlett shows that he was combining, from memory, two unconnected passages from *Dorian Gray*.[33] And Lucy McDiarmid notices a further level of intertext. Wilde gave a similar speech at a ritual at the Crabbet Club, '"a convivial association" of forty-five men who met annually at [Wilfrid] Blunt's family estate in Crabbet Park'.[34] These previous performances, however, only confound the possibility of understanding what Wilde really meant. First, these two passages appear in very different contexts in *The Picture of Dorian Gray*. The first comes near the beginning of the novel and refers to Lord Henry's description of what he imagines his friendship with Dorian Gray will be like: 'Was it not Plato, that artist in thought, who had first analysed it? Was it not Buonarroti who had carved it in the coloured marbles of a sonnet sequence? But in our own century it was strange...'.[35] As the novel progresses, it will be seen that this friendship will have at least an ambivalent, if not a fully detrimental effect, on Gray's personality. The Platonic love of Lord Henry is very obviously questioned. But, in the second passage, Gray is thinking about Basil Hallward, wistfully wishing that he could rekindle that purer kind of friendship: Basil's love 'was really love—had nothing in it that was not noble and intellectual. It was not that mere physical admiration of beauty that is born of the senses, and that dies when the senses tire. It was such love as Michael Angelo had known, and Montaigne, and Winckelmann, and Shakespeare himself.'[36] The novel, then, is itself highly equivocal about the value and significance of such male friendships between older and younger men. Indeed, both dangerous and pure relations of affection are expressed in the same sort of language, so that they cannot be told apart. Joseph Bristow has saliently observed that 'Dorian is surely seduced by aphorisms... Many of [Lord Henry's] maxims explicitly parody proverbs unthinkingly dictated to the young... Lord Henry's eloquence overturns commonly held assumptions to reveal the unethical bases of values all too readily deemed fit for young minds'. Bristow asks 'who or what is to blame' for Gray's corruption? 'Pater or the law?'[37] That is to say, is it dangerously influential books on aestheticism like Walter Pater's *The Renaissance*

---

[33] Bartlett (1993: 204).   [34] McDiarmid (2001: 454).
[35] Wilde (2005b: 199).   [36] Wilde (2005b: 269).
[37] Bristow (1992: 54, 61).

or does Victorian society actually lead boys and young men into corruption, as if, without realizing, through the lessons it inculcates into its young? Wilde's novel plays upon the highly contested significance the ancient Greek example had for Victorian masculinity, suggesting that his speech is going to be no clearer, no more explicit, about what these friendships really 'mean'.[38]

Secondly, the tenor of Wilde's performance at the literary Crabbet Club is also very hard to gauge. As Richard Ellmann in his biography notes, Wilde had been invited to join the club, and George Curzon 'agreed to play devil's advocate and oppose Wilde for membership'. Ellmann quotes the hedonist, poet, and breeder of Arab horses, Wilfrid Scawen Blunt, on Wilde's reply to Curzon, who 'did not spare him [Wilde], playing with astonishing audacity and skill upon his reputation for sodomy and his treatment of the subject in *Dorian Gray*. Poor Oscar sat helplessly smiling, a fat mass, in his chair . . . But he pulled himself together as he went on and gradually warmed into an *amusing* and *excellent* speech.' Ellmann appends, 'he never went back to the Crabbet Club'.

Blunt was himself a remarkable individual. As well as a poet with aristocratic connections, he was a 'diplomat, traveller, advocate of Irish, Egyptian and Indian self-government, breeder of Arab horses and philanderer'. He hosted the club at his Crabbet Park estate, where interesting individuals from society assembled annually, 'united by a taste for amusing company and nude tennis'.[39] This description is not designed to discredit Blunt's account of the Curzon/Wilde debate. Rather what we should attend to is Blunt's description as 'amusing and excellent', which bespeaks an uncertainty about how to take Wilde's speech—both serious and comic. The context itself was also ambivalent—a literary club established to celebrate verse composition that was also dedicated to riotous hedonism. Does Wilde's abstention from the club imply that he felt his speech had fallen on deaf ears?

[38] See also Sedgwick (1990: 157–67), who reads the novel as one in which different conceptualizations of same-sex desire (the pederastic and the modern) are compared and contrasted. We should also remember Pater's review (1891) of *Dorian Gray*, in which he tries to police the differences between Lord Henry's and Hallward's pedagogies.

[39] Ellmann (1988: 302). See also Longford (1979: 290–1). A remarkable figure, he fashioned himself after Lord Byron, who was Blunt's father's fag at Harrow, and Blunt married his granddaughter. See Walker (2006: 554).

This particular occasion for his oration cannot, then, be read for the truth behind the speech he made in the dock.

Wilde's oration also echoes a passage from Mallock's satirical novel *The New Republic*, published in 1876. This very popular work mocked, among other things, the apparently high-minded ideals of contemporary Victorian philhellenic gentlemen. It is set in a country house where a group of men and women pontificate about the problems besetting contemporary society—religion, science, and education. Pater's aestheticism was a clear target in Mallock's satire. And notably, a year later, St John Tyrwhitt published his scathing critique of effeminate aesthetic prose. In one passage in the novel, a Mr Rose (very obviously Walter Pater) croons:

> Think of the immortal dramas which history sets before us; of the keener and profounder passions which it shows an action, of the exquisite groups and figures it reveals to us, of nobler mould than ours—Harmodius and Aristogeiton, Achilles and Patroclus, David and Jonathan, our English Edward and the fair Piers Gaveston . . . or, above all, those two by the *agnus castus* and the plane-tree where Ilyssus flowed . . . and where the Attic grasshoppers chirped in shrill summer choir.[40]

If any aspect of Wilde's speech be performative, it would be the listing of male names: David and Jonathan, Plato, Achilles and Patroclus, and so on. Mallock's satirical reference to Plato's *Phaedrus* resonates in Wilde's 'affection of an elder for a younger man'. Mallock's lampoon also refers to the famous speech by Mortimer (the elder) in Marlowe's *Edward II*, which lists pairs of passionate males.[41] Of course, highly literate listeners (and later readers) of Wilde's speech would pick up on these chains of reference, chains that stretch back to Cicero's *De Amicitia*, where he lists examples of the best male friendships. And Cicero's exemplification itself alludes back to Pausanias' paean to Achilles and Patroclus in Plato's *Symposium*.[42] Wilde's catalogue of exemplary male affection was, then, nothing but unoriginal.

---

[40] Mallock (1975: 189).

[41] See *Edward II* (I. iv. 387–400). On this speech, see Bredbeck (1991: 71–7).

[42] See Cicero, *De Amicitia* 15 (mentioning 'three or four pairs of friends' without actually naming them, so famous they have already become. Most commentators suggest: Theseus and Pirithous; Achilles and Patroclus; Orestes and Pylades; and Damon and Phintias); and see Plato, *Symposium* 179e–180b.

But, just as the speech says very little of substance about the 'love that dare not speak its name', so the examples of such friendship are bland clichés that had become highly elastic in their usability. First, let us take Mallock's example. The discussion about what would constitute a better society takes up the whole of the visit of Otho Laurence's guests—Laurence hosts them at his uncle's estate, which he had recently inherited. At the end of discussion, the last part of which takes place in Laurence's uncle's library in his summerhouse, the guests file out, leaving Mr Rose and Laurence alone:

'I was looking before dinner,' said Mr Rose, who with Laurence was bringing up the rear, 'at the books in your uncle's pavilion in the garden; and I saw there, in a closed case, a copy of the 'Cultes secrets des Dames Romaines'. 'Well?' said Laurence a little stiffly, 'It has been locked up for years.' 'I conceived as much,' said Mr Rose gently. 'As you do not seem to set much store by the work, I will give you thirty pounds for it'.[43]

It is with this conversation that the fourth book out of five concludes Mallock's novel. But what sort of joke is this? For the discerning reader, the character based on Pater was not referring to some dry antiquarian text, but to a pornographic work first produced back in the 1770s and 1780s by a shadowy individual who titled himself Baron d'Hancarville. This character, whose real name was Pierre François Hugues, had collaborated with Sir William Hamilton in the eighteenth century to produce his monumental four-part anti-quarian work on Hamilton's prodigious vase collection. Hamilton employed d'Hancarville to produce volumes so that he might create an art market, so that he could sell his vases to the new British Museum. D'Hancarville used the opportunity to write his own history of art, which (he believed) rivalled Comte de Caylus and Winckelmann. D'Hancarville also published numerous pornographic books, which ostensibly looked like antiquarian scholarship—until one looked inside. *Cultes secrets des dames romaines* (originally published, it seems, in 1784) was one such salacious volume that examined Roman women's participation in ancient sexual cults.[44] And so Mallock's novel presents a picture of Pater that might seem highly aestheticizing and that might also allude explicitly to his interest in same-sex desire. But at the close of the dialogue, Mallock wittily

---

[43] Mallock (1975: 339).   [44] See Haskell (1987: 30–45).

overturns his readers' expectations on their heads, to reveal that behind Mr Rose/Pater's aesthetic stance is a man who lusts after women—not men. Mallock's novel gently mocks its readers' beliefs about what Greek friendship was all about, dryly suggesting that it was merely a façade for a male predator of women.[45]

If we turn back further into the nineteenth century, we can read Charles Kingsley, in his review of Tennyson's elegy to Hallam, where he wrote jubilantly of 'finding that hero-worship is not yet passed away; that the heart of man still beats young and fresh; that the old tales of David and Jonathan, Damon and Pythias, Socrates and Alcibiades, Shakespeare and his nameless friend, of "love passing the love of woman" . . . can still blossom out'.[46] Kingsley 'works hard to assimilate *In Memoriam* to his idea of Christian manliness'.[47] The rhetoric of manly exempla bequeathed to Victorian writers by Plato and Cicero was contested and malleable for various different agendas. Against this historical canvas, Wilde's own speech is even more difficult to evaluate. The catalogue of ancient male friends was hardly straightforwardly a performative speech act in the nineteenth century, as it could be used to mean different things in different contexts for different writers.

So what are we to make of Wilde's law-court (re-)citation of words from *Dorian Gray* that parody the parody from Mallock's *New Republic*, a speech that is then supplemented by a philological explanation that advertises its Platonic—pedagogic credentials, only to emphasize how difficult it is to understand? Was Wilde making liberal use of a by-now cliché, old joke? If so, did he intend the audience to think that he was mocking in such a way that these were meant to be empty words, just hot air—was Wilde just making light of Douglas's poem, offering a parody of an explanation that everyone knew meant absolutely *nothing* (no whiff of a homosexual there)? Or was Wilde being impassionedly genuine—was he really trying to re-appropriate a tradition that had been used by writers such as Mallock? But then, if Wilde were being serious, was he trying to defend modern homosexuals, modern copies of ancient Athenian pederasts, or was he attempting to align his speech with Kingsley's

---

[45] Although Dowling (1994: 104–12) and Denisoff (2001: 31–42) both offer interesting accounts of Mallock's satire of Pater, both omit to consider the crucial punchline.

[46] Kingsley, quoted in Buckton (1998: 37).

[47] Sinfield (1994: 59).

earlier discourse of Christian muscularity? Moreover, we can ask: if Wilde was being deliberately ambiguous, how are we to distinguish deliberate from accidental ambiguity? (How) can we feel as confident as Foldy in disambiguating what sort of ambiguity might be present in this speech?

Finally, what makes Wilde's speech even more difficult to assess is that he was the first and only man to defend himself so openly and publicly on such charges throughout the nineteenth century. There was neither a framework for understanding his speech nor one for setting it within some well-known pattern.[48] But it is not simply the issue that Wilde's court appearance might have performed a public coming-out that is at stake. Rather, as Harry Cocks shows, sodomy was prosecuted continuously in growing numbers through this period. But it was a charge that was particularly difficult to convict precisely because 'the Victorian sodomite became modern... as a figure of equivocation, both reported and unseen, flagrantly visible and at the same time invisible and mysterious'.[49] The famous 1870 Boulton and Park case, where two men dressed as 'Stella' and 'Fanny' were arrested when leaving the Strand Theatre, demonstrated that the prosecution of such men was extremely tricky. Ernest Boulton and Frederick Park were *not* found guilty as charged: 'The historical paradox of Boulton and Park lies in the fact that they were undoubtedly figures of unnatural desire, and yet it could not be legally proved that their behaviour added up to a specific form of guilt'.[50] Victorian legal and popular discourses supported a highly contradictory attitude to the sodomite, who was all at once *both* a member of an identifiable and 'detestable race', *and* the end point in depravity at which *any* person could find himself.[51] It would, therefore, be anachronistic to say that Wilde could 'come out'—become completely understood—in any straightforward manner.

Historians have argued for some time now about whether the 1885 Criminal Law Amendment Act, along with Henry Labouchere's clause, really did help to solidify and concretize the figure of the modern homosexual.[52] Labouchere's amendment criminalized gross

---

[48] See Cocks (2006: 87, 102–3).
[49] Cocks (2003: 90).
[50] Cocks (2003: 114).
[51] See Sedgwick (1990: 82–6) and Cocks (2006: 94) for 'detestable race'.
[52] For a useful summary of the arguments, see Foldy (1997: 87–8).

indecency between men, but crucially did not define what that actually constituted. Harry Cocks has shown that by the beginning of the nineteenth century all sorts of acts and intimacies could be prosecuted as an attempt to commit sodomy and that Labouchere's amendment continued the bewilderment about male indecency, despite attempting to reify it.[53] Cocks also shows that what can be more conclusively stated is that the Act permitted the accused to speak from the box, a privilege that had largely *not* been bequeathed in the nineteenth century to the one sitting in the dock. Although this clause to the Act was designed to give 'the poor and uneducated' a voice at their trial, critics at the time argued that it placed 'those most in need of protection from barristers and judges under unbearable scrutiny. Wilde's trial provided an ironic reversal of these fears'.[54] Although Wilde was allowed to speak, then, his voice was also silenced. His famous oration reflects his paradoxical position: his desires were made both utterly visible to a broader public, and, for that reason, all the more difficult to read, and therefore open to interpretation. We have repeatedly seen the ardent desire of readers to have been present at Plato's lessons with Socrates, in order to understand him. The emphasis on being there in the *Phaedrus* is echoed in the desire to have been there in the law court to hear Wilde speak. Yet, right from the start, his discourse about Platonic love produced polarized responses from his first audience, beginning a long history of questions about what Wilde might mean, about who might be the true recipients of Wilde's speech. The Law does not produce an uncontested understanding of Greek love. Recovering Wilde's voice and knowing precisely what his Platonic lesson was supposed to teach us are now impossible.

FROM PLATO TO CHRIST

Wilde might have considered his public position to have been so eminent that he was able to teach the entire British public a lesson about Platonic love. He risked everything the moment he engaged his listeners in a debate that had previously been conducted within the

---

[53] See Cocks (2003: 32 and *passim*). See also further discussion in Powell (2009: 135–41).

[54] Cocks (2006: 103).

exclusively male homosocial scene of the Oxbridge tutorial. Rather than an eloquent Socratic figure, Wilde came very quickly to look like a character from Greek tragedy, satisfying Aristotelian conventions of a great man suffering a reversal of fortune. Indeed, Wilde himself characterized his life in tragic terms in 'Epistola: In carcere et vinculis' (originally published in abridged form as *De Profundis*), ensuring that 'Wilde's "downfall" has provided *and effectively continues to provide a de facto "official version"*'.[55] This depiction of Wilde has had the effect of turning him into an example. As Dellamora has explained, in the 1890s, with regard to late Victorian anxieties about masculinity and the 'new Woman', 'scandals provide a point at which gender roles are publicly, even spectacularly, encoded and enforced'. Scandal operates 'as a mechanism of the social construction of gender'.[56] Wilde becomes the scapegoat, the *pharmakos*, for Victorian society.

Although the tragic is a significant leitmotif in *De Profundis*, Wilde's letter also examines in great detail the contemporary interpretation that saw Wilde as a corrosive Socratic teacher who corrupted a younger man. This central and crucial aspect of *De Profundis* has received very scarce attention. Wilde closes his text, a prison letter addressed to 'Bosie': 'You came to me to learn the pleasure of life and the pleasure of art. Perhaps I am chosen to teach you something much more wonderful—the meaning of sorrow and its beauty'.[57] Wilde, then, is very interested in the transmission and reception of knowledge from the elder generation to the younger. He explicitly compares and contrasts various modes of pedagogy. As we shall examine, Wilde is very anxious to discuss the letter he wrote to Douglas, a letter that, in Wilde's opinion, landed him in prison. In this 'charming letter' (as Wilde describes it), he compares Douglas to Hyacinth and, implicitly, himself to Apollo. This letter, which blackmailers got hold of and copies of which apparently circulated around London, and which found its way into Douglas's father's possession, allows Wilde to meditate upon what happens when classical pedagogy literally goes astray: the transmission of Greek knowledge arrives in the hands of those who have no understanding of it. As we shall see, the destination of letters is an important theme in *De Profundis*, as Wilde describes how his and Douglas's lives come to be lived out in letters between Douglas, his father, and his mother. We have

---

[55] Cohen (1993: 3).
[56] Dellamora (1990: 194, 205). See also Fisher (1995) and Kaplan (2005).
[57] Wilde (2005a: 155).

repeatedly witnessed the importance of the relationship between letters and life: what do (epistolary/scholarly) texts tell us about male sexuality? With Wilde, we are reading a letter that itself purports to teach a lesson about how misunderstood Wilde's Hellenism has been. Misreading his Greek letters has, Wilde contends, brought him to this lowly state.

For Wilde, then, it is not so much the Platonic lessons he tried to teach the young Douglas that brought about those tragic events. Instead, Wilde moves the truth of the matter away from the issue of perverse sexuality to degenerate racial hereditary. As we shall see, for Wilde, it is not the transmission of classical knowledge but the inheritance of a corrosive familial heritage from his father's line that caused the events of 1895. Wilde, then, disavows the truth claims of contemporary sexological discourse, in order to rely on the raciological. We have already seen how the Dorian heritage was viewed in racial terms by Pater and Symonds. In *De Profundis*, however, Wilde makes use of similar nineteenth-century discourses in order to elucidate a very different sort of model for the transmission of knowledge from one generation to the next. Furthermore, the issue of what a woman can teach her son becomes explicit in *De Profundis*. Wilde repeatedly claims that it was Douglas's mother's *lack of tuition* that also brought about Wilde's imprisonment. The mother's inability to enter upon the homosocial scene, the relationship between father and son, was to have grave consequences for all involved. In his attempts to rewrite the contemporary version that saw Wilde as Socrates and Douglas as a corrupted youth, Wilde emphasizes the importance of the mother for the formation of the modern male, here exemplified by Douglas. Of course, the presence of the mother will, for Freud, have difference effects (which we will discuss in the following chapter). For now, it is important to observe that Wilde suggests that a mother's pedagogy is just as influential as the paternal law and Platonic reading. As we shall see, the presence of women will be an important factor for understanding male sexuality in Forster's *Maurice*. Wilde's rewriting of public perceptions of Platonism post-1895 sees him shift his focus in *De Profundis* to another exemplary pedagogue: Jesus. It is this aspect of Wilde's letter that provoked contemporary readers the most. For some it is a sincere act of contrition, whereas for others it is merely a counterfeit confession.[58] With his portrait of Christ, Wilde

[58] See Doylen (1999: 546–9).

attempts to produce a very different model for pedagogy and the transmission of ancient knowledge into modernity, a model that will also self-consciously meditate on what sort of model Wilde thought he himself might be for those seeking to imitate and/or learn from him. Although the tragic depiction of Wilde has made him seem an exemplar for gay and queer people as well as other counter-cultural persons, Wilde's analysis of Christ's teaching will cause us to question this exemplarity. With these issues in mind, then, let us turn to *De Profundis*.

Just as in the law court, where Wilde praised Platonic love between an elder and a younger, so in *De Profundis* he reiterates his case:

You send me a very nice poem of the undergraduate school of verse for my approval: I reply by a letter of fantastic literary conceits: I compare you to Hylas, or Hyacinth, Jonquil or Narcisse or some one whom the great God of Poetry favoured, and honoured with his love. The letter is like a passage from one of Shakespeare's sonnets transposed to a minor key. *It can be understood only by those who had read the Symposium of Plato*, or caught the spirit of a certain grave mood made beautiful for us in Greek marbles. It was, let me say frankly, the sort of letter, I would, in a happy if wilful moment, have written to any graceful young man of either University who had sent me a poem of his own making, certain that he would have sufficient wit, or culture, to interpret rightly its *fantastic phrases*. Look at the history of that letter! It passes from you into the hands of a loathsome companion: from him to a gang of blackmailers: copies of it are sent about London to my friends, and to the manager [Herbert Beerbohm Tree] of the theatre where my work is being performed: *every construction but the right one is put on it*: Society is thrilled with the absurd rumours that I have had to pay a huge sum of money for having written an infamous letter to you: *this forms the basis of your father's worst attack*: I produce the original letter myself in Court to show what it really is: it is denounced by your father's Counsel as a revolting and insidious attempt to corrupt innocence: ultimately it forms part of a criminal charge: the Crown takes it up: the Judge sums up on it with little learning and much morality: *I go to prison for it at last. That is the result of writing you a charming letter.*[59]

Just as at his trial, so here writing in incarceration, Wilde reproduces his defence: the letter, which he wrote to Douglas that found its way into a blackmailer's hands, which then followed a path into Queenberry's fists, is the 'basis' for Douglas's father's 'attack'. 'I go to prison

---

[59] Wilde (2005a: 59), emphases added.

for it at last'. If the prosecution could not convict Wilde on the basis of his amoral *Dorian Gray*, this 'letter of fantastic literary conceits' will imprison him. And, more significantly still, 'it can be understood only by those who read the *Symposium* of Plato'. Indeed, 'every construction but the right one is put on it'. Wilde claims that he would happily write such a letter again—to someone classically educated at Oxford or Cambridge, who might 'interpret rightly its fantastic phrases'. The translation of perverse sexuality out of Platonic textuality is the key issue for Wilde. The letter, which provided the 'basis' for the trial, also itself comments upon the relations between sender and receiver. Let us consider briefly the epistle that, in Wilde's opinion, at least, landed him in so much trouble:

[January 1893?]   [Babbacombe Cliff]
My Own Boy [Lord Alfred Douglas],
Your sonnet ['In Sarum Close'] is quite lovely, and it is a marvel that those red rose-leaf lips of yours should have been no less for music of song than for madness of kisses. Your slim gilt soul walks between passion and poetry. I know Hyacinthus, whom Apollo loved so madly, was you in Greek days.
    Why are you alone in London, and when do you go to Salisbury? Do go there to cool your hands in the grey twilight of Gothic things [cf. 'In Sarum Close', lines 3–4], and come here whenever you like. It is a lovely place—it only lacks you; but go to Salisbury first.
Always, with undying love, yours,
OSCAR.[60]

This letter was read out in the first trial by Sir Edward Clarke, who was representing Wilde. Queensberry's defence had intended to use this against Wilde, but this was anticipated by Clarke, who attempted to defuse any problems the epistle might raise later. After reading the letter Clarke offered a commentary:

The words of that letter, gentleman, may appear extravagant to those in the habit of writing commercial correspondence or those ordinary letters which the necessities of life force upon one every day. But Mr Wilde is a poet, and the letter is considered by him as a prose sonnet, and one of which he is no way ashamed and is prepared to produce anywhere as the expression of true poetic feeling, and with no relation whatever to the hateful and repulsive suggestions put to it in the plea in this case.[61]

[60] Wilde (2000: 544).   [61] Hyde (1973: 101–2).

As Foldy notes, it was Clarke's express intention to 'give the jury pause over the vast cultural gulf that separated them from Wilde'.[62] The aestheticization of this letter had already begun two years before the trial in 1893, when Pierre Louys published a sonnet in French based on the letter in the 4 May issue of Douglas's Oxford undergraduate magazine *Spirit Lamp*. Indeed, it would not be difficult to offer an analysis of this letter that examined its literariness: one could mention the doubled alliteration of 'red rose-leaf lips'; the thematic balancing between poetry and love ('no less for music of song than for madness of kisses'), which introduces the delicate gait of Douglas tip-toeing between 'passion and poetry'; the repeated accent upon sensual intoxication ('madness of kisses...loved so madly'); as well, of course, as the classical allusion to Apollo and Hyacinthus.

It is, however, this classical allusion that would have alerted contemporary attention. The homoeroticism, as Queensberry's defence knew too well, was difficult to hide and sublimate as Clarke had wished. And, although this point was not made at the trial, well-read spectators of the events in 1895 would have perceived the irony of the allusion: as Ovid records (in the best-known textual version of the myth), Apollo was playing discus with his young friend Hyacinthus when Zephyrus noticed them and grew jealous. The god of the south wind blew Apollo's discus off course so that it hit Hyacinthus so violently that it struck the boy and killed him. The blood-drops that fell to the ground changed into clusters of flowers (*Met.* 10.162–219). Wilde's letter alludes to a story in which one sends a missive to another, which does not arrive at its intended destination: the jealous wind blows it off course so that it harms its receiver. And it was the very errant nature of this letter in all its materiality that ultimately did much harm not only to its original addressee Bosie, but also to Wilde himself. Just as those others who read the letter put every construction on it but the right one, so Wilde must have pondered in his prison cell upon the ironic significance of seeing himself and Douglas as Apollo and Hyacinthus.[63] Tantalizingly, Wilde *never* tells his readers the letter's correct interpretation. Instead they are

[62] Foldy (1997: 3).

[63] The darker side of Apollo would have been clear to Wilde by this time: Pater's 'Lacedæmon' described a violent Apollo, as well as the Hyacinthia, a Spartan festival where 'the Lacedæmonians with their guests were met together to celebrate the death of the hapless lad' (Pater 1910: vi. 229). Pater's disturbing story 'Apollo in Picardy' had also appeared in *Harper's Magazine* in November 1893. The name Hyacinth had already

made to feel like eavesdroppers on an (albeit one-sided) private conversation between Wilde and Douglas. *De Profundis* becomes, then, just
like the Hyacinth letter, both a public and a private document, a sealed
epistle and an open postcard.[64] By discussing his private 'letter of
fantastic literary conceits' in such a public manner, Wilde *both* lures
his reader in *and* blocks his reader's access. Is *this* what Platonic
pedagogy really looks like, the reader is left to wonder. If so, what are
we meant to learn from Wilde's Platonic letter?

The destination of letters is a theme that dominates *De Profundis*.
Wilde cites a letter addressed to Douglas but meant for the readership
of another, Wilde himself, as one of the origins for all his troubles:
'Two days after we had returned to London, your father saw you
having luncheon with me at the Café Royal, joined my table, drank
my wine, and that afternoon, *through a letter addressed to you, began
his first attack on me*.'[65] A little further on, Wilde returns to this letter:
'When your father first began to attack me it was as your private
friend, and in a private letter to you. As soon as I had read the letter
with its obscene threats and coarse violences I saw at once that there
was a terrible danger looming on the horizon of my troubled days.'[66]
Wilde continues: 'You had already, before you saw me on the subject,
sent your father a foolish and vulgar telegram as your answer . . . That
telegram conditioned the whole of your subsequent relations with
your father, and consequently the whole of my life'.[67] The problem
here, then, is that Wilde, who was *not* the addressee of Douglas's
letter, did *not* get to read the epistle before it was sent to its supposedly correct destination, Queensberry. In the context of his analyses
of Douglas's and Queensberry's mutual hatred (an issue to which we
will return), Wilde also notes how he plays piggy-in-the-middle
between Douglas and his mother: 'Instead of speaking directly to
you about your life, as a mother should, she always wrote privately

gained homoerotic associations in Gerard Manley Hopkins' poetry (Dellamora 1990:
48–9). It was also a term used by Byron and his Cambridge peers for sexually available
adolescents earlier in the nineteenth century (Crompton 1985: 127–9). Tennyson also
draws on the myth of Apollo and Hyacinthus in *In Memoriam* (Dellamora 1990: 37–8).
Finally, we should remember Thomas Cannon's mid-eighteenth-century tale of Amorio
and Hyacinth.

[64] For Wilde's instructions to Ross, see Wilde (2000: 780–1).
[65] Wilde (2005a: 50–1), emphasis added.
[66] Wilde (2005a: 66).
[67] Wilde (2005a: 67).

to me with earnest, frightened entreaties not to let you know that she was writing to me.'[68] Wilde implies that, if mother and son had indeed corresponded directly, then much of the trouble that ensued would not have happened.[69] So it is hardly surprising that *De Profundis* should be a letter designed to be read by those to whom it is not addressed: Wilde's and Douglas's relationship was structured, as Wilde represents it in *De Profundis*, as one governed by letters sent to one person but really addressed to another. 'From pert telegrams to priggish lawyers' letters was a natural progress...'[70]

The imprisoned Wilde had time to consider the ironies of his existence, and was well aware of the difficulty of transmitting and understanding Greek just like Jowett, Pater, and Symonds before him. The story of the older man (sexually and intellectually) corrupting the younger is the story that became widely circulated and accepted during and after the trials. Wilde writes: 'Your father's version of our friendship...that version has now actually passed into serious history: it is quoted, believed and chronicled: the preacher has taken it for his text, and the moralist for his barren theme.'[71] With *De Profundis*, however, Wilde attempts to offer a different sort of 'history' of the formation of Douglas's masculinity. Wilde suggests that he let himself be influenced by Douglas.[72] One of the most emotional and best-known sections of *De Profundis* recounts a stay in Brighton where Douglas fell 'ill with that dreadfully low fever that is foolishly called the influenza'.[73] Wilde relates how he tended and cared for 'Bosie', but when he caught the cold, Bosie was nowhere to be seen except to take money. Although many readers might indeed feel quite moved by Wilde's pitiful, heartrending account, we can see that the 'influenza' acts as a metaphor for the terrible contagion that had affected Douglas and that was henceforth transferred onto Wilde:

[68] Wilde (2005a: 134).
[69] Douglas's mother's 'unfortunate weakness...had been an element no less fatal than [Douglas's] father's violence' (Wilde 2005a: 49).
[70] Wilde (2005a: 67). See also Koestenbaum (1995) for the epistolary nature of *De Profundis*.
[71] Wilde (2005a: 80). See also (2005a: 137). Note Wilde also says elsewhere (2005a: 139): 'The "influence of an elder man over a younger man" is an excellent theory till it comes to my ears. Then it becomes grotesque.'
[72] See Wilde (2005a: 38–42), where Wilde repeatedly martyrs himself ('I blame myself') for repeatedly letting Douglas into his life.
[73] Wilde (2005a: 52).

'I have caught the influenza from you.'[74] Wilde's facetious observation on the 'foolish' name 'influenza' (just quoted) further brings home the punning message that Wilde was acting under the *influence* of Douglas.

The pathologization of Douglas is a significant part of the fabric of *De Profundis*. Just as Queensberry's version of events plays on Victorian anxieties about masculine sexuality, so Wilde's version takes its explicatory power from another set of Victorian discourses—those of race and heredity. The Socratic teaching scene is replaced by Wilde's description of a corrupting transmission of degenerate familial heritage. Fairly early on, he addresses Douglas: 'You had yourself often told me how many of your race there had been who had stained their hands in their own blood; your uncle certainly, your grandfather possibly, among others in the mad, bad line from which you came.'[75] For Wilde, there is no sense in polarizing himself and Douglas in contrast to men like Queensberry. Rather, it is the fateful similarity between Queensberry and Douglas that is the real problem: 'Through your father you come of a race, marriage with whom is horrible, friendship fatal, and that lays violent hands either on its own life, or lives on the lives of others.'[76] Much later in the text he writes: 'The curious thing to me is that you should have tried to imitate your father in his chief characteristics. I cannot understand why he was to you an exemplar, where he should have been a warning, except whenever there is hatred between two people there is bond or brotherhood of some kind.' The letters each man wrote to Wilde were qualitatively highly alike: Queensberry would 'write filthy letters...from a neighbouring hotel. You [Douglas] used to do *just the same* to me.'[77] The Queensberry/Douglas dyad illustrates what Sedgwick has called the 'homosocial continuum'[78]: the social and sexual behaviour of men that on one level seems polarized is on another virtually identical: to the one (Queensberry, a paragon of masculinity) the heterosexual institution of marriage is 'horrible', whereas to the other (Douglas, an effete, young poet) the homosocial institution of 'friendship' is 'fatal'. The effect of the behaviour of *both* father *and* son is to dissolve any bonds either might have to those around

[74] Wilde (2005a: 52).   [75] Wilde (2005a: 50).   [76] Wilde (2005a: 58).
[77] Wilde (2005a: 131), emphasis added.   [78] Sedgwick (1985).

them and atomize them. Queensberry was an 'exemplar' for Douglas to 'imitate'. Wilde asks Douglas:

> Do you think I am here on account of my relations with the witnesses on my trial? My relations, real or supposed, with people of that kind were matters of no interest either to the Government or to Society ... I am here for having tried to put your father into prison ... Your father completely turned the tables on me ... That is why there is contempt felt for me. That is why people despise me.[79]

Again tantalizing the reader with 'real or supposed' relations, thereby evading a straightforward confession, Wilde locates the true reason for his imprisonment with the Marquis of Queensberry. As we have already discussed, it was a telegram from Douglas to his father that conditioned the path of Wilde's life.[80] Elsewhere Wilde directly lays the blame at Douglas's door: 'it was not your father but you who had put me into prison ... from beginning to end you were the responsible person ... it was through you, for you, and by you that I was there [in prison]'.[81] Anticipating his identification with Christ later, Wilde solemnly declares that the 'sins of another [Douglas] were being placed to my account'.[82] The hatred for his father that Douglas displays in the newspapers is viewed by Wilde as symptomatic of an illness, which reiterates the pathological rhetoric: 'To write to the papers to say that one hates someone is as if one were to write to the papers to say that one had some secret and shameful malady.'[83] Indeed, Wilde's nosology strategically shifts any allusion from sexual inversion to Douglas's hate. Near to the conclusion of *De Profundis*, Wilde diagnoses the situation:

> The fact that your father loathed you, and that you loathed your father, was not a matter of any interest to the English public. Such feelings are very common in English domestic life, and should be confined to the place they characterize: the home ... You took domesticity out of its proper sphere, just as you took yourself out of your proper sphere.[84]

Returning to the public/private problematic, Wilde rewrites the events as a domestic (melo)drama of fathers and sons in a letter that is itself designed for a public audience. A little further on, Wilde says:

---

[79] Wilde (2005a: 79).   [80] Wilde (2005a: 67).   [81] Wilde (2005a: 70–1).
[82] Wilde (2005a: 74).   [83] Wilde (2005a: 71–2).   [84] Wilde (2005a: 143).

Having got hold of my life, you did not know what to do with it. You couldn't have known. It was too wonderful a thing to be in your grasp. You should have let it slip from your hands and gone back to your own companions at their play . . . That, when everything is said, is perhaps the *ultimate secret* of all that has happened. For secrets are always smaller than their manifestations. By the displacement of an atom a world may be shaken.[85]

Drawing on the fondness for the theme of secrecy in Victorian culture and writing, Wilde displaces the possibility that there will be a revelation in this document.[86] Perhaps the true secret is that there was no real secret after all. Indeed, the only character who should be confessing without exactly confessing is Alfred Douglas himself: 'The key of the situation rested entirely with yourself'.[87] 'You were the only person who, and *without in any way exposing yourself* to scorn or danger or blame, could have given another colour to the whole affair, have put the matter in a different light, have shown to a certain degree how things really stood.'[88]

Wilde puts the relationship between father and son in counter-point with that between mother and son, except here it is the mother's *lack* of pedagogical leadership that is the problem. Douglas's mother 'talks of the influence of an elder over a younger man, for instance. It is one of her favourite attitudes towards the question, as it is always a successful appeal to popular prejudice and ignor-ance'.[89] 'But the first duty of a mother', Wilde counsels, 'is not to be afraid of speaking seriously to her son. Had your mother spoken seriously to you about the trouble she saw you were in . . . it would have been much better and much happier ultimately for both of you'.[90] Instead of acting like a parent who was meant to teach her son, 'she was afraid of her responsibilities, and tried to shift them on to me'.[91] Freud will warn of too much maternal desire. Here Wilde

---

[85] Wilde (2005a: 146), emphasis added.
[86] See C. A. Miller (1988) and Sedgwick (1990) on secrecy, the open secret, and Victorian (homo)sexuality.
[87] Wilde (2005a: 69).
[88] Wilde (2005a: 79), emphasis added. Even if Douglas cannot face the public with what really happened, he will need 'to take the mask off for breathing purposes' and admit the truth to himself (Wilde 2005a: 138).
[89] Wilde (2005a: 138).   [90] Wilde (2005a: 135).   [91] Wilde (2005a: 136).

worries over the fear a mother has for her son. Wilde unwrites the story of a Socratic elder corrupting ephebic youth. The formation and education of Douglas were due to a damaging racial heritage from his father and his mother's inability to teach. Wilde consciously does *not* continue to paint Bosie as another Alcibiades. Wilde attempts to put a stop to the repetitiousness of the teacher—pupil relationship gone wrong. Indeed, we have already read about Jowett's vexed relations with his students, Pater and Symonds. We have discussed Pater's own difficult friendship with Wilde. Now Wilde finds himself in a similarly tricky position with his disciple, Bosie, who simply did not heed his Greek lessons. It is in this context, then, that Wilde can be seen to redefine the Platonic model, by turning to the example of Jesus Christ.

The nineteenth century had already witnessed a continual interest in Christ's relations with other men. Jeremy Bentham discussed Christ in his apology for desire between men;[92] Tennyson's poetry bespeaks a concern with a homoerotic Christ;[93] the Catholic conversion of the poet Gerard Manley Hopkins provides us with another nineteenth-century example of homoerotic interest in Christ's beauty.[94] Eve Kosofsky Sedgwick has examined how nineteenth-century interest in Greek homoerotic culture is almost always accompanied by a consideration of Christian ethics.[95] We have seen how Jowett's examination of Plato was accompanied by weekly preaching in Balliol College chapel. Pater's Spartans were explicitly compared to David and Jonathan, whose love passed even that of a woman. And Symonds's essay 'The Genius in Greek Art' examined the possibility of synthesizing Greek and Christian ethics in a modern education. Indeed the Christlike holiness of Socrates was programmed by Gesner's accentuation on holy pederasty, which itself points back to Renaissance readings of Socrates and Plato, influenced by Erasmus's

---

[92] See Crompton (1985: 260).

[93] See Dellamora (1990: 37–8, 227 n. 47). Interestingly, Tennyson's reworking of the myth of Apollo and Hyacinthus makes the young boy who returns as a flower look very much like the return of the Messiah.

[94] See Dellamora (1990: 47–8). Other 'Uranian' poets of 'boy-love' were also interested in Christ's beauty: see d'Arch-Smith (1970: 188–91) and Hilliard (1982: 199–200).

[95] See Sedgwick (1990: 136–41).

'Sancte Socrates, ora pro nobis'. David Hilliard has also examined how 'Anglo-Catholic religion within the Church of England ha[d] offered emotional and aesthetic satisfactions' to men who formed intensely close bonds to other men in the second half of the nineteenth century.[96] Walter Pater regularly visited 'St Austin's Priory', an Anglo-Catholic monastic brotherhood in Walworth, south London.[97] Finally, it is interesting to note that Wilde received aid from a prominent Anglo-Catholic socialist priest, Stewart Headlam, 'himself something of an aesthete'.[98]

Just as Pater found himself in need of redefining his aestheticism in the face of mounting critique, so Wilde sought to restructure his (and implicitly Pater's) aesthetic ideals, which had become so tarnished from 1895 onwards.[99] Quoting from Pater's essay 'Winckelmann', which itself cited Goethe, Wilde writes that Christ 'is just like a work of art. He does not really teach one anything, but by being brought into his presence one becomes something'.[100] Just like Pater's Winckelmann and Plato, Jesus is a figure whose influence over modernity is undeniable and yet at the same time fragmentary and therefore open to imaginative revision and rewriting. This complex reception of Jesus is reflected in Wilde's excitement that nineteenth-century scholarship has apparently proven that Jesus spoke Greek and that it was possible to read his very own words ('ipsissima verba'): 'It was always supposed that Christ spoke Aramaic. Even [Ernest] Renan thought so. Now we know the Galilean peasants, like the Irish peasants of our own day, were bilingual, and that Greek was the ordinary language of intercourse all over Palestine, as indeed all over the Eastern world'.[101] Wilde positions Jesus within Greek antiquity, reflecting a Victorian anxiety to distance Jesus from 'Semitic' culture. The historical Jesus could be seen as related culturally and racially to white Europeans.[102]

---

[96] Hilliard (1982: 181).   [97] Hilliard (1982: 193).
[98] Hilliard (1982: 199). See also Roden (2002) for a detailed account of homoerotic desire in Victorian religious culture.
[99] See Hanson (1997: 5).
[100] Wilde (2005a: 123). Pater (1910: i. 185): 'One learns nothing from him . . . but one becomes something.'
[101] Wilde (2005a: 118).
[102] See Wilde (2005a: 266–7) on late Victorian scholarship on Greek being spoken by Jesus.

Yet, just as Goethe never got to meet Winckelmann, so Jesus never met Plato or Socrates: Wilde muses that 'it is a delight to me to think that as far as his conversation was concerned, Charmides might have listened to him, and Socrates reasoned with him, and Plato under-stood him: that he really said ἐγώ εἰμι ὁ ποιμὴν ὁ καλός' 'I am the good shepherd'.[103] We have repeatedly witnessed the desire to have been present at and actually hear the Socratic lesson, a wish instilled by the critique of writing in the *Phaedrus*. Here Wilde wishes Jesus, Socrates, and Plato could have conversed and debated with one another. Reading Jesus' words makes him seem audible, and yet what he said was only the beginning of a process, necessarily an imaginative fragment. Wilde's Jesus is both a historical figure, posi-tioned within the history of Greek-speaking Europe, and an imagined work of beautiful art.

Wilde's turn to Christ polarized readers as soon as Robbie Ross published the abridged edition of *De Profundis* in1905. Some thought that it signalled repentant contrition, while others saw it as insincere, yet another aestheticizing pose.[104] Even with the publication of the fuller text, Wilde's voice has remained difficult to hear. Jonathan Dollimore sees Wilde's text as a capitulation to conventional moral-ity. Wilde's aesthetic celebration of Christian humility is politically vacuous, merely a fantasy of maverick autonomy. Wilde's repeated description of 'shallowness' as the 'supreme vice' is nothing more than the assertion of bourgeois individualism.[105] Michael Doylen meanwhile views Wilde's text as a vigorously imaginative attempt to create new models of self-fashioning and self-invention.[106] Just as the relationship between Platonic textuality and Greek pederasty proved a significant source of debate for eighteenth- and nineteenth-century scholars, so the relationship between nineteenth-century letters and male sexuality has been the source of speculation for more recent historians. And *De Profundis* has proven to be one of the most difficult of letters to translate. It is impossible to know what to make of it—it resists classification: partly a private document, in

---

[103] Wilde (2005a: 118). Wilde is quoting John 10:11, 14. In the late nineteenth century, John was viewed quite differently from the Synoptic Gospels. Ernest Renan wrote in his *Life of Jesus* of John's 'obscure Gnosticism and the distorted metaphysics' (Renan 1890: xliv).
[104] See the early reviews of *De Profundis* in Beckson (1970).
[105] See Dollimore (1991: 95–8).
[106] See Doylen (1999). See also Buckler (1989) and Roden (2002).

which Wilde writes out in petty detail the money he spent on Douglas; partly a public apologia countering Queensberry's version of events; partly a dense and opaque examination of Christ as the exemplary artist. Linda Dowling represents many others when she hopes that 'Wilde is steadily becoming audible again, as a cultural hero rather than merely a homosexual martyr'.[107] It is not as a religious icon but as a Greek hero that she anticipates Wilde becoming 'audible'. 'Perhaps, a century after the tragedy of Wilde's fall', she continues, 'we are at last able to *hear* . . . the recovery of a perspective that had originally entered Anglo-American consciousness through the spiritual procreancy ideal of Oxford Hellenism'.[108] Her celebration of the possibility that we might at last be hearing Wilde's message, that we at the end of the twentieth century are the true recipients of his texts, clearly alludes to Plato's *Symposium*. Dowling's reception of Wilde reflects the difficulties of knowing what sort of example he is for the present: on the one hand, her emphasis on making him audible signifies her scholarly eagerness to excavate his biography. Yet, on the other hand, her neglect of *De Profundis* implies that not everything Wilde said is worth remembering for the present. Just as Wilde's Christ hovers between lived historical personage and imaginary work of art, so Wilde himself has become a myth for the present and an irrecoverably foreign figure, which brings forth several difficult questions: should we mythologize Wilde? (How) should we forget the inconvenient historical details of his life? What does it mean to make a man, predisposed to pederastic relations, an exemplar for gay people? What are we to make of Wilde's treatment of his wife and family? Finally, how are we to include Wilde's Christ in his (hi)story: a final capitulation to bourgeois mentality or a radical attempt to redefine conventional Christian morality?

Wilde himself meditates on the knowability of the self when he writes during his Christology:

People whose desire is solely self-realization never know where they are going. They can't know. In one sense of the word it is of course necessary, as the Greek oracle said, to know oneself: that is the first achievement of knowledge. But to recognize that the soul of a man is unknowable is the ultimate achievement of wisdom. The final mystery is oneself.[109]

[107] Dowling (1994: 153).
[108] Dowling (1994: 154), emphasis added.
[109] Wilde (2005a: 124).

De Profundis is explicitly *not* a confessionary text. Wilde does not divulge the sexual truth about his relationship with Douglas. As we have already seen, the 'secret' of the events, for Wilde, is not to be located there. It is hardly surprising, then, that he should have produced such a contested legacy: Wilde himself questioned what was to be known about his self.

TRANSLATING CLIVE'S TRANSLATIONS OF GREEK

This constant rewriting of the past, this incessant remaking of Britain's classical heritage, became all the more urgent after Wilde's trial. And *De Profundis* provoked numerous publications, all trying to make sense of Wilde's relationship with Bosie.[110] If his Platonism was shattered in the minds of the broader public, then those within the old universities, Cambridge and Oxford, felt the attack on their own classical values. The Cambridge Apostles, who represent an important chapter in the history of sexuality and masculinity in early twentieth-century England, were a secretive brotherhood of members of Cambridge University, who met for discussion on a wide range of subjects.

Scholars have argued that they used Platonism as a 'screen to hide behind',[111] but, as Julie Anne Taddeo discusses, 'the embracing of the classical heritage helped them to explain and comprehend their feelings for one another', as these 'men tried to fashion for themselves a nonmedical, nonpathological identity that erased the newly constructed boundaries between the homosexual and heterosexual male'. 'Within their private rooms at Cambridge, the Apostles continued to invoke Dorianism' and 'read Walt Whitman's poetry'.[112] The group, whose origins date back to the 1820s (early members included Tennyson and Hallam[113]), included such illustrious

---

[110] Ed Cohen (1993) has discussed the contemporary press coverage of the Wilde trial, but as yet there has been no extended scholarly analysis of the many publications written from 1905 onwards, the year *De Profundis* was published: see Sherard (1905, 1934); Ingleby (1907, 1912); S. Mason (1908); Ransome (1912); Birnbaum (1914); Harris (1918). We should also note Douglas's own commentary, first published in 1929.

[111] Jenkyns (1980: 293).

[112] Taddeo (1997: 200).

[113] See Dellamora (1990: 16–41) on Tennyson and the Apostles.

members as Lytton Strachey and Maynard Keynes, all interested in virile, chaste, platonic love. The Wilde trial haunted the Edwardian Apostles, and they expressed great concern that they might be seen as 'disciples of the deplorable practices of Oscar Wilde' and that male friendships were simply a 'cloak' for the 'most unnatural and shock-ing form of vice'.[114] The events of some ten years before made Strachey wonder if Plato's modern disciples might 'suffer in eminent silence til the day after tomorrow'.[115] And Wilde's turn to Christ in *De Profundis* must have seemed compromising for a group of men who named themselves after Jesus' followers.

It was into this brotherhood that E. M Forster stepped in 1902. And the intense discussion about male friendship certainly had an influ-ence on the budding writer. Indeed, his 1914 novel *Maurice* is one of the earliest texts to respond to Wilde's words, in such a way as to express its pointed awareness of the difficulty of understanding what Wilde meant by the 'love that dare not speak its name'. His book portrays a world of both innocence and knowledge. In the 'Terminal Note' to the novel, Forster says of his book that it 'certainly dates . . . it belongs to an England where it is still possible to get lost. It belongs to the last moment of greenwood'.[116] Elsewhere he wrote that he had created 'something absolutely new, even to the Greeks'.[117] At the same time, however, *Maurice* is set in a post-Wilde-trial world, where a homosexual was at risk of blackmail. Forster also notes that the book was 'the direct result of a visit to Edward Carpenter', where 'he and his comrade George Merrill combined to make a profound impression on me and to touch a creative spring'. But, as Forster then cheekily remarks, 'George Merrill also touched my backside—gently and just above the buttocks'.[118] Forster presents the novel as a result of a sexual awakening. Critics have more recently noticed that *Maur-ice* was also a consequence of Forster's visit to India. *Maurice* can easily be seen to reflect Forster's queer colonialist desires for the oriental other. The class-defined relationship of Clive and Alec talks of India without talking of the sexual encounter between colonizer

---

[114] A letter from Keynes to Strachey, 10 April 1907, quoted in Taddeo (1997: 226).
[115] In a letter to Keynes, 27 November 1905, quoted in Taddeo (1997: 228).
[116] Forster (1972: 221).
[117] Forster (1972: 9).
[118] Forster (1972: 217).

and colonized.[119] The novel presents itself, then, as both inside and outside concrete, historical processes, with characters that paradoxically portray innocent knowingness and studied ignorance.

Many readers of the novel have commented upon the novel's concern with Hellenism and homosexuality. In a well-known essay, Robert K. Martin remarks:

> the novel opposes two kinds of homosexuality—one that is identified with Cambridge and Clive, and one that is identified with Alec and the open air . . . The first [kind of homosexuality] is dominated by Plato, and indirectly, by John Addington Symonds and the apologists for 'Greek Love'; the second is dominated by Edward Carpenter and his translation of the ideas of Whitman.[120]

Other critics have more recently commented upon Forster's hostility to Hellenism in the novel *Maurice*. As Ann Ardis has noted, Edwardian England is a place where 'the Grand Tour does not carry . . . the cultural weight and authority that it could in the eighteenth century'. Mrs Durham, Clive's mother, does not want her son to travel to the Mediterranean, but to America instead, before he can follow his father into a political career.[121] Nevertheless, Clive does get his way. After having sat for his bar exams, he caught 'a slight touch of influenza with fever', which resulted in a further fainting fit at Maurice's house. Clive, soon recovered, travels to Greece, leaving Maurice stuck back in England.[122] Forster makes Maurice's 'antipathy' to Greece very clear, including a catalogue of Greek names that cites those previous roll-calls we have noted, but with a difference, for Maurice is a man who 'ha[s] no use for Greece'. 'His interest in the classics had been slight and obscene, and had vanished when he loved Clive. The stories of Harmodius and Aristogeiton, of Phaedrus, of the

---

[119] Quentin Bailey (2002: 340) writes: 'Syed Ross Masood, to whom Forster had made several declarations of love in 1910 and 1911, had returned to India, and Forster longed to see him again. There was, thus, a certain sexual charge to Forster's trip, an aspect that is interestingly absent from Forster's account at the beginning of *Maurice* [the "Terminal Note"] with its emphasis on the whole European genesis of the novel.' Gregory Bredbeck (1997) also writes of the influence of Carpenter's interest in Hinduism on Forster.

[120] R. K. Martin (1985: 52).

[121] Ardis (2007: 63). See Forster (1972: 89). On Forster's hostility to Hellenism, see Ardis (2007: 65).

[122] Ardis (2007: 94). It is thanks to the medical attentions of a doctor named 'Mr Jowitt' that Clive gets off to Greece (Forster 1972: 94–5). It is hard *not* to see a reference to Professor Benjamin Jowett in this name.

Theban Band were well enough for those whose hearts were empty, but no substitute for life.'[123] Maurice 'hated the very word ['Greece'] and . . . connected it with morbidity and death'.[124]

Forster makes Maurice's difficult relationship with the classics a recurring subject in the novel. In the very first chapter, Mr Ducie's sex education, which alludes to Plato's *Phaedrus*, elicited the following response from Maurice: 'Liar,' he thought. 'Liar, coward, he's told me nothing.'[125] The truthfulness or mendacity of Platonism is, as we shall see, an important issue in *Maurice*. For now, we can also note that Maurice's academic career was dogged by his miscomprehension of Latin and Greek. While daydreaming of a beautiful male face during Latin class, the authorial voice ponders knowingly, 'Was he a Greek god, such as illustrates the classical dictionary? More probable, but most probably he was just a man.'[126] Very close to the end of the novel, we will see that 'Alec was not a hero or a god, but a man embedded in society like himself [Maurice]'.[127] Maurice was never sexually attracted to ancient Greece. And when his classics master awakens his dreamy pupil with the admonishment: 'Hall! Dreaming again! A Hundred Lines!', all Maurice can respond with is: 'Sir—oh! Dative absolute,' a grammatical construction that of course does not exist in Latin.[128] At his school's prize day, he is bestowed with the honour of delivering the Greek oration. The authorial voice remarks, however, that 'the Greek was vile: Maurice got the prize on account of the Thought, and barely thus. The examining master had stretched a point in his favour since he was leaving and a respectable chap, and moreover leaving for Cambridge, where prize books on his shelves would help advertise the school'.[129] Right at the end of the novel, when Maurice announces his love for Alec to Clive, the latter re- marks: 'But surely—the sole excuse for any relationship between men is that it remain purely platonic'.[130] The text comments on why Maurice made this final visit to Clive at Penge:

It was the closing of a book that would never be read again, and better close such a book than leave it lying about to get dirtied. The volume of their past must be restored to its shelf, and here, here was the place, amid darkness and

[123] Forster (1972: 99).   [124] Forster (1972: 100).
[125] Forster (1972: 20). On the Platonic overtones, see Raschke (1997: 155–6).
[126] Forster (1972: 26).
[127] Forster (1972: 206).   [128] Forster (1972: 26).
[129] Forster (1972: 28).   [130] Forster (1972: 213).

perishing flowers. He owed it to Alec also. He could suffer no mixing of the old and the new.

'You belong to the past,' Maurice says to Clive.[131] Old and new—ancient and modern—have to be distinguished and remain separate for Maurice. 'The [Platonic] volume of their past' at the end of the novel that needs to be closed alludes to an important scene at the beginning of the book. The successful closure of this Platonic volume is to be contrasted with the sexual diagrams that Mr Ducie draws on the beach during the Platonic lesson he gives the young Maurice in the novel's very first chapter. Walking along the beach after the lesson had been imparted, Mr Ducie suddenly remembers: '"I never scratched out those infernal diagrams." . . . At the further end of the bay some people were following them also by the edge of the sea. Their course would take them by the very spot where Mr Ducie illustrated sex, and one of them was a lady.'[132] The contrast between Mr Ducie's text on the beach that might possibly linger on, and the Platonic volume of Maurice's and Clive's friendship, shaped as it was by their reading of Plato's *Symposium* at Cambridge, is noteworthy.

Even if we are never sure whether the 'lady' saw those infernal diagrams (in the Merchant/Ivory film production of *Maurice* (1987), a lady certainly does!), the possibility that Platonism might linger on is most obviously emblematized in the figure of Clive himself. Robert Martin has analysed the 'double structure' of *Maurice* in terms of two types of sexuality, whereby Maurice must move from the airless Platonism of Clive to the real-life love of a man with Alec. However, the novel's description of Clive's sexual orientation is not quite so clear-cut. *Maurice* does not simply equate 'Greece' with 'Greek love'. Even if the Cambridge college dean leaves 'the unspeakable vice of the Greeks' untranslated at his 'translation class', Clive does seem to think that Platonic love is translatable into the modern world.[133] Most notably, in *Maurice*, Greece is *not* a place where a male character will find sexual fulfilment with another man. Rather, it is the place where Clive meets Anne, his future wife.[134] Debrah Raschke has remarked:

Many critics have puzzled, quite understandably, on Clive's inexplicable turn to heterosexuality. One explanation is that he has seemingly confused

---

[131] Forster (1972:. 213, 214).   [132] Forster (1972: 20).
[133] Forster (1972: 50).   [134] See Forster (1972: 105, 128).

the perceived desires of his culture with his own. I agree with this assess-
ment but would like to suggest that there is more to this enigma . . . that it is
Clive's Platonism that is both the obstacle thwarting love between him and
Maurice and the catalyst to his pallid marriage . . . Clive's marriage, rather
than a confirmation of his heterosexuality, seems more an extension of his
Platonism.[135]

We cannot, of course, find evidence in Forster's text to confirm
Raschke's reading of Clive's psychology (his supposed confusion
about his desires). The text is actually most mysterious about Clive's
change of direction. An enigmatic, impersonal voice outside himself:
'just an announcement, "You who loved men, will henceforth love
women . . . " He tried to clothe the change with reason . . . and he
failed'. During his illness, the text simply says, 'he noticed how charming his nurse was and enjoyed obeying her'.[136] John Fletcher is also
perplexed by Clive's 'conversion to heterosexuality', which he views as
'an anomaly at the heart of the book that remains inexplicable and
unassimilable'. Indeed, he offers up numerous possible reasons:
'Clive's influenza and his hysteria; his discovery of the pleasures of
heterosexual flirtation; his family and class obligations . . . '.[137]

The lack of psychological depth—or anomalousness—bestowed
on Clive's character with regard to his sexuality should not, however,
be seen as a fault of Forster's writing, nor yet another sign of this
author's reserve. We do indeed get access into Clive's interior, but
one that is altogether more platonic, and this is where we can agree
with Raschke's observation that his marriage is a continuation of his
Platonism rather than any signifier of his heterosexuality. While Clive
and Maurice were together during and after Cambridge, the text says
of their relationship: 'Clive had expanded in this direction ever since
he had *understood* Greek. The love that Socrates bore Phaedo now
lay within his reach, love passionate but temperate . . . He educated
Maurice, or rather his spirit educated Maurice's spirit, for they themselves became equal.'[138] In contrast to Maurice, Clive is presented as
someone who understands his Greek. And his literacy is reflected in the
care he uses in comparing his own desire to the classics: the relationship
is presented as one where Clive—Socrates saves the sensual other

---

[135] Raschke (1997: 160).   [136] Raschke (1997: 106).
[137] Fletcher (1992: 83).   [138] Fletcher (1992: 91), emphasis added.

Maurice—Phaedo (Phaedo was a prostitute). There is no allusion to the altogether more ambiguous passages from the Platonic œuvre that mention Socrates' blushing at the beauty of Charmides or the complex relationship with Alcibiades. Later in the novel, when the authorial voice comes to describe Clive's feelings for Anne, it notes: 'But for Maurice he would never have developed into being worthy of Anne . . . The centre of his life was Anne . . . Besotted with love, he gave her his body and soul, he poured at her feet all that an earlier passion had taught him, and could only remember with an effort for whom that passion had been.' The text is quite explicit about Clive's feelings and does not mention any sense that Clive has to repress his feelings for Maurice—indeed quite the opposite. And, if anyone might accuse Forster of being reticent about sexual matters, they might be refuted with what continues with regard to Clive's and Anne's sexual relations. It is necessary to quote the details of Forster's quasi-sexological account:

> He never saw her naked, nor she him. They ignored the reproductive and the digestive functions . . . It was *unmentionable* . . . though he valued the body, the actual deed of sex seemed to him unimaginative, and best veiled in night. Between men it is inexcusable, between man and woman it may be practised since nature and society approve, but never discussed nor vaunted. *His ideal of marriage was temperate and graceful, like all his ideals*, and he found a fit helpmate in Anne, who had refinement herself . . . They loved each other tenderly . . . [139]

Problematically for many readers, Forster's presentation of Clive is not of a man who has to repress sexuality for the sake of society. The change is presented in highly mysterious terms ('just an announcement'), but at the same time, there has been no change, for Clive is Platonic from start to finish. His philosophy of marriage is idealistic in its temperance and grace, terms that are resonant with Benjamin Jowett's translation of Plato's dialogues.[140] Notably, it is *not* Platonic love that is an '*unspeakable* vice' but modern married sexual relations that must remain '*unmentionable*'. Clive is ultimately presented as an individual who has little interest in sex, homo- or hetero-erotic.

---

[139] Fletcher (1972: 144), emphases added.
[140] For instance, note that the English title of the homoerotic dialogue *Charmides* is 'Charmides or Temperance' (Jowett 1892: i. 9).

Conversely, it is Maurice who is presented by the novel as deceiv-
ing himself and misunderstanding Greek. When at Cambridge Clive
pronounces his love to Maurice, the latter simply does not understand, despite having read the *Symposium* in the preceding vacation.
Instead he 'was scandalized, horrified. He was shocked to the bottom
of his suburban soul,' and exclaims 'oh rot!'[141] In the very next
chapter in which we see Maurice pondering Clive's declaration, the
authorial voice narrates: 'He [Maurice] had lied ... He would not
deceive himself so much ... He loved men and always had loved
them.'[142] Eventually he announces to Clive: 'I have always been like
the Greeks and didn't know it.'[143] But their relationship is ultimately
doomed precisely because *each man differs in the way in which he has
translated his Greek.* Clive promotes a reading of the Platonic texts
that validates spiritual, non-sensual love, whereas Maurice reads
Plato as valorizing physical as well as spiritual desire. On their one
day together in Platonic passion at Cambridge, when they skip
lectures (including the Dean's Greek translation class), they take the
side-car out into the country. Forster, with deliberate ambiguity,
writes: 'the machine [the side-car] took on a life of its own, in
which they met and realized the unity preached by Plato'.[144] That
their own translations of Plato took a life of their own is evidenced by
Forster's word 'unity', a seemingly innocent and abstract term simultaneously suggestive of sexual innuendo. Indeed, the hypnotist that
Maurice will later see to cure his 'congenital homosexuality' will ask
whether Maurice and Clive 'had ever united'.[145] At the very end of the
novel, when Maurice meets Clive to tell the latter that he has shared
'all' with Alec, Penge's former gamekeeper, Clive asks Maurice: 'Who
taught you to talk like this?' Maurice answers: 'You, if anyone'.[146]
Maurice has read sensuality in(to) the Platonic œuvre. At the beginning of the novel, as we have seen, Maurice calls the Platonic pedagogue a 'liar'. By the end of the novel, it seems he has uncovered quite
a different truth from Plato. Indeed, Maurice is quite defiant in his
reassessment of the Greek philosopher. With regard to Alec's forsak-
ing of his emigration to Argentina for his love of Maurice, the latter
says: 'I don't know whether that's platonic of him or not, but it's what

---

[141] Forster (1972: 52).   [142] Forster (1972: 58–9).
[143] Forster (1972: 62).   [144] Forster (1972: 76).
[145] Forster (1972: 158, 157). [146] Forster (1972: 214).

he did.'[147] Even more pointedly, he says to Clive: 'You don't worry whether your relation with her [Anne] is platonic or not, you only know it's big enough to hang a life on.'[148] The irony of what Maurice says is resonant, as Clive certainly does view his marriage in such philosophical parameters. Nevertheless, it has been Clive's philosophy that has taught Maurice to see his own truth. Clive can only wonder: 'had he corrupted an inferior's intellect? He could not realise that he and Maurice were alike descended from the Clive of two years ago . . .'.[149] The high-minded Victorian reading of Platonism could, worryingly, furnish *more than one* interpretation: a Clive could reproduce himself *and* a Maurice. Forster's metaphor of 'descent' ironically accentuates the burning question at the heart of the novel: what does it mean to say that modern homosexuality is 'descended' from Platonic philosophy? Forster's metaphor reflects Symonds's and Pater's own imagery of ancestry and relationality.

The novel ends on a mysterious note—Maurice disappears into the night, never to be seen again.[150] But there is a still more mysterious denouement after Maurice vanishes, and this is with Clive himself: 'He waited for a little in the alley, then returned to the house, to correct his proofs and to devise some method of concealing the truth from Anne.'[151] This is the final sentence of the novel. The attentive and careful reader is finally rewarded—with ambiguity: what is this 'truth' that Clive must conceal from Anne— his own sexuality or that of Maurice? This delicious equivocation that closes Forster's own volume also keeps it open, as we are tantalizingly left to wonder whether Clive really was lying or telling the truth to himself about Plato. How are we to translate Clive's translations of ancient Greek? Is it possible to believe consciously in Platonic love after the Wilde trial?

Forster makes it explicit that his novel takes place after that sensationalized event. When Maurice, sprawling in loneliness after Clive has left him, sees the old family doctor, Barry, he confesses to being 'an unspeakable of the Oscar Wilde sort'. All Barry can respond is, 'Rubbish, rubbish!' and terminate the consultation.[152] Rather than clarifying homosexual identity, Oscar Wilde's public proclamation of Platonism poses a problem for those Edwardian men sexually

---

[147] Forster (1972: 213).   [148] Forster (1972: 214).   [149] Forster (1972).
[150] See Bredbeck (1997: 54) on the enigmatic closure.
[151] Forster (1972: 215).   [152] Forster (1972: 139).

attracted to other men. Indeed, just as ancient Greek sexuality proved untranslatable in the Dean's translation class, because of its 'unspeakable' nature, so Wilde's sexuality is also difficult to translate for Maurice, again because it is 'unspeakable'. Maurice does not know how to translate into his own present the unspeakable Wilde's translation of the love that remains unspeakable. 'Wilde' signifies in language a problem, which paradoxically must remain outside language, ineffable.

It is important to observe that this final scene of the novel, in which male—male love is more tortuously discussed than in any other scene, itself becomes difficult to remember. The end of the novel flashes forward to Clive's future daydreams: 'To the end of his life Clive was not sure of the exact moment of [Maurice's] departure, and with the approach of old age *he grew uncertain whether the moment had yet occurred* . . . Out of some eternal Cambridge his friend began beckoning him, clothed in the sun . . . '.[153] The novel ultimately presents for us a character for whom it seems impossible that such a discussion about the Platonic theory of love could ever have occurred, could ever have been possible. We are never permitted a view of Maurice's and Alec's future —only Clive's. Instead, Maurice is consigned to an ancient past, to the Cambridge of the 'May Term', 'clothed'—in nothing but (?)—'the sun'. Is this memory of Maurice blinded or enhanced by solar rays? (How) are we to remember Maurice and his love? We have already examined Symonds's difficulty in remembering how he learnt from Jowett, and we have already discussed the difficulty of knowing what influence Jowett exerted over Pater's career and his Platonism. The Platonic encounter remains a mysterious one in *Maurice*.

Interestingly, the 1987 Merchant/Ivory film *Maurice* interprets Clive quite differently. Here he is most definitely presented as a repressed homosexual in the film's denouement. Richard Dyer has contextualized *Maurice* the film within the genre of heritage cinema— that is, period films that are mostly and very explicitly adaptations of canonical literary works. Indeed, 'heritage cinema has been notably hospitable to homosexual subject matter'.[154] Dyer emphasizes the difference between historical scholarship, which often explores the

---

[153] Forster (1972: 215), emphasis added.   [154] Dyer (2002: 205).

'perhaps incommensurable differences in the manifestations of "homosexuality" in the past', and homosexual heritage cinema, which has been 'more inclined to cherish in the past antecedents of the practices and beliefs of gay liberation: being yourself, coming out, heroism'.[155] Such cinema is not so much about putting homosexuals into history, as about aiming to provide contemporary gay people with a heritage.[156] As Glyn Davis makes clear, this agenda erases historical difference and risks essentializing sexuality so that 'more disruptive, queer forms of sexuality are markedly absent . . . Indeed it would seem that the form of the heritage film . . . is too closely tied to a "gay liberation" perspective.'[157] Clive's ambiguous nature is accordingly suppressed in the 1980s filmic presentation of *Maurice*. Here his Platonism can stand for nothing but a suppression of a sexuality that Maurice heroically embraces. This is, however, perfectly understandable if we consider the film's context: in 1987 HIV/AIDS was already ravaging gay communities, and it was important to locate a moment of gay history that looked healthy, warm, and loving.

The problem for the film-makers, then, was to find a motivation for Clive's turn to marriage. Forster's own mysterious presentation of Clive's Platonism was not used by the screenwriter, and instead an entirely new subplot was introduced for the film, which did not appear in the novel: the trial of Viscount Risley. In Forster's 'Terminal Note' to the novel, he happily remarks that 'Risley, as Lytton [Strachey, an early reader] gleefully detected, was based upon Lytton'.[158] In the novel, the 'clever Trinity undergraduate'[159] appears in the Cambridge scenes and in one other chapter, when Maurice meets him after a concert where Tchaikovsky's *Symphony Pathétique* was played. (Maurice was attending with Miss Tonks, a friend of Kitty's, in the hope that he might develop an attraction to her.) This, of course, was 'the symphony of Tchaikovsky Clive had taught him to like', and Risley mockingly calls it the 'Symphony Pathique'.[160] The chance meeting takes place in the very next chapter after Maurice has visited Dr Barry, worrying that he is 'an unspeakable of the Oscar Wilde sort'.[161] In the film, the novel's oblique association of Risley with Wilde (*pace* Strachey) is explicitly

[155] Dyer (2002: 207).   [156] Dyer (2002: 210).
[157] G. Davis (2006: 199, 205).   [158] Forster (1972: 220, 219).
[159] Forster (1972: 220).   [160] Forster (1972: 141).
[161] Forster (1972: 139).

expanded in a separate storyline in which Risley is caught by the police *in flagrante* in a back alley with a soldier. 'The film narrative, by adding the Risley sequence, creates a causal chain for Clive's behaviour. His illness, although not overtly described as a response to Risley's situation, follows immediately after it . . . Only in the film does Clive say, "We've got to change . . . ".'[162] The film's audience cannot not think of Wilde when they see Risley (Lytton Strachey was hardly a household name by the end of the twentieth century). In the film, the Oscar Wilde/Viscount Risley trial moves Clive into repression—the trial is a decisive and deciding event, whereas, in the book, Wilde's trial makes understanding modern male—male desire in relation to ancient Greece all the more complicated.[163]

Robert K. Martin, as we have noted, has emphasized how *Maurice* (the book) moves from Platonic to Carpenterian homosexuality, a journey of Maurice's personal growth. But, as we have seen, the Platonism of the first part of the novel does not simply disappear in the second, neither in Clive nor in Maurice. Forster's attitudes to Hellenism are altogether more complex and ambivalent. As Gregory W. Bredbeck has examined, Maurice is explicitly seen as 'bacchanalian' by Mrs Durham near the end of the novel;[164] and his disappearance at the very end also makes Maurice mysteriously Dionysian. Ultimately, 'Maurice himself is simply somewhere *different*, somewhere discernible neither by Clive, nor the reader, nor the narrative itself'.[165] Lytton Strachey, to whom Forster early on passed on a manuscript of *Maurice* to read, complained that Maurice's relationship with Alec was 'very wobbly . . . I would have prophesied a rupture after 6 months—chiefly as a result of lack of common interests owing to class differences'. Furthermore, Strachey was highly critical of Forster's reticence of the presentation of the sexual side of Maurice's and Alec's relationship.[166] Christopher Lane has interrogated Strachey's assessment in his readdressing of Forster's interest in 'democratic affection'. Lane argues that we should attend to Forster's reserve all the more carefully. Rather than see a homosexuality that has been repressed behind democratic ideals, we should take

---

[162] Levine (1996: 316).   [163] See also M. Williams (2006) on queer cinema.
[164] Forster (1972: 164).   [165] Bredbeck (1997: 54).
[166] Strachey, quoted in Lane (2007: 114). Forster also records this criticism in his 'Terminal Note', although here it is only 'six weeks' (Forster 1972: 219).

Forster's concern with 'democratic affection' in itself more seriously. 'Forster's struggle to represent sexuality brought to the fore other narrative and philosophical dilemmas that are worth considering in their own right.'[167] Although Forster's portrayal of Clive and Alec may be reticent in its presentation of physical, sexual details, it nevertheless does bring up difficult questions about how male—male friendship, affection, and love might be successfully interlaced, integrated, and lived, within Edwardian society. Forster's apparent reserve about sexual matters in fact very candidly spotlights interesting ideas about the democracy of sexuality. Indeed, Forster's presentation of Carpenterian 'Love of Comrades . . . the Uranians' through the faces of Maurice and Alec is profoundly influenced by readings of ancient Greek texts.[168] In a poem contained in the publication *Towards Democracy* (originally published in four parts between 1883 and 1902), Edward Carpenter describes an allegorical figure of Democracy with 'huge limbs' and a 'stalwart erect member', and says: 'I will drain thy limbs and the secret things of thy body, | I will conceive by thee, Democracy'. Carpenter's socialist philosophy sought to see 'homosexuality as part of a wider vision of social renewal and reform'.[169] As Matt Cook has noted on Carpenter's poetically political deification of Democracy, he 'is like one of the free-standing Greek statues, and the encounter yields spiritual, philosophical and political progeny'.[170] Edward Carpenter's manipulation of Walt Whitman's manipulation of ancient Greek conceptualizations of democracy is to find expression in Forster's 1914 text.[171] Indeed, John Addington Symonds's view of Whitman's poetry as 'performing a function analogous to that performed by Socrates for Greek *paiderastia*' suggests that Platonism could *not* be monopolized by those who read like Clive.[172]

Maurice's relationship with Alec, then, signals a move away from nineteenth-century pederastic encounters. Maurice reads Plato's *Symposium* not because an older man has told him to but because Clive, his peer, suggests it.[173] That their love is one between two adult men is made clear when the announcement of Clive's engagement to Anne is made at the Halls' breakfast table. In order to escape from

---

[167] Lane (2007: 117–18).   [168] Forster (1972: 217).
[169] Carpenter (1985: 141).   [170] Cook (2003: 134, 138).
[171] On Carpenter's Hellenism, see Cook (2003: 133–8) and Cocks (2003: 192–6).
[172] Fletcher (1992: 67).   [173] Forster (1972: 50).

the scene, Maurice goes upstairs to wake Dickie Barry, Dr Barry's 'young nephew', who has been staying that weekend while the doctor was away.[174] The night before, on wishing Dickie goodnight, Maurice suggestively said to the boy that he slept in the room above his, in case he wanted anything, adding: 'all night alone. I always am'. The boy 'understood the situation perfectly' but did not take up Maurice's offer: 'Dickie's impulse was to bolt the door after him, but he dismissed it as unsoldierly, and awoke to the ringing of the breakfast bell, with the sun on his face and his mind washed clean'.[175] The pederastic encounter, then, is a forgotten encounter of the night before—of the past, now no longer part of Maurice's present.

Maurice's accentuation on virile equality as opposed to pederastic asymmetry is nevertheless complicated, if we remember that Forster wrote *Maurice* after his trip to India and after having met, tutored, and fallen in love with Syed Ross Masood.[176] Forster's democratic erotics veil a history of colonial desire. As we saw in the previous chapter, Symonds's investment in 'the right sort of Socialism' was at the same time a fetishization of the working-class 'other'. Furthermore, the admiration of manly Dorian culture was explicitly accompanied by approbation of the enslavement of Helots in Pater's *Plato and Platonism*. But Pater's Dorians oscillated between being an invisible, impossible ideal and visual, anatomized, imperialistic male bodies. That is to say, his Dorians looked like a distant other and a racialized carbon copy of the English public-school body. And Symonds's texts made clear that *he* did not know whether he was imitating Dorian (rather than Ionian) culture. Forster was writing against a background of texts in which the Dorians, the Edwardian model for manly love, wobbled between relation and foreigner, just as Alec looks like Forster's 'other half', his love of the same, *and* like the colonial other.

The break *Maurice* attempts to make from nineteenth-century pederastic discourses is reflected by the significant presence of women in the novel, a presence rarely discussed. We are no longer examining scenes of male homosocial pedagogy, such as Jowett's and Pater's texts, which resolutely exclude women, as Amy Levy's poem 'Xantippe' (1884) famously complained. Instead, right from the beginning of the novel, women problematically intrude upon that

---

[174] Forster (1972: 128).   [175] Forster (1972: 131).
[176] See Bailey (2002) on Masood and Forster.

previously exclusive, homosocial space. Maurice's Platonic lesson in chapter one with Mr Ducie ends his concern that he did not wipe away those 'infernal diagrams' in the sand and 'some people' who were walking on the beach would take themselves to 'the very spot where Mr Ducie had illustrated sex, and one of them was a lady'.[177] Chapter one is programmatic not only for the novel's exploration of Platonism but also for the problem of women's knowledge about men and male desire. That the reader never finds out whether 'a lady' does get to read the diagrams programmes the novel's continuous examination of the issue of female wisdom: women in *Maurice* both know and do not know, they hover awkwardly between knowledge and ignorance about male sexuality. Although Maurice might feel that 'home emasculated everything', and despite Clive's discourse on the superiority of male—male love over what his sister Pippa might feel for her fiancé, women constantly intrude upon the love of Maurice and Clive—and not just Anne Woods.[178] Mrs Hall enters the room the moment Maurice kisses Clive after the latter has fainted. Maurice swears his mother to secrecy: '"As you know, we are great friends, relations almost." It sufficed. She liked to have little secrets with her son.'[179] Mrs Hall is both privy to knowledge and at the same time ignorant of the real secret at the heart of the novel. And, when Maurice goes on a date with Gladys Olcott during a vacation between university terms, 'he played the domineering male . . . But she knew something was wrong. His touch revolted her. It was a corpse's'.[180] Again, a woman is portrayed as knowing and not knowing at the same time. Moreover, Maurice's sister Ada is depicted as a knowledgeable woman, but knowledgeable about what? When Clive is attracted to her, he says, 'No one knows as much as you!'[181] And when Maurice jealously blames Ada for his ensuing argument with Clive, she knows it is not her fault, but cannot say why: 'It doesn't signify', she remarks. Women are in special possession of knowledge in *Maurice* but cannot put into language the unspeakable problem.

Later in the novel, Clive patronizingly characterizes this knowledge as 'female intuition', when Anne somehow guesses that Maurice's

---

[177] Forster (1972: 20).
[178] Forster (1972: 51, 84). See also (1972: 78): Maurice's mother's 'very softness enraged him'.
[179] Forster (1972: 95).   [180] Forster (1972: 53).   [181] Forster (1972: 111).

erratic behaviour meant that he was in love. 'Women are extraordinary', Clive triumphantly exclaims, as Maurice lies to his old friend about plans to get married.[182] After a night in each other's arms and the cricket match in which Alec and Maurice play together as if 'they were against the whole world',[183] Maurice leaves Penge for London for another bout of hypnosis to cure his sexuality. With Maurice absent, 'there was to be a laughing open secret about this girl in town', his supposed fiancé.[184] Ann's and Mrs Durham's knowledge that Maurice's love life is an 'open secret' reflects their complicated relationship to knowledge: they know that Maurice has a secret but do not know what that secret is.

The representation of Maurice's life as an open secret is not accidental: by the end of the novel, the reader is left with the sense that we know everything about Maurice, but at the same time our knowledge eludes linguistic expression. He is like a ghost: fully embodied, part of the modern present, *and* an image from the past that Clive can only half remember, vanishing into the night. The relationship between Maurice and Alec is founded upon real, physical desires, but its story remains untold—it is outside the very frame of the novel itself, beyond the bounds of representation. In his 'Terminal Note', Forster remarks that 'Lytton Strachey, an early reader . . . wrote me a delightful and disquieting letter and said that the relationship of the two rested upon curiosity and lust and would only last six weeks'.[185] Having written a novel for a small audience of friends, designed to be published posthumously, Forster was criticized by Strachey for the chaste nature of the writing (as mentioned above). But Strachey missed the point: rather than locate the truth of Maurice in his sexual acts, as a sexologist or legal theorist might have done, Forster questions the knowability of Maurice's *erōs*. Moving between two worlds, classical Cambridge and modern suburbia, Platonic idealism and bodily realism, *Maurice* ponders whether love is ever straightforwardly knowable: what is the more erotic object of desire, the visible or the invisible, the tangibly present or the tantalizingly absent? The novel stages a young man's transition from Plato's Cambridge to a world where the gaze of the public—and the gaze of women especially—is unavoidable. And it is women's responses to Maurice that

---

[182] Forster (1972: 152).   [183] Forster (1972: 176).
[184] Forster (1972: 179).   [185] Forster (1972: 219).

structure the reader's response: the novel suggests that, after Wilde, male love is both known and unknowable, fully reified and yet ideally beyond representation. Although Forster's book stages a transition from nineteenth-century Platonism into twentieth-century sexuality, the book is haunted by the paradoxes explored in an Oxbridge education, as exemplified by Wilde's own notebooks on Platonic *erōs* between knowledge and ignorance. The Platonic emphasis in the *Phaedrus* on just having to be there to know it is reflected in Forster's refusal to represent Maurice's and Alec's relationship. The knowability of male desire was also a crucial issue for Sigmund Freud, who was writing at the same time at E. M. Forster. Also writing in a medical and legal context in which male sexuality was supposedly capable of being historicized, accounted for, and fully known, Freud radically questioned whether a man ever really knew what he wanted. As we turn to Freud now, we will see that men's desires evolve within quite fantastical and mythical relationships, relationships many twentieth-century men would never have imagined.

5

Freud and the History of Masculinity: Between Oedipus and Narcissus

iste ego sum

> (Narcissus, Ovid, *Met.* 3.463)

I am all Leonardo

> (Sigmund Freud, letter, 6 March 1910, in
> *The Freud/Jung Letters*)

At the turn of the nineteenth century into the twentieth, Havelock Ellis's *Sexual Inversion* was one of the best-known works on same-sex desire. For the scientist, 'society would right itself when people achieved a certain level of self-knowledge, especially sexual knowledge'.[1] The truth of one's self, the truth of one's self-understanding, lay in the comprehension of one's sexual desires, desires that themselves are the truthful, indelible core of our natures. As such, as we saw in our discussion of John Addington Symonds, any legislation that sought to criminalize against those desires (homo- or hetero-erotic) was pointless: we could not choose whom we desired and loved. Very quickly, however, Ellis's pre-eminence was eclipsed by the psychoanalytic theories of Freud.[2] Whereas Ellis considered that homosexual was innate or congenital, Freud made various arguments across the period of his career that, as we shall see, produced a very different model of male sexuality. One of the most fundamental differences between the two doctors was their interest in the relationship between history and sexuality. Freud himself makes the relevant

---

[1] Crozier (2000: 449).   [2] Crozier (2000: 450).

observations in a footnote to *Three Essays on Sexuality*, first published in 1905:

> Havelock Ellis has published a number of autobiographical narratives… These reports naturally suffer from the fact that they omit the prehistoric period of the writers' sexual lives, which is veiled by infantile amnesia and which can only be filled in by psychoanalysis in the case of an individual who has developed a neurosis.[3]

One of those autobiographies was, of course, provided by Symonds himself. We are witness here to a significant shift in the way in which sexuality was historicized, from the autobiography to the uncovering of the 'prehistoric period' by psychoanalysis, from Symonds to Freud, from waking up with Plato in one's arms, to the myths of Oedipus and Narcissus. In previous chapters we saw how the Socratic teaching scene, the Platonic dialogue, the relationship between the Dorians and the Ionians and the love between Achilles and Patroclus, provided the various leitmotifs through which modern masculinity was furnished with a sense of history. We examined how different versions of the pederastic relationship (the Socratic/Platonic, the Dorian, the Ionian) were imagined by German and British thinkers across the eighteenth and nineteenth centuries. The history of this pedagogy produced Oscar Wilde, who impressed the Oxford examiners' board to such an extent that he was awarded a double first and was requested to attend a *viva voce* examination to elucidate his thoughts on the relationship between Aristotle and Walt Whitman.[4] The best Oxford classicist of 1877 provoked a discussion on the relationship between ancient Greek philosophy and a nineteenth-century poet who wrote on the loving bonds men had with other men. By 1895, however, rather than academic glory, the relationship between modern male friendship and Plato's theory of love saw to Wilde's incarceration. Sigmund Freud was also the product of the neo-humanist educational system. But, rather than a pedagogy that sought to explain the influence of ancient philosophy on modern society, Freud's *abitur* examination in 1873 famously featured a translation from Sophocles' *Oedipus Tyrannus*, which put Freud on the path of

---

[3] From *Three Essays on Sexuality*, pages 190–1 in *The Standard Edition of the Complete Psychological Works of Sigmund Freud*, ed. and trans. J. Strachey et al. 24 vols. London: Hogarth Press, vii. 190–1. Unless otherwise stated, all quotations from Freud will follow this edition (henceforth *SE*).

[4] Ellmann (1988: 94). See also (1988: 61) on Wilde on Aristotle's aestheticism.

understanding how *Greek myth* created who we are today.[5] Rather than attempt to uncover the historical *realien* of Greek pederasty and friendship, Freud sought to show that the history of male sexuality was nothing but a myth, caught between the tales of Oedipus and Narcissus.[6]

In 1865 Freud entered the *Realgymnasium* in Leopoldstadt, Vienna, a bold, new experiment in the history of Humboldt's *Gymnasium*. As we examined in Chapter 1, Humboldt's reforms of the Prussian education system, saw that the learning of languages was central to the pedagogic curriculum, through which one's character and personality were formed. Greek and Latin were the foundations of Humboldt's *Bildung*, which aimed to produce modern citizens for modern civilization. Austria, however, had not experienced the same history of educational reforms as Prussia. The important moment in Viennese educational history came in 1848–9 during the Revolution and counter-revolution. Under the neo-absolutist period, secondary and university education was widely reformed. In 1818, the curriculum was largely dominated by Latin; in 1849, the Latin element was reduced to a quarter of the student's time, and Greek and scientific subjects were introduced.[7] And so, under the influence of Humboldt's ideas, the Austrian *Gymnasium* sought a 'conciliation entre "deux cultures" scientifique et littéraire'. Jacques Le Rider has called the *Gymasium*'s legacy 'la double dette', which Freud owed to his *alma mater*, placing in him 'l'intérêt pour les langues et les civilisation anciennes et le goût du savoir scientifique'. Furthermore, 'cette double dette correspond à la double identité intellectuelle' of Freud: humanist faithful to the grand tradition of the return to classical Greece, *and* cautious and rigorous doctor, the professor of science.[8]

Just as Freud's own intellectual self was doubled, so his model of masculinity was also divided, between the myths of Oedipus and Narcissus. And it was Leonard da Vinci, as both artist and scientist, who, for Freud, exemplified the nature of male identity and sexuality. In this chapter, we will see how for Freud it is his interest in his past

[5] See Le Rider (2002: 54).

[6] It should be noted, however, that other readers have been interested in comparing Freud's theories of love with those of Plato: see Nachmansohn (1915), to whom Freud refers (*SE* vii. 134), and Santas (1988).

[7] Le Rider (2002: 51–2).

[8] Le Rider (2002: 63). Forrester (1980) also examines the importance of nineteenth-century linguistics and philology for the origins of psychoanalysis.

that creates a man's sexuality. Furthermore, as we shall discuss, the mythical figures Oedipus and Narcissus will be seen to exemplify what masculinity is, precisely because for Freud these myths concern how a man relates to his past. For him, these *mythoi* that meditate on the history of the individual are what create our access to knowledge about sexuality. And psychoanalytic discourses about sexuality shape, according to Freud, our knowledge of the meaning of these myths— that is, their meditations about what constitutes history. This chapter will show that the history of masculinity is not with Freud a history of how modern man might relate to his ancient counterpart. Rather the history from ancient to modern times is encapsulated within each of ourselves. But this history of masculinity, for Freud, is a mythical one—we tell myths about our past, in order to explain our present. Every man is ancient and modern, capable of both hetero- and homosexuality, Oedipus *and* Narcissus. The history of male sexuality *is* a myth. Locating the formation of every man in repressed, infantile urges saw that Greek love could no longer be a historical object of scholarly enquiry. Rather Freud created a Greek past for modern man, which was irrecoverable but at the same time profoundly influential on his present. In questioning Ellis's methods, in questioning modern men's abilities to write autobiographies of their (sexual) identities, Freud questioned what modern men thought they knew about their past desires and the relation of those desires to the present.

With Freud, the neo-humanist desire for the past becomes formalized into a full-scale theory of identity: as opposed to the pederastic scene in which the elder man influences his young lover, for Freud it is our infantile desires for our parents that define who we are. Freud famously abandoned his seduction theory that posited that children were commonly sexually molested by the adults who cared for them. Instead, our childhood histories became myths of desire played out in our heads. With Freud, Platonic pederasty became male infantile sexuality. And, more pointedly still, it was the little boy's relationship with his mother that interested Freud so much. The influence of the mother over the son was a concern that reflects a broader context for Freud's writing. The end of the nineteenth century saw a peak in the debate about women's higher education in the German states, with entry opened to women in Germany soon after. But the educated woman, as opposed to the educated and educating man, posed a problem for German intellectuals. Racial hygienists, eugenicists, and feminists argued over the benefits and problems of combining motherhood with a career. The politics of reproduction were fiercely contested: what would be the effect of higher education on a woman's body and mind? Could a highly educated woman be a good mother? Such were the questions being posed in the infancy of the twentieth century, as Freud turned to Leonardo's infantile desires.[9]

MOVING ON?

Freud's identification with Oedipus himself is well known. Oedipus was the man who solved the riddle of the Sphinx and who uncovered some other rather more unpalatable truths about himself. A copy of Ingres's painting *Oedipus and the Sphinx* (1808) hung on one of the walls of the room in which he analysed his patients. The replicability of Oedipus is reflected by the medallion that was presented to Freud in 1906 for his fiftieth birthday and his personal bookplate (both images bearing the line from Sophocles' play in Greek 'he who knew the famous riddles and was a powerful man'). Furthermore, the image on the bookplate is reproduced on the front cover of Rudnytsky (1987). Leonard da Vinci was also an exemplary figure for Freud, who compares his own iconoclasm with Leonardo's own radical avant-garde thinking in the Renaissance.[10] Leonardo's claim that 'il sole non si move' (the sun does not move) was met with great resistance, just like Copernicus' hypothesis and Darwinian theory precisely because these ideas shattered 'human self-love [*Eigenliebe*]'.[11] James Strachey translates *Eigenliebe* as 'narcissism'. Freud's message is clear: the history of scientific achievement necessitated a termination of humanity's narcissism at large. And so not dissimilarly, then, Freudian psychoanalysis underlines the need for the little boy to move on from his early narcissistic tendencies, through the Oedipus complex, into a safe and secure masculinity. It is the burden of Freud's biographical study of Leonardo, *Leonardo da Vinci and a*

---

[9] See Rowold (2010: 99–130) on German mothers and education.

[10] See also Armstrong (2005: 63): Freud's interest in Leonardo is 'key for understanding Freud's personalized genealogy of empirical science'.

[11] Leonardo's statement, quoted in *SE* xi. 76; Copernicus and Darwin, discussed in *SE* xix. 221.

Memory of his Childhood, first published in 1910, to show how Leonardo himself moved from Narcissus to Oedipus, from aesthetician and artist ('Künstler') to the great man of modern science ('Forscher').[12]

This sense of historical progress encapsulated within a single individual, working through a series of mythical identities, is reflected in Freud's interest in contemporary recapitulation theory. For Freud, the subject's life recapitulates *in nuce* the history of humanity in its development from primitive to civilized culture.[13] *Three Essays on the Theory of Sexuality* presents a developmental model of a child's sexuality beginning with

the *oral*, or as it might be called, cannibalistic pregenital sexual organisation . . . A second pregenital phase is that of the *sadistic—anal* organisation. Here the opposition between two currents, which runs through all sexual life, is already developed: they cannot yet, however, be described as 'masculine' and 'feminine', but only as 'active' and 'passive'. The activity is put into operation by the instinct for mastery through the agency of somatic musculature; the organ which, more than any other, represents the passive sexual aim is the erotogenic mucous membrane of the anus . . . Alongside these, other component instincts operate in an auto-erotic manner.[14]

This appears in the sixth section of the second essay—the section's name being 'The Phases of Development of the Sexual Organisation'. One can easily perceive that the historical development of the individual child summarizes the progress of human history as a whole. The oral phase mimics a 'primitive' society of cannibals; the anal phase in its organization of sexuality in terms of active/passive rather than masculine/feminine, as well as the accentuation on the anus, recalls ancient sexual practices, as they would have been understood in the nineteenth and early, and indeed later, twentieth centuries. This developmental model prepares the subject for a mature sexual disposition enabling sexual reproduction. In the end, then, heterosexuality and modern civilization, ideally, obtain. (In 1925, Freud added a footnote observing the insertion of the phallic phase between these pregenital organizations and sexual maturity.)

[12] *SE* xi. 63; *Gesammelte Werke*, ed. Anna Freud. 17 vols. Frankfurt-am-Main: Fischer Taschenbuch Verlag (henceforth *GW*), viii. 128.
[13] See Bowlby (2007: 230–3), with references to Gould (1977: 156–71), Sulloway (1980), and Ritvo (1990: 74–98).
[14] *SE* vii. 198.

This march of progress is, however, somewhat less certain than it appears. The opposition of currents found in the sadistic—anal organization, as Freud himself says, 'can persist throughout life'. Notably, Freud goes on to say that 'the predominance in it of sadism and the cloacal part played by the anal zone give it a quite peculiarly archaic colouring'.[15] The use of the word 'archaic' would not have gone unnoticed by Freud's readers. The sadistic—anal phase looks as if it were something that might happen in the ancient world. And, more strangely still, it seems that this ancient sexual distribution might persist into modern times. The developmental model, then, is far messier than at first appears. As Rachel Bowlby writes,

the child's uncoordinated sexual and emotional organization passes through several different phases, beginning with the oral and the anal, but there is no simple sequence, one after the other, still less a simple ending in which they are all surpassed and left behind in favour of the adult formation of hetero-sexual maturity. The earlier ways of experiencing remain in the background of the adult's reality, disturbingly not harmoniously; modern man is stuck with a primitive past.[16]

A FREUDIAN BIOGRAPHY OF LEONARDO

So how did Freud's only foray into the genre of historical biography contribute to his understanding of the psycho-history of masculinity? Did Leonardo move from Narcissus to Oedipus and beyond? Let us summarize more precisely the content and structure of Freud's *Leonardo*, which certainly gives no straightforward account of the great man's life. Rather Freud's bases his entire study on a single archive of a single memory that Leonardo has of his childhood: 'It seems that I was always destined to be so deeply concerned with vultures; for I recall as one of my very earliest memories that while I was in my cradle a vulture [*Geier*] came down to me, and opened my mouth with its tail, and struck me many times with its tail against my lips.'[17] For Freud 'the scene with the vulture' is 'not a memory of

---

[15] *SE* vii. 199.   [16] Bowlby (2007: 231). See also (2007: 161).
[17] *SE* xi. 82; *GW* viii. 150.

Leonardo's but a phantasy, which he formed at a later date and transposed to childhood'. Freud can state this simply because it 'sounds so improbable, so fabulous, that another view of it... has more to commend it to our judgement'.[18] The fantasy covered over a true memory, one in which the baby Leonardo suckled on his mother's breast, where 'he enjoyed the highest erotic bliss, which is never again attained'.[19] This unconscious memory suggests to Freud that Leonardo's relationship with his mother was highly charged and intense. The vulture's tail represents the mother's phallus. Before the little boy has a realization and full understanding of sexual difference, he will assume his mother is just like him, possessive of a penis.[20] For Freud, this memory testifies to an uncommonly close relationship with the mother, which suggests to the psychoanalyst that Leonardo lived with only her in the first years of his life.[21] The vulture also carries symbolic freight for Freud. 'The Egyptians also worshipped a Mother Goddess,' just like the infant Leonardo. She was represented as having a vulture's head, or else several heads, of which at least one was a vulture's.' Freud enthusiastically notes that this goddess's name was pronounced *Mut*, tantalizingly close to the German word *Mutter*.[22] And not only this: this mother goddess was also represented with 'a male organ in a state of erection'. Egyptian mythology, then, provides evidence for a history of belief in a phallic mother.[23]

'After this preliminary stage a transformation sets in whose mechanism is known to us but whose motive forces we do not yet understand'. That is to say, the boy's intense love for his mother cannot continue indefinitely and so 'succumbs to repression. He puts himself in her place, identifies himself with her, and takes his own person as a model in whose likeness he chooses the new objects of his love'.[24] It is in this way, then, that Leonardo became homosexual ('er ist so homosexuall geworden'[25]). Furthermore, for Freud, it was the absence of the father that was also crucial in this scenario: 'the

---

[18] *SE* xi. 82.   [19] *SE* xi. 129.   [20] See *SE* xi. 96.

[21] One should note that there is no evidence in the historical record for Freud's belief that Leonardo lived with just his mother in his earliest years, nor is there any evidence that Leonardo's mother overstimulated her son. See Armstrong (2005: 65).

[22] *SE* xi. 88.   [23] *SE* xi. 94.

[24] *SE* xi. 99–100.   [25] *GW* viii. 170.

presence of a strong father would ensure that the son made the correct decision in his choice of object, namely someone of the opposite sex.'[26]

But Leonardo did not simply become homosexual. In the introductory chapter to his study, Freud observes that 'most young children, or at least the most gifted ones, pass through a period, beginning when they are about three, which may be called the period of *infantile sexual researches*'.[27] Disbelieving the story about the stork, they 'form theories of babies originating from eating, of their being born through the bowels, and of the obscure part played by the father'. They have some notion of the sexual act, but still no clear idea about where babies come from, their 'investigation...must inevitably come to nothing [*so muß auch seine Forschung...im Sande verlaufen*]' and be abandoned.[28] This period of researches is 'terminated by a wave of energetic repression'. For Leonardo, according to Freud, 'the libido evade[d] the fate of repression by being sublimated from the very beginning into curiosity and by becoming attached to the powerful instinct for research as a reinforcement'.[29] Freud can conclude at the end of his introduction, then, that 'the core of his nature, and the secret of it [*der Kern und das Geheimnis seines Wesens*] would appear to be that after his curiosity had been activated in infancy in the service of sexual interests' and the overstimulation here received from his single-parent mother, 'he succeeded in sublimating the greater part of his libido into an urge for research'.

Although Freud cannot explain how Leonardo was able to sublimate his physical desires so completely (Freud can find no evidence of Leonardo having sex with men, women, or boys), he is nevertheless able to uncover the traces of his desires in his artwork. This allows Freud to solve the 'riddle' of the smile of the *Mona Lisa* and the significance of several other portraits painted by Leonardo da Vinci.[30] The narcissist—homosexual's artistic career was, according to Freud and the secondary sources he uses, dominated by depictions of children and beautiful women. 'If the beautiful children's heads were reproductions of his own person as it was in his childhood,

[26] *SE* xi. 99.   [27] *SE* xi. 78.
[28] *SE* xi. 79; *GW* viii. 146. We should note here that 'im Sande verlaufen' is fairly informal German. Freud's depiction of infantile cognitive processes is not simply a technical treatise but a paternally affectionate one.
[29] *SE* xi. 80.   [30] *SE* xi. 109.

then the smiling women are nothing other than repetitions of his mother Caterina, and we begin to suspect the possibility that it was his mother who possessed the mysterious smile' that he again found on the 'Florentine lady' Mona Lisa.[31]

There is one piece of apparently certain evidence about Leonardo's childhood: 'a Florentine land-register for the purpose of taxation... mentions Leonardo among the members of the household of the Vinci family as the five-year-old illegitimate child of Ser Piero'.[32] This more conventional evidence, as well as a slip that Leonardo makes in a notebook about the time of his father's death,[33] leads Freud to argue that Leonardo's 'father too came to play an important part in Leonardo's psychosexual development'. This was in two ways: through his absence in the first years, and then through his presence—Freud surmises that Leonardo must have been living with his father by his fifth birthday. Although Leonardo's narcissistic—homosexual tendencies were already fixed, a sort of Oedipus complex ensued (though of course Freud does not use this term) whereby Leonardo then falls into 'the normal relationship of rivalry' and felt 'a compulsion to copy and outdo his father'.[34] Finally, it was oedipal rivalry with his father that pushed Leonardo to give up his interest in fine art and to take up an irreverent position to authority and become a scientific investigator. He thereby became, according to Freud, the 'first modern natural scientist... being the first man since the Greeks to probe the secrets of nature while relying solely on observation and his own judgement'. He replaced his father by becoming a new, modern Oedipus, overcoming his narcissistic, artistic tendencies.

HISTORY BETWEEN OEDIPUS AND NARCISSUS

Freud's interest in how the myths of Oedipus and Narcissus inform male (sexual) identity took place on a canvas of eighteenth- and nineteenth-century fascination with these two Greek tales. As Peter

---

[31] *SE* xi. 111.   [32] *SE* xi. 81.   [33] *SE* xi. 119.   [34] *SE* xi. 121.

Rudnytsky has examined, Freud's engagement with Oedipus came at the end of a long tradition of interest in the lame-footed reader of the Sphinx. From the famous painting by Ingres to philosophical admiration for the intelligence of the man who saved Thebes: the tale of Oedipus fascinated the Enlightenment.[35] As Rocco has discussed, 'the tragedy of Oedipus is the tragedy of the enlightenment, dramatizing the triumphs and failures attending the heroic attempts of enlightened reason to fix the identity of the rational, autonomous, emancipated and fully self-constituted subject'.[36] And, as Leonard has examined, it is Hegel who turns Oedipus' answer to the Sphinx into the origin of philosophy itself.[37] On the other hand, Narcissus became an important figure for romanticism. As Louise Vinge has explained, Narcissus was 'the symbol of the creative genius to come to know the deepest spiritual forces within himself'.[38] Romanticist intellectuals became very interested in the idea that everything we perceive is a projection of our own making. Percy Bysshe Shelley, in his 'Discourse on the Manners of the Ancient Greeks Relative to the Subject of Love', wrote that the lover's mind 'selects among those who resemble it, that which most resembles it; and instinctively fills up the interstices of the imperfect image. . . '.[39] Such theorizing reflects the influence of Bishop Berkeley, for whom 'perhaps *all* vision is by definition narcissistic'.[40] Oedipus the Enlightened scientist and Narcissus the romanticist hero represented twin poles, exemplifying eighteenth- and early nineteenth-century interests in the possibilities of perception. Whereas Oedipus provided a model for the rational scientist who believed that empirical truths might be discovered out there in the world, so Narcissus presented the opposite vision, the suggestion that all the truth of the world is to be found within.

Oedipus and Narcissus, however, were never stable models of admiration. Before Hegel's reading, Schelling's Oedipus was already an ambivalent paradigm for the enlightened thinker. As Leonard discusses, Schelling's Oedipus is a paradoxical figure 'whose very political freedom is constituted in his recognition of the inexorable

---

[35] See Rudnytsky (1987).   [36] Rocco (1997: 34).
[37] See Leonard (2005: 27).   [38] Vinge (1967: 313).
[39] Shelley, quoted in Notopoulos (1969: 408).
[40] Bruhm (2001: 21).

workings of necessity'.[41] And, by the second half of the nineteenth century, Narcissus came to be viewed as the mythical figure that exemplified the sexual problem of narcissism. Havelock Ellis found in his research conducted in the 1890s that 'narcissism is a marked feature in both women and "feminine-minded men"'.[42] And for both Ellis and Max Nordau, the author of *Degeneration* (written in 1895), Oscar Wilde epitomized the effete narcissistic male.[43] Ellis's work on narcissism was translated into German by the psychiatrist Paul Näcke, which brought these medical theories to the attention of Freud. If Oedipus and Narcissus had so preoccupied literary, philosophical, artistic and medical imaginations for their powers of perception, then it was left to Freud to problematize radically these readings of these Greek myths. That is to say, for Freud, Narcissus and Oedipus fully and explicitly embodied the dangers of knowing oneself. In the versions of the myths told by Sophocles and Ovid, Teiresias the seer pronounced warnings with regard to both about the perils of self-knowledge. And, just as Freud underlines the dangers of actually knowing what you see, so his psychoanalysis encourages us all to move beyond what Narcissus and then Oedipus knew about themselves. The healthiest psyches are those that no longer desire themselves and no longer desire their mothers and wish to kill their fathers. The healthy psyche is one that has moved beyond the myths of Narcissus and Oedipus into modern, historical reality. And it is the job of psychoanalysis to bring us to face ourselves, to confront those dangerous knowledges of self-love, incestuous desire, and patricide, in order to move beyond them. But Freud was never so optimistic for the vast majority of us, who *never* quite manage to move beyond the myths of our childhood. As he wrote at the end of his career, the castration complex and penis envy seem to be 'the bedrock' of psychoanalysis, beyond which analysis cannot go.[44] All too many of us, it is Freud's burden to tell, remain ensnared within the paradigms of Narcissus and Oedipus.

Oedipus and Narcissus were also useful for Freud because they helped him to think about the ways in which modernity has

---

[41] Leonard (2005: 27). See (2005: 22–32) for a more detailed history of Oedipus' place in enlightenment philosophy.

[42] Bruhm (2001: 4), quoting Ellis.

[43] See Bruhm (2001: 54–7).

[44] See Freud's late essay 'Analysis Terminable and Interminable' (*SE* xxiii. 209–54), where Freud talks about the 'bedrock' of psychoanalysis.

conceptualized its relationship with its (ancient) past. On the one hand, the modern relationship with Oedipus is one in which 'we shrink back from him with the whole force of repression', as Freud writes in *The Interpretation of Dreams*.[45] It seems that Oedipus represents the otherness of antiquity, his tale of patricide and incest being the tragedy of the other. The continuing relevance and meaning of the play lies somewhere else ('it is neither at base an allegory of nature, as classical scholars of the time suggested, nor is it a pious reflection on the awesome power of the gods'[46]). On the other hand, the modern relationship with Narcissus is one of similarity and reflection. This story offers the hope that we might indeed see ourselves in the pool of antiquity. Oedipus represents the distance between ancient and modern, whereas Narcissus allegorizes the closeness of fit.

For Freud, however, the situation is somewhat more complicated. Oedipus' story is about one who thinks he knows his past (he can look back on his history and identify where he comes from: Polybus and Merope (*Oedipus Tyannus* 774–5)). But, even though he thinks he can look back into his past and know who he is, this look back is false, as Oedipus and his past are soon revealed to be quite different. Similarly, although modernity might feel able to glance back at antiquity, indeed at Oedipus' tragedy itself, and trace its history and link past with present, that history and genealogy prove radically false. That is to say, we might like to identify with antiquity, here the tale of Oedipus, but that identification is misguided: our identification with antiquity, with Oedipus, is actually something else entirely—and alarmingly so. On the other hand, Narcissus' story is about a boy who looks into a pool and falls in love with a boy; only later does he realize that he has fallen in love with himself. Narcissus' tale teaches us that, when we do look into the (ancient) past and desire its otherness, we will really be looking at ourselves. It is hardly surprising, then, that Freud should have turned to these classical myths. The one (Oedipus) shows how we identify with a past, but the correct identification is something else entirely, something apparently completely undesirable; the other (Narcissus), conversely, shows how we dis-identify with the past, emphasizing its otherness, when in fact we are merely staring ourselves in the face. The myths of Oedipus and Narcissus reflect (upon) each other. Together they measure out *both*

[45] *SE* iv. 262.
[46] Armstrong (2005: 51); see also *SE* iv. 264.

248 Classical Culture and Modern Masculinity

the disturbing closeness of past and present, ancient and modern (Oedipus), *and* the alarming distance between those two poles (Narcissus). When we think we can see ourselves in the past, that is the moment we do not (Oedipus); when we are looking longingly into a distant past just out of grasp, that is the moment we are looking at and (be)holding merely ourselves (Narcissus).

The myths of Narcissus and Oedipus reflect Freud's disruptions of our relationship with our pasts still further. Freud's theories make the radical suggestion that there was never a present in the past and nor was there ever a past in the present. Let us begin with the former proposition. For Freud, the male child is never truly in the presence of his mother as such. He never *really* identifies with her; rather he *narcissistically* projects his own phallic fantasies on to her, creating a phallic mother, whom he loves in his own image. Furthermore, when he has begun to undergo the Oedipus complex, he is still never in her presence the way he would like to be. That is, he cannot be with her sexually, because of the paternal threat materializing as the incest taboo. Both narcissistic and oedipal longing entail that there never was a present in the past for the male child. Conversely, as we turn to the second proposition, Freud's theories show that the past never quite makes it into the present. These narcissistic and oedipal desires are themselves unconscious memories and are never quite remembered as such by the boy and the adult male. As Richard Armstrong has shown, Freud was influenced by the historicism of Barthold Georg Niebuhr, the authoritative ancient historian and author of *Römische Geschichte* (1811–32), who argued that historical narratives of early Rome by Roman writers served psychological needs rather than attempted to provide an accurate description of the past.[47] As Freud writes himself in the *Leonardo* study:

Their nature [i.e. that of childhood memories] is perhaps best illustrated by a comparison with the way in which the writing of history originated among peoples of antiquity . . . It was inevitable that this early history should have been an expression of present beliefs and wishes rather than a true picture of the past; for many things had been dropped from the nation's memory, while others were distorted, and some remains of the past were given a wrong interpretation in order to fit in with contemporary ideas . . . A man's

---

[47] As mentioned in Chapter 1, Niebuhr was, along with Müller, one of Ranke's 'Vorbilder', in the development of modern German historicism (see Walther 1998: 423 n. 2).

conscious memory of the events of his maturity is in every way comparable to the first kind of historical writing [which was a chronicle of current events]; while the memories that he has of his childhood, as far as their origins and reliability are concerned, [are comparable] to the history of a nation's earliest days, which was compiled later and for tendentious reasons.[48]

If, for Freud, 'myth is analogous to the dream, then legendary history becomes the analogue to the 'screen memories' and fantasies of childhood . . . When it comes to origins, we remember what we want to remember.'[49] Freud's (and Breuer's) treatment of female hysterics in the 1890s, which 'opened the way towards psychoanalysis',[50] showed patients worrying after analysis about their repressed, forgotten desires being brought to consciousness. As Freud notes, they often said: 'But I can't remember having thought it . . .'. This led Freud to wonder: '[Are] we to suppose that we are . . . dealing with thoughts which never came about, which merely had a *possibility* of existing, so that the treatment would lie in the accomplishment of a psychical act which did not take place at the time?'[51]

LEONARDO BETWEEN NARCISSUS AND OEDIPUS

Neither a present in the past nor a past in the present: for Freud, Narcissus and Oedipus accentuate the problematic nature of the relationship between past and present. The deluded, mythicizing self-longings of both Narcissus and Oedipus become exemplary for Freud's understanding of the internal myth-history of every little boy. And Freud's interest in the mythical structures of our thinking reflected the work of his contemporary, the ancient historian and Renaissance scholar Jacob Burckhardt, whose scholarship was widely read at the end of the nineteenth century.[52] Burckhardt was concerned about the growing mountain of conflicting and contesting facts of history piling up in the academic establishment. With his

---

[48] *SE* xi. 83–4. See Armstrong (2005: 162–5).
[49] Armstrong (2005: 165).
[50] Bowlby (2007: 59).
[51] *SE* ii. 300.
[52] See Le Rider (2002: 72) and Armstrong (2005: 175–82).

noted preference for *Kulturgeschichte* and his interest in the 'Greek talent for lying', which produced 'uncertain, controversial', and 'coloured' narratives of events, Burckhardt examined what Greek mythology might be able to tell us about the way Greeks conceptualized their world and culture.[53] His concern was 'to establish the vital forces, both constructive and destructive, that were active in Greek life'.[54] Freud quotes Burckhardt on Leonardo at the very beginning of his study: 'He was a universal genius "whose outlines can only be surmised—never defined".'[55] And Freud's psychoanalysis of Leonardo, although committed to finding out the truth, is *not* concerned with locating the truths of sexuality that Ellis and Symonds before him sought. Even if Freud's analysands were just like the Greeks with regard to the 'tissue of lies [*Lügengewebe*]' and 'veil of lies [*Lügenhülle*]' that they told themselves about their pasts, the Greek lies that Wilde might have told will *not* be the key to *Freud's* understanding of male sexuality.[56] Rather the Greek myths of Narcissus and Oedipus will reveal that our sexual dispositions are inhabited by mythical monsters (phallic mothers and castrating fathers) and mythical desires (narcissistic and oedipal relations). In the very opening paragraph of his *Leonardo* study, Freud quotes a couplet from Schiller's poem 'Das Mädchen von Orleans', saying that '"to blacken the radiant and drag the sublime [*das Erhabene*] into the dust" is not part of [the] purpose' of psychiatric research'.[57] Freud is expressly not interested in de-sublimating Leonardo, a man, whom Freud shows actually sublimated his own homosexuality into great artistic and scientific achievements. The opening paragraph, then, bespeaks a tension that will attend the *Leonardo* study all the way through. On one level, Freud is *not* invested in 'outing' Leonardo as a homosexual in any straightforward manner; this will not be a lurid and smutty history of his private life. On another level, Freud *is* interested in uncovering Leonardo's latent sexuality, in the way that sexuality, for Freud, is not a practised enjoyment of certain sexual acts, but the mental dispositions of one's unconscious.

---

[53] Burkhardt ([1898–1902] 1998: 5).   [54] Burkhardt ([1898–1902] 1998: 4).

[55] *SE* xi. 63.

[56] *SE* xi. 41; *GW* viii. 42. The public lecture (delivered at Clark University) in which these terms appeared was published in the same year as the *Leonardo* study.

[57] *SE* xi. 63.

Despite the summary we gave above of Freud's biography, a closer reading shows (as we shall now see) that the mental—historical progress Leonardo supposedly made from narcissistic tendencies to oedipal rivalry is *not* actually borne out by Freud's text. Rather, Leonardo's narcissism is already haunted by oedipal desires, and his adult oedipal investigations remain disturbed by a lingering narcissism. These myths, which interested Freud precisely because they complicated the relationship between past and present, themselves resist Freud's attempts to control and fit them into a temporal framework in the history of (Leonardo's) masculinity. Let us turn, then, to reconsider Leonardo's earliest childhood and his step into narcissism to see how Freud ends up *not* uncovering any straightforward truth of latent homosexuality. Freud comments that Leonardo, an illegitimate child, was brought up solely at first by his mother, with the following consequences:

The child's love for his mother cannot continue to develop continuously any further; it succumbs to repression. The boy represses his love for his mother; he puts himself in her place, identifies himself with her; and takes his own person as a model in whose likeness he chooses the new objects of his love. In this way he has become a homosexual.

Freud then states, however: 'What he has in fact done is slip back to auto-erotism'.[58] Freud observes that the child will love other boys as 'only substitutive figures and revivals of himself in childhood—boys whom he loves in the way in which his mother loved *him* when he was a child'.[59] It is at this very point that Freud mentions 'Narcissus', the 'youth who preferred his own reflection to everything else'. There is a regressive move, not only in Leonardo's identity, but also in Freud's text itself: Leonardo becomes a homosexual, but then Freud moves back from this statement to say that 'in fact' he 'slip[s] back to auto-erotism'. Narcissism does not seem to be quite the same thing as homosexuality. Freud's doubts reveal themselves again in the next paragraph of his text when he says that 'we are far from wishing to exaggerate the importance of these explanations of the psychical genesis of homosexuality'. Freud is more than aware that his psychoanalysis of Leonardo is 'in sharp contrast to the official theories of

---

[58] *SE* xi. 63. [59] *SE* xi. 63.

those who speak for homosexuals'.[60] With this in mind, he continues: 'what is *for practical reasons* called homosexuality may arise from a whole variety of psychosexual inhibitory processes; the particular process [in Leonardo] we have singled out is perhaps one among many, and is perhaps related to only one type of "homosexuality"'.[61] 'Homosexuality', then, is a term that is used only 'for practical purposes', suggesting that, if Freud could have, he would have used another word, to describe Leonardo, which implies that he is not quite definable as a homosexual. Furthermore the inadequacy of the term is expressed by his use of scare quotes in the text.

At this point James Strachey inserts a footnote to Freud's text: 'A more general discussion of homosexuality and its genesis will be found in the first of Freud's *Three Essays* (1905d), particularly in a long footnote added between 1910 and 1920, *Standard Ed.*, 7, 144–7.'[62] It is remarkable to note that some of Freud's most detailed discussions about the origins of homosexuality—with the exception of *Leonardo*—appear in just these very footnotes that began to be added in 1910 for the second edition of *Three Essays*, the same year the *Leonardo* study appeared. Significantly, Freud writes in the first footnote (added in 1910): '*In all cases we have examined we* [emphasis added] have established the fact that the future inverts, in the earliest years of childhood, pass through a phase of very intense but short-lived fixation to a woman (usually their mother), and that, after leaving this behind, they identify themselves with a woman and take *themselves* as their sexual object.'[63] Whereas in *Leonardo* the Renaissance man's narcissism is 'perhaps related to only one type of "homosexuality"', in the footnote to *Three Essays* published in the same year as *Leonardo*, exactly the same sort of narcissism is seen to be present 'in all cases'. Freud's 'we' emphasizes that it is not only he but also his psychoanalytical colleagues who have established this generality. When the footnote is supplemented in 1915 for the third edition of *Three Essays*, Freud confirms and strengthens his position: 'In inverted types, a predominance of archaic constitutions and primitive psychical mechanisms is regularly to be found. Their most

---

[60] *SE* xi. 63. Freud could be alluding to Havelock Ellis, German campaigners for the decriminalization of sexual acts between men, or both.

[61] *SE* xi. 101, emphasis added.

[62] *SE* xi. 101.   [63] *SE* vii. 145.

essential characteristics seem to be coming into operation of *narcissistic object-choice* and a *retention* of the erotic significance of the *anal zone*. Although there might be various types of inverts (such as 'transitional types'), 'analysis shows that the differences between their determinants are only quantitative', and *not* 'qualitative'. In 1915, narcissism is one of 'the most essential characteristics' of 'inversion', a term that Freud continues to use right into the 1920s, when *Three Essays* receives its sixth edition. And so, whereas in the 1910 *Leonardo* essay the relationship between 'homosexuality' and 'narcissism' is tricky to elucidate clearly and fully, that between 'inversion' and 'narcissism' becomes firmer and firmer with each re-edition of *Three Essays*. If the relationship is firm in *Three Essays*, it always remains loose in *Leonardo*, itself a study that receives three editions by 1923. The concurrent republications of *Three Essays* and *Leonardo* during the 1910s and 1920s broadcast highly conflicting messages about the Freudian understanding about the relationship between homosexuality and narcissism. Leonardo da Vinci, then, slips between being a unique case and being an example for all 'homosexuals'—or should that be inverts?[64]

Even if the link between same-sex desire and narcissism should seem securer in the footnotes in *Three Essays* than in the *Leonardo* biography, what Freud understands by same-sex desire remains ambiguous, precisely because he oscillates between 'Homosexuell' and 'Inversionstype'.[65] In the main text of *Three Essays*, Freud discusses other theories of same-sex desire, in particular, theories of inversion, captured in Karl Heinrich Ulrich's phrase 'anima muliebris in corpore virili', reproduced in Freud's text as 'a feminine brain in a masculine body'.[66] Although Freud does not agree with the position that this 'psychical hermaphroditism' establishes a link with an 'anatomical one' (that is, inverts show some sort of anatomical difference from 'normal' men and women), it does seem to suggest that the invert 'feels he is a woman in search of a man'.[67] Freud then qualifies this by saying that inverts are frequently *not* effeminate but 'retain the mental quality of masculinity'.

---

[64] Bruhm (2001: 87) also notes that Freud's Leonardo 'thesis ossifies into his standard account' of homosexuality.

[65] Both these terms appear in the footnotes to *Three Essays*.

[66] *SE* vii. 142.

[67] *SE* vii. 144. On theories of sexual inversion, see Chauncey (1982–3), Kennedy (1988), and Sedgwick (1990: 157–60).

It is clear that in Greece, where the most masculine men were numbered among the inverts, what excited a man's love was not the *masculine* character of the boy, but his physical resemblance to a woman as well as his feminine mental qualities—his shyness, his modesty and his need for instruction and assistance [*Lern- und Hilfsbedürfigkeit*]. As soon as the boy became a man he ceased to be a sexual object for men and himself, perhaps, became a lover of boys [*Knabenliebhaber*].[68]

Freud's reliance on classical studies here is clear: Greek pederasty closely resembles a heterosexual relationship, just as it did in Meier's article, and Freud's insistence on the pedagogic aspects of the relationship reflects the influence of Müller's scholarship. Freud, however, carries on:

the sexual object is not someone of the same sex but someone who combines the characters of both sexes [*die Vereinigung beider Geschlechtscharaktere*]; there is, as it were, a compromise between an impulse that seeks for a man and one that seeks for a woman, while it remains a paramount condition that the object's body (i.e. genitals) shall be masculine. Thus the sexual object is a kind of reflection [*Spiegelung*] of the subject's of own bisexual nature.[69]

Freud's dense, even confusing, account shows that the oscillation between 'homosexuality' and 'inversion' reflects the tension at the heart of Freud's conceptualization of narcissism. On the one hand, narcissism is a desire for another who is just like oneself, a relationship of sameness, as the term *homo*sexuality suggests. On the other hand, however, narcissism is the desire of the boy who has identified himself with his mother, who then desires a boy, which suggests that the narcissistic tendency is one of one gender for another, as the term *inversion* implies. Ultimately, all Freud can say is that the object of desire is someone who retains both male and female qualities, being a 'reflection' (*Spiegelung*) of the subject's own 'bisexual nature'. That is to say, then, *the subject and object of desire mirror each other precisely because they each have doubled ('bisexual') identities.* We will return to the issue of Freud, that man of double identity, being so interested in the doubled Leonardo, the artist and scientist, Narcissus and Oedipus.

<hr/>

[68] *SE* vii. 144.
[69] *SE* vii. 144. Freud's theorizing here reflects the thinking of Krafft-Ebing (see Oosterhuis 2000).

For now, we should note that these thoughts lead Freud to one of his most famous statements on sexuality (and we need to cite Freud fully):

Psychoanalytic research is most decidedly opposed to any attempt at separating off homosexuals from the rest of mankind as a group of special character. By studying sexual excitations other than those that are manifestly displayed, it has found that all human beings are capable of making a homosexual object-choice and have in fact made one in their unconscious . . . Psychoanalysis considers that a choice of an object independently of its sex—freedom to range equally over male and female objects—as it is found in childhood, in primitive states of society and early periods of history, is the original basis from which, as a result of restriction in one direction or the other, both the normal and the inverted types develop. Thus from the point of view of psychoanalysis the exclusive sexual interest felt by men for women is also a problem that needs elucidating and is not a self-evident fact based upon an attraction that is ultimately of a chemical nature.[70]

Freud's well-known blurring of the distinction between hetero- and homosexuality (a distinction posited only recently by sexologists) is suggested by the 'bisexual nature' of every subject. And so we can turn back to Leonardo, the Renaissance man, suspended as it were in anachronism, between ancient and modern, Narcissus and Oedipus. We are now in a position to consider more directly how Leonardo's narcissism conceals oedipal desires, and conversely how his oedipal rivalry with his father is haunted by narcissistic tendencies for this mother. As Freud says, once Leonardo has become a narcissist-homosexual, he nevertheless

remains *unconsciously fixated* [*im Unbewußten . . . fixiert*] to the mnemic image of his mother. By repressing his love for his mother he preserves it in his *unconscious* [*in seinem Unbewußten*] and from now on remains *faithful* [*treu*] to her. While he seems to pursue boys and to be their lover, he is in reality running away from the other women, who might cause him to be *unfaithful* [*untreu*]. In *individual cases* [*durch direkte Einzelbeobachtung*] . . . the man who gives the appearance [*scheinbar*] of being susceptible only to the charms of men is in fact [*in Wahrheit*] attracted by women in the same way as *normal men* [*ein Normaler*].[71]

---

[70] *SE* vii. 145–6.   [71] *SE* xi. 100, emphases added; *GW* vi. 170.

First, the homosexual is appearance only ('scheinbar'): 'unconsciously,' he really ('in Wahrheit') desires women just like a normal—a heterosexual—man. And, secondly, the narcissist does not really desire himself, but another—he wishes to remain 'faithful' (Freud's tale is a strange romance) to his mother.

Furthermore, Freud's proposition that Leonardo, a narcissist-homosexual, 'is in fact attracted by women in the same way as a normal man' is a statement that is exquisitely ambiguous. *Either* the narcissist is really oedipal because he desires women who are really his mother, which is the fate of 'ein Normaler'; *or* the normal man who has gone through the Oedipus complex nevertheless still desires a woman in the way he desired the pre-oedipal phallic mother. The homosexual and the heterosexual man desire women *in the same way*. *Either* the narcissist desires women like a normal man, making him, on an unconscious level, at least, heterosexual. *Or* the normal man desires women just like a narcissist, meaning that all he ever desires really when he desires a woman is to return to that narcissistic relation he had with his pre-oedipal, phallic mother. Either behind the narcissist-homosexual lies an incestuous, heterosexual, oedipal relationship; or behind a heterosexual, oedipal relationship lies the love of a narcissist for his pre-oedipal, phallic mother.[72]

Freud's tales show that 'myths work with a narrative logic of their own that cannot be safely contained by the rationalizing discourse of *Wissenschaft*'.[73] Freud used the myths precisely because they showed how our relationship with our past was constructed in terms of self and other, closeness and distance. Oedipus teaches us that, although we may think we are at one with our past, it is actually quite repulsive to us, something we would rather ignore, so that we might divide ourselves into two—but this past is actually and disturbingly closer than we think. Narcissus teaches us that, although we might look into the pool of the past and feel that it seductively eludes our desiring grip, we are nevertheless just holding onto ourselves, looking into a mirror. But Freud's own theories fall foul of these mythical lessons. *On the one hand*, Freud's theory of the normal, oedipal man will always be haunted by a desire for the pre-oedipal, phallic mother, his

---

[72] See also Warner (1990) and Bruhm (2001: 82–8) on Freud's ambiguous discussions of narcissism.

[73] Armstrong (2005: 73), discussing Freud's problematic appropriation of the Egyptian Mut, to which we will have reason to return.

supposedly singular, unified self divided into two. The pre-oedipal mother seeps into the present of the oedipal man. Even though pre-oedipal narcissism is meant to stay firmly in the past—although the desire of the narcissist is meant to remain for ever elusive—it nevertheless remains part and parcel of the self, so that Freud's own theory cannot halt the return of that repressed, however much he might desire it. For Freud's own theory ignores the fact that Narcissus' desire never stops right up until his death: that narcissistic past seeps dangerously into the present.[74] *On the other hand*, the theory of the narcissist-homosexual is always already oedipal. Just like Narcissus, this theory itself thinks he is divided in two, but he is always already one. It is *his* pre-oedipal desires that are at the same time the 'normal' man's oedipal desires. Just as Freud's theory did not seek to 'separat[e] off homosexuals from the rest of mankind as a group of special character', so his theorizing shows that the normal man is really looking at himself, when he looks at the narcissist-homosexual. The otherness of Narcissus, the otherness of the past, is actually his 'normal' present, as those oedipal desires are actually what the regressively stunted narcissist really, unconsciously, feels. Just like Narcissus who thinks he sees another, when oedipal men stare into the ungraspable past, they are really just beholding themselves right in the present.[75]

Freud's study ends up suggesting that Leonardo's narcissistic sexuality looks very much like his oedipal researches, and that his oedipal researches are in fact narcissistic desires about the all-powerful mother. Let me explain further. *First*, his narcissistic relationship with his mother is actually a precursor to his later oedipal rivalries for dominance over his father. Living at first with only his mother, Leonardo 'escaped being intimidated by his father' and 'cast away the fetters of authority'.[76] Leonardo is able to solve riddles, to become another Oedipus, thanks to the absence of his father. Furthermore, with his mother, 'in his childhood days he has enjoyed the highest erotic bliss, which is never again attained'.[77] And Leonardo accomplishes what most oedipal boys never manage: theirs is 'a completely

---

[74] On the pre-oedipal mother, who refuses to go away in Freud's theory of male sexuality, see Sprengnether (1990), Jonte-Pace (2001), and, with reference to Leonardo, Armstrong (2005: 79–83).

[75] On how everyone is really—or could be—a narcissist by Freud's theory, see Warner (1990).

[76] *SE* xi. 123.   [77] *SE* xi. 129.

satisfying love-relation ... In the happiest young marriage the father is aware that the baby, especially if he is a baby son, has become a rival, and this is a starting-point of an antagonism towards the favourite which is deeply rooted in the unconscious'.[78] It is as if Leonardo out-Oedipuses Oedipus. *Secondly*, when Freud comes to talk about Leonardo's wish to compete oedipally with his father, 'to out-Herod Herod,' he says: 'his identification with his father lost all significance for his sexual life,' and these oedipal researches actually look narcissistic, even when Leonardo has turned to science.[79] For, as Richard Armstrong discusses, Leonardo's intellectual curiosity represents 'his submission to the feminine realm of *die Natur* (which is, we know, ultimately, *die Mutter*, Mut) as subjection to the grammatically feminine Ἀνάγκη'.[80] That is, for Freud, Leonardo's scientific interests 'breathe resignation of the human being who subjects himself to Ἀνάγκη, to the laws of nature [*Natur*], and who expects no alleviation from the goodness or grace of god'. Just as Leonardo began his life with a profound interest in an apparently omnipotent, narcissistic, phallic mother figure, so his life ended in this way.

Leonardo's 'homosexuality' is the love both of the same and of the different. We have repeatedly seen how the ancient Greeks oscillated between being historical ancestors and mythical others. For example, Winckelmann's homoeroticism marked his affinity with the Greeks and his love of the same, and signified the impossibility of loving as a Greek. The Greek object of desire seemed both close at hand, near enough to be touched (as he fingered Greek statues), and irrecoverably lost, merely a tissue of texts to absent lovers. Freud's psychoanalysis reflects this theme. Is the object of our desires real or mythical? Is it knowable? Leonardo's love of a phallic mother, both the same as and different from him, lovingly present and fantastically absent, becomes the story of all our sexualities, according to Freud. It is hardly surprising that Freud should have chosen an *Egyptian goddess* to illustrate his argument. By 1910, Egyptology had become its own, discrete discipline separate from other forms of *Altertumswissenschaft*. Since Franz Bopp's work on comparative linguistics in the 1820s and 1830s, 'Aryan' (or Indo-European) languages became

---

[78] *SE* xi. 116–17.
[79] *SE* xi. 121. Freud's Herod quotation is from *Hamlet*, that other seminal text that supposedly evidences the Oedipus complex.
[80] Armstrong (2005: 79–80).

segregated from 'Semitic' ones. With the supposed discovery that hieroglyphics were not related to Greeks, these linguistic arguments quickly became racialized. Ancient Egyptians were a 'Semitic' other.[81] This perspective was consolidated by significant advances in archaeological and philological scholarship in early twentieth-century Egyptology.[82] Freud's suppositions about the Egyptian goddess Mut could hardly have been more provocative: not only did they fly in the face of serious contemporary Egyptology, but tracing the sexuality of a great European hero back to 'Semitic' origins would have seemed highly problematic. Furthermore, Freud's theory of narcissism that the love for the male self was the same as the love for a female Egyptian other would have seemed especially challenging: from Greek god Apollo Belvedere, to Egyptian goddess Mut.

Freud was well aware that his 'Aryan' readers not only viewed psychoanalysis as a Jewish science, but also saw the Jewish male body itself as different.[83] 'Circumcision', as Sander Gilman has examined, 'marked the Jewish body as unequal to that of the Aryan, and the male Jew as the exemplary Jew'.[84] The male Jewish physique was stereotyped as both a dark, African body and a feminized body.[85] Freud's depiction of male desire as a desire for a female, Egyptian body, which was also a narcissistic desire, was certainly confrontational. One page after discussing Mut, Freud explains that the boy's fantasy for a phallic mother emerges out of his castration complex. And in the 1919 edition he added the following footnote: 'The conclusion strikes me as inescapable that here we may also trace one of the roots of the anti-semitism which appears with such elemental force and finds such irrational expression among the nations of the West. Circumcision is unconsciously equated with castration.'[86]

Writing within an anti-Semitic context, then, Freud portrays the ancient 'Semitic' (m)other as the body that actually every little 'Aryan' boy, every boy who takes after the Greeks, wants. Freud wrote on more than one occasion about 'the narcissism of minor differences'. 'It is', Freud contends, 'the minor differences in people who are

[81] See Olender (1992) and Marchand (2009: 124–30).
[82] See Marchand (2009: 203–6).
[83] See Gilman (1993: 31).   [84] Gilman (1993: 49).
[85] Gilman (1993: 18–19, 38–9).   [86] *SE* xi. 95–6 n. 3.

otherwise alike that form the basis of feelings of strangeness and hostility between them'.[87] But Freud's argument that the desire for the maternal phallus is universal, be that phallus 'Semitic' or 'Aryan', also saw to it that female sexuality was to be characterized as the 'dark continent' of the human psyche.[88] As Sander Gilman has observed: 'Freud translates the complicated, pejorative discourse about the "dark" Jew with its suggestion of disease and difference into a discourse about the "blackness" (the unknowability) of the woman.'[89]

Figure 2. Lanzone (1883), plate 86. By permission of The British Library. Freud would have been amused and interested by the way in which the phallus was represented in the Egyptology textbook to which he refers his readers for a picture of Mut: both visible and obscured, present and absent, this sketched-in/crossed-out phallus makes the (Semitic) phallic mother look both similar to, and different from, the desirous, penis-possessing, little (Aryan) boy.

[87] *SE* xi. 199. See also xviii. 101 and xxi. 114.
[88] *SE* xix: 212.
[89] Gilman (1993: 38).

LEONARDO THE PHALLIC MOTHER

Leonardo was, for Freud, 'the first man since the time of the Greeks to probe the secrets of nature'.[90] But, when Freud looks at oedipal Leonardo, although he apparently sees a repeatable exemplar for himself, Leonardo always remained a narcissist. Similarly, Oedipus thought he was at one with his past, but his own past was actually someone else. And so, when Freud looks at the narcissistic Leonardo and sees an unrepeatable other, he is looking at himself just like Narcissus. For, just as Freud depicts Leonardo mythologizing the phallic mother, so we may also criticize Freud for the *very same* mythologizing. That is, Leonardo never 'remembered' seeing a vulture, a phallic mother, but a 'kite,' 'nibio' in the Italian. The German text in which Freud had read about Leonardo's 'memory' was in fact a mistranslation.[91] Freud's now famous mistake, therefore, entails that his construction of the Egyptian's fantasy about a phallic mother embodied as the goddess Mut is itself a fantasy. Furthermore, Freud does not so much make Leonardo look like Oedipus as he makes him look like another phallic mother. Just as Leonardo apparently desired erotic bliss with a being that possessed 'union of the male and female natures', so does Freud depict Leonardo himself as 'the result of the blending of male and female dispositions'.[92] In addition, Freud does not only identify with Leonardo; he also admits to being attracted to him: 'Like others *I have succumbed to the attraction* [*Ich bin wie andere der Anziehung unterlegen*] of this great and *mysterious* [*rätselhaften*] man, in whose nature [*Wesen*] one seems to detect powerful instinctual passions which can nevertheless only express themselves in so remarkably subdued a manner'.[93] The phrase 'der Anziehung unterlegen' is exactly the one Freud used to describe the way 'a normal man' is attracted to women in his discussion of Leonardo's narcissism.[94] That is to say, then, Freud is attracted to Leonardo in precisely the same terms as 'a normal man' is attracted to a woman, which is itself the same way in which a

---

[90] *SE* xi. 122.   [91] See Strachey's editorial note, *SE* xi. 60–2.
[92] *SE* xi. 136.   [93] *SE* xi. 134; *GW* viii. 207.
[94] *SE* xi. 100; *GW* viii. 170.

narcissistic-homosexual is himself attracted to his own (phallic) mother. Indeed, at the very beginning of his study, Freud expresses his enthrallment to Leonardo, the 'mysterious master [*geheimnisvollen Meister*]'.[95] Freud ultimately remains mystified by this Sphinx of a man, a being of composite identity, literally 'full of riddes [*rätselhaften*]'. 'But whatever the truth about Leonardo's life might be . . .'[96]

Although Freud tries to show how the history of sexuality is a series of discrete, separate stages, his reliance on the myths of Oedipus and Narcissus disrupts the logic of his own theorizations. These myths problematize the very concepts of past and present. The retarded, regressive, archaic nature of narcissism supposedly reflects a character stuck in the past. But the myth of Narcissus shows that this past never had a present, since Narcissus could never quite be present-to-himself. The narcissist really desires someone else entirely, someone that does not really exist (Freud's phallic mother). Conversely, the story of Oedipus thematizes progress, development, and a future. But the Oedipal present is always haunted by a past—a past that we do not consciously realize is in our present. Although Freud's study repeatedly emphasizes Leonardo's uniqueness,[97] Leonardo's history ends up explaining the history of masculinity itself. And so, if Freud's history of sexuality does not present a succession of eras, ancient, Renaissance, and modern, then we are all Renaissance men, stuck between antiquity and modernity. In his presentation of Leonardo's *double* nature, artist and scientist, Narcissus and Oedipus, of 'bisexual nature', ancient Greek and modern intellectual, Leonardo comes to exemplify everyone, just as everyone exemplifies Leonardo.

Freud's study illustrates the irony in identifying the homosexual with Narcissus and the heterosexual with Oedipus, and so illustrates the precariousness of mythical identification. The narcissist-homosexual, who might find solace in a historical representation of himself, turns out really to desire his mother. That is to say, just as the homosexual might have thought he saw himself when he gazes back at images, produced in the past, of Narcissus, so his past was actually

---

[95] *SE* xi. 64; *GW* viii. 129.   [96] *SE* xi. 134.

[97] *SE* xi. 63, 122: 'one of the greatest men of the Italian renaissance'; 'only' Leonardo could have dispensed with 'the need for support from an authority of some sort' when he studies Mother Nature.

quite different—in fact his past was *just like Oedipus*, in that he once
desired his mother. Conversely, the oedipal heterosexual who might
look back at the figure of Narcissus might see his other, the homosexual. He does not, however, realize that he is just looking at
himself—*just like Narcissus*—doomed to desire the pre-oedipal, phallic mother, the narcissistic extension of himself. Freud's thinking
neatly shows that our histories of sexuality are indeed myths—they
are simply not true, historical accounts.

Freud's psychoanalysis of the male reflects a complex intellectual
heritage. His critique of contemporary sexology and psychology,
which offered detailed taxonomies and classifications of the sexual
self, questioned the historical truthfulness of the autobiographical
accounts collected by doctors such as Havelock Ellis and Richard
von Krafft-Ebing. Freud's stories of Greek love were not simply polite
euphemisms for concrete and detectable sexualities. Instead he
coupled his scientific training with his classical interests to show
that a man's objects of desire were mythical inventions not straightforward historical persons. Writing at a time when racial and hereditary aetiologies were often given for sexual abnormalities, Freud
relocated modern man's ancestors in Greek myth. He changed who
a man thought he was. Freud ensured, then, that, as soon as homosexuality was supposedly reified by sexologists and other doctors, it
was also questioned as a category. The turn of the nineteenth century
witnessed not the emergence of The Homosexual but a complex and
contested engagement with ancient Greek culture that produced
competing discourses on same-sex desire in the twentieth century
and beyond. The truth of sexuality was a Greek lie. A man's repressed
urges, his narcissism and oedipality, saw to it that his desires were not
simply historically knowable, but a strange, irrecoverable past, at the
same time profoundly influential on his present.
 Freud's portrait of the Renaissance man Leonardo reflects a pervasive interest for turn-of-the-century Europe: the Renaissance had
been invented as a pivotal epoch between ancient and modern, and
provided a model for modernity's turn to the ancient world. What
had already captivated the imaginations of Pater, Symonds, and
Wilde, who all wrote extensively about the Renaissance, was the
intense cultivation of personality that that period seemed to enjoy.
Renaissance self-realization spoke to liberatory sexual discourses at
the beginning of the twentieth century, and offered an example for

modern engagements with the classical past.[98] Freud's questioning of the homo/hetero distinction has had a profound influence on late-twentieth-century gay and queer activism, which has sought to unravel the repressive, pathologizing diagnoses of sexology and psychology. The mythological nature of the past, both Renaissance and ancient, permitted creative reimaginings for the present.

But this legacy we might trace back to Freud comes at great cost. Freud's researches into the mythical history of sexuality took place in the context of nineteenth-century philhellenism. But, whereas, for Pater and Wilde, cultured *Bildung* offered the opportunity to question modern sexual and social norms, for Freud the ideal quite simply was heterosexuality. The formation of the Freudian self might not have been made out of pre-packaged hereditary attributes, but his *Bildungsroman* ideally, if impossibly, ended in happy marriage. Freud redirects the eroticism of nineteenth-century scholarship on the Renaissance. He quotes Walter Pater's description of *La Gioconda* as 'expressive of what in the ways of a thousand years men had come to desire', which suggests that Mona Lisa's smile still has the power to arouse men in Pater's day.[99] Leonardo's sexuality, however, is utterly sublimated into art and science. And any enjoyment Pater detects in looking at Mona Lisa is, for Freud, rather more problematic: it symbolizes Leonardo's desire for his mother. In the context of psychoanalysis, the sexual development of the young male does not take place in a homosocial, pederastic context. Instead, with Freud, the role of the mother within the family comes under the spotlight like never before. And it is Freud's characterization of the mother that is most problematic from a feminist perspective. The misogynistic pretext for his arguments presupposes that a mother's influence on her son is a danger always in need of attention. Although Freud does not imagine a Platonic education to be a profound influence on the formation of a boy, unlike the Oxford Hellenists, he does nonetheless feel the need for a male role model in every boy's life. The German scholarship we examined in Chapter 1, Meier in particular, blamed the misogyny of ancient Greek culture for the institution of Greek pederasty: women were not suitably educated to attract men. Despite

---

[98] See Ivory (2009) on the sexual celebration of the Renaissance between 1850 and 1930.

[99] *SE* xi. 110. The quotation comes from Pater's essay 'Leonardo Da Vinci', from *The Renaissance* (see Pater 1910: i. 124).

the history of this scholarship and despite a century of intense feminist debate across Europe, at the beginning of the twentieth century Freud misogynistically blames the homosexuality of boys on the excessive influence of the mother. His misgivings about what a mother might teach her son reflects a chauvinistic belief in what men can teach boys. Indeed, we might go so far as to say that Freud's perception of the need for a father-figure in a boy's life reflects a concern about the reproductive powers of men that we have witnessed right through this book, since Plato's *Symposium*. Even though Freud does not discuss Diotima's/Socrates' tale of pregnant men, he is clearly writing within a neo-humanistic tradition that valorized the lessons older men taught boys—indeed, valorized them so profoundly that the intrusion of a woman into that space would alert suspicion. We should remember that the debate about women in higher education peaked in Germany at the end of the nineteenth century, and women students were first admitted into German universities at the beginning of the twentieth. Although Freud pointedly critiqued contemporary sexological theory, and although he welcomed women psychoanalysts into the fold, his phallic mother reflects contemporary sexological research that associated women's *Bildung* with female sexual inversion, the masculine woman.[100] There is no trace of Socrates' Diotima here. Freudian psychoanalysis comes to look like a prolonged critique of the monstrous mother, who is consigned to a primitive, dark age, with her story left untold.

---

[100] See Rowold (2010: 69–151) on the politics of women's education in Germany; and Appignanesi and Forrester (2000: 171–393) on female psychoanalysts and Freud's friendships with women.

Conclusion: The Truth of *Erōs* and the *Erōs* for Truth

Since the eighteenth century, the Greek pederast has been seen as both the subject of truth and the object of knowledge: he has been lionized as the producer of truthful knowledge and interrogated as the most difficult object for the scientific claims of modern academic historicism. For Foucault, and a generation of historians after him, sexuality connoted the truth of the self for many medical doctors and legal theorists and practitioners by the beginning of the twentieth century. The writers we have considered in *Classical Culture and Modern Masculinity*, on the other hand, continually questioned the knowability of one's desires. Although many have been keen to see a homosexual signified behind the euphemistic signifier of Greek love in the modern era—that homosexual desire can finally be known—we have examined a series of intellectuals who questioned that equation. We have seen that Greek love did not straightforwardly reflect the 'truths' of the sexologist or the legal practitioner. The complexities of Greek pleasures and passions were not comprehensible within modern legal and medical frameworks. Not directly intervening in growing debates about nature and nurture, the German professors, the English dons, the Anglo-Irish writer, and the Austrian psychoanalyst all pondered what it meant for men to read Greek in a modern age. What was the relationship between ancient texts and modern desiring selves? Greek pederasty became one of the most difficult of questions for those writers interested in reifying the nature of the relationship between antiquity and modernity. Such a question should make us now consider all the more carefully what (sorts of) sexualities we historians produce from eighteenth-century, Victorian, and Edwardian textualities. What does it mean to know about Greek pederasty? How does that knowledge inform notions of modern masculinity?

Tellingly, such questions have not gone away. Most recently, James Davidson concluded his 2007 study *The Greeks and Greek Love* saying:

Greek Love may be one of the knottiest subjects in all of Western history . . . A full investigation of 'the Greek custom' and all its ramifications would not merely take at least a lifetime, therefore; in the end it would resemble something not very far from a full-scale social, cultural and political history of that loose cultural federation of polities that we call 'ancient Greece'.[1]

For this eminent historian, at least, Greek love remains one of the most important of issues for 'Western history'. Knowing Greek love becomes commensurate not only with living a life but also with writing a history of ancient Greece itself: writing a history of Greek love would be to write a 'full-scale' history of Greece itself. Davidson's wonder at the significance and the endlessness of what might be known about this subject reflects a long intellectual tradition, which we have been tracing in this book. It is interesting to see that at the end of the twentieth century and the beginning of the twenty-first ancient Greek male desire still questions what can be knowable. The second volume of Foucault's *History of Sexuality* on the use of pleasures in ancient Greece opens with an introduction that addresses this very issue. In a very rare footnote, Foucault commented:

I am neither a Hellenist nor a Latinist. But it seemed to me that if I gave enough care, patience, modesty, and attention to the task, it would be possible to gain sufficient familiarity with the ancient Greek and Roman texts; that is a familiarity that would allow me—in keeping with a practice that is doubtless fundamental to Western philosophy—to examine both the difference that keeps up at a remove from a way of thinking in which we recognize the origin of our own, and the proximity that remains in spite of that distance which we never cease to explore.[2]

Foucault is at once outside the discipline of classical philology and sufficiently familiar with its texts, just as modernity locates its origins in the ancient world *and* marks its historical specificity by reference to that world. Foucault is intellectually wandering abroad while at the same time practising that which is 'doubtless fundamental to Western philosophy', and thereby firmly staying at home. Foucault's ambivalence about his relationship to antiquity reflects a long history

---

[1] Davidson (2007: 466).   [2] Foucault (1986: 7 n.).

of ambivalence we have marked out since the eighteenth century, as antiquity shifts in and out of Foucault's grasp.

This is reflected in Foucault's account for what inspired him to write a history of ancient and modern sexuality in the first place:

> As for what motivated me, it is quite simple; I would hope that in the eyes of some people it might be sufficient in itself. It was curiosity [*curiosité*] . . . the only kind of curiosity, in any case, that is worth acting upon with a degree of obstinacy: not the curiosity that seeks to assimilate what it is proper to know, but that which enables one to get free of oneself [*se déprendre de soi-même*]. After all, what would be the value of the passion for knowledge [*l'acharnement du savoir*] if it resulted only in a certain amount of knowledgeableness and not, in one way or another and to the extent possible, in the knower's straying afield of himself [*l'égarement de celui qui connaît*]?[3]

Foucault's *curiosité* is expressly not sexual: he does not want to learn about ancient pleasures because he might be 'homosexual'. Indeed, quite the opposite: this is a relentless determination for knowledge ('l'acharnement du savoir') that will free Foucault of himself. His is a curiosity not to know himself (his sexual self) but to lose the way of his self—indeed to lose the reason and mind of his self ('l'égarement de celui qui connaît'). The most famous historian of madness here (rhetorically) flirts with madness, with a wish to lose his senses and to find another self through his essay into antiquity.

But, despite the seemingly ecstatic potential for self-invention and self-fashioning that the work of history affords, Foucault felt at the same time that he was doing nothing new. His essay 'is the living substance [*le corps vivant*] of philosophy, at least if we assume that philosophy is still what it was in times past, i.e., an "ascesis", *askēsis*, an exercise of oneself [*un exercice de soi*] in the activity of thought'.[4] Philosophy is a 'living body', something that is not dead, joining together ancient and modern, likened to a physical work-out for the self. Foucault explicitly positions himself within a long history of Western philosophy, traceable back to Socrates'/Diotima's emphasis on philosophy being a physical activity that affects the male body. This is like philosophy at the gymnasium, the site for much of Socratic elenchus. 'The studies that follow', observes Foucault, 'are not the work of a "historian"' but are 'a philosophical exercise'.[5]

---

[3] Foucault (1986: 8).   [4] Foucault (1986: 9).
[5] Foucault (1986: 9).

Indeed, even when Foucault was portraying the best historian as 'straying afield from himself', the 'égarement de celui' he preaches looks just like the mad philosopher's loss of his senses in the *Phaedrus*. Foucault's thinking, then, exhorts both bodily escape and bodily exercise, a flight from one's body and a concentration on one's physicality.

So, at the same time as writing a *history* of sexuality, in an attempt to show the sheer difference of ancient sexual norms and discourses, Foucault was also invested in the idea that he himself was part of that ancient masculine philosophical tradition that thought to think oneself differently, a tradition that is living, still part of Foucault's present. Foucault suspends himself between history and philosophy, between writing a history of an aspect of classical Greek culture and demonstrating the origins of modern philosophical discourse itself. He writes that the 'long history of these [Greek and Roman] aesthetics of existence and these technologies of the self remained to be done'.[6] That history of sexuality is what remains for historians to write—it is an important object for historical analysis. Yet, at the same time, those ancient discourses Foucault will excavate will also prove to be the origins for the way in which modern thinkers conduct their thinking, their exercise of the self that might change the self. Foucault is cognizant of this conflict at the heart of his analysis: despite wishing to get away from himself, all he has done is to know himself all the better: 'Sure of having travelled far [*on croyait s'éloigner*], one finds that one is looking down on oneself from above. The journey rejuvenates things, and ages the relationship with oneself. I seem to have gained a better perspective on the way I worked ... on this project, whose goal is a history of truth'. Ultimately, Foucault's work on his project provided him access into a sounder knowledge of how he worked on his project, which has turned out to be nothing but a history of truth itself, a history of how ancient 'games of truth' have produced the modern world. His voyage took him to antiquity and back again.

Foucault's exercise of the self looks very much like the neo-humanistic project of *Bildung* that we have been analysing throughout this book. Foucault's history of Greece, which explicitly concentrates on male technologies of the self and neglects discussion of ancient

---

[6] Foucault (1986: 11).

women's desires, echoes the ethos of masculine self-realization voiced from Winckelmann to Wilde and Freud: one does not so much learn facts from the Greeks, as learn how to become someone, to become a *male* subject. Foucault's Greeks' '"arts of existence" . . . to make their life into an *œuvre* that carries certain aesthetic values and meets certain stylistic criteria' looks very much like the aestheticisms of Winckelmann, Goethe, and Pater, so influential over Symonds and Wilde: the making of the self as a conscious project, turning oneself into a work of art.[7] Foucault turns the text of philosophy into a male body and sees the male body as an artistic text—making philosophy a transaction between embodied men, a transaction that can, however, be accessed only through texts, Plato's, Winckelmann's, Pater's, and so on. Foucault's strategy clearly reflects the neo-humanistic wish to translate Platonic textuality in a modern male body, while at the same time emphasizing the textual artificiality of that body.

In making the self a conscious project but also an endlessly impossible one, Foucault's positioning within the neo-humanistic tradition has been met with mixed responses. Some have seen his 'pensée du dehors' as a positive and important moment in postmodern thought, questioning repressive labels of selfhood and sexuality.[8] Foucault thus makes identity malleable and changeable, something that need not be subject to the regime of power/knowledge. Others have found his appropriation of the Enlightenment project of *Bildung* more problematic: 'Foucault's Greeks and Romans are the projections of these Enlightenment ideals onto the past'. Foucault seems willing to view 'the modern paradigm [of the exercise of the self] as the evolved form of the ancient practice'.[9] Foucault thus risks replicating all the exclusionary discourses rehearsed between 1750 and 1930 we have analysed: in exemplifying the Greeks for the modern exercise of the self, Foucault risks reconfirming a white, male, European ideal for modernity. As we have seen, Foucault's Greeks are both the other to modern systems of sexual knowledge *and* the originators of proper, Western philosophical ascesis and thinking. It in this way, then, that Foucault repeats the intellectual tensions that we have been examining throughout this book—making the Greeks subjects of truth and objects of knowledge, removing them from and inserting them into history, Greeks as embodied, historical personages and Greeks as idealized

---

[7] Foucault (1986: 10–11).   [8] See P. A. Miller (2007).
[9] Porter (2006: 178).

textual artifices. Right at the beginning of this book, we saw how Diotima's/Socrates' pregnant men questioned what sort of male body might be required for doing real philosophy and intellectual work.

Foucault's project will look liberatory to some and politically problematic to others: despite his attempts to 'other' the Greeks, they come to look very much like a model for himself. He could not help appropriating neo-humanism's own appropriation of antiquity. And so, whether we are searching for an essentialist gay history or a Foucauldian history of queer, artistic self-fashioning and self-invention, tracing ourselves back to the Greeks via nineteenth- and eighteenth-century Hellenisms always raises difficult questions about gay and queer commitments to feminism and anti-racism. The neo-humanistic exemplification of the Greeks was accompanied by efforts to dovetail Hellenism within explicitly Christian frameworks; by profound suspicions about the admittance of women into the lives of *gebildet*, beautiful men; and an emphasis on a racialized heritage linking Greek antiquity to European modernity.

Foucault's aim to ensure that one's sexual orientation need not be an object of scientific knowledge is, nevertheless, quite understand-able: the pathologization and criminalization of homosexuality at-tempted to contain the sexually 'aberrant' from contaminating the rest of the population. But making one's desires queerly unknowable has also frustrated many gay scholars and critics: with the risk of turning one's desires into an impossible idealization, what if we start to believe that we might never know love? Is that such a positive political position? It is precisely this issue that informs James David-son's *The Greeks and Greek Love* (2007). Instead of Foucault's ex-ploration of the individual's intense relation with himself, for Davidson, 'Greek Erōs' concerns '*falling* in love with a member of the same sex, and, one might add, making a great big song and dance about it . . . "Greek Homobesottedness" would give a more accurate impression of how the phenomenon manifests itself, though it would fit less neatly on a title page'.[10] Davidson contrasts his approach with Foucault by explicitly turning back to historical sources via the work of scholars such as Meier, to show how multifarious, complex, and utterly bizarre customs around Greek same-sex desire were. Davidson thus demonstrates the enormous loquacity over *erōs* in the Greek

---

[10] Davidson (2007: 36).

world beyond the topics Foucault discusses. Davidson's emphasis on the historian's work of collating together as much ancient source material as possible reveals his intellectual investment in his trade as a historian, as opposed to Foucault the philosopher. His analysis of not only ancient Athens and Sparta but also Crete, Elis, Thessaly, Macedonia, and Boeotia maps out areas of Greece little analysed since Foucault's *History of Sexuality*. Furthermore, his contextualization of same-sex desires within religious and military contexts provides other ways for understanding ancient Greek culture.

Despite his commitment to historicize Greek love as comprehensively as possible, Davidson's conclusion, however, makes it clear that he is also politically invested in his own idealization of the Greeks. Near the end of his conclusion he tentatively offers an 'all about' answer to the problem of Greek Love.

It was a bridge between the culture's structurally given gaps, between age-classes, between men who were not related, between endogamous 'in-marrying' families with their weddings of cousins to cousins and uncles to nieces, between the human and the divine . . . And it thereby helped to build a sense of a unified political society out of divided groups, a pan-Athenian Eros of the Academy, a pan-Theban Sacred Band 'of the polis' . . . a sense of Team Greece itself in opposition to the Barbarians.[11]

Unlike Foucault's exercise of the self over the self, Davidson's *erōs* binds Greeks together, strengthens Greeks against barbarians. This emphasis on the Greekness of Greek love allows Davidson to argue about the origins of Greek love in the final section of his conclusion, 'Where did it come from?' Surveying comparisons of Greek pederasty with anthropological work on pederastic initiation ceremonies in Papua New Guinea, Davidson suggests that scholars have been quick to notice similarities but not the differences. Closing this section with a subsection titled 'Pairs, yokes and chariots', Davidson contends that 'the stable universal core of Greek Homosexuality is simply the pairing of two members of the same sex', arguing that 'the *idea* of a personally devoted chariot-pair was probably flourishing in the early first millennium, and there were already sacrifices to Eros by men in all-male groups, i.e. war bands, armies'.[12] Davidson uncovers the prevalence of 'same-sex pairing, the image of pairing, myths about pairs, cults of the pair, the practices of pairing, the specialized

[11] Davidson (2007: 499).   [12] Davidson (2007: 509, 513).

terminology for each partner in a pair', deeply embedded in early recorded Greek material and literary culture.[13] Greek *erōs* should not be compared to the initiatory pederasty of Papua New Guinea— rather, it looks more like 'same-sex wedding—one-to-one troth plighting'.[14] And that heritage has, for Davidson, Indo-European credentials:

> the divine Spartan twins [Castor and Pollux] called the Dioscuri, the 'youths of Zeus'. . . seem to have an awful lot in common with the Asvins, the divine horse-twins of Vedic mythology . . . The Dioscuri therefore allow us to trace a genealogy of the Greek same-sex chariot-pair via the Spartans, the Dorians and the West Greeks all the way back to the Aryans.[15]

And not only this: such relationships of yoking and pairing supposedly bind together the whole history of the European West, from the 'Celts' to 'wed brothers' in medieval Europe.[16] 'There is indeed a strong case to be made that it reflects a common inheritance, not an institution of paederastic insemination and initiation into adulthood, but rather of homosexual pair-bonding, association, perhaps, with the divine twins. With that proviso, I conclude . . . the origins of Greek Homosexuality may well be discovered among the Aryans'.[17]

Despite seeking to offer an image of Greeks who publicly celebrated same-sex love, thereby offering modern gay readers a world where such love might have been more affirmatively viewed, Davidson's contention that gay marriage has a long history dating back to the dawn of antiquity nevertheless appropriates a history of scholarship that emphasizes a racial connection between ancient Greeks and the modern West. Davidson's model of a 'common inheritance' reestablishes a hermetically sealed-off Europe (with northern India attached), whose ancestry can be traced back to Aryans. Greek same-sex desires are to look nothing like any other cultures around the globe: just as for Müller, Meier, and Symonds before, the Greeks (with their Aryan heritage) were special. This attempt to celebrate twenty-first-century gay marriage, although understandable, is politically precarious. Reflecting a heritage of writing, from Forster's and Carpenter's democratic lovers, to Pater's (sensually) enslaving Spartans back to Müller's manly Dorians, ancestors of northern

---

[13] Davidson (2007: 513).
[14] Davidson (2007: 514. [15] Davidson (2007: 514).
[16] Davidson (2007: 515–16).   [17] Davidson (2007: 516).

Europeans, Davidson's Greeks come to look like the hyper-virile, white warriors imagined in the nineteenth and early twentieth centuries. Is Aryanism a myth-history that all gay people would want to lay claim to today?

We live in a world where there are no institutions whose explicit objective is to 'make someone gay'—indeed, the idea of such a place seems nonsensical. Homosexuality has, however, been seen to be an unfortunate by-product of those other 'great' institutions: boarding schools, the Church, the armed forces. We also live in a world where there is no shortage of institutions that are designed to make you straight. This profound imbalance simply shows how little we valorize gayness or homosexuality, or whatever you might want to call 'it'. And so it is hardly surprising, then, that the Greek education system should have provided such a remarkably alluring example of an institution that valued the desires between men. In *Epistemology of the Closet*, Eve Kosofksy Sedgwick poignantly observed that gay people 'seldom grow up in gay families ... [They] always belatedly [have] to patch together from fragments a community, a usable heritage, a politics of survival or resistance'.[18] But the use of a classical past to craft the present needs to confront the history of the uses of that classical past. It is our neo humanistic 'heritage' that makes the Greeks seem so close *and* so distant from us: it is, then, that 'heritage' that we must face at the same time as searching for our (other) Greeks.

---

[18] Sedgwick (1990: 81).

References

Abbott, E., and Campbell, L. (1897). *The Life and Letters of Benjamin Jowett, MA.* 2 vols. London: Murray.

Ackerman, R. (1998). 'K. O. Müller in Britain', in Calder and Schlesier (1998: 1–18).

Adams, J. E. (1995). *Dandies and Desert Saints: Styles of Victorian Masculinity.* Ithaca, NY, and London: Cornell University Press.

Adamy, P. (2009). *Isidore Liseux 1835–1894, un grand 'petit editeur'.* Bassac: Plein Chant.

Aldrich, R. (1993). *The Seduction of the Mediterranean: Writing, Art and Homosexual Fantasy.* London and New York: Routledge.

Andersen, W. (2001). *Freud, Leonardo da Vinci, and the Vulture's Tail.* New York: Other Press.

Appignanesi, L., and Forrester, J. (1992). *Freud's Women.* London: Weidenfeld and Nicolson.

Ardis, A. (2007). 'Hellenism and the Allure of Italy', in Bradshaw (2007: 62–76).

Armstrong, M. (1998). '"Jene eigenthümlich Dorische Männerliebe": K. O. Müller's *Die Dorier* and Greek Homosexuality', in Calder and Schlesier (1998: 19–54).

Armstrong, R. H. (2005). *A Compulsion for Antiquity: Freud and the Ancient World.* Ithaca, NY, and London: Cornell University Press.

Arnold, M. (1960–77). *The Complete Prose Works of Matthew Arnold*, ed. R. H. Super. 11 vols. Ann Arbor: University of Michigan Press.

Bahlcke, J. (1997). 'Enzyklopädie und Aufklärung im literarischen Deutschland: Zu Leben und Wirken des schlesischen Bibliothekars Johann Samuel Ersch (1766–1828)', *Berichte und Forschungen, Jahrbuch des Bundesinstituts für ostdeutsche Kultur und Geschichte*, 5: 81–99.

Bailey, Q. (2002). 'Heroes and Homosexuals: Education and Empire in E. M. Forster', *Twentieth Century Literature*, 48/3: 324–47.

Barr, J. (1982). 'Jowett and the Reading of the Bible "Like Any Other Book"', *Horizons in Biblical Theology*, 4: 1–44.

Bartlett, N. (1993). *Who Was that Man? A Present for my Oscar Wilde.* Harmondsworth: Penguin.

Bauer, H. (2009). *English Literary Sexology: Translations of Inversion, 1860–1930.* Basingstoke: Palgrave Macmillan.

Beard, M. (2000). *The Invention of Jane Harrison.* Cambridge, MA: Harvard University Press.

Beckson, K. (1970) (ed.). *Oscar Wilde: The Critical Heritage*. New York: Routledge and Kegan Paul.

Benson, A. C. (1906). *Walter Pater*. London: Macmillan and Co.

Berlinerblau, J. (1999). *Heresy in the University: The* Black Athena *Controversy and the Responsibilities of American Intellectuals*. New Brunswick and London: Rutgers University Press.

Bernal, M. (1987). *Black Athena: The Afroasiatic Roots of Classical Civilization*, i. *The Fabrication of Ancient Greece 1785–1985*. New Brunswick and London: Rutgers University Press.

Bettelheim, B. (1982). *Freud and Man's Soul*. New York: Knopf.

Birnbaum, M. (1914). *Oscar Wilde: Fragments and Memories*. New York: James F. Drake.

Bland, L., and Doan, L. (1998). *Sexology in Culture: Labelling Bodies and Desires*. Chicago: Chicago University Press.

Blanshard, A. (2000). 'Hellenic Fantasies: Aesthetics and Desire in John Addington Symonds' *A Problem in Greek Ethics*', *Dialogos*, 7: 99–123.

Blanshard, A. (2010). *Sex: Vice and Love from Antiquity to Modernity*. Oxford: Wiley-Blackwell.

Bleys, R. C. (1996). *The Geography of Perversion: Male-to-Male Sexual Behaviour outside the West and the Ethnographic Imagination 1750–1918*. London: Cassell.

Blok, J. (1994). 'Quest for a Scientific Mythology: F. Creuzer and K. O. Müller on History and Myth', *History and Theory*, 33/4: 26–52.

Blok, J. (1996). 'Proof and Persuasion in *Black Athena*: The Case of K. O. Müller', *Journal of the History of Ideas*, 57/4: 705–24.

Bloom, H. (1974). 'The Crystal Man', in *Selected Writings of Walter Pater*, ed. H. Bloom. Columbia: Columbia University Press, pp. vii–xxxi.

Bluestone, N. (1987). *Women and the Ideal Society: Plato's Republic and Modern Myths of Gender*. Amhurst: University of Massachusetts Press.

Bowlby, R. (1987). 'Promoting Dorian Gray', *Oxford Literary Review*, 9: 147–62.

Bowlby, R. (2007). *Freudian Mythologies: Greek Tragedy and Modern Identities*. Oxford: Oxford University Press.

Boyne, R. (1990). *Foucault and Derrida: The Other Side of Reason*. London: Unwin Hyman.

Bradshaw, D. (2007) (ed.). *The Cambridge Companion to E. M. Forster*. Cambridge: University of Cambridge Press.

Brady, S. (2005). *Masculinity and Male Homosexuality in Britain, 1861–1913*. Basingstoke: Palgrave Macmillan.

Brake, Laurel (2004). 'Pater, Clar a Ann (*bap.* 1841, *d.* 1910)', in *Oxford Dictionary of National Biography*, online edn. Oxford. www.oxforddnb.com/view/article/48505 (accessed 31 May 2010).

Brake, L., and Small, I. (1991) (eds). *Pater in the 1990s*. Greensboro, NC: ELT Press.

Bray, A. (1988). *Homosexuality in Renaissance England*. 2nd edn. London: Gay Men's Press.

Bredbeck, G. W. (1991). *Sodomy and Interpretation: Marlowe to Milton*. Ithaca, NY: Cornell University Press.

Bredbeck, G. W. (1997). 'Queer Superstitions: Forster, Carpenter and the Illusion of (Sexual) Identity', in Martin and Piggford (1997: 58).

Bristow, J. (1992). 'Wilde, *Dorian Gray*, and Gross Indecency', in J. Bristow (ed.), *Sexual Sameness: Textual Differences in Lesbian and Gay Writing*: London and New York: Routledge, 44–63.

Bristow, J. (1997). '"A Complex Multiform Creature": Wilde's Sexual Identities', in Raby (1997: 195–218).

Bristow, J. (1998). 'Symonds' History, Ellis's Heredity: *Sexual Inversion*', in Bland and Doan (1998: 79–99).

Bristow, J. (2004). 'Biographies', in Roden (2004: 6–30).

Bristow, J. (2007). 'Remapping the Sites of Modern Gay History: Legal Reform, Medico-Legal Thought, Homosexual Scandal, Erotic Geography', *Journal of British Studies*, 46: 116–42.

Bruhm, S. (2001). *Reflecting Narcissus: A Queer Aesthetic*. Minneapolis and London: University of Minnesota Press.

Buckler, W. E. (1989). 'Oscar Wilde's Aesthetic of the Self: Art as Imaginative Self-Realization in *De Profundis*', *Biography*, 12: 95–115.

Buckton, O. S. (1998). *Secret Selves: Confession and Same-Sex Desire in Victorian Autobiography*. Chapel Hill, NC, and London: University of North Carolina Press.

Burkhardt, J. ([1898–1902] 1998). *The Greeks and Greek Civilization*, ed. O. Murray, trans. S. Stern. New York: St Martin's Press.

Burnyeat, M. (1977). 'Socratic Midwifery, Platonic Inspiration', *BICS* 24: 7–16.

Calder, W. M., and Schlesier, R. (1998) (eds). *Zwischen Rationalismus und Romantik: Karl Otfried Müller und die Antike Kultur*. Hildesheim: Weidmann.

Carhart, M. C. (2007). *The Science of Culture in Enlightenment Germany*. Cambridge, MA, and London: Harvard University Press.

Cartledge, P. (2001a). 'The Politics of Spartan Pederasty', in Cartledge (2001b: 91–105).

Cartledge, P. (2001b). *Spartan Reflections*. London: Duckworth.

Carpenter, E. (1985). *Towards Democracy*. London: Gay Men's Press.

Chauncey, G. (1982–3). 'From Sexual Inversion to Homosexuality: Medicine and the Changing Conceptualization of Female Deviance', *Salmagundi*, 58–9: 114–46.

Christian, L. G. (1972). 'The Figure of Socrates in Erasmus' Work', *Sixteenth Century Journal*, 3/2: 1–10.

Clark, W. (2006). *Academic Charisma and the Origins of the Research University*. Chicago and London: Chicago University Press.

Classen, C. J. (1989) (ed.). *Die Klassische Altertumswissenschaft an der Georg-August-Universität. Eine Ringvorlesung zu ihrer Geschichte*. Göttingen: Vandenhoeck & Ruprecht.

Cohen, E. (1993). *Talk on the Wilde Side: Toward a Genealogy of a Discourse on Male Sexualities*. New York and London: Routledge.

Cocks, H. (2003). *Nameless Offences: Homosexual Desire in the Nineteenth Century*. London and New York: I. B. Tauris.

Cocks, H. (2006). 'Making the Sodomite Speak: Voices of the Accused in English Sodomy Trials, *c*.1800–98', *Gender and History*, 18/1: 87–107.

Collison, R. (1966). *Encyclopaedias: Their History throughout the Ages: A Bibliographical Guide with Extensive Historical Notes to the General Encyclopaedias issues throughout the World from 350 BC to the Present Day*. 2nd edn. New York and London: Hafner Publishing Company.

Cook, M. (2003). *London and the Culture of Homosexuality, 1885–1914*. Cambridge: Cambridge University Press.

Coppa, F. (2004). 'Performance Theory and Performativity', in Roden (2004: 96–118).

Craft, C. (1994). *Another Kind of Love: Male Homosexual Desire in English Discourse, 1850–1920*. Berkeley and Los Angeles: University of California Press.

Craft, C. (2002). 'Come See about Me: Enchantment of the Double in "The Picture of Dorian Gray"', *Representations*, 91: 109–36.

Craft, C. (2005). 'Come See about Me: Enchantment of the Double in *The Picture of Dorian Gray*', *Representations*, 91/2: 109–36.

Crompton, L. (1978a). 'Jeremy Bentham's Essay on "Paederasty": An Introduction', *Journal of Homosexuality*, 3/4: 383–405.

Crompton, L. (1978b). 'Jeremy Bentham's Essay on "Paederasty" Part 2', *Journal of Homosexuality*, 4/1: 91–107.

Crompton, L. (1985). *Byron and Greek Love: Homophobia in 19th-Century England*. Berkeley and Los Angeles: University of California Press.

Crozier, I. (2000). 'Taking Prisoners: Havelock Ellis, Sigmund Freud, and the Contruction of Homosexuality, 1897–1951'. *Social History of Medicine*, 13/3: 447–66.

Crozier, I. (2008). 'Introduction: Havelock Ellis, John Addington Symonds and the Construction of *Sexual Inversion*', in Ellis and Symonds (2008: 1–86).

Cruise, C., with. Ferrari, R. C., Mancoff, D. N., Prettejohn, E., Seymour, G. M., Sharp, F. C., and Osborne, V. (2005) (eds). *Love Revealed: Simeon Solomon and the Pre-Raphaelites*. London: Merrill.

Danson, L. (1997a). *Wilde's Intentions: The Artist in his Criticism*. Oxford: Clarendon Press.

Danson, L. (1997b). 'Wilde as Critic and Theorist', in Raby (1997: 80–95).

D'Arch Smith, T. (1970). *Love in Earnest: Some Notes on the Lives and Writings of English 'Uranian' Poets from 1889 to 1930*. London: Routledge and Kegan Paul.

Davidson, J. (2007). *The Greeks and Greek Love: A Radical Reappraisal of Homosexuality in Ancient Greece*. London: Weidenfeld and Nicolson.

Davis, G. (2006). 'Taming Oscar Wilde: Queerness, Heritage and Stardom', in Griffiths (2006: 195–206).

Davis, W. (1995). 'Freuds Leonardo und die Kultur der Homosexualität', *Texte zur Kunst*, 5/17: 56–73.

Davis, W. (1996). 'Winckelmann's "Homosexua"' Teleologies', in N. B. Kampen (ed.), *Sexuality in Ancient Art*. Cambridge: Cambridge University Press, 262–76.

Davis, W. (1999). 'The Image in the Middles: John Addington Symonds and Homoerotic Art Criticism', in Prettejohn (1999: 188–216).

Davis, W. (2004). 'Narzissmus in der homoerotischen Kultur und in der Theorie Freuds', in M. Fend and M. Kroos (eds), *Mannlichkeit im Blick: Visuelle Inszenierungen in der Kunst seit der fruher Neuzeit*. Cologne: Bohlau, 213–32.

De Vries, G. J. (1969). *A Commentary on the* Phaedrus *of Plato*. Amsterdam: Hakkert.

DeJean, J. (1989). 'Sex and Philology: Sappho and the Rise of German Nationalism', *Representations*, 27: 148–71.

DeJean, J. (1997). *Ancients against Moderns: Culture Wars and the Making of a Fin de Siècle*. Chicago and London: Chicago University Press.

DeLaura, D. J. (1969). *Hebrew and Hellene in Victorian England*: *Newman, Arnold, and Pater*. Austin and London: University of Texas Press.

Dellamora, R. (1990). *Masculine Desire: The Sexual Politics of Victorian Aestheticism*. Chapel Hill, NC, and London: University of North Carolina Press.

Dellamora, R. (1994). *Apocalyptic Overtures: Sexual Politics and the Sense of an Ending*. New Brunswick: Rutgers University Press.

Dellamora, R. (1999) (ed.). *Victorian Sexual Dissidence*. Chicago: Chicago University Press.

Denisoff, D. (2001). *Aestheticism and Sexual Parody 1840–1940*. Cambridge: Cambridge University Press.

Denisoff, D. (2004). 'Oscar Wilde, Commodity, Culture', in Roden (2004: 119–42).

Derks, P. (1990). *Die Schande der Heiligen Päderastie: Homosexualität und Öffentlichkeit in der Deutschen Literatur 1750–1850*. Berlin: Verlag Rosa Winkel.

Derrida, J. (1976). *Of Grammatology*, trans. G. Spivak. Baltimore: Johns Hopkins University Press.

Derrida, J. (1981). 'Plato's Pharmacy', in *Dissemination*, trans. B. Johnson. Chicago: Chicago University Press, 65–171.

Detel, W. (2005). *Foucault and Classical Antiquity: Power, Ethics, and Knowledge*, trans. D. Wigg-Wolf. Cambridge: Cambridge University Press.

Diderot, D. (1975–). *Œuvres complètes*, ed. H. Dieckmann, J. Prouse, and J. Varloot. Paris: Hermann.

Dollimore, J. (1991). *Sexual Dissidence: Augustine to Wilde*. Oxford: Oxford University Press.

Donoghue, D. (1995). *Walter Pater: Lover of Strange Souls*. New York: Knopf.

Douglas, A. (1929). *The Autobiography of Lord Alfred Douglas*. London: Martin Secker.

Dover, K. (1980) (ed.). *Plato: Symposium*. Cambridge: Cambridge University Press.

Dowling, L. (1988). 'Walter Pater and Archaeology: The Reconciliation with Earth', *Victorian Studies*, 31: 209–31.

Dowling, L. (1989). 'Ruskin's Pied Beauty and the Constitution of a "Homosexual" Code', *Victorian Newsletter*, 75: 1–8.

Dowling, L. (1991). 'Foreword', in Brake and Small (1991: pp. ix–xiii).

Dowling, L. (1994). *Hellenism and Homosexuality in Victorian Oxford*. Ithaca, NY: Cornell University Press.

Doylen, M. (1998). 'Homosexual Askesis: Representations of Self-Fashioning in the Writings of Walter Pater, Oscar Wilde and John Addington Symonds'. Ph.D. thesis, University of California, Santa Cruz.

Doylen, M. (1999). 'Oscar Wilde's *De Profundis*: Homosexual Self-Fashioning on the Other Side of Scandal', *Victorian Literature and Culture*, 27/2: 547–66.

Duberman, M. B., Vicinus, M., and Chauncey, G., Jr (1989) (eds). *Hidden from History: Reclaiming the Gay and Lesbian Past*. London: Penguin.

Dyer, R. (2002). *The Culture of Queers*. London and New York: Routledge.

Dynes, W. R. (2005). 'Light in Hellas: How German Classical Philology Engendered Gay Scholarship' *Journal of Homosexuality*, 49: 341–56.

Ellis, H. (2007). 'Newman and Arnold: Classics, Christianity and Manliness in Tractarian Oxford', in Stray (2007: 46–63).

Ellis, H. H., and Symonds, J. A. (1896). *Die konträre Geschlechtsgefühl*. Leipzig: Wigand.

Ellis, H. H., and Symonds, J. A. (1897). *Sexual Inversion*. London: Wilson and Macmillan.

Ellis, H. H., and Symonds, J. A. (1915). *Studies in the Psychology of Sex*, ii. *Sexual Inversion*. 3rd edn. Philadelphia: F. A. Davis.

Ellis, H. H., and Symonds, J. A. (2008). *Sexual Inversion: A Critical Edition*, ed. I. Crozier. Basingstoke: Palgrave Macmillan.

Ellmann, R. (1988). *Oscar Wilde*. Harmondsworth: Penguin.

Engel, A. J. (1983). *From Clergyman to Don: The Rise of the Academic Profession in Nineteenth Century Oxford*. Oxford: Clarendon Press.

Erasmus, D. (1997). *Collected Works of Erasmus*, xxxix. *Colloquies*, trans. and annotated by C. R. Thompson. Toronto and London: University of Toronto Press.

Evangelista, S. (2003a). 'Against Misinterpretation: Benjamin Jowett's Translations of Plato and the Ethics of Modern Homosexuality', *RANAM* 36: 141–53.

Evangelista, S. (2003b). 'Walter Pater's Romantic Hellenism'. D.Phil. thesis. University of Oxford.

Evangelista, S. (2006). '"Lovers and Philosophers at Once": Aesthetic Platonism in the Victorian *Fin de Siècle*', *Yearbook of English Studies*, 36/2: 230–44.

Evangelista, S. (2007a). 'Platonic Dons, Adolescent Bodies: Benjamin Jowett, John Addington Symonds, Walter Pater', in Rousseau (2007a: 203–36).

Evangelista, S. (2007b). 'Walter Pater's Teaching in Oxford: Classics and Aestheticism', in Stray (2007: 64–77).

Evangelista, S. (2009). *British Aestheticism and Ancient Greece: Hellenism, Reception, Gods in Exile*. Basingstoke: Palgrave Macmillan.

Faber, G. (1957). *Jowett, a Portrait with Background*. London: Faber and Faber.

Faught, C. B. (2003). *The Oxford Movement: A Thematic History of the Tractarians and their Times*. University Park, PA: Pennsylvania State University Press.

Fellows, J. (1991). *Tombs, Despoiled and Haunted: 'Under-Textures' and 'After-Thoughts' in Walter Pater*. Stanford, CA: Stanford University Press.

Ferrari, G. R. F. (1987). *Listening to the Cicadas: A Study of Plato's* Phaedrus. Cambridge: Cambridge University Press.

Field, M. (1933). *Works and Days: From the Journal of Michael Field*, ed. T. and D. C. Sturge Moore. London: J. Murray.

Fisher, T. (1995). *Scandal: Sexual Politics of Late Victorian Britain*. Stroud: Alan Sutton.

Fletcher, J. (1992). 'Forster's Self-Erasure: *Maurice* and the Scene of Masculine Love', in J. Bristow (ed.) *Sexual Sameness: Textual Differences in Lesbian and Gay Writing*. London and New York: Routledge, 64–90.

Foldy, M. (1997). *The Trials of Oscar Wilde: Deviance, Morality, and Late-Victorian Society*. New Haven and London: Yale University Press.

Forrester, J. (1980). *Language and the Origins of Psychoanalysis*. London: Macmillan.

Forster, E. M. (1972). *Maurice*. repr. Harmondsworth: Penguin, 1983.

Foucault, M. (1970). *The Order of Things: An Archaeology of the Human Sciences*. London: Tavistock Publications.

Foucault, M. (1984). 'On the Genealogy of Ethics: An Overview of Work in Progress', in P. Rabinow (ed.) *The Foucault Reader*. New York: Pantheon Books, 340–72.

Foucault, M. (1986). *The History of Sexuality: The Use of Pleasure*, trans. R. Hurley. Harmondsworth: Penguin.

Foucault, M. (1988). *The History of Sexuality: The Care of the Self*, trans. R. Hurley. Harmondsworth: Penguin.

Foucault, M. (1998). *The History of Sexuality: The Will to Knowledge*, trans. R. Hurley. Harmondsworth: Penguin.

Foxon, D. (1964). *Libertine Literature in England, 1660–1745. With an appendix on the publication of John Cleland's 'Memoirs of a Woman of Pleasure', commonly called 'Fanny Hill'*. London: Shenval Press.

Freud, S. (1999). *Gesammelte Werke*, ed. Anna Freud. 17 vols. Frankfurt-am-Main: Fischer Taschenbuch Verlag.

Freud, S. (1953–74). *The Standard Edition of the Complete Psychological Works of Sigmund Freud*, trans. James Strachey [et al.]. 24 vols. London: Hogarth Press.

Freud. S. (1974). *The Freud-Jung Letters: The Correspondence between Sigmund Freud and C. G. Jung*, ed. W. McGuire, trans. R. Manheim and R. F. C. Hull. London: Routledge.

Friedrich, R. (1991). *Johann Matthias Gesner: Sein Leben und sein Werk*. Roth: Genniges.

Gerard, K., and Hekma, G. (1989) (eds). *The Pursuit of Sodomy: Male Homosexuality in Renaissance and Enlightenment Europe*. New York and London: Haworth Press.

Gericke, T. (1911). *Johann Matthias Gesners und Johann Gottfried Herders Stellung in der Geschichte der Gymnasialpädagogik*. Doctoral thesis. Borna-Leipzig.

Gesner, J. M. (1763). *Primae lineae Isagoges in eruditionem uniuersalem nominatim philologiam, historiam, et philosophiam*. Leipzig: Caspari Fritsch.

Gesner, J. M. (1877). *Socrate et l'amour grec (Socrates sanctus παιδεραστής)*, trans. A. Bonneau. Paris: I. Liseux.

Gilbert, A. (1978). 'Sodomy and the Law in Eighteenth and Nineteenth Century Britain', *Societas*, 8: 225–4.

Gilbert, A. (1980–1). 'Conceptions of Homosexuality and Sodomy in Western History', *Journal of Homosexuality*, 6: 69–70.

Gildenhard, I., and Zissos, A. (2000). 'Ovid's Narcissus (Met. 3.339–510): Echoes of Oedipus', *American Journal of Philology*, 121/1: 129–47.

Gilman, S. L. (1993). *Freud, Race and Gender*. Princeton: Princeton University Press.

Gilroy, P. (1993). *The Black Atlantic: Modernity and Double Consciousness*. London and New York: Verso.

Gladfelder, H. (2007a). 'In Search of Lost Texts: Thomas Cannon's *Ancient and Modern Pederasty Investigated and Exemplfy'd*', *Eighteenth-Century Life*, 31/1: 22–38.

Gladfelder, H. (2007b) (ed.). 'The Indictment of John Purser, Containing Thomas Cannon's *Ancient and Modern Pederasty Investigated and Exemplify'd*', *Eighteenth-Century Life*, 31/1: 39–61.

Goethe, J. G. von (1985). *Sämtliche Werke nach Epochen seines Schaffens, Münchner Ausgabe, Volume 6 (in 2 volumes): Weimarer Klassik, 1798–1806*, ed. K. Richter, H. G. Göpfert, N. Miller, and G. Sauder. Munich: Hanser.

Goldhill, S. (2002). *Who Needs Greek? Contests in the Cultural History of Hellenism*. Cambridge: Cambridge University Press.

Gosse, E. (1896). *Critical Kit-Kats*. London: Heinemann.

Goulbourne, R. (2007). 'Voltaire's Socrates', in Trapp (2007: 229–47).

Gould, S. J. (1977). *Ontogeny and Phylogeny*. Cambridge, MA, and London: Belknap Press of Harvard University Press.

Grafton, A. (1983). 'Polyhistor into Philolog: Notes on the Transformation of German Classical Scholarship, 1780–1850', *History of Universities*, 3: 159–92.

Grant, M. (1975) (ed.). *Erotic Art in Pompeii: The Secret Collection of the National Museum in Naples*. London: Octopus Books.

Grell, C. (1995). *Le Dix-Huitième Siècle et l'antiquité en France, 1680–1789*. Oxford: Voltaire Foundation.

Griffiths, R. (2006) (ed.). *British Queer Cinema*. London and New York: Routledge.

Gustafson, S. E. (2002). *Men Desiring Men: The Poetry of Same Sex Identity and Desire in German Classicism*. Detroit: Wayne State University Press.

Haggerty, G. E. (1999). *Men in Love: Masculinity and Sexuality in the Eighteenth Century*. New York and Chichester: Columbia University Press.

Hall, D. (1994) (ed.). *Muscular Christianity: Embodying the Victorian Age*. Cambridge and New York: Cambridge University Press.

Halperin, D. M. (1989). *One Hundred Years of Homosexuality*. New York and London: Routledge.

Halperin, D. M. (1990). 'Why is Diotima a Woman? Platonic *Erōs* and the Figuration of Gender', in D. M. Halperin, J. J. Winkler, and F. I. Zeitlin (eds), *Before Sexuality: The Construction of Erotic Experience in the Ancient Greek World*. Princeton: Princeton University Press, 257–308.

Halperin, D. M. (1992). 'Plato and the Erotics of Narrativity', in R. Hexter and D. Selden (eds), *Innovations of Antiquity*. New York and London: Routledge, 95–126.

Halperin, D. M. (2007). *What Do Gay Men Want? An Essay on Sex, Risk, and Subjectivity*. Ann Arbor: University of Michigan Press.

Hamilton, W. (1777). 'Account of the Discoveries at Pompeii, Communicated by Sir William Hamilton', *Archaeologia*, 4: 160–75.

[Hancarville, Baron d'] (1784). *Monumens du Culte Secret des Dames Romaines*. Caprées [= Nancy?]: Privately printed.

Hanfmann, G. M. A. (1951). "Socrates and Christ" *Harvard Studies in Classical Philology* 60: 205–233.

Hanson, E. (1997). *Decadence and Catholicism*. Cambridge, MA, and London: Harvard University Press.

Harris, F. (1918). *Oscar Wilde: His Life and Confessions*. 2 vols. New York: Privately printed.

Harrison, J. (1925). *Reminiscences of a Student's Life*. London: Hogarth Press.

Hartog, F. (2003). *Régimes d'historicité: Présentisme et expériences du Temps*. Paris: Seuil.

Hartog, F. (2005). *Anciens, modernes, sauvages*. Paris: Galaade.

Harvey, A. D. (1978). 'Prosecutions for Sodomy at the Beginning of the Nineteenth Century' *Historical Journal*, 21: 939–49.

Harvey, A. D. (1994). *Sex in Georgian England*. London: Duckworth.

Haskell, F. (1987). 'The Baron d'Hancarville: An Adventurer and Art Historian in Eighteenth-Century Europe', in Haskell, *Past and Present in Art and Taste: Selected Essays*. New Haven and London: Yale University Press.

Hatfield, H. C. (1943). *Winckelmann and his German Critics, 1755–1781: A Prelude to the Classical Age*. Morningside Heights, NY: King's Crown Press.

Heidt, S. (2003). '"Let JAS words stand": Publishing John Addington Symonds's Desires', *Victorian Studies*, 46/1: 7–31.

Hext, K. (2008). 'Recent Scholarship on Walter Pater: "Antithetical Scholar of Understanding's End"', *Literature Compass*, 5/2: 407–23.

Higgins, L. (1993). 'Jowett and Pater: Trafficking in Platonic Wares', *Victorian Studies*, 37/1: 43–72.

Higgins, L. (2002). 'No Time for Pater: The Silenced Other of Masculinist Modernism', in L. Brake, L. Higgins, and C. Williams (eds), *Walter Pater: Transparencies of Desire*. Greensboro, NC: ELT Press, 37–54.

Hilliard, D. (1982). 'Unenglish and Unmanly: Anglo-Catholicism and Homosexuality', *Victorian Studies*, 25: 181–210.

Hinchliff, P. (1987). *Benjamin Jowett and the Christian Religion*. Oxford: Clarendon Press.

Holland, M. (1997). 'Biography and the Art of Lying', in Raby (1997: 3–17).

Holliday, P. J. (2000). 'Symonds and the Model of Ancient Greece', in Pemble (2000: 81–101).

Honey, J. R. de S. (1977). *Tom Brown's Universe: The Development of the English Public School in the Nineteenth Century*. New York: Quadrangle/ New York Times Book Company.

Houlbrook, M. (2005). *Queer London: Perils and Pleasures in the Sexual Metropolis, 1918–1957*. Chicago and London: University of Chicago Press.

Howard, T. A. (2006). *Protestant Theology and the Making of the German University*. Oxford: Oxford University Press.

Humboldt, W. von (1960). *Werke*, i. *Schriften zur Anthropologie und Geschichte*, ed. A. Flitner and K. Giel. Stuttgart: Cotta.

Hurst, I. (2006). *Victorian Women Writers and the Classics: The Feminine of Homer*. Oxford: Oxford University Press.

Hurst, I. (2007). '"A fleet of . . . inexperienced Argonauts": Oxford Women and the Classics, 1873–1920', in Stray (2007: 14–27).

Hyde, H. M. (1973). *The Trials of Oscar Wilde*. New York: Dover Publications.

Iggers, G. (1982). 'The University of Göttingen 1760–1800 and the Transformation of Historical Scholarship', *Storia della Storiografia*, 2: 11–37.

Iggers, G., and Powell, J. M. (1990) (eds). *Leopold von Ranke and the Shaping of the Historical Discipline*. Syracuse, NY: Syracuse University Press.

Ingleby, L. [Cyril Arthur Gull] (1907). *Oscar Wilde*. London: T. Werner Laurie.

Ingleby, L. [Cyril Arthur Gull] (1912). *Oscar Wilde: Some Reminiscences*. London: T. Werner Laurie.

Inman, B. A. (1990). *Walter Pater and his Reading, 1874–1877: With a Bibliography of his Library Borrowings, 1878–1894*. New York: Garland.

Inman, B. A. (1991). 'Estrangement and Connection: Walter Pater, Benjamin Jowett and William M. Hardinge', in Brake and Small (1991: 1–20).

Inman, T. (1869). *Ancient Pagan and Modern Christian Symbolism Exposed and Explained*. London and Liverpool: Privately printed.

Ivory, Y. (2009). *The Homosexual Revival of Renaissance Style, 1850–1930*. Basingstoke: Palgrave Macmillan.

Jeismann, K.-E. (1996). *Das preußische Gymnasium in Staat und Gesellschaft. Die Entstehung des Gymnasiums als Schule des Staates und der Gebildeten, 1787–1817*. 2 vols. Stuttgart: Klett-Cotta.

Jenkyns, R. (1980). *The Victorians and Ancient Greece*. Oxford: Basil Blackwell.

[Johnson (later Cory), W.] (1858). *Ionica*. London: Smith, Elder and Company.

Jonte-Pace, D. (2001). *Speaking the Unspeakable: Religion, Misogyny, and the Uncanny Mother in Freud's Cultural Texts*. Berkeley and Los Angeles, and London: University of California Press.

Jowett, B. (1860). 'On the Interpretation of Scripture', in [F. Temple et al.], *Essays and Reviews*. London: J. W. Parker.

Jowett, B. (1892). *The Dialogues of Plato: Translated into English with Analyses and Introductions*. 5 vols. Oxford: Clarendon Press.

Jowett, B. (1899). *Letters Arranged and Edited by Evelyn Abbott and Lewis Campbell*. London: J. Murray.

Jowett, B. (1901). *Sermons on Faith and Doctrine*, ed. W. H. Fremantle. London: J. Murray.

Kaplan, M. (2005). *Sodom on the Thames: Sex, Love and Scandal in Wilde Times*. Ithaca, NY, and London: Cornell University Press.

Kaye, R. A. (2004). 'Gay Studies/Queer Theory and Oscar Wilde', in Roden (2004: 189–223).

Kaylor, M. M. (2006). *Secreted Desires: The Major Uranians: Hopkins, Pater and Wilde*. Brno: Privately printed.

Kemp, J. (2000). 'A Problem in Gay Heroics: Symonds and *l'Amour de l'impossible*', in Pemble (2000: 46–61).

Kennedy, H. (1988). *Ulrichs: The Life and Works of Karl Heinrich Ulrichs. Pioneer of the Modern Gay Movement*. Boston: Alyson Publications.

Kennell, N. (1995). *The Gymnasium of Virtue: Education and Culture in Ancient Sparta*. Chapel Hill, NC, and London: University of North Carolina Press.

Kiberd, D. (1997). 'Oscar Wilde: The Resurgence of Lying', in Raby (1997: 276–94).

Kincaid, J. R. (1992). *Child-Loving: The Erotic Child and Victorian Culture*. New York and London: Routledge.

King, T. A. (2004). *The Gendering of Men, 1600–1750: The English Phallus*. Madison: University of Wisconsin Press.

King, T. A. (2008). *The Gendering of Men, 1600–1750: Queer Articulations*. Madison: University of Wisconsin Press.

Koestenbaum, W. (1989). *Double Talk: The Erotics of Male Literary Collaboration*. New York and London: Routledge.

Koestenbaum, W. (1995). 'Wilde's Hard Labour and the Birth of Gay Reading', in A. Bennett (ed.), *Readers and Reading*. Harlow: Longman, 164–80.

Kofman, S. (1985). *The Enigma of Woman: Woman in Freud's Writing*, trans. Catherine Porter. Ithaca, NY, and London: Cornell University Press.

Kuzniar, A. (1996) (ed.). *Outing Goethe and his Age*. Stanford: Stanford University Press.

Landfester, M. (1988). *Humanismus und Gesellschaft im 19. Jahrhundert. Untersuchungen zur politischen und gesellschaftlichen Bedeutung der humanistischen Bildung in Deutschland*. Darmstadt: Wissenschaftliche Buchgesellschaft.

Lane, C. (2007). 'Forsterian Sexuality', in Bradshaw (2007: 104–19).

Laqueur, T. (1990). *Making Sex: Body and Gender from the Greeks to Freud.* Cambridge, MA and London: Harvard University Press.

Lanzone, R. V. (1883). *Dizionario di Mitologia Egizia,* iii. Turin: Litografia Fratelli Doyen.

Larmour, D, H., Miller, P. A., and Platter, C. (1998) (eds). *Rethinking Sexuality: Foucault and Classical Antiquity.* Princeton: Princeton University Press.

Lauer, R. (2001) (ed.). *Philologie in Göttingen. Sprach und Literaturwissenschaft an der Georgia Augusta im 18. und beginnenden 19. Jahrhundert.* Göttingen: Vandehoeck & Ruprecht.

Lauritsen, J. (2005). 'Hellenism and Homoeroticism in Shelley and his Circle', *Journal of Homosexuality,* 49/3–4: 357–76.

Le Rider, J. (2002). *Freud, de l'Acropole au Sinaï: Le Retour à l'antique des modernes viennois.* Paris: Presses universitaires de France.

Leonard, M. (2005). *Athens in Paris. Ancient Greece and the Political in Post-War French Thought.* Oxford: Oxford University Press.

Leonard, M. (2008). *How to Read Ancient Philosophy.* London: Granta.

Levine, J. P. (1996). 'The Functions of the Narrator's Voice in Literature and Film: Forster and Ivory's *Maurice*', *Literature/Film Quarterly,* 24/3: 309–21.

Lewis, C. T., and Short, C. (1896). *A Latin Dictionary.* Oxford: Clarendon Press.

Lissarrague, F., and Reed, M. (1997). 'The Collector's Books', *Journal of the History of Collections,* 9/2: 275–94.

Loesberg, J. (1991). *Aestheticism and Deconstruction: Pater, Derrida and De Man.* Princeton: Princeton University Press.

Longford, E. (1979). *A Pilgrimage of Passion: The Life of Wilfrid Scawen Blunt.* London: Weidenfeld and Nicolson.

McClelland, C. (1980). *State, Society and University in Germany 1700–1914.* Cambridge: Cambridge University Press.

McDiarmid, L. (2001). 'Oscar Wilde's Speech from the Dock', *Textual Practice,* 15/3: 447–66.

McKeon, M. (2005). *The Secret History of Domesticity: Public, Private, and the Division of Knowledge.* Baltimore: Johns Hopkins University Press.

MacLeod, C. (1998). *Embodying Ambiguity: Androgyny and Aesthetics from Winckelmann to Keller.* Detroit: Wayne State University Press.

Maddox, B. (2006). *Freud's Wizard: The Enigma of Ernest Jones.* London: John Murray.

Mallock, W. H. (1975). *The New Republic: Culture, Faith and Philosophy in an English Country House.* Leicester: Leicester University Press.

Manuel, F. (1959). *The Eighteenth Century Confronts the Gods.* Cambridge, MA: Harvard University Press.

Marcel, R. (1951). '"Saint" Socrate, patron de l'humanisme', *Revue internationale de philosophie*, 5: 135–43.

Marchand, S. (1996). *Down from Olympus: Archaeology and Philhellenism in Germany, 1750–1970*. Princeton: Princeton University Press.

Marchand, S. (2009). *German Orientalism in the Age of Empire: Religion, Race, and Scholarship*. Washington: German Historical Institute; Cambridge: Cambridge University Press.

Marcus, S. (1966). *The Other Victorians: A Study in Sexuality and Pornography in Mid-Nineteenth Century England*. London: Weidenfeld and Nicolson.

Martin, M. M. (2002). '"Boys who will be men": Desire in Tom Brown's Schooldays', *Victorian Literature and Culture*, 30/2: 483–502.

Martin, R. K. (1985). 'Edward Carpenter and the Double Structure of *Maurice*', in S. Kellogg (ed.), *Essays on Gay Literature*. New York and Binghamton: Harrington Park Press, 35–46.

Martin, R. K., and Piggford, G. (1997) (eds). *Queer Forster*. Chicago and London: University of Chicago Press.

Martindale, C. (2005). *Latin Poetry and the Judgement of Taste*. Oxford: Oxford University Press.

Mason, H. (1981). *Voltaire: A Biography*. London: P. Elek, Granada Publishing.

Mason, S. (1908). *Oscar Wilde: Art and Morality: A Defence of* The Picture of Dorian Gray. London: J. Jacobs.

Maynard, J. (1993). *Victorian Discourses on Sexuality and Religion*. Cambridge: Cambridge University Press.

Mazón, P. (2003). *Gender and the Modern Research University: The Admission of Women to German Higher Education, 1865–1914*. Stanford: Stanford University Press.

Meier, M. H. E. (1837). 'Päderastie', in *Allgemeine Encyclopädie der Wissenschaften und Kunst in alphabetischer Folge von genannten Schriftstellern*, ed. J. S. Ersch and J. G. Gruber. Leipzig: J. F. Gleditsch, vol. ix, sect. iii, pp. 149–89..

Meier, M. H. E. (1930). *Histoire de l'amour grec dans l'antiquité*, trans. L.-R. De Pogey Castries. Paris: Stendhal et compagnie.

Meier, P. (2001). *Mord, Philosophie und die Liebe der Männer: Franz Desgouttes und Heinrich Hössli; eine Parallelbiographie*. Zurich: Pendo.

Meinecke, F. (1959). *Werke*, iii. *Die Entstehung des Historismus*, ed. C. Hinrichs. Munich: R. Oldenbourg Verlag.

Meiners, C. (1775). 'Betrachtungen über die Männerliebe der Griechen, nebst einem Auszuge aus dem Gastmahle des Plato', in *Vermischte Philosophische Schriften*. Leipzig: In der Weygandschen Buchhandlung, i. 61–119.

Meisel, P. (1980). *The Absent Father: Virginia Woolf and Walter Pater*. New Haven and London: Yale University Press.

Miller, D. A. (1988). *The Novel and the Police*. Berkeley and Los Angeles, and London: University of California Press.

Miller, P. A. (2007). *Postmodern Spiritual Practices: The Reception of Plato and the Construction of the Subject in Lacan, Derrida and Foucault*. Columbus: Ohio State University Press.

Mitter, P. (1977). *Much Maligned Monsters: History of European Reactions to Indian Art*. Oxford: Clarendon Press.

Monsman, G. (1971). 'Pater, Hopkins and Fichte's Ideal Student', *South Atlantic Quarterly*, 70: 365–76.

Monsman, G. (1980). *Walter Pater's Art of Autobiography*. New Haven: Yale University Press.

Monsman, G. (2002). 'The Platonic Eros of Walter Pater and Oscar Wilde: "Love's Reflected Image"', *English Literature in Transition*, 45: 26–45.

Montaigne, M. (1928). *The Essayes of Michel Lord of Montaigne*, trans. John Florio. 3 vols. London: Dent.

Montuori, M. (1981). *De Socrate Iuste Damnato: The Rise of the Socratic Problem in the Eighteenth Century*. Amsterdam: Gieben.

Morris, I. M. (2007). 'The Refutation of Democracy? Socrates in the Enlightenment', in Trapp (2007: 209–27).

Müller, K. O. (1824). *Die Dorier*. Breslau: Josef Max.

Müller, K. O. (1832). *Denkmäler der Alten Kunst nach der Auswahl und Anordnung von C. O. Müller*, ed. C. Oesterley. Göttingen: In der Dieterichschen Buchhandlung.

Müller, K. O. (1839). *The History and Antiquities of the Doric Race*, trans. Henry Tufnell and George Cornewall Lewis. 2 vols. 2nd edn. London: John Murray.

Naas, M. (2010). 'Earmarks: Derrida's Reinvention of Philosophical Writing in "Plato's Pharmacy"', in M. Leonard (ed.), *Derrida and Antiquity*. Oxford: Oxford University Press.

Nachmansohn, M. (1915). 'Freuds Libidotheorie verglichen mit der Eroslehre Platos', *Internationale Zeitschrift der Psychoanalyse*, 3: 65–83.

Namowicz, T. (1978). *Die Aufklärische Utopie: Rezeption der Griechenauffassung J. J. Winckelmanns um 1800 in Deutschland und Polen*. Warsaw: Warsaw University Press.

Nelson, S. (2007). 'Shelley and Plato's *Symposium*: The Poet's Revenge', *International Journal of the Classical Tradition*, 14/1–2: 100–29.

Notopoulos, J. A. (1969). *The Platonism of Shelley: A Study of Platonism and the Poetic Mind*. New York: Octagon Books.

Norton, R. (1992). *Mother Clap's Molly House: The Gay Subculture in England 1700–1830*. London: Gay Men's Press.

O'Connor, E. M. (1989). *Symbolum Salacitatis: A Study of the God Priapus as a Literary Character*. Frankfurt: Lang.

Ohi, K. (2005). *Innocence and Rapture: The Erotic Child in Pater, Wilde, James and Nabokov*. Basingstoke: Palgrave Macmillan.

Olender, M. (1992). *Languages of Paradise: Race, Religion and Philology in the Nineteenth Century*, trans. A. Goldhammer. Cambridge, MA: Harvard University Press.

Olverson, T. D. (2010). *Women Writers and the Dark Side of Late-Victorian Hellenism*. Basingstoke: Palgrave Macmillan.

Oosterhuis, H. (2000). *Stepchildren of Nature: Krafft-Ebing, Psychiatry and the Making of Sexual Identity*. Chicago: University of Chicago.

Paget, S. (1921) (ed.). *Henry Scott Holland: Memoir and Letters*. London: John Murray.

[Pater, W.] (1867). 'Winckelmann', *Westminster Review*, NS 31: 80–110.

[Pater, W.] (1868). 'Poems by William Morris', *Westminster Review*, NS 34: 300–12.

Pater, W. (1891). 'A Novel by Mr Oscar Wilde', *Bookman*. 1: 59–60.

Pater, W. (1910). *The Works of Walter Pater*. 10 vols. London: Macmillan.

Pater, W. (1980). *The Renaissance: Studies in Art and Poetry, The 1893 Text*, ed. D. Hill. Berkeley and Los Angeles: University of California Press.

Pater, W. (1986 [1893]). *The Renaissance: Studies in Art and Poetry*, ed. Adam Phillips. Oxford: Oxford University Press.

Pemble, J. (2000) (ed.). *John Addington Symonds: Culture and the Demon Desire*. Basingstoke: Macmillan.

Penner, E. E. (1992). 'Spiritual Pregnancy in Plato's *Symposium*', *Classical Quarterly*, 42: 72–86.

Petschauer, P. (1986). 'Eighteenth-Century German Opinions about Education for Women', *Central European History*, 19/3: 262–92.

Peyrefitte, R. (1992). *Voltaire et Frédéric II*. 2 vols. Paris: A. Michel.

Pfeiffer, R. (1976). *History of Classical Scholarship 1300–1850*. Oxford: Clarendon Press.

Plato (1951). *The Symposium*, trans. W. Hamilton. Harmondsworth: Penguin.

Plato (1988). *Phaedrus*, trans. and ed. C. Rowe. 2nd edn. Warminster: Aris and Phillips.

Plato (1994). *Symposium*, trans. R. Waterfield. Oxford: Oxford University Press.

Plato (1999). *The Symposium*, trans. C. Gill. London: Penguin.

Porter, J. (2006). 'Foucault's Antiquity', in C. Martindale and R. F. Thomas (eds), *Classics and the Uses of Reception*. Malden, MA, and Oxford: Blackwell, 168–79.

Potts, A. (1994). *Flesh and the Ideal: Winckelmann and the Origins of Art History*. New Haven and London: Yale University Press.

Powell, K. (2009). *Acting Wilde: Victorian Sexuality, Theatre, and Oscar Wilde.* Cambridge: Cambridge University Press.

Prettejohn, E. (1999) (ed.). *After the Pre-Raphaelites: Art and Aestheticism in Victorian England.* Manchester: Manchester University Press.

Prettejohn, E. (2007). *Art for Art's Sake: Aestheticism in Victorian Painting.* New Haven and London: Yale University Press.

Prins, Y. (1999a). 'Greek Maenads, Victorian Spinsters', in Dellamora (1999: 43–81).

Prins, Y. (1999b). *Victorian Sappho.* Princeton: Princeton University Press.

Prior, W. (1996) (ed.). *Socrates: Critical Assessments*, i. *The Socratic Problem and Socratic Ignorance.* London: Routledge.

Raby, P. (1997) (ed.). *The Cambridge Companion to Oscar Wilde.* Cambridge: Cambridge University Press.

Ransome, A. (1912). *Oscar Wilde: A Critical Study.* London: Martin Secker.

Raschke, D. (1997). 'Breaking the Engagement with Philosophy: Re-Envisioning Hetero/Homo Relations in *Maurice*', in Martin and Piggford (1997: 151–65).

Rawson, E. (1969). *The Spartan Tradition in European Thought.* Oxford: Clarendon Press.

Renan, E. (1890). *The History of the Origins of Christianity. Book 1. Life of Jesus.* London: Mathieson.

Richardson, E. (2007). 'Jude the Obscure: Oxford's Classical Outcasts', in Stray (2007: 28–45).

Riquelme, J. P. (2000). 'Oscar Wilde's Aesthetic Gothic: Walter Pater, Dark Enlightenment, and *The Picture of Dorian Gray*', *Modern Fiction Studies*, 46/3: 609–31.

Ritvo, L. B. (1990). *Darwin's Influence on Freud: A Tale of Two Sciences.* New Haven and London: Yale University Press.

Robert, R. H. (1934). *Oscar Wilde Twice Defended from André Gide's Wicked Lies and Frank Harris's Cruel Libels to which is added a Reply to George Bernard Shaw, a Refutation of Dr G. J. Renier's Statements, a Letter to the Author from Lord Alfred Douglas, an Interview with Bernard Shaw by Hugh Kingsmill.* Chicago: Argus Book Shop.

Robertson, M. (2008). *Worshipping Walt: The Whitman Disciples.* Princeton: Princeton University Press.

Rocco, C. (1997). *Tragedy and Enlightenment: Athenian Political Thought and the Dilemmas of Modernity.* Berkeley and Los Angeles, and London: University of California Press.

Roden, F. S. (2002). *Same-Sex Desire in Victorian Religious Culture.* Basingstoke: Palgrave Macmillan.

Roden, F. S. (2004) (ed.). *Palgrave Advances in Oscar Wilde Studies.* Basingstoke: Palgrave Macmillan.

Rogers, A. K. (1933). *The Socratic Problem.* London: H. Milford.

Rousseau, G. S. (1987). 'The Sorrows of Priapus: Anticlericalism, Homosocial Desire and Richard Payne Knight', pp. 101–53 in Rousseau and Porter (1987: 101–53).

Rousseau, G. (2007a) (ed.). *Children and Sexuality: From the Greeks to the Great War.* Basingstoke: Palgrave Macmillan.

Rousseau, G. (2007b). 'Privilege, Power and Sexual Abuse in Georgian Oxford', in Rousseau (2007a: 142–69).

Rousseau, G. (2007c). '"You Have Made me Tear the Veil from those Most Secret Feelings": John Addington Symonds amidst the Children', in Rousseau (2007a: 173–205).

Rousseau, G. S., and Porter, R. (1987) (eds). *Sexual Underworlds of the Enlightenment.* Manchester: Manchester University Press.

Rowbotham, S. (2008). *Edward Carpenter: A Life of Liberty and Love.* London and New York: Verso.

Rowold, K. (2010). *The Educated Woman: Minds, Bodies, and Women's Higher Education in Britain, Germany, and Spain, 186–1914.* New York and London: Routledge.

Rüdiger, B. (2005). 'Der "Ersch-Gruber": Konzeption, Drucklegung und Wirkungsgeschichte der Allgemeinen Encyklopädie der Wissenschaften und Kunsten', *Leipziger Jahrbuch zur Buchgeschichte*, 14: 11–78.

Rudnytsky, P. (1987). *Freud and Oedipus.* New York: Columbia University Press.

Santas, G. (1988). *Plato and Freud: Two Theories of Love.* Oxford: Basil Blackwell.

Schindel, U. (1989). 'Johann Matthias Gesner, Professor der Poesie und Beredsamkeit 1734–1761', in Classen (1989: 9–26).

Schindel, U. (2001). 'Die Anfänge der Klassischen Philologie in Göttingen', in Lauer (2001: 9–24).

Sedgwick, E. K. (1985). *Between Men: English Literature and Male Homosocial Desire.* New York: Columbia University Press.

Sedgwick, E. K. (1990). *Epistemology of the Closet.* Berkeley and Los Angeles: University of California Press.

Sedgwick, E. K. (1992). 'Gender Criticism', in S. Greenblatt and G. Gunn (eds), *Redefining the Boundaries: The Transformation of English and American Literary Studies.* New York: Modern Language Association of America, 271–303.

Seiler, R. (1980). *Walter Pater: The Critical Heritage.* London: Routledge and Kegan Paul.

Sherard, R. H. (1905). *Oscar Wilde: The Story of an Unhappy Friendship.* London: Greening and Co.

Sherard, R. H. (1934). *Oscar Wilde twice Defended from André Gide's Wicked Lies and Frank Harris's Cruel Libels to which is Added a Reply to George Bernard Shaw, a Refutation of Dr G. J. Renier's Statements, a Letter to the*

Author from Lord Alfred Douglas, an Interview with Bernard Shaw by Hugh Kingsmill. Chicago: Argus Book Shop.

Shuter, W. F. (1982). 'Pater on Plato: "Subjective" or "Sound"?' *Prose Studies*, 5: 215–28.

Shuter, W. F. (1994). 'The "Outing" of Walter Pater', *Nineteenth-Century Literature* 48: 480–506.

Shuter, W. F. (1997). *Rereading Walter Pater.* Cambridge: Cambridge University Press.

Shuter, W. F. (2003). 'Pater, Wilde, Douglas and the Impact of "Greats"', *English Literature in Transition*, 46/3: 250–78.

Sigusch, V. (2000). *Karl Heinrich Ulrichs: Der erste Schwule der Weltgeschichte.* Berlin: Verlag Rosa Winkel.

Sinfield, A. (1994). *The Wilde Century: Effeminacy, Oscar Wilde and the Queer Moment.* London: Cassell.

Small, I. (1972). 'Plato and Pater: Fin de Siècle Aesthetics', *British Journal of Aesthetics*, 12: 869–83.

Smith, A. (1996). *The Victorian Nude: Sexuality, Morality, and Art.* Manchester: Manchester University Press.

Smith, A. (2001) (ed.). *Exposed: The Victorian Nude.* London: Tate Publishing.

Smith, P. E., II, and Helfand, M. S. (1989) (eds). *Oscar Wilde's Oxford Notebooks: A Portrait of Mind in the Making.* Oxford: Oxford University Press.

Somerville, S. (2000). *Queering the Color Line: Race and the Invention of Homosexuality in American Culture.* Durham, NC, and London: Duke University Press.

Sprengnether, M. (1990). *The Spectral Mother: Freud, Feminism, and Psychoanalysis.* Ithaca, NY: Cornell University Press.

Stewart, A. (1997). *Close Readers: Humanism and Sodomy in Early Modern England.* Princeton: Princeton University Press.

Stoler, A. L. (1996). *Race and the Education of Desire: Foucault's* History of Sexuality *and the Colonial Order of Things.* Durham, NC: Duke University Press.

Stone, L. (1977). *Sex and Marriage in England 1500–1800.* London: Weidenfeld and Nicolson.

Stone, L. (1993). *Broken Lives: Separation and Divorce in England, 1660–1857.* Oxford: Oxford University Press.

Stray, C. (1998). *Classics Transformed: Schools, Universities, and Society in England, 1830–1960.* Oxford: Oxford University Press.

Stray, C. (1999) (ed.). *Classics in Nineteenth- and Twentieth-Century Cambridge: Curriculum, Culture and Community.* Cambridge Philological Society, Supplement 24. Cambridge: Cambridge Philological Society.

Stray, C. (2007) (ed.). *Oxford Classics: Teaching and Learning 1800–2000*. London: Duckworth.

Sulloway, F. (1980). *Freud, Biologist of the Mind: Beyond the Psychoanalytic Legend*. London: Fontana.

Sünderhauf, E. S. (2004). *Griechensehnsucht und Kulturkritik: Die Deutsche Rezeption von Winckelmanns Antikenideal 1840–1945*. Berlin: Akademic Verlag GmbH.

[Symonds, J. A.] (n.d. [1883]). *A Problem in Greek Ethics*. London: Privately printed.

Symonds, J. A. (1920). *Studies of the Greek Poets*. 3rd edn. London: A. and C. Black.

Symonds, J. A. (1928). *Studies in Sexual Inversion (Embodying: A Study in Greek Ethics and A Study in Modern Ethics)*. [London: Privately Printed].

Symonds, J. A. (1967–9). *The Letters of John Addington Symonds*, ed. H. M. Schueller and R. L. Peters. 3 vols. Detroit: Wayne State University Press.

Symonds, J. A. (1984). *The Memoirs of John Addington Symonds: The Secret Homosexual Life of a Leading Nineteenth-Century Man of Letters*, ed. P. Grosskurth. London: Hutchinson.

Taddeo, J. A. (1997). 'Plato's Apostles: Edwardian Cambridge and the "New Style of Love"', *Journal of the History of Sexuality*, 8/2: 196–228.

Tobin, R. (2000). *Warm Brothers: Queer Theory and the Age of Goethe*. Pennsylvania: University of Pennsylvania Press.

Trapp, M. (2007) (ed.). *Socrates from Antiquity to the Enlightenment*. Aldershot: Ashgate.

Trilling, L. (1955). *Matthew Arnold*. 2nd edn. London: Allen and Unwin.

Trumbach, R. (1977). 'London's Sodomites: Homosexual Behaviour and Western Culture in the Eighteen Century', *Journal of Social History*, 10: 1–33.

Trumbach, R. (1987). 'Sodomitical Subcultures, Sodomitical Roles, and the Gender Revolution of the Eighteenth Century: The Recent Historiography', in R. P. Maccubbin (ed.), *'Tis Nature's Fault: Unauthorized Sexuality during the Enlightenment*. Cambridge: Cambridge University Press, 109–21.

Trumbach, R. (1989a). 'The Birth of the Queen: Sodomy and the Emergence of Gender Equality in Modern Culture, 1660–1750', in Duberman, Vicinus, and Chauncey (1989: 129–40).

Trumbach, R. (1989b). 'Sodomitical Assaults, Gender Role, and Sexual Development in Eighteenth-Century London', in Gerard and Hekma (1989: 407–29).

Trumbach, R. (1993). 'Erotic Fantasy and Male Libertinism in Enlightenment England', in L. Hunt (ed.), *The Invention of Pornography: Obscenity and the Origins of Modernity 1500–1800*. New York: Zone Books, 253–82.

Trumbach, R. (1998). *Sex and the Gender Revolution*, i. *Heterosexuality and the Third Gender in Enlightenment London*. Chicago: Chicago University Press.

Turner, F. M. (1981). *The Greek Heritage in Victorian Britain*. New Haven and London: Yale University Press.

Tyrwhitt, R. St. J. (1877). 'The Greek Spirit in Modern Literature', *Contemporary Review*, 29: 552–66.

Urbainczyk, T. (1997). *Socrates of Constantinople: Historian of Church and State*. Ann Arbor: University of Michigan Press.

Vance, N. (1985). *The Sinews of Spirit: The Ideal of Christian Manliness in Victorian Literature and Religious Thought*. Cambridge: Cambridge University Press.

Vasunia, P. (2005). 'Greek, Latin and the Indian Civil Service', *Classical Cambridge Journal*, 51: 35–71.

Vinge, L. (1967). *The Narcissus Theme in Western European Literature to the Early 19th Century*, trans. R. Dewsnap. Lund: Gleerup.

Vlastos, G. (1981). *Platonic Studies*. 2nd edn. Princeton: Princeton University Press.

Voltaire (1968–). *The Complete Works of Voltaire*, ed. T. Besterman, W. H. Barber, Ulla Kölving, Haydn T. Mason, and Nicholas Cronk. Oxford: Voltaire Foundation.

Walker, P. J. (2006). *Writers, Readers, and Reputations: Literary Life in Britain, 1870–1918*. Oxford: Oxford University Press.

Walkowitz, J. (1994). *City of Dreadful Delights: Narratives of Sexual Danger in Late Victorian London*. Chicago: Chicago University Press.

Wallace, C. (2008). *Catching the Light: The Art and Life of Henry Scott Tuke*. Edinburgh: Atelier Books.

Walther, G. (1998). 'Radikale Rezeption: Niebuhrs *Römische Geschichte* als Vorbild und Herausforderung für K. O. Müllers historisches Denken', in Calder and Schlesier (1998: 423–39).

Warner, M. (1990). 'Homo-Narcissism; or, Heterosexuality', in J. A. Boone and M. Cadden (eds), *Engendering Men: The Question of Male Feminist Criticism*. London and New York: Routledge, 190–206.

Weaver, W. N. (2004). '"A Schoolboy's Story": Writing the Victorian Public Schoolboy Subject', *Victorian Studies*, 46: 455–87.

Weeks, J. (1989 [1981]). *Sex, Politics and Society: The Regulation of Sexuality since 1800*. Rev. edn. London: Longman.

Weeks, J. (1990 [1977]). *Coming Out: Homosexual Politics in Britain from the Nineteenth Century to the Present*. Rev. edn. London: Quartet Books.

White, C. (1999). *Nineteenth-Century Writings on Homosexuality: A Sourcebook*. London and New York: Routledge.

Wilde, O. (1877). 'The Grosvenor Gallery', *Dublin University Magazine*, 90 (July), 118–26.

Wilde, O. (1925). *Intentions*. London: Methuen.

Wilde, O. (2000). *The Complete Letters of Oscar Wilde*, ed. Merlin Holland and Rupert Hart-Davis. London: Fourth Estate.

Wilde, O. (2005a). *The Complete Works of Oscar Wilde*, ii. *De Profundis 'Epistola: In carcere et vinculis'*, ed. I. Small. Oxford: Oxford University Press.

Wilde, O. (2005b). *The Complete Works of Oscar Wilde*, iii. *The Picture of Dorian Gray: The 1890 and 1891 Texts*, ed. J. Bristow. Oxford: Oxford University Press.

Williams, C. (1989). *Transfigured World: Walter Pater's Aesthetic Historicism*. Ithaca, NY: Cornell University Press.

Williams, M. (2006). '"Come and have a bathe!" Landscaping the Queer Utopia', in Griffiths (2006: 105–19).

Williamson, G. S. (2004). *The Longing for Myth in Germany: Religion and Aesthetic Culture from Romanticism to Nietzsche*. Chicago and London: University of Chicago Press.

Willoughby, G. (1993). *Art and Christhood: The Aesthetics of Oscar Wilde*. Cranbury, NJ, London, England, and Mississauga, Ontario: Associate University Presses.

Wilson, E. (2007). *The Death of Socrates: Hero, Villain, Chatterbox, Saint*. London: Profile.

Winckelmann, J. J. (1764). *Geschichte der Kunst des Alterthums*. Dresden: In der Waltherischen Hof-Buchhandlung.

Winckelmann, J. J. (1952–7). *Briefe*, ed. W. Rehm. 4 vols. Berlin: W de Gruyter.

Winckelmann, J. J. (2006). *History of the Art of Antiquity*, trans. H. F. Mallgrave. Los Angeles: Getty Research Institute.

Wohlgemuth, A. (1923). *A Critical Examination of Psycho-Analysis*. London: Allen and Unwin.

Wood, G. (1998). *A History of Gay Literature: The Male Tradition*. New Haven and London: Yale University Press.

Woodbury, L. (1973). 'Socrates and the Daughter of Aristides', *Phoenix*, 27/1: 7–25.

Woods, Gregory (1998). *A History of Gay Literature: The Male Tradition*. New Haven and London: Yale University Press.

*Index**

Abbott, Evelyn 45, 98, 103, 146
Achilles and Patroclus 48, 175–6, 178–9,
    182, 184, 199, 236
  see also Dorians, the; Symonds, John
    Addington; Wilde, Oscar
Aeolia and Aeolians 89, 181
  see also Meier, W. H. E.; Sappho;
Amorio and Hyacinth, story of 4–8, 36,
    209 n. 63
Apollo 169, 208 n. 63
  'Apollo Belvedere' 19–22, 33, 259
  and the Dorians 84 n. 145, 137
  and Hyacinth 43, 45, 204, 207–9,
    214 n. 93
  and Walter Pater 137
  see also Dionysus
Apostles, the Cambridge 218–19
Aphrodite 45, 137
Aristotle 89, 236
Athens 40, 153, 272
  and marriage customs 71
  and pederasty 93–4, 118, 171, 174,
    176–80, 183
  compared with Sparta 77–8, 80, 86,
    139, 159, 171, 180, 183

Benson, Arthur 104, 105, 106, 107,
    129 n. 110, 159 n. 43
  see also Pater, Walter
Berg, Friedrich von 125–6
Bernal, Martin 78
Boeckh, August 61
Boulton, Ernest and Frederick Park 202
Burton, Richard 177 n. 108
Butler, Josephine 45, 102
  see also Jowett, Benjamin
Butler, Judith 196

Cambridge, University of 39, 98,
    140, 142, 145, 159, 209 n. 63,
    218–28, 233

  see also Apostles, the Cambridge
  see also Durham, Clive
  see also Forster, E. M.
  see also Hall, Maurice
Campbell, Lewis 45, 98, 103, 146
Cannon, Thomas 1–8, 16
  and Elizabeth Cannon 1, 2
Carpenter, Edward 32, 37, 183 n. 128,
    219, 220, 230
Caylus, Comte Anne Claude de 201
Charmides 216, 224
  see also Plato, works discussed:
    Charmides
Cicero 65 n. 72, 87, 199, 201
Conington, John 102, 156, 158
Crete 86, 176, 272
Creuzer, Georg Friedrich 79–80

David and Jonathan 137, 193, 199, 201,
    214
Davidson, James 89, 267–74
Demeter 137, 142
Dionysus 137, 142, 167, 169
  and the Dionysian 137, 229
Diotima 11–16, 141, 186, 265
  see also Plato: works discussed:
    Symposium
Dorians, the
  and E. M. Forster 231
  and Karl Otfried Müller 77–88, 99
  and Walter Pater 134–9,
  and John Addington
    Symonds 159–60, 167, 175–6,
    179–83,
  and Oscar Wilde 134–6
  see also Ionians, the
Douglas, Lord Alfred 17, 43–5, 129
    n. 110, 190, 204–214, 217–18
Dupuis, Charles 79
Durham, Clive 44–5, 98, 219–33
  and Mrs Durham 220, 229

* This book is most easily navigated through the personalities it examines, and so the Index
lists the figures ancient and modern, mythical and historical, who populate this book.